D1616723

THE AESTHETIC COLD WAR

The Aesthetic Cold War

DECOLONIZATION AND GLOBAL LITERATURE

PETER J. KALLINEY

PRINCETON UNIVERSITY PRESS

PRINCETON & OXFORD

Published by Princeton University Press
41 William Street, Princeton, New Jersey 08540
6 Oxford Street, Woodstock, Oxfordshire OX20 1TR

press.princeton.edu

ISBN 9780691230634
ISBN (e-book) 9780691230641

British Library Cataloging-in-Publication Data is available

Editorial: Anne Savarese & James Collier
Production Editorial: Ali Parrington
Jacket Design: Katie Osborne
Production: Erin Suydam
Publicity: Alyssa Sanford & Charlotte Coyne
Copyeditor: Michele Rosen

Jacket image: Courtesy of the Hanna Holborn Gray Special Collections Research Center, University of Chicago Library.

This book has been composed in Arno

Printed on acid-free paper. ∞

Printed in the United States of America

10 9 8 7 6 5 4 3 2 1

CONTENTS

.

List of Illustrations   vii

Acknowledgments   ix

List of Abbreviations   xiii

Note on Translation and Transliteration   xv

PART I   1

1   Cultural Diplomacy, the Political Police, and Nonalignment   3

2   A Brief Intellectual History of the Aesthetic Cold War   17

PART II   49

3   Modernism, African Literature, and the Congress
for Cultural Freedom   51

4   Indigeneity and Internationalism: Soviet Diplomacy
and Afro-Asian Literature   83

5   A Failure of Diplomacy: Placing Eileen Chang
in Global Literary History   117

PART III   149

6   The Activist *Manquée,* or How Doris Lessing Became
an Experimental Writer   151

7   Caribbean Intellectuals and National Culture:
    C.L.R. James and Claudia Jones   180

8   Notes from Prison: Individual Testimony Meets
    Collective Resistance   217

    Conclusion   245

                    Notes   251
                Bibliography   285
                    Index   307

ILLUSTRATIONS

2.1. Intersection of debates about language choice and aesthetic independence.   46

3.1. Chinua Achebe, Frances Ademola, Theodore Bull, André Deutsch, Arthur Drayton, Dennis Duerden, Bernard Fonlon, and Bob Leshoai, at the Makerere conference, June 1962.   52

3.2. Françoise Robinet, Dennis Duerden, Gerald Moore, and Langston Hughes at the Makerere conference, June 1962.   69

3.3. "7 T ONE = 7 E TON," by Rajat Neogy. From *Transition* magazine #1, November 1961.   72

3.4. Neville Rubin, Elizabeth Spio-Garbrah, and Wole Soyinka at the Makerere conference, June 1962.   76

4.1. Unidentified woman, W.E.B. Du Bois, and Mulk Raj Anand at the Tashkent Conference, 1958.   94

4.2. Sembène Ousmane (center, smoking pipe), Majhemout Diop, and unidentified others at the Tashkent conference, 1958.   97

4.3. Sembène Ousmane, Thu Bon, and Ngũgĩ wa Thiong'o celebrating the Lotus Award at the Alma-Ata Conference, 1973.   98

4.4. Youssef El-Sebai presenting the Lotus Award to Sembène Ousmane at the Alma-Ata Conference, 1973.   99

4.5. Alex La Guma and Chinghiz Aitmatov at the Alma-Ata Conference, 1973.   104

5.1. Installment of *Little Ai* [*Xiao'ai*], under pen name Liang Jing. *Yibao* newspaper (Shanghai), 4 January 1952.   128

5.2. First installment of *The Rice-Sprout Song* in the USIA
magazine *World Today* [*Jinri shijie*], 1954.   131

5.3. USIA memo distributed with *World Today* [*Jinri shijie*],
1954, page 1.   132

5.4. USIA memo distributed with *World Today* [*Jinri shijie*],
1954, page 2.   133

5.5. First manuscript page of "The Spyring" by Eileen Chang.   142

6.1. Doris Lessing's Communist Party registration card, 1955,
from MI5 dossier.   157

6.2. Doris Lessing's passport photo circa 1950s, from MI5
dossier.   159

6.3. Intercepted letter from Campaign for Nuclear Disarmament,
November 1962, with handwritten cross-references to
intelligence file numbers of Lessing and other writers in
attendance.   165

7.1. Prosecutive Summary, 1951, from Claudia Jones's FBI
dossier.   189

7.2. Claudia Jones reading the *West Indian Gazette*.   192

7.3. One of the earliest documents in C.L.R. James's FBI
dossier, dated 22 July 1947.   197

7.4. FBI memo in C.L.R. James's dossier showing heavy
redactions, likely concealing names of confidential
informants and agents.   199

7.5. C.L.R. James's MI5 dossier springs back to life with this 1953
report, which includes information from an agent about his
ocean crossing after he was deported from the United
States. Page 1 of this report includes details of his stay in the
US and his ocean crossing.   200

7.6. C.L.R. James's MI5 dossier springs back to life after
deportation from the US in 1953. Page 2 of this report
includes information from an agent about his ocean crossing.   201

8.1. Harold Pinter reading Jack Mapanje's poetry at a PEN protest
in front of the Malawi High Commission, London, 1987.   231

ACKNOWLEDGMENTS

· THIS BOOK would not have been possible without the help of archivists and librarians. The staff at the University of Kentucky Library system, the Library of Congress, the Hanna Holborn Gray Special Collections Research Center (University of Chicago), the Harry Ransom Center (University of Texas), the British Library, the National Archives and Records Administration II (United States), the National Archives (United Kingdom), the Mayibuye Centre (University of the Western Cape), the Beinecke Library (Yale University), the Bodleian Library (University of Oxford), the Rare Books and Manuscript Library (Columbia University), the Schomburg Center for Research in Black Culture, Manuscripts, Archives and Rare Books Division (New York Public Library), the National Museum of Labour History (United Kingdom), the British Archive for Contemporary Writing (University of East Anglia), The Keep (University of Sussex), the East Asian Library Special Collections (University of Southern California), the Georgetown University Library, and the Russian State Archive of Literature and Art (RGALI) have been enormously helpful. Courtney Taulbee at the University of Kentucky went to great lengths to track down rare materials.

Research support and leave time also helped. Fellowships from the John Simon Guggenheim Memorial Foundation and the National Endowment for the Humanities were crucial. The dean's office and the English department at the University of Kentucky offered additional support. Jonathan Allison, Jeff Clymer, and Mark Kornbluh deserve special mention.

I have benefitted from conversations with colleagues near and far. I learned a lot from Adélékè Adéèkó, Rita Barnard, Greg Barnhisel, Elleke Boehmer, Molly Blasing, Marshall Brown, Eric Bulson, Nesrine Chahine, Laura Chrisman, Katy Clark, Elliott Colla, Eleni Coundouriotis, Jacqueline Couti, Julie Cyzewski, Carole Boyce Davies, Tommy Davis, Rossen Djagalov, Jim English, Jed Esty, Harris Feinsod, Leah Feldman, Roger Field, Susan Stanford Friedman, Simon Gikandi, Yogita Goyal, Weihsin Gui, Allan Hepburn, DaMaris Hill,

Janice Ho, Beth Holt, Nicole Huang, Emily Hyde, David James, Michelle Kelly, Benjamin Kohlmann, Sean Latham, Chris Lee, Haiyan Lee, Ben Lindfors, Liang Luo, Marina MacKay, John Marx, Bill Maxwell, Peter McDonald, Tariq Mehmood, Shauna Morgan, Alan Nadel, Monica Popescu, Jahan Ramazani, Sangeeta Ray, Nicole Rizzuto, Asha Rogers, Gayle Rogers, Paul Saint-Amour, Claire Seiler, Shuang Shen, James Smith, Janet Stanley, Nathan Suhr-Sytsma, Matthew Taunton, Michael Trask, Christina Walter, Hermann Wittenberg, Russ Wyland, and Laetitia Zecchini. Yan Wang provided important research assistance. Huajing Maske, Tianyi Wang, and Jingjie Wang made a trip to China possible. Renfrew Christie and Menan du Plessis were exceptionally generous hosts in Cape Town.

At Princeton University Press, I was the beneficiary of two insightful reports. Anne Savarese has been a conscientious and encouraging editor. Lisa Black and James Collier provided timely advice on images and permissions. Michele Rosen, Theresa Liu, and Ali Parrington have provided support with copy editing and production.

My appreciation for my family grows with every passing day. My parents, Sami and Elizabeth Edmunds Kalliney and Raymonde Rignall, continue to encourage me when others would have told me to find a better use for my energies. Karen Rignall and our children, Nedjma and Zaydan, shared with me the joys and disappointments of working on this project.

Portions of chapter three appeared in *Modern Language Quarterly*, and portions of chapter 7 appeared in *A History of 1930s British Literature*, edited by Benjamin Kohlmann and Matthew Taunton (Cambridge University Press). Reprinted with permission.

Permissions and credits for images are included in the captions. I secured permission to quote from written material as indicated below. Complete archival location details are in the notes and bibliography.

Bruce King grants permission to quote from unpublished letters held at the Harry Ransom Center archives.

Katharyn Duerden Owen grants permission to quote from Dennis Duerden's unpublished letters held at the Harry Ransom Center archives.

Curtis Brown Agency, acting on behalf of the authors' estates, grants permission to quote from C.L.R. James's and Stephen Spender's unpublished letters held at the Schomburg Center for Research in Black Culture and the Hanna Holborn Gray Special Collections Research Center at the University of Chicago, respectively.

Quotations from Doris Lessing's letters are reprinted with kind permission of Jonathan Clowes Ltd.

Selections from an interview with Richard M. McCarthy are quoted by permission of the Foreign Affairs Oral History Collection, Association for Diplomatic Studies and Training, Arlington, VA, www.adst.org.

Wole Soyinka grants permission to quote from his unpublished letters held at the Harry Ransom Center archives.

I have made extensive efforts to trace and contact copyright holders for permission to reproduce or quote from unpublished material. I would be happy to rectify any omissions that are brought to my attention at the earliest opportunity.

ABBREVIATIONS

AAPSO   Afro-Asian Peoples' Solidarity Organization

AAWA   Afro-Asian Writers' Association (sometimes AAWU, or Afro-Asian Writers' Union); first meeting Tashkent, 1958; *Lotus* is the association's house journal

ACLALS   Association for Commonwealth Literature and Language Studies

CCF [LATER IACF]   Congress for Cultural Freedom, funded covertly by the CIA; became IACF, or International Association for Cultural Freedom, after CIA funding scandal; records under IACF acronym at Hanna Holborn Gray Special Collections Research Center, University of Chicago

CIA   Central Intelligence Agency (of the United States), overseas spy agency

CID   Criminal Investigation Department (in the United Kingdom and its colonies); plainclothes police, but distinct from Special Branch

CP, CPUSA, CPGB   Communist Party (sometimes CPUSA or CPGB, as in Communist Party USA or Great Britain); NB—I capitalize Communist Party when I gesture to the organized political movement, whereas I use communist when I allude to more general communist principles and their adherents, often regarded by the Party as heterodox during the cold war

FBI   Federal Bureau of Investigation (of the United States), domestic law enforcement and spy agency

INS   Immigration and Naturalization Service (of the United States)

MI5   Military Intelligence agency 5 (of the United Kingdom and colonies); the domestic spy agency, working closely with Special Branch (the political police) and CID (Criminal Investigation Department, or plainclothes police); unlike the FBI, MI5 do not have powers of arrest

MI6   Military Intelligence agency 6 (of the United Kingdom); the secret spy agency, largely responsible for gathering information beyond national borders

NGO   non-governmental organization

PEN   originally Poets, Essayists, and Novelists; the leading international NGO working on behalf of writers and journalists

PWA   All-India Progressive Writers' Association (1934–)

USIA   United States Information Agency, overseas cultural diplomacy program begun by US State Department; sometimes called USIS, or United States Information Service

NOTE ON TRANSLATION AND TRANSLITERATION

THIS BOOK is primarily a study of anglophone writers and texts, but there are many instances in which I turn to writers and texts from other linguistic traditions. In general, when texts are available in English versions, I rely on these existing translations. I cite the source of the translations in the notes, but I do not provide the text in the original language. My readings do not hinge on the finer points of translations, but curious readers will be able to track down the translations and originals readily enough through the scholarly apparatus. There are a few sources related to Eileen Chang not available in English, and for these I relied on assistance from a translator. I think the few materials unavailable in English supplement rather than cinch my argument, and of course I am solely responsible for any factual or interpretive errors. The primary materials in Chinese, French, Hindi, Portuguese, Russian, and Urdu discussed in chapter 2 are all available in English versions.

When transliterating or romanizing words, publication titles, and names of writers and characters (mostly from Chinese, occasionally from Arabic and other languages), I have used the transliterated and romanized forms that are most common in the existing primary and secondary literature. When romanizing Chinese words, for instance, most translators and scholars now prefer Pinyin. Much of the important early scholarship on Eileen Chang (Zhang Ailing), especially that of C. T. Hsia, however, was published when the Wade-Giles system was the most common convention, and even some of Chang's recent translators prefer this older system because it was the one Chang herself used. I settled on what I believe will be the least confusing option for anglophone readers—that of using the romanized forms that are most common in the existing translations and scholarship—even if this leads to some anachronisms and inconsistencies. When discussing *Lotus* magazine, likewise, I rely on transliterations that appear in the magazine. The city of Almaty in Kazakhstan is transliterated as Alma-Ata, for instance, and the name of Yusuf al-Sibai, as it might be transliterated now, appears as Youssef El-Sebai.

Part I

1

Cultural Diplomacy, the Political Police, and Nonalignment

IN "AFRICA AND HER WRITERS," a feisty Chinua Achebe begins by proclaiming, "*Art for art's sake is just another piece of deodorized dog shit.*" The joke, of course, comes at high modernism's expense, and he was neither the first nor the last figure from decolonizing regions of the world to rail against writing for a privileged few. I do not know the reaction of his audience at Harvard University, where he originally delivered these remarks in 1972, but Achebe himself performed as if he knew the ghost of alumnus T. S. Eliot would be among the listeners.[1] He laments that at some point in "the history of European civilization the idea that art should be accountable to no one, and needed to justify itself to nobody except itself, began to emerge." Artists themselves abandoned the principle that art fills specific human needs, rejecting the idea that literature ought to answer to a wider reading public. "Words like *use, purpose, value*," he summarizes, "are beneath the divine concerns of this Art" (30). "Africa and Her Writers" offers a pointed synopsis, or caricature, depending on one's perspective, of what scholars call aesthetic autonomy. For Achebe, this theory of artistic freedom is a distinguishing feature of European literary development—or of European literary decline—providing one more piece of evidence that the rest of the world should think carefully before following their example.

A more succinct recapitulation and repudiation of modernism's aesthetic theories would be difficult to find. Achebe insists, against these snobs, "that art is, and was always, in the service of man" (29). For many years, Achebe's readers tended to see his work in precisely this way, as he represents it here: straightforward, where the metropolitan modernists prefer indirection; committed instead of aloof; pragmatic and utilitarian, not esoteric and self-contained; solicitous of broad audiences rather than chasing the approbation of an elite. The most current generation of scholars, myself included, has questioned this neat antithesis, but we ought to remember that this way of positioning his work in the global literary field is authorized by Achebe himself, at least in moments such as these. To regard the work of Achebe and the writing of his many peers from the decolonizing world as contiguous and compatible with metropolitan modernism, one must sometimes read these figures against themselves.

If we turn away from "Africa and Her Writers" at this early juncture, however, we miss the full significance of the great Nigerian's aesthetic contrasts. Metropolitan modernists are not his only concern in this essay. Another camp of European writers, appropriately enough, rejects aesthetic autonomy in terms no less damning. This group—congregating further east in Europe, or on the other side of the same literary hill, to use Achebe's metaphor—begins with the proposition that "a poet is not a poet until the Writers' Union tells him so." Not content with peaceful coexistence, each tribe has gone out of its way to antagonize the other: "Between these two peoples, an acrimonious argument rages. [. . .] *Monstrous philistines! Corrupt, decadent!* So loud and bitter does the recrimination become that it is often difficult to believe that these two peoples actually live on two slopes of the same hill" (31). The high modernists in one camp, the Party's advocates of socialist realism in the other, but both groups are unmistakably European all the same. Despite employing words as simple as use, purpose, and value to describe his own writing, Achebe is no more sanguine about the "Writers' Union" approach to literary production than he is enamored of modernist autonomy. Again, working by way of shorthand caricatures, Achebe tells us that the dreary, predictable, administered world of state-sanctioned literature represents no better alternative than metropolitan modernism for the emerging talents of Africa. A curse on both these European houses, Achebe says! Writers from decolonizing areas ought to be wary of reproducing the excesses of Europe's leading aesthetic theories.

Before concluding with a consideration of the poetry of Christopher Okigbo, Achebe's friend and recently deceased countryman, the essay pauses to give us a glimpse of how the world's system of literary production appears from the perspective of a midcentury African writer. "As African writers emerge onto the world stage, they come under pressure to declare their stand," Achebe reports. A stand on what issue, we might ask: on imperialism and neocolonialism, on racism as an endemic international problem, on the use of European languages in postcolonial literature, all of which he considers in detail elsewhere? No. In "Africa and Her Writers," Achebe describes a world literary system in which writers, European and African alike, are expected to declare their allegiances in what I call the aesthetic cold war. Outlining one's position in the "recrimination between capitalist and communist aesthetics in our time" is, Achebe considers, the most urgent question African writers must answer if they wish to find audiences both within and beyond national borders (32). Achebe's sense that African writers are walking onto a "world stage" is every bit as significant as his complaints about an aesthetic divide: it was during the middle decades of the twentieth century that one could begin to talk, realistically, about the field of literature in English including both writers and readers from colonial and postcolonial regions.

Following Achebe, *The Aesthetic Cold War* argues that the literatures of decolonization ought to be read as integral to, not apart from, the literatures of the global cold war. The cold war was of course a geopolitical event—a conflict between states—as well as an ideological showdown—a contest of ideas, we might say—but it was also an aesthetic standoff, arguably the defining and determining condition of literary production throughout much of the twentieth century. While scholars of metropolitan modernist, colonial, postcolonial, and global literatures have overlooked or downplayed the significance of this aesthetic competition—preferring instead to regard imperialism, anticolonialism, and global capitalism as the primary historical contexts for the literatures of the decolonizing world—this book will insist that the cold war and its aesthetic debates were coextensive with the global literary field in the twentieth century, especially in the anglophone regions. The aesthetic debates of the cold war do not provide—merely—a context for the emergence of African and other literatures of decolonization: the literatures of decolonization and the literatures of the cold war are tightly conjoined, not to be separated, contextually or otherwise. The imaginative representation of decolonization is one of the cold war's major, lasting contributions to literary history. If anything like a global literature came into existence during the period of decolonization, this global literary field was shaped by the cold war's aesthetic debates. To read the literatures of the cold war and decolonization separately, or side-by-side, or in a background-foreground relationship, is to misunderstand them both.

In political and ideological terms, late colonial and early postcolonial writers were a diverse bunch, although most gravitated toward some version of cold war nonalignment. The Bandung meeting of 1955, also known as the Afro-Asian or Asian-African Conference, provides the fullest and most visible articulation of decolonization as a global political aspiration.[2] The meeting's final communiqué urges economic cooperation and cultural exchange among

decolonizing nations and calls for an end to the racism and human rights viola-
tions that typify the colonial period. But equally, the document calls on large
states, most obviously the United States and the Soviet Union, to abstain from
applying economic, military, and diplomatic pressure on less powerful nations.[3]
Writing just after the close of the Bandung conference, George Padmore says,
"colonial peoples are resentful of the attitude of Europeans, of both Communist and anti-Communist persuasion, that they alone possess the knowledge
and experience necessary to guide the advancement of dependent peoples."[4]
A few years later, in *The Wretched of the Earth*, Frantz Fanon speaks for many
of his fellow intellectuals of the global south when he categorically rejects the
notion that decolonizing peoples must "choose between the capitalist system
and the socialist system." Although Fanon recognizes that the anticolonial
movement makes strategic use of "the savage competition between the two
systems in order to win their national liberation," he firmly insists that "the
underdeveloped countries must endeavor to focus on their very own values as
well as methods and style specific to them."[5]

In broad sympathy with Padmore and Fanon, most writers from the decolonizing areas of the world, including Achebe and Okigbo, saw the cold war
as both an exciting opportunity and a moment of profound danger. After
World War II, the relative weakness of the European imperialist powers afforded colonial peoples their best chance of self-determination. The cold war,
however, with its complicated grid of alliances, client states, influence, and
proxy wars, threatened new and more insidious forms of external control for
the colonized peoples of the world. In *The Origins of Totalitarianism*, for instance, Hannah Arendt says that the second half of the century witnessed "the
unexpected revival of imperialist policies and methods" more commonly
associated with the late nineteenth century scramble for Africa.[6] Most late
colonial and early postcolonial intellectuals were not eager to trade direct
European imperialism for another type of remote control, but unconditional
political independence, military integrity, and economic self-sufficiency were
rare commodities in this geopolitical context.[7] The cold war exacerbated political instability throughout the global south as wars of liberation, resistance
to foreign occupation, and civil wars proliferated with direct and indirect
superpower involvement. Writers from decolonizing regions experienced the
cold war less as observers of an uneasy truce and more as witnesses to and
participants in armed conflict. Writing specifically of the African context,
Monica Popescu observes, "Some of the most compelling positions on the
function of the writer came out of the search for a third, unaffiliated or

nonaligned, mode of cultural production."[8] Anglophone writers from Africa, Asia, and the Caribbean tended to be conscientious objectors of one kind or another in the cold war's ideological standoff.

As fascinating as I find the political side of the cold war, the history of which continues to be told as new archives open for research, most midcentury writers were equally concerned with the status of literature, after all. In the sphere of arts and letters, the cold war exerted two opposing pressures on intellectuals from decolonizing regions: new opportunities for global circulation through cultural diplomacy programs, on the one hand, and increasingly severe sanctions, including surveillance, censorship, and imprisonment, on the other hand. Large states began an unprecedented effort to court writers from the decolonizing parts of the world. Yet these very same writers faced significant political pressures both at home and as they traveled.

Both the United States (and to a lesser extent its western European partners) and the Soviet Union (and to a degree, its inconstant allies such as China and Cuba) actively supported writers from sub-Saharan Africa, the Middle East, south Asia, southeast Asia, the Caribbean, and Latin America. Cultural diplomacy, or soft power, complemented the armaments race: each side battling for proverbial hearts and minds, especially for the loyalty of writers and intellectuals in the decolonizing parts of the world. For the United States and the Soviet Union, part of this task involved packaging their own talent for export. Musical performers, dancers, art exhibitions, libraries, book tours, and other cultural goodwill programs were staples of US, British, French, Soviet, and Chinese cultural diplomacy throughout much of the century.[9]

This kind of programming was enhanced by recruitment of intellectual allies in the decolonizing world. Both the United States and the Soviet Union sponsored literary conferences and prizes, magazines, book publishing, libraries, arts centers, drama, music, and radio programs featuring artists and intellectuals from the decolonizing world. Often, such programs were open about the nature of the sponsorship: the Soviets were widely recognized for their support of *Lotus* magazine and its prize, while the US Information Agency was clear about its involvement in the career of Eileen Chang and other writers. In some instances, however, sponsorship could be clandestine, as in the Central Intelligence Agency (CIA) covertly bankrolling the Congress for Cultural Freedom, which had a formative influence on the emergence of African literature in English. I shall have much more to say about cultural diplomacy in the following chapters, but for the moment I will mention that it did not always work as we might expect it to work—that is, writers from decolonizing parts of the world did not become cold war partisans simply because they were beneficiaries of US or Soviet patronage. In fact, many writers, including Achebe, were happy to receive accolades and tangible support from both sides.

In addition to cultural diplomacy, however, superpower competition affected literary life in the decolonizing world because the cold war's most powerful states, as well as the governments of postcolonial nations, resorted to surveilling, blacklisting, censoring, imprisoning, and expelling writers of diverse political beliefs. The disciplining of intellectuals among the Warsaw Pact states is an old story, limited in some ways because its telling is so often partisan. Intimidation of writers was commonplace in the capitalist democracies as well as in the postcolonial nation-states of Africa and Asia, with the practice in no way limited to Soviet or Chinese areas of influence. This fact is generally known, but its effect on the literature of decolonization has not been considered in any depth. As William J. Maxwell, James Smith, and Mary Helen Washington have shown in some detail, the Federal Bureau of Investigation (FBI) in the United States and MI5 (Security Service) and MI6 (Secret Intelligence Service) in the United Kingdom kept tabs on many intellectuals, especially queer and African diasporic writers.[10] C.L.R. James, Claudia Jones, Doris Lessing, and the All-India Progressive Writers' Association were some of the individuals and groups scrutinized by British intelligence; James and Jones were both detained and then deported from the United States as political undesirables. Being a fierce anti-Stalinist and critic of Soviet Communism, as James was, did not make him any more palatable from the perspective of the US government. Postcolonial states do not have a better record: Faiz Ahmed Faiz, Sajjad Zaheer, Rajat Neogy, Ngũgĩ wa Thiong'o, and Wole Soyinka, to name only a few, all ran afoul of the authorities after independence for their nations. Apartheid-era South Africa, which does not fit easily into the model of colonial dependency or postcolonial nation-state, made life extremely difficult for many of its intellectuals, such as Ruth First, Alex La Guma, and Es'kia Mphahlele, each of whom I consider in subsequent chapters. The flip side of cultural diplomacy, then, is the harassment, intimidation, and coercive pressures that established and nascent states employed in attempts to contain or marginalize dissident writers.

As with cultural patronage, however, collecting intelligence on writers, even banishing or imprisoning them, did not always produce the effects intended by the governments responsible. Far from containing a figure such as Lessing, already living in exile, routine surveillance seemed to whet her intellectual appetite. Some writers could take it as a sign of their own significance that they were worth monitoring. Others who were objects of state surveillance, such as Richard Wright, collaborated with security and intelligence operations when they believed it was in their interest to do so. Imprisonment of writers most certainly altered the development of postcolonial literature—how many texts were stillborn we will never know—but writers contested this practice by cultivating transnational, nonaligned networks of their own. Similar to cultural diplomacy, the fate of persecuted writers was a matter of fierce cold war rivalry, in which national governments, from the powerful to the weak, were prone to criticize one another by pointing to abuses in other states. Writers seized on such animosities. Jailing intellectuals, as I show in the second half of this book, encouraged writers to see themselves as part of an international guild of dissidents, refusing to recognize the cold war's geographical boundaries and ideological allegiances. In stark contrast to our times, when literary intellectuals freely acknowledge their insignificance to the workings of the state, the cold war was a period when writers mattered, when they were important enough for large governments to patronize them, to collaborate with them, to censor them, and even to imprison, banish, or kill them.

The Aesthetic Cold War argues that a global literary field, largely but not exclusively anglophone, emerged during the twentieth century through the incorporation of writers from the decolonizing world into transnational systems of literary production and consumption. The process of integrating writers from Africa, Asia, and the Caribbean into a global network happened as part of the cold war. The Soviet Union and the United States, which sometimes worked through allies and client states, made significant efforts to control this process through cultural diplomacy programs and through punitive measures. It would be a significant mistake, however, to infer that such large states successfully enlisted or intimidated a great many writers from the decolonizing world, turning them into cold war partisans out of gratitude or fear. When it came to diplomacy efforts, the same writers had no qualms about accepting patronage from a variety of sources. Because of intense competition, neither the United States nor the Soviet Union made many overt demands on intellectuals from the decolonizing world, who tended to be fiercely independent and stubbornly nonaligned. Likewise, when it came to disciplinary measures, large states looked much the same from the perspective of the writer. Whatever their supposed ideological orientation, powerful governments and their allies had a marked tendency to surveil, censor, banish, imprison, and sometimes inflict capital punishment on outspoken figures.

Autonomy and Indigeneity

A few important observations follow from this book's fundamental contention that the literature of decolonization and the literature of the cold war are part of the same conceptual field, that to read one without the other is to misunderstand them both. First, readers will notice that I speak less in the following chapters of a debate between metropolitan modernism (or experimental writing, or art for art's sake) and socialist realism and more about the tension between aesthetic autonomy and aesthetic utilitarianism. Although the major cold war antagonists often reduced the aesthetic cold war to modernism versus socialist realism, intellectuals from the decolonizing world offered more capacious and sophisticated responses to the problem of aesthetic form in an ideological age. As Achebe's comments in "Africa and Her Writers" show us, the debate between art for art's sake and state-mandated literary forms was blinkered by political expedience and non-aesthetic judgments. Literature's proper use, purpose, and value, Achebe believes, can be located somewhere between declarations of pure autonomy and absolute submission to state control of the literary field. Read with care, Achebe's essay becomes a call for African writers both to assert their independence—against outside interference from neocolonial or cold war interests—and to create works of art that observe utilitarian principles by serving the needs of readers. Writers from the decolonizing world, I will suggest in the following chapters, reinterpreted the standoff between modernism and socialist realism as a more fundamental and enriching tension between the need for intellectual freedom and the desire to have writing serve practical ends, such as showcasing the dignity and value of one's culture. As chapter 2 will make apparent, writers from the decolonizing world were keen to assert their autonomy—their independence from the marketplace, from colonial culture, from cold war pressures, and from emerging nation-states—yet they did not necessarily forsake the goal of serving their primary constituents with their work. They thought about these competing imperatives in ways that may seem inconsistent from the perspective of a cold war partisan, but which I believe repay our attention as creative solutions to an impasse not of their own making.

In addition to autonomy and utilitarianism, writers from the decolonizing world thought deeply about the tension between indigeneity and cultural syncretism, as Achebe's discussion of Okigbo demonstrates. Should colonial writers resuscitate autochthonous cultural traditions and write in indigenous languages to fight against cultural imperialism? Or should they embrace the unique forms of hybridity that come with intercultural contact? Likewise, could nonmetropolitan writers turn metropolitan languages into tools of anticolonial thought? Should writers Africanize English, as Achebe proposes elsewhere, or should they forswear writing in imported tongues, as Ngũgĩ argues? Thoughts on the language debate, narrowly, and the cultural particularity versus hybridity discussion, more generally, provide some of the foundational questions in postcolonial studies, as the work of Adélékè Adéèkó, Kwame Anthony Appiah, Ranajit Guha, F. Abiola Irele, and Gayatri Chakravorty Spivak shows.

These arguments about language and culture cannot be understood without considering the impact of cold war diplomacy. The US diplomacy system developed an implicit language centralization model, with English functioning as a convenient and self-serving medium of literary exchange. Soviet diplomacy programs, by contrast, worked with an explicit model of linguistic plurality— potentially limitless portals for translation, with no one language given priority over another. This difference between the US and Soviet networks—one implicit and inconsistently managed, the other explicit and given more practical emphasis; one favoring vertical integration through cultural exchange within a dominant language, the other preaching horizontal exchange between languages and cultures—was just as important as the confrontation between autonomy and utilitarianism. Yet here, too, writers from the decolonizing world rarely line up neatly in predetermined camps. Chapter 2, which sketches out a detailed intellectual history of these debates in the anticolonial tradition, provides a more involved account about how the autonomy/utilitarianism and linguistic centralization/linguistic plurality discussions were stoked by the fires of the aesthetic cold war.

A Few Words on Methods

My approach in this book is archival, meaning that my readings of individual literary texts and cultural institutions are supported by evidence found in a variety of written deposits, from intelligence files to organizational memos to correspondence between authors and editors. When I started research for this project, I anticipated finding records showing how the United States bent anglophone writing from Africa, Asia, and the Caribbean into a shape it would find politically acceptable through circuits of patronage and elaborate networks of surveillance. Similarly, I expected Soviet networks to demand some version of socialist realism and ideological sympathy from their partners in the global south and to exclude writers who employ experimental techniques. The archives I consulted, however, had other things to teach me. After familiarizing myself with materials related to cultural diplomacy, I became more and more convinced that we should think of this as a system with built-in competition. Accounting for the Soviet presence in the global literary system forced me to acknowledge the limits of US influence; the Soviet cultural diplomacy apparatus presented a vibrant, attractive network of its own. Although it is clear that the superpowers influenced the emergence of late colonial and early postcolonial literature by promoting some writers and attempting to limit the circulation of others, it is not at all clear that the United States or the Soviet Union successfully created partisan intellectual networks among writers of the decolonizing world. The presence of competing cold war programs and the willingness of canny, nonaligned intellectuals to be courted by multiple interests while remaining uncommitted complicates such a narrative. Arguably, the United States wanted to promote pro-US and anti-Soviet writers, but it ended up promoting anglophone writing from diverse political perspectives. Although consolidating the dominance of English was an unintended consequence of US cultural diplomacy efforts—manipulating intellectuals for political gain was the primary, but largely unrealized objective—the elevation of English writing in the literary field was more lasting than any political gains. Superpower rivalry also retarded the development of local publishing industries, which found themselves competing against heavily subsidized imports.[11] The underdevelopment of local book markets was another lasting but accidental by-product of cultural diplomacy.

Archival materials generated by the political police, likewise, pose interpretive hazards of their own. The most obvious problem is the unevenness of the written record, where materials have been deliberately suppressed or unintentionally misplaced by their keepers. While Claudia Jones's FBI dossier is reasonably complete, for instance, there is no trace of her MI5 file. Even the most complete dossiers are full of redactions. The motivations of the political police and their informants present another clear challenge. I make a deliberate effort to balance the accounts we find in the intelligence dossiers against the accounts provided by writers who were the target of surveillance. When I suggest that writers from the decolonizing world carved out a measure of intellectual independence despite the pressures to which they were subjected, I rely on their testimony to substantiate this claim. But my book proposes we go beyond a state containment/dissident resistance template for explaining the relationship between the political police and recalcitrant writers. The ubiquity of state intelligence programs, from capitalist democracies to Communist governments to colonial situations to fledgling postcolonial states, led writers to think of themselves as vital nodes of an international, nonaligned network of intellectuals, neither beholden to ideology nor constrained by citizenship. Rivalries between states meant that writers who were bullied in one place sometimes found support and relief elsewhere. The United States and its allies, the Soviet Union and its allies, and the emerging states of the global south all contributed to the midcentury discourse of human rights by pointing out the weaknesses and limitations of other states, creating a system of competition that writers were quick to recognize and exploit to defend themselves. The writers I consider in the following pages understood state discipline and human rights networks as part of a multinational, advantage-seeking system full of gaps and inconsistencies. This context supported specific forms of intellectual nonalignment.

My account of the literary field is informed, broadly speaking, by materialist and sociological approaches to literary studies, especially by the work of Pierre Bourdieu and some of his leading interlocutors, such as John Guillory, Pascale Casanova, James F. English, Mark McGurl, and Sarah Brouillette. My claim that the history of late colonial and early postcolonial literature may be narrated as a struggle over intellectual autonomy, bolstered by ideological nonalignment, will be recognizable to scholars familiar with Bourdieu's descriptions of literary texts as self-legislating artifacts or the field of art as the economic world turned upside-down.[12] I differ from Bourdieu and from some of those influenced by his work when I suggest that the aesthetic cold war created an environment in which large states attempted to intervene in arts and letters in unprecedented ways. More so than at any time before or since, the literary field came under direct pressure from powerful government agencies that supported and suppressed literary production through complementary mechanisms. When midcentury writers thought about the question of autonomy and quarreled over utilitarian principles, they were thinking not only about the impact of global capitalism on the market for symbolic goods, but also about the workings of large states. During this period, powerful states devoted extraordinary resources to subsidizing literary production, which included financing work produced by international writers and destined for readers across the world. Likewise, they devoted extraordinary resources to controlling literary production by harassing dissident writers. In terms of literary history, the aesthetic cold war represents an anomaly, an interlude during which powerful nations attempted to shape the production of literature both within and far beyond their areas of direct political control. This anomalous situation created a predominantly anglophone global literary field that has outlived the specific political conditions through which it took shape.

What Follows

The book has three main parts. The opening section includes this short introduction and a longer chapter on the intellectual history of the period. Here, I show how the aesthetic debates of the cold war, especially debates about autonomous versus utilitarian theories of literary production, were inextricable from anticolonial discussions about literary language, especially those about the use of metropolitan, vernacular, and indigenous languages. This chapter provides a lengthy, technical background of the aesthetic debates over decolonization and the cold war. Specialists will want to read it, but nonspecialists may wish to skip ahead to the second and third sections.

The second section of the book includes three chapters on cultural diplomacy programs. Chapter 3, on the activities of the Congress for Cultural Freedom in Africa, shows how the CIA's literary activities functioned in a decolonizing environment. Against those who read the CIA as a skillful puppet master, I suggest that African intellectuals had considerable room for maneuver when they engaged with US cultural diplomacy. Chapter 4 turns to Soviet-led cultural diplomacy efforts, especially the Afro-Asian Writers' Association and its house magazine, *Lotus*, which were very similar to US programs. The Soviets were no more successful than their rivals in recruiting ideological mouthpieces among global south writers. The major difference between the superpowers' programs, I argue, is that Soviet-led cultural diplomacy insisted on the value of linguistic and cultural heterogeneity. Chapter 5 returns to US cultural diplomacy through the career of Eileen Chang and her dealings with the United States Information Agency (USIA), the cultural diplomacy offshoot of the US State Department. Unlike the Congress for Cultural Freedom, the USIA and the State Department were open about their sponsorship of cultural goods, which changes how we might understand their position in the decolonizing parts of Asia.

The final section of the book turns to programs of state surveillance and discipline of intellectuals. Chapter 6 delves in the intelligence files of the political police, in this case MI5, which kept tabs on Doris Lessing for nearly two decades. Rather than stifling her creativity, the experience of being monitored encouraged Lessing to write in new, more experimental ways. Chapter 7 looks at the FBI files compiled on Claudia Jones and C.L.R. James, Trinidadians who were deported from the United States in the mid-1950s. My research suggests that surveillance, incarceration, and deportation brought these political antagonists—Jones was a card-carrying Communist Party member, while James was a Trotskyite—much closer to each other as they turned to the nationalist projects of the 1960s. Chapter 8 examines the genre of the prison memoir, with forays into the archives of PEN International. Jailing writers is a basic way of curbing intellectual freedoms, but the experience of reading prison memoirs also reminds us that these writers used the language of human rights to resist. Prison memoirs show us how writers collaborated with the cold war's human rights organizations to imagine themselves as part of an international, affirmatively nonaligned network of intellectuals, crisscrossing national boundaries and entrenched ideologies.

Before providing more details about how the cold war's systems of patronage and policing influenced the development of literature from the global south, I pause here to reflect briefly on my own ideological perspective. As I have presented some of my preliminary research over the past few years, both in talks and in print, I have been surprised by the number of audience members and readers expecting me to adopt a definitive position on a cold war that ended, effectively, three decades ago. Some react with fury, or glee, when they discover that the United States or the Soviet Union attempted to influence the world of arts and letters in Africa and Asia, or when I insist that Achebe's unwitting acceptance of CIA support or his conscious acceptance a Soviet-sponsored literary prize should not then lead us to suspect his motives or to question his integrity. My attempt to reconstruct a literary history of decolonization and the cold war together will neither exculpate nor condemn the cultural diplomacy of the era's superpowers. I take it for granted that the disciplining of intellectuals for merely stating their political views is cowardly, unconscionable, and all too common in this period. Likewise, I will not take a position on the tiresome question of whether one side of the cold war acted less dishonorably than another, with the nearly inevitable conclusion that the US state and its allies were somehow more justified than their rivals when they crossed ethical lines. I leave this to the people who feel called to take a belated partisan stand on these issues.

For a literary historian, as I attempt to write in these pages, these are unsatisfying and ultimately misleading approaches to midcentury global literature. Whether anticolonial writing might have evolved along more or less promising lines, or whether it would have been more or less free to imagine a different future, without state interference are not questions we are in a position to answer: the most sustained attempts to decolonize literary culture happened in this specific intellectual and ideological context, and it is a speculative endeavor to wish it otherwise. If I have any ideological conviction in these pages, it is a species of loyalty to the anticolonial intellectuals who achieved a measure of cultural and political freedom for themselves and their primary audiences. Arguing that the literature of decolonization was sanitized or coopted by cold war cultural diplomacy and discipline does not help us understand the texts that Achebe, Lessing, Ngũgĩ, or Soyinka have left us, few of which promote colonialism, apologize for US imperialism, or defend Soviet authoritarianism. Where others have read cold war intellectuals as compromised by their acceptance of state patronage, this book tends to recognize how late colonial and early postcolonial intellectuals carved out a degree of independence in the face of considerable pressure. This conclusion will not satisfy those who are inclined to believe that the cold war superpowers were nearly omnipotent in their dealings with a group of disorganized, scattered, relatively powerless intellectuals. But it will, I hope, have the advantage of explaining how a genuinely anticolonial literary tradition found a footing on the cold war's rocky terrain.

2

A Brief Intellectual History
of the Aesthetic Cold War

BEFORE PROVIDING more details about how cold war patronage and surveillance of writers impacted twentieth century anglophone literature, this chapter sketches an intellectual history of this aesthetic cold war. Achebe's turn to
Okigbo in "Africa and Her Writers" provides a clue to how this intellectual
history might be imagined. In rejecting the excesses of both "capitalist" and
"communist" literary practices in his search for a nonaligned aesthetics,
Achebe concludes the essay by championing Okigbo's unique, experimental
indigeneity. Why should a rejection of cold war partisanship lead Achebe to
celebrate Okigbo as a specifically Nigerian writer? In what way does cultural
particularity function as the antidote to cold war rivalries? Achebe acknowl-
edges that Okigbo was the most self-consciously difficult and elitist poet of his
generation, the figure of his cohort most informed by metropolitan modernism. Yet Achebe also maintains that Okigbo's final volume, *Path of Thunder*,
brings his cosmopolitanism and deep learning (Okigbo studied classics) to
bear on a distinctive Nigerian experience:

> [Okigbo] brought into his poetry all the heirlooms of his multiple heritage;
> he ranged with ease through Rome and Greece and Babylon, through the
> rites of Judaism and Catholicism, through European and Bengali literatures,
> through modern music and painting. But at least one perceptive Nigerian
> critic has argued that Okigbo's true voice only came to him in his last se-
> quence of poems, *Path of Thunder*, when he had finally and decisively opted
> for an African inspiration. [...] It was as though the goddess he sought in
> his poetic journey through so many alien landscapes, and ultimately found
> at home, had given him this new thunder. (44–45)

In Achebe's estimation, Okigbo wandered far and wide, learning from multiple peoples and cultural traditions, but he could not express himself fully until he drew his inspiration from domestic sources. Autochthony, indigeneity, cultural authenticity: this cluster of concepts, undergirding Achebe's reading of Okigbo as a repatriated poet, are familiar to any student of late colonial and early post-colonial literature in English. African writers, according to this essay, ought to be able to use the raw materials at hand to connect with audiences close to home. They may find favor with overseas readers—Achebe excelled all African writers on that front—but they must stay true to their own cultural traditions. This kind of nativism, I should point out, is not a version of racial essentialism or an insistence on cultural purity: Achebe is comfortable enough with hybridity and plurality and borrowing, so long as the literary product helps cultivate a national (or perhaps regional) literary tradition.

My intellectual history of the aesthetic cold war is an attempt to explain how a few key concepts in late colonial and early postcolonial literature—especially cultural authenticity, cultural independence, and indigeneity—can be understood as part of fundamental debates about aesthetic autonomy and aesthetic utilitarianism. The goal is not to put the emergence of global literature in English in the context of the cold war—thereby fitting the literature of decolonization into a cold war frame, leaving the implicitly Euro-American container more or less intact—but instead to suggest that the aesthetic cold war and the history of global English literature in the twentieth century cannot be written without one another.[1] The aesthetic cold war, in short, allowed writers from decolonizing regions opportunities to plug into new networks, but those networks were in turn shaped and reshaped by late colonial and postcolonial intellectuals who were debating the relationship between aesthetics and politics, cultural dependency and autonomy, indigeneity and cosmopolitanism. In this chapter, I argue that discussions about cultural particularity were an integral part of the aesthetic cold war.

Interwar Debates

By the early 1970s, as Achebe's comments suggest, many observers had come to regard the aesthetic cold war as a disturbingly reductive and frustratingly predictable disagreement about the function of art. Even as subtle a thinker as Fredric Jameson, in *Marxism and Form*, writes off Popular Front era aesthetic debates on the left as "relatively untheoretical, essentially didactic in nature, destined more for use in the night school than in the graduate seminar."[2] Very few of the most important salvos in this confrontation, however, are quite as simple as many students of twentieth-century literature are in the habit of assuming. I hypothesize that returning to some of these discussions may allow us to think about the literary history of the century in new ways by showing how diverse sectors of the world literary market—metropolitan modernist, socialist, late colonial, postcolonial, and global anglophone—were trying to answer some of the same questions.

A few interwar documents and gatherings stand out as particularly relevant for my purposes. Leon Trotsky's *Literature and Revolution* (1923), "Revolution of the Word" (1929), *transition* magazine's collective statement about the value of linguistic experimentation, the first and second manifestoes of Surrealism (1924, 1930) and the *Affaire Aragon*, the writers' conferences in Kharkov (1930) and Moscow (1934), Paris's International Congress in Defense of Culture (1935), the Left Book Club (1936–48) and the journal *Left Review* (1934–38), Cecil Day-Lewis's "Revolutionaries and Poetry" (1935), Ralph Fox's *The Novel and the People* (1937), and the "Manifesto for an Independent Revolutionary Art" (1938), signed by André Breton and Diego Rivera but usually attributed to Breton and Trotsky: these are among the key interwar manifestoes, cultural institutions, conferences, and events associated with the start of an aesthetic debate that would resonate across the world of arts and letters throughout the century. Spanning only fifteen years in appearance, the events and publications on this list make it easy to see why a figure such as Achebe would regard this as a conflict between European tribes. Excepting Rivera's signature on "Manifesto for an Independent Revolutionary Art" and a few Left Book Club titles, the non-European contributions to this discussion appear limited.

We can observe the battle lines most clearly by contrasting the short "Revolution of the Word" manifesto with the far lengthier proceedings of the 1934 Soviet writers' conference, *Problems in Soviet Literature*. Published in a little magazine now famed for its embrace of experimental, multilingual modernism, "Revolution of the Word" makes an appeal to readers who have grown weary of literature "still under the hegemony of the banal word, monotonous syntax, static psychology, descriptive naturalism, and desirous of crystallizing a viewpoint." Several of the manifesto's bullet points are worth quoting in full:

1. The revolution in the English Language is an accomplished fact.
2. The imagination in search of a fabulous world is autonomous and unconfined.
   [...]

6. The literary creator has the right to disintegrate the primal matter of words imposed on him by textbooks and dictionaries.
   (*The road to excess leads to the palace of wisdom ... Blake*)
7. He has the right to use words of his own fashioning and to disregard existing grammatical and syntactical laws.
   (*The tigers of wrath are wiser than the horses of instruction ... Blake*)
   [...]
9. We are not concerned with the propagation of sociological ideas, except to emancipate the creative elements from the present ideology.
   [...]
12. The plain reader be damned.
    (Damn braces! Bless relaxes! ... Blake)[3]

It is immediately clear that Achebe's characterization of metropolitan modernists as contemptuous of readers, bewitched by the search for absolute independence of the aesthetic, has not missed the mark entirely. Yet a few principles outlined here would be of importance to nonmetropolitan writers as they contemplated the workings of the global literary system they were in the process of recalibrating. First, and most obvious, "Revolution of the Word" borrows the language of radical political manifestoes even if it displays an indifference to "sociological ideas." The manifesto's form seems to invite revolutionary rhetoric even if the content expresses skepticism about political engagement.[4]

Second, late colonial and early postcolonial writers borrowed liberally from the flexible doctrine of aesthetic autonomy as they developed their own solutions to the problem of decolonizing literary culture.[5] If such writers were sometimes suspicious of aesthetic autonomy of the purest kind, they were willing to adapt the language of autonomy to insist on the independence of late colonial and early postcolonial writing, demanding freedom from state interference as well as the end of colonial rule. This is not aesthetic autonomy in an unadulterated form, but rather a distinctive amendment to the doctrine of authorial and textual independence.

Third, late colonial and early postcolonial writers, even the less experimental ones, were not afraid to bend the shape of English to fit their own particular needs, often by indigenizing it. In "African Writers and the English Language," for instance, Achebe says that his writing will help create "a new English, still in full communion with its ancestral home but altered to suit its new African surroundings" (*Morning Yet* 103). Again, this is not precisely the "revolution in the English Language" that the *transition* signatories proclaim as an "accomplished fact." But the effort to work the English language into a nonmetropolitan form, as exhibited in the writing of figures as different as Louise Bennett, Kamau Brathwaite, James Kelman, Okot p'Bitek, Salman Rushdie, and Amos Tutuola, channels the same spirit of linguistic innovation in order to indigenize, or provincialize, literary language.[6]

The rejection of socialist aesthetics, likewise, was not nearly so wholesale as Achebe's remarks in "Africa and Her Writers" would have us believe. A quick overview of *Problems of Soviet Literature: Reports and Speeches at the First Soviet Writers Congress* shows that the tropes of cultural authenticity and autochthony that appear in late colonial and early postcolonial accounts of cultural politics have a wide-ranging history. James Joyce, perhaps the single figure most closely associated with *transition* and the magazine's insistence on creative freedoms, attracted special attention from the plenary speakers. Maxim Gorky, one of the leading figures of Soviet literature and often credited as the founder of socialist realism, states the collective case against "formalism" most succinctly: "The liberty of art, the freedom of creative thought have been upheld with passionate redundancy."[7] Karl Radek's keynote report singles out Joyce for his linguistic experiments and his elitism. Beyond these deficiencies, Radek claims the fault of *Ulysses* is not that it is too ambitious, but that it is not ambitious enough:

> [Joyce's] basic feature is the conviction that there is nothing big in life—no big events, no big people, no big ideas; and the writer can give a picture of life by just taking "any given hero on any given day," and reproducing him with exactitude. A heap of dung, crawling with worms, photographed by a cinema apparatus through a microscope—such is Joyce's work. (153)

Achebe's humorously petulant comparison of art-for-art's-sake to animal feces, we see, has its precedent in official Soviet responses to Joyce's work. But Radek's and Achebe's scatological comparison makes it easy to miss the deeper significance of the reading. Socialist writers have much to admire about Joyce's technique, as Radek clarifies later in the talk—Joyce's rendering of physical details and mental processes of unremarkable people are far in advance of the technical capabilities of 1930s Soviet writers—but progressive writers should be cautious about literature that is pleased merely to document the daily routine of an undistinguished and unambitious individual. The problem with *Ulysses* is that it insulates readers from any "big ideas" and significant forms of social conflict. Instead, we have the banal, the mundane; there is no sense of inspiring victories or harrowing defeats, no struggle for a better or different future, no history-changing conflicts rendered even on a personal scale. In the welter of surface details, we lose the depth that transforms mere reportage into serious art. This is a debatable reading of *Ulysses*, but it certainly made an impact on the way late colonial and postcolonial writers interpreted the legacy of metropolitan modernism.

To restate this difference in more theoretical terms, this reading recategorizes *Ulysses* as far from the high literary forms—tragedy and especially epic—as one can move in the novel.[8] For all its allusions to the great epics, Joyce's novel offers a kind of small stakes, intentionally myopic view of modern life, according to this line of thought. As Radek puts it later in his address: in contrast to *Ulysses*, "[t]he literature of socialist realism is a literature of world scales" (158). This invocation of world scales makes Radek sound more like a twenty-first-century literary critic than a Party functionary from a dim Soviet past, which is another way of saying that the current ways of reading world literature owe more to cold war thought than we readily acknowledge. Or, as the revolutionary Nikolai Bukharin describes in his lecture, "One cannot understand art without analysing its connections with the entire life-activity of society, because art must not be transformed into a metaphysical 'thing-in-itself'" (201). Radek and Bukharin suggest that "formalism" and microscopic attention to detail have two particularly debilitating consequences: renouncing literature's connection with its audiences and sacrificing world-historical depth for an impressionistic, fleeting surface. *Ulysses* provides the wrong kind of realism—for all its linguistic virtuosity, it is too appearance-obsessed in a way, refusing to see the underlying social significance in the quotidian. Joyce's novel figures here as anti-epic, the narrative that refuses to connect the fate of the individual with the fate of a larger society. Later in this book, I turn to C.L.R. James, hardly an apologist for socialist realism or Stalinist politics, showing that he operates with similar criticisms of metropolitan modernism and similar ideas about the potential of epic to serve as a genre for telling the story of decolonization.

Aside from sharing some beliefs about world scale and linguistic play, socialist aesthetic theory would provide an alternative to the "Revolution of the Word" position on the language question. If the *transition* manifesto provides some sense that literary languages should deviate from standard metropolitan forms, the Soviet Writers Congress is more explicit about the place of indigenous languages in imagining literature on a "world scale." Gorky—"Soviet literature is not merely a literature of the Russian language. It is an All-Union

literature [. . . including] the literary creation of the national minorities"
(59)—and Bukharin—"An All-Soviet literature is growing up in our country,
in which the literature of national minorities possesses enormous significance"
(211)—both emphasize the place of subordinated languages in a progressive
literary movement. Gorky and Bukharin may have been playing to the gallery:
Steven S. Lee points out that at least half of the six hundred delegates at the
conference came from the "national minorities."[9] This position was in line with
Stalin's writing on the national question.[10] The Afro-Asian Writer's Association and its house journal, *Lotus*, would continue to emphasize the cultural
heterogeneity of the Soviet Union. The outlines of the language debate are
now in evidence: revolutionize metropolitan languages or develop horizontal
connections between languages through translation. Whereas many late colonial and postcolonial writers had mixed feelings about working in European
tongues—sparking a lively debate in African letters, where both English- and
French-language literatures came under scrutiny—Soviet official policy welcomed, at least in theory, contributions from writers in all languages.[11]

Nancy Cunard's pamphlet and questionnaire, "Authors Take Sides on the
Spanish War" (1937), is another interesting artifact from the interwar years
because it urges Cunard's like-minded modernists to abandon their invest-
ments in aesthetic autonomy, at least in the face of fascist aggression. It follows
close on the heels of the argument that split Surrealism into two camps in what
became known as the *Affaire Aragon*: should literature submit to Party discipline and political expediency, or should aesthetic production remain independent of political interference?[12] Cunard's pamphlet features participation
from many figures who are closely associated with the kind of modernist experimentation favored by the *transition* manifesto, and yet the urgency of the
struggle against fascism leads Cunard's cosignatories to proclaim that "we are
determined, or compelled, to take sides. The equivocal attitude, the Ivory
Tower, the paradoxical, the ironic detachment, will no longer do."[13] The association of habitual fence-sitting or equivocation with sophisticated aesthetic
forms—metropolitan modernism and its defense of aesthetic autonomy—is
both asserted and undermined by the contents of "Authors Take Sides." Several signatories, including Cunard, W. H. Auden, Heinrich Mann, Stephen
Spender, and Tristan Tzara, as well as several pro-Republican respondents,
such as Samuel Beckett and Cyril Connolly, would at different points in their
careers advocate "the paradoxical, the ironic attitude" openly rejected here.
The association of political nonparticipation with the doctrine of creative autonomy would become one of the most intractable assumptions of the

aesthetic cold war, and yet literary intellectuals were liable to alter or rearrange their opinions on this matter in different situations.

This pervasive belief that elite art constitutes a form political abdication is one of the main reasons we should read the literatures of decolonization and the cold war as part of the same tradition. Late colonial and postcolonial intellectuals, as I discuss below, were every bit as responsible for perpetuating this attitude, and every bit as likely to play both sides of this debate when the situation allowed it. Perhaps the porosity between these two literary traditions, read separately for so long, can be illustrated by realizing that colonial intellectuals were drafted into these discussions from the earliest stages. James, Mulk Raj Anand, Cedric Dover, George Padmore, and Christina Stead are among the nonmetropolitan intellectuals who responded affirmatively to Cunard's call for support for Spain. Although a schematic outline of the differences between the doctrines of metropolitan modernism and socialist aesthetics makes the rift seem like an all-European affair, several key contributions to the debate, also from the interwar period, come from non-European sources, and it is to them I now turn.

Interwar: Anticolonial Revolutionaries

A few of the important interwar forays into the aesthetic cold war from anticolonial thinkers include Velimir Khlebnikov's "An Indo-Russian Union" (1918), Oswald de Andrade's "Cannibalist Manifesto" ("Manifesto Antropófago," 1928), some of the early publications of negritude, such as *Légitime Défense* (1932) and the Nardal sisters' *La Revue du monde noir* (1931–32), the Trinidadian little magazine *The Beacon* (1931–33), the All-India Progressive Writers' Association manifesto and movement (1930s), and the Chinese May Fourth New Culture Movement (1919–30) and League of Left-Wing Writers (1930–36). While scholars traditionally read these texts, periodicals, and movements as founding statements in nationalist and anticolonial literary traditions, erecting a firewall between the cold war and the literatures of anticolonialism has impoverished our understanding of both. As far back as the 1920s, colonial intellectuals were freely borrowing and freely criticizing the aesthetic theories of both major cold war camps, articulating a version of indigeneity and cultural autonomy. The texts and movements I discuss in this section borrow from the Marxist concept of revolution, but none of them are all that faithful to the aesthetic or political Communist Party line of the day.

That the "Cannibalist Manifesto" draws on the tradition of Marxism is obvious from the title alone. It is deeply indebted to the Surrealist movement as well, which of course has its own debt to Dada. As in several of Dada's manifestoes and performance pieces and the first Surrealist manifesto, Andrade's well-travelled text—not his first stab at the genre—is full of inside jokes, abrupt transitions, nonsense or apparent nonsense, and arcane references. It does not offer easy reading, appealing much as "Revolution of the Word" does to the cognoscenti. Unlike the *transition* document, however, the "Cannibalist Manifesto" insists that cultural politics cannot be cordoned off from literary endeavors:

> We want the Carib revolution. Greater than the French Revolution. The unification of all productive revolts for the progress of humanity. Without us, Europe wouldn't even have its meager declaration of the rights of man. [. . .] From the French Revolution to Romanticism, to the Bolshevik Revolution, to the Surrealist Revolution.[14]

The document's use of revolution toggles back and forth between political and cultural definitions of the concept. Andrade finds antecedents for his "Carib revolution" in other political revolutions, naming both the French and the Bolshevik uprisings as part of the region's history. Inverting European discourses about civilization and development, Andrade reads metropolitan progress—the "meager declaration of the rights of man"—as a byproduct of imperialist theft and appropriation. James, too, in *The Black Jacobins*, reads the revolution in what would become Haiti as the first full expression of a postcolonial identity—both political and cultural—drawing on but ultimately surpassing the metropolitan wing of the French Revolution. Andrade insists that the project of political emancipation in colonial regions be consolidated by forms of cultural emancipation.

Prefiguring many later declarations of cultural autonomy from the late colonial and early postcolonial canon, the "Cannibalist Manifesto" also suggests that nonmetropolitan intellectuals have the freedom to salvage bits of European culture for their own projects. Rudimentary elements of communism and capitalism, the French and Bolshevik revolutions, and even the modernist aesthetics of Surrealism were already present in the preconquest culture Andrade hopes to reclaim for modern Brazil: "We already had Communism," he says, and "We already had Surrealist language. The Golden Age" (40). Ritualistic cannibalism, in which the victor consumes the vanquished enemy, provides a template for how colonial peoples might assert independence from imperialist control and yet claim features of European culture, such as Surrealism or communism. Cultural cannibalism, in other words, is an early theory of indigenization, of turning metropolitan practices into the raw material for an independent polity.

Not to be boxed in by ideological differences, Andrade tropes this version of cultural cannibalism as a capitalist practice, too: "Everyday love and the capitalist way of life. Cannibalism. Absorption of the sacred enemy" (43). Marx's famous descriptions of capitalism as a vampire, feeding on the blood of the proletariat, are here transformed into playful banter about the usefulness of aggression and cultural appropriation when fighting for the rights of colonized peoples. Whether capitalist or communist, Andrade's cannibalism is unmistakably Brazilian. It would be futile to look for ideological consistency in the "Cannibalist Manifesto." Similar to many late colonial and early postcolonial intellectuals, Andrade creates a patchwork out of available materials, reclaiming indigenous practices and stitching them together with scraps from everywhere: capitalist and communist, metropolitan and autochthonous, highbrow and vernacular.[15]

The earliest stirrings of the negritude movement follow right on the heels of the "Cannibalist Manifesto," and as with Andrade, some of the most influential members of the francophone Black Atlantic shuttled between Surrealism and Communism. For decades, intellectual historians credited Aimé Césaire with coining the term negritude, although there were disputes about when and where this might have appeared first in print. The recent recovery of a long-lost early issue of L'étudiant noir has allowed scholars to trace the term to Césaire's 1935 essay "Conscience Raciale et Révolution Sociale." The essay should interest scholars of the anticolonial literary tradition for a few reasons. It shows that Césaire and his negritude collaborators, such as Léopold Sédar Senghor and Léon Gontran Damas, were in close dialogue with Marxist thought as they were developing this cultural theory, even though Senghor and Damas were never ardent Marxists and Césaire probably only joined the Communist Party later, in 1942.[16] It also demonstrates that despite Césaire's sympathy for the Marxist faith in revolution, his firm belief that people of African descent needed to acquire racial consciousness before joining a socialist revolution put him at odds with many of his Party colleagues.

"Conscience Raciale et Révolution Sociale" adapts a Marxist theory of alienation but translates it from the economic to the cultural sphere. Césaire is well aware that the labor of Black, colonial peoples is exploited in an imperial-capitalist system, but he insists in this essay that there is no chance of a lasting change if people of African descent cannot overcome the affliction of racial inferiority first:

> if it is true that the work of the revolutionary dialectic is to destroy "all the falser perceptions lavished upon men," should we not denounce the soporific identifying culture and place beneath the prisons that white capitalism has built for us, each one of our racial values like so many liberating bombs? They have forgotten the principal, those who tell the Negro to revolt without first making him become conscious of himself, without first telling him that it is beautiful and good and legitimate to be a Negro.[17]

What the European wings of the Party do not realize when they try to recruit colonial intellectuals is that the racial hierarchies imposed by colonialism are an impediment to revolution. Class consciousness will not make revolution succeed in the colonial world. Fifty years later, after political decolonization was well underway, Ngũgĩ would insist that cultural imperialism lasts longer, and does more damage, than mere political control of colonial peoples.

If, however, people of African descent assert their cultural significance, this newfound racial consciousness could serve the revolution well, becoming "liberating bombs" in the service of lasting change. Césaire's first known use of the term negritude comes directly out of this engagement with the philosophies of the left:

> before starting the Revolution and in order to start the revolution—the real one—[. . .] one condition is essential: break the mechanical race identification, tear out superficial values, seize in ourselves the immediate Negro, plant our Négritude like a beautiful tree so that it can bear its most authentic fruit. [. . .] To be a revolutionary is all well and good; but for us other Negros it is insufficient, we must not be revolutionaries who are coincidentally black, but properly Negro revolutionaries.[18]

The Party's insistence that revolutionaries give pride of place to economic exploitation, thereby underestimating the effects of cultural alienation, is one of Césaire's longstanding grievances with the Communist line. In this he anticipates Achebe's contention in "The Novelist as Teacher" that one of the urgent tasks of the Black Atlantic intellectual is to convince readers that people of African descent had not been delivered out of "one long night of savagery" only yesterday by the saving graces of European civilization (*Morning Yet* 72).

In contrast to the avant-garde language and structure of the "Cannibalist Manifesto" and Césaire's early poetry, the manifesto of the All-India Progressive Writers' Association (PWA) relies on straightforward language and equally uncomplicated form to communicate its message. Although at least four versions of the manifesto are known to have circulated—drafted in London in English in 1934–35, published in *Hans* in Hindustani in 1935, published in English in *Left Review* in 1936, and formally ratified at the Second PWA meeting in 1938—each of the versions emphasizes the group's support for nationalist aspirations, loosely socialist politics, and engaged literature written in Indian languages, especially Hindustani.[19]

The PWA is the anticolonial literary movement influenced most heavily by the Union of Soviet Writers, itself founded just before the early stirrings of the PWA. Rakhshanda Jalil, in her comprehensive scholarly history of the Urdu branch movement, goes so far as to say that original member and first PWA Secretary Sajjad Zaheer "was either instructed to do something similar or decided on his own to establish an association modelled on Soviet lines."[20] Most original PWA members were not Party members, but Zaheer joined during his years in England. Zaheer's own accounts of the PWA indicate how the group was influenced by his and Mulk Raj Anand's attendance at the 1935 conference in Paris (especially by the presence of the Soviet delegation), by Aragon, the French Surrealist who pledged his loyalty to the Party during a trip to the Soviet Union, and by Ralph Fox, the English Communist heavily involved with *Left Review* who died fighting in Spain in 1937.[21] Fox encouraged Zaheer, Anand, and Jyotirmoy Ghosh (or J. C. Ghose) as they drafted the manifesto and gathered like-minded Indians in London, and the group's manifesto enjoyed a metropolitan airing in *Left Review*.[22]

Formation of the PWA was influenced by contact with metropolitan British and Soviet writers, but it is also clear that everyone was responding to developments in China, where leading members of the May Fourth New Culture Movement and the League of Left-Wing Writers had been calling for a literature in accessible, vernacular language since the 1910s and '20s. Lu Xun, who provided a bridge between the May Fourth modernizers and the politically militant League of Left-Wing Writers, spent much of the 1920s arguing that his contemporaries ought to abandon writing in traditional Chinese script: "All we want is this: instead of overtaxing our brains to learn the speech of men long since dead, we should speak that of living men. Instead of treating language as a curio, we should write in the easily understood vernacular."[23] Mao

Zedong would pick up this thread about fifteen years later during his wartime lectures on culture. Scholars of Chinese literature have long understood how these calls to bring vernacular speech into literary practices changed the trajectory of a national literary tradition. Scholars of global literature, however, have been slow to recognize how these arguments about vernacular speech and translation were happening simultaneously across the world throughout this period—in China, in Brazil, in the francophone Black Atlantic, in the Soviet Union, as well as in metropolitan centers such as London and Paris. The appearance of the PWA manifesto in the 1930s, announcing the creation of a literary association and carrying a message of Indian nationalism, appearing in both an Indian and a European little magazine in the mid-1930s adds several vectors to this transnational debate about language and culture.

The PWA manifesto urges Indian writers to "bring the arts into the closest touch with the people" and to "deal with the basic problems of our existence to-day—the problems of hunger and poverty, social backwardness and political subjugation."[24] Like Achebe in "Africa and Her Writers," Zaheer asserts that the idea of pure creative freedom for artists is a metropolitan fabrication, totally foreign to the indigenous cultures of India.[25] Although Zaheer reports an interest in Surrealism in his memoirs, the PWA manifesto's language, in sharp contrast to the "Cannibalist Manifesto" and its Surrealist counterparts, employs simple, declarative prose. In so doing, the text implies that experimental literature is not best equipped to represent "hunger and poverty, social backwardness and political subjugation" in ways that would further progressive causes—a conclusion shared by Lu Xun, for instance, but not by all anticolonial writers, such as Andrade or the young Césaire. As with the Soviet Writers Congress, the PWA calls for the promotion of literature in all Indian languages, although it controversially says the organization will "strive for the acceptance of a common language (Hindustani) and a common script (Indo-Roman) for India" (n.p.)—a resolution dropped in the manifesto adopted at the Second PWA meeting in Calcutta in 1938 (Jalil 437–38). One version of Indian nationalism—a language unity model—gives way to a vernacular pluralist agenda as the document makes its way in the world.[26]

A remarkable feature of the PWA is that it caught the attention of British intelligence agencies almost from the start. Partly because the Communist Party was banned in India at the time, the India Office (distinct from but analogous to the Colonial Office) tracked the group with the assistance of Scotland Yard and the Indian Intelligence Bureau. The reports begin as early as January 1936, shortly after Zaheer returned to India to publicize the PWA. "Zaheer has a growing reputation as a writer," one report summarizes, speculating that

> his new plans are founded on instructions received from Moscow, the Comintern have decided to use his talents in this direction while satisfying themselves about his *bona fides*. If he survives the test, it is probable that he will be employed on the more important Communist work for which his training in England and Germany has fitted him. Till then, it seems, he will be expected to confine his activities within the limits suggested above and to the formation of the Progressive Writers' Association.[27]

The PWA here figures as Zaheer's audition for real Party work, and indeed Zaheer took on a more active role as an organizer in later years. When he was not campaigning for the PWA, making nationalist speeches, or working for the socialist wing of the Congress, Zaheer spent several years in prison between his return to India in late 1935 through 1942, when the ban on the Communist Party in India was lifted. The experience only strengthened his political resolve, it seems, for he would spend additional time behind bars in Pakistan in the 1950s. As with many Popular- or United-Front era cultural activities, the British political police concluded that the PWA must be operating as a clandestine wing of the Communist Party, alleging that "every effort is being made to conceal the Association's communist inspiration and intentions."[28] It is not obvious how the group's sympathy with Communist Party objectives has been attenuated in the manifesto—it seems to be right on the surface of the text, even if one cannot therefore conclude that the PWA was simply a front organization doing Moscow's bidding. As a result, government officials suppressed the PWA's first stab at a periodical, *New Indian Writing*, confiscating it when it arrived in India.[29]

One perverse consequence of state surveillance of Zaheer and the PWA is that our literary histories are richer and more comprehensive because of the existence of these files. As William J. Maxwell states the case in *F.B. Eyes: How J. Edgar Hoover's Ghostreaders Framed African American Literature*, the US government's prurient interest in African American literature turns the state into an untrained curator and its archives into a kind of literary museum, preserving a branch of cultural production that operated on the fringes of mainstream literary culture at the time (16–17). Likewise, the substantial reports generated for the India Office present a tendentious view of the PWA, but they certainly fill out a record that would be sketchier otherwise. For instance, excerpts from the PWA manifesto, which had yet to be published in English, show up in the intelligence files.[30] If one thinks of Anand's career path, the ironies are significant. As we know from the publication history of *Untouchable* (1935), Anand struggled mightily to get his novel published with a metropolitan firm until the leftist publisher Wishart agreed to issue it on condition that E. M. Forster lend his endorsement by adding a preface.[31] In the mid-1930s, much of literary London was ignoring Anand, despite his many metropolitan acquaintances and Oxbridge credentials. The Communists at *Left Review* and the British government, by contrast, were lavishing attention on Anand, Zaheer, and their colleagues, attending PWA meetings and reading everything they wrote with care. Although the relationship between the state, socialist revolutionaries, and late colonial intellectuals could be extremely fraught, it was also close.

1940–1956: Anticolonialism Consolidated

Conventional accounts of the cold war often start in the mid-1940s, with the end of World War II or the blockade of Berlin. George Orwell is usually credited as the first to use the term in this specific way in a great little essay from 1945, "You and the Atom Bomb."[32] My intellectual history revises this chronology, suggesting that the aesthetic cold war began in earnest during the interwar years, and it revises the implied geography of the cold war, arguing that writers from a variety of regions and cultural traditions were thinking about how language choice could impact discussions about cultural autonomy and utilitarianism. This conversation proliferated in the midcentury decades. Mao Zedong, for instance, refashioned some of the principles articulated by the May Fourth New Culture Movement, the League of Left-Wing Writers, and the Union of Soviet Writers at the Yan'an Forum on Literature and Art (1942), a conference held in the Communist-controlled region of China. Anti-Communists in the United States and Western Europe stated their case with *The God That Failed* (1950) and followed that with their own movement and manifesto, the Congress for Cultural Freedom (1950–67), which I consider at greater length in chapter 3. As if anticipating *The God That Failed*, the French Communist Party produced *Why I am a Communist* (1947). Exchanges between global north and global south writers intensified during these years, as if metropolitan intellectuals realized that the cold war stalemate might be settled by appeals to nonmetropolitan figures. *The God That Failed* includes a substantial essay by Richard Wright, an expatriate African American writer and *Présence Africaine* board member with a prevailing interest in decolonization and racism as global issues. Likewise, *Why I am a Communist* features a contribution from Césaire, who had recently been elected as mayor of Fort-de-France and deputy to the French Assembly. We also see instances of this in the work of European intellectuals who attempted to fashion a progressive politics outside the Party. Jean-Paul Sartre's collaboration with Frantz Fanon and the *Présence Africaine* group, Stuart Hall's editorship of *New Left Review* (1960–62) and directorship of the Birmingham Centre for Contemporary Cultural Studies (1969–79), and Doris Lessing's participation in the founding of *New Left Review* provide a few illustrative examples of this process. Anticolonial intellectuals enjoyed, as perhaps they have not enjoyed in times previous or since, support for their ideas from metropolitan networks.

During the immediate postwar period, two debates from the aesthetic cold war impacted writers from decolonizing areas in particular: the appropriate language for writing and the place of politics in literature. On the question of language, especially on the utility of folk or vernacular materials, many late colonial and early postcolonial writers were deeply influenced by developments in Communist Party thinking. Building on Hu Shi's and Lu Xun's call for Chinese literature to turn to the vernacular, Mao suggests at the Yan'an conference that "the rich, lively language of the popular masses" should inspire the literature of the revolution.[33] The Yan'an talks develop this point at some length:

> Our professional writers should give their attention to the masses' wall newspapers and to reportage literature in the army and the villages. Our professional playwrights should give their attention to little theater groups in the army and villages. Our professional musicians should give their attention to songs sung by the masses. Our professional artists should give their attention to mass art. All of these comrades should develop close relationships with comrades who are doing the work of reaching wider audiences on the lowest level among the masses, helping and guiding them at the same time as learning from them and drawing sustenance from them, replenishing, enriching, and nourishing themselves so that their profession does not become an ivory tower isolated from the masses and from reality, devoid of meaning and vitality. (73)

It would be difficult to overstate the lasting significance of these sentiments in late colonial and postcolonial literature. As Mao puts it here, vernacular culture should replenish and enrich aesthetic production, while experts should help improve the technical capacities of popular artists. Mao gives little thought to socialist realism, which did not have much impact outside the Soviet Union and its sphere of influence, but his emphasis on demotic culture—an important component of his party's nationalist program—was part of a much broader movement to revalue popular and folk arts during the postwar decades.[34] It is tempting to speculate that Mao's insistence on a people's aesthetic enjoyed a longer lifespan in postcolonial literature than it did in China itself.

Beyond the appeal to the vernacular and the skepticism about the ivory tower, Mao's remarks at Yan'an, like the ideas floated at the first Soviet Writers Congress and the PWA manifestoes, are significant because they emphasize the social identity of the writer as an important part of the critical apparatus. In direct contrast to strains of metropolitan modernism that deemphasize the social position of the artist, Mao and his forerunners insist that the writer be authentically working class or become authentically revolutionary. The question of cultural authenticity and social identity would be no less important to anticolonial intellectuals from this period, who were in the process of formulating their own contributions to aesthetic theory. Achebe's reading of Okigbo as a repatriated poet offers a case in point: only when Okigbo tempers his cosmopolitan experiences with local influences does he speak in an authentically Nigerian voice. The more contemporary attempts to name women's literature, Black Atlantic literature, queer literature, and other minority literatures as distinctive are prefigured, in part, by cold war debates about working-class culture.

Présence Africaine (1947–) is probably the most resolutely nonaligned intellectual venue of the midcentury period, documenting the cultural richness of the Black Atlantic as an important resource in the struggle against old and new imperialisms. Alioune Diop, its founding editor, puts it very bluntly in the opening line of the magazine's first editorial statement: "This review is not under the bidding of any philosophical or political ideology."[35] Diop's early approach seems to have more in common with the Nardal sisters' *La Revue du monde noir* than the more defiantly left-oriented (and notably short-lived) precedents such as a *Légitime Défense* and *L'étudiant noir*. *Présence Africaine* thus started life by putting as much distance as possible between itself and cold war ideology—even though Party members such as Césaire were taking an active part in the project. The editorial continues by announcing its commitment to racial partnership, not revolution: "It is open to the collaboration of all men of goodwill (white, yellow and black), who are willing to help us define the [African's] creativity and to hasten his integration in the modern world" (185). Whereas the "Cannibalist Manifesto" uses irony and verbal play to avoid making firm political commitments, Diop's first editorial statement is far more earnest and direct about avoiding the cold war's ideological traps. It is difficult to discern if this reflects one of Diop's core beliefs—that Black Atlantic culture should not commit itself to any specific political system—or if it is a pragmatic decision, a way to avoid alienating a segment of the constituency he hopes to reach with the magazine.

The first issue substantiates its commitment to cross-racial collaboration by soliciting contributions from a few of the leading non-Communist (but left-oriented) metropolitan intellectuals of the day, including Sartre and André Gide, both of whom are named as board members along with Albert Camus ("Comité de Patronage"). The editorial closes with another proclamation of racial reconciliation and humanism:

> The intellectual collaboration we appeal for can be useful to all. Europe creates the leaven of all future civilizations. But we men of overseas, from ancient China, from pensive India to silent Africa, possess immense moral resources which constitute the substance to be fecundated by Europe. We are indispensable to each other. (192)

This passage exhibits a touch of the feel-good racial essentialism for which negritude would be arraigned in later years by some of its fiercest critics, especially Wole Soyinka. Negritude's skeptics do not wish people of African descent to be honored for their intuition or their morality—they want political and cultural independence and the respect that goes with it. In contrast to earlier and later expressions of anticolonial militancy (of the PWA in the 1930s, for example, or of Ngũgĩ from the 1970s), which borrow extensively from the Marxist revolutionary tradition, the 1940s and early 1950s are marked by several projects that attempt to harness less combative rhetoric in service of antiracist and anticolonial movements. This avoidance of a revolutionary position, combined with a criticism of imperialist capitalism, is clearly an attempt to negotiate the pressures of the cold war. For reasons I discuss below, the more militant side of anticolonial theory, while not completely absent in the 1940s, reemerges noticeably after 1956, culminating perhaps with Ngũgĩ's *Decolonising the Mind* or Jean Bernabé, Patrick Chamoiseau, and Raphaël Confiant's manifesto on *Créolité*.

The little magazines *Bim* (1942–) and *Black Orpheus* (1957–75; 1982), Barbadian and Nigerian respectively, served as flexible instruments for articulating a version of cultural independence partly because their editors avoided taking a firm political stand. Unlike Diop, who announced his journal's political hesitancies from the beginning, *Bim*'s longtime editor Frank Colly-more simply ignored the question altogether, eventually saying, and often repeating in later issues, that the journal has "no intention of restricting [itself] to any set programme."[36] In place of an ideological or even a clear aesthetic policy, the journal emphasizes the richness of Barbadian, and after a few issues, West Indian, culture by covering the region's literary scene and by carrying extensive notes on Bajan vernacular speech.[37] Hence a cover bearing the title *Bim*, vernacular for Barbadian. As Collymore puts it rather flippantly in one of his early editorial statements, with "West Indian Federation loom[ing] hazily on the shifting background of world politics, [. . .] it is only by developing our inherent bimness to the utmost that we can hope to do our bit in the formation of a successful and vital commonwealth."[38] Being authentically Barbadian or West Indian means asserting cultural specificity as a way of augmenting the political project of decolonization.

For Ulli Beier, the German expatriate and founding editor of *Black Orpheus*, the avoidance of ideological commitment was a conscious, utilitarian decision. Inspired by the example of *Présence Africaine*, Beier envisioned *Black Orpheus* as a journal that could be as vibrantly eclectic as the Black Atlantic culture it was designed to showcase: tenebrous poetry and bright folk art, abstract and representational painting, texts translated from an array of languages from the diaspora and from the African continent all find room in the magazine's pages. Beier saw himself as a purveyor of "propaganda" not for a political organization, but for Black Atlantic culture of whatever provenance.[39] It would be easy to claim that *Bim* and *Black Orpheus* were less politically radical because Colly-more was very light-skinned (but not White, on his account) on a predomi-nantly Black island, or that Beier was German (though of Jewish descent), but this does little to explain why these little magazines were natural homes for some of colonialism's fiercest literary critics, such as Kamau Brathwaite and George Lamming (regular *Bim* contributors) or John Pepper Clark-Bekederemo and Soyinka (regular *Black Orpheus* contributors). These journals had local credibility among anticolonial figures because they aspired to cultural indepen-dence in a colonial setting. Their editors believed that partisan politics could undermine their efforts to articulate a nonmetropolitan cultural tradition.

Doris Lessing, anticolonial activist and British New Left participant, echoes the rhetoric of nonalignment in her own writing from the period. In "The Small Personal Voice," appearing originally in *Declaration* (1957) alongside the manifestoes of several metropolitan intellectuals loosely associated with the Angry Young Men, Lessing puts an interesting spin on the idea of committed art. The idea of commitment had fallen into disrepute because of the quantities of bad art that had been produced under its banner, but Lessing defines commitment as the vision an artist shares with an audience—the small personal voice—not commitment to a party or an ideology. Lessing compares the simple optimism of socialist realism to "a little boy whistling in the dark" and categorizes the best writing from western Europe and North America as "despairing statements of emotional anarchy."[40] These are two sides of the same counterfeit literary coin, she asserts, while it is the task of the most courageous midcentury writers to search "Somewhere between these two" for "a resting-point, a place of decision, hard to reach and precariously balanced" (194). Lessing figures aesthetic nonalignment not as a cowardly refusal to take sides, but as a bold choice and a positive act, an assertion of humanist values against the threat of imminent nuclear destruction.

Lessing's most incisive point in the essay is her claim that metropolitan British writing, like the culture out of which it has emerged, is parochial. It is perfectly reasonable to regard this as an anticolonial intellectual striking back at the metropolitan center, which it is in part. But Lessing's belief that commitment represents an alternative to parochialism is an argument that anticolonial writers, because they have the chance to speak with and speak for an audience finding its own voice after years of subordination, have a special opportunity that writers from the First and Second Worlds, with their forms of despair and ennui, on one side, and their state-mandated optimism, on the other, do not possess. Anticolonial intellectuals will, she hopes, save the novel (the only "popular art-form left where the artist speaks directly" to an audience) because they are deprovincializing it, turning the energies of the decolonizing world into a form with the power to shift the direction of literary history (201). Whether or not Lessing is correct in claiming uniqueness for the novel is not really my point here.[41] What matters, I think, is her provocative conclusion that midcentury literature might be resuscitated by combining the "fresh rush of vitality" as a previously "inarticulate class is released into speech" with the flexibility of ideological nonalignment found widely among late colonial intellectuals (196). It proved to be a very potent mixture.

1956–1990: Toward a Postcolonial Tradition

Histories of the political left in the twentieth century typically pivot around 1956, when the Suez Crisis, Nikita Khrushchev's not-so-secret speech at the meeting of the Twentieth International, and Soviet military intervention in

Hungary prompted sustained reflections on imperialism and mass defections from the Communist Party in western Europe. 1956 was no less important a year for the development of a postcolonial literary tradition. Césaire penned his famous letter of resignation from the Communist Party, citing the legacy of Stalinism and the Party's reluctance to embrace anticolonialism among his grievances.[42] In noting this, one might conclude that intellectuals from decolonizing regions were walking the same political paths as their metropolitan counterparts. There is some truth to this, as Césaire's example shows us, but 1956 is particularly interesting in the development of anticolonial literature for the convening of the First International Congress of Black Writers and Artists (1er Congrès International des Écrivains et Artistes Noirs) by *Présence Africaine* at the Sorbonne. Other significant gatherings followed in its wake: the first Afro-Asian Writers Association Conference in Tashkent in 1958 (discussed in chapter 4), the Second Congress of Black Writers and Artists in Rome in 1959, the African Writers of English Expression, better known as the Makerere conference, in Kampala in 1962 (discussed in chapter 3), the First World Festival of Negro Arts in Dakar in 1966, and the third Association for Commonwealth Literature and Language Studies (ACLALS) meeting in Kingston in 1971. These conferences were attempts to consolidate and build upon the cultural foundations of the previous decades, turning postcolonial literature into a durable fixture of the global intellectual field.

The delegates at the 1956 Paris meeting openly acknowledged that the anticolonial movement could not be disentangled from the aesthetic cold war, for better or worse. Diop's address of welcome framed the conference as a replay of the previous year's Bandung summit, for intellectuals instead of politicians and diplomats. James Baldwin, who was reporting on the event for a rival organization, the Congress for Cultural Freedom, recalled that the atmosphere was filled with tension, with the knowledge that the "ultimate resolution" of the US-Soviet stalemate might "very well depend on the earth's non-European population."[43] And then came the letter of salutation from W.E.B. Du Bois:

> I am not present at your meeting today because the United States government will not grant me a passport for travel abroad. Any Negro-American who travels abroad today must either not discuss race conditions in the United States or say the sort of thing which our state Department wishes the world to believe. The government especially objects to me because I am a Socialist and because I [believe] in peace with Communist states like the Soviet Union and their right to exist in security.[44]

The small US delegation, including Baldwin and Richard Wright, who had extensive connections to the Congress for Cultural Freedom as well, came under immediate suspicion from their fellow attendees. Participants from other parts of the world reached the obvious conclusion that the US government forced African American intellectuals to toe the line or face restrictions on movement. Du Bois's travel ban only increased the conviction of the *Présence Africaine* delegates that neither cold war superpower had their interests foremost.

It is possible to view this incident from a US-centric perspective, as Juliana Spahr does in *Du Bois's Telegram: Literary Resistance and State Containment.* Her goal in the book is "to take Du Bois's telegram seriously" by tracing the impact of the US state's "interference" in the literary field, its efforts to contain dissident thought.[45] Reading Du Bois's message to the *Présence Africaine* congress delegates simply as an instance of the cold war security state disciplining a wayward African American intellectual, however, does not tell the full story. The US government was punitive, to be sure, but it was also inconsistent and largely ineffective. Its handling of Du Bois backfired, as Baldwin and Wright probably reported to their contacts in intelligence circles. The move may have kept Du Bois at home temporarily, where he could be watched, but it alienated anticolonial intellectuals, proving that the United States was not to be trusted. Within two years, at least partly because of the negative international reaction to his travel ban, Du Bois had his passport reinstated. This happened in time for him to be the guest of honor at the first Afro-Asian Writers' Association conference in 1958, held in Tashkent, Uzbekistan, then part of the Soviet Union. When we put these two adjacent moments into the frame, a fuller picture becomes clear: the United States cared enough about the opinions of global south intellectuals that they could be forced into an embarrassing U-turn.

In the key texts and manifestoes of the post-1956 years, intellectuals in decolonizing areas reaffirmed their commitment to nonalignment with increased militancy. *Présence Africaine's* change of editorial direction just before the conference provides an example of this trend. From the first issue of 1955, the Comité de Patronage, with its list of sympathetic White intellectuals, silently disappears from the front matter. More direct is the editorial statement:

But the crushing weight of colonialism is now to be doubled. Europe, overshadowed by two giants, sees her prestige and power condemned by the excessive development of these two great nations. European culture is in turn experiencing colonialism. [...] It is therefore turning now to the African continent to seek a guarantee of its survival and security, if not of its lost hegemony. [...] The situation is aggravated by the appearance of new appetites, those of the non-colonizing nations which call for a "more equitable" sharing out of African resources. It is not hard to foresee the future of insecurity, violence and exploitation that such European national cupidity holds out for us.[46]

The imperial nations of Europe, ravaged by two continental wars and squeezed by two new superpowers in the aftermath, threaten to intensify exploitation of their overseas colonies to compensate for a newfound dependency. Europe is "in turn experiencing colonialism," in their words, but this is not likely to lead to emancipation in Africa and Asia unless colonial peoples demand it. Add to that the avarice of the cold war antagonists, the "non-colonizing nations" that now clamor for access to colonial resources. Exchanging one form of foreign domination for another is not what Diop and his collaborators hoped was in store for the colonial world when they founded the magazine in 1947.

For colonial intellectuals, the revamped *Présence Africaine* argues, the only viable response is to band together, to voluntarily suppress differences that might otherwise imperil the anticolonial movement. The editorial board asks that contributors refrain from attacking the "ideological and confessional peculiarities of others" (8) and instead work on constructing "societies, institutions, organizations, for the advancement of our freedom" (10). "We are not going beyond the cultural sphere," the editorial statement concludes, "for our mission in Europe is not that of a political party" (10). In this formulation, cultural institutions and practices, especially literature, have a bearing on politics—and on the aims and aspirations of colonial peoples—but the producers of cultural objects ought to avoid political partisanship of the kind that threatens to undermine the anticolonial movement. The final declaration from the 1956 meeting follows this line of thinking: the group's main task is to conduct an inventory of Black culture. The best response to superpower interference is to do a stocktaking of indigenous cultural resources. Asserting cultural autonomy is the best way to resist manipulation by outside interests.

Two aspects of the journal's new editorial line would become recurring features of the post-1956 era. First, late colonial and postcolonial intellectuals launched many influential, independent cultural institutions during this period, some of them national or regional in scope, some of them ambitiously transnational. The sturdiest of these institution-building efforts were underwritten by a nonaligned or nonpartisan aesthetic theory. Second, late colonial and early postcolonial intellectuals were inclined more than ever to close ranks by calling for the suppression of ideological and aesthetic differences among themselves. They became increasingly disenchanted with the ideological pressures exerted by both cold war superpowers, understandably, but they also became more suspicious of other late colonial and postcolonial writers who were too cozy with metropolitan intellectuals and too solicitous of international audiences. The debate between "capitalist" and "communist" poetics, as Achebe put it, was subtly but decisively transformed into a debate between cultural nationalism and cosmopolitanism (or what would now be called postcolonial versus global literatures). As the silent abolition of the Comité de Patronage and the editorial policy adjustment in the first 1955 issue of *Présence Africaine* tell us, this inclination to close ranks could be subdued and piecemeal rather than spectacular and absolute. But this change of strategy led, in the first decades of postcolonial literature, to more frequent efforts to police the thought of other colonial and postcolonial writers as part of the struggle against metropolitan cultural domination. The US State Department was not alone in making demands on late colonial and postcolonial intellectuals: they were beginning to formulate prohibitions of their own.

The conflicts at the 1971 ACLALS conference provide a brief glimpse of how the logic of the aesthetic cold war informed the emergence of cultural institutions in the early years of postcolonial independence. It was the organization's third conference—the inaugural event at Leeds was sponsored by the Congress for Cultural Freedom—but the first to be hosted in a predominantly Black, recently independent nation. Fireworks ensued. In a keynote address, Edward (later Kamau) Brathwaite, the people's champion, insisted that Caribbean vernacular speech and folk traditions "provided the metaphor, armour to express the mass culture," recreating the close relationship between artists and their audiences.[47] V. S. Naipaul and Raja Rao, who shared the dais with Brathwaite, took a contrary position, asserting the writer's need for self-cultivation. The Naipaul-Rao view did not go down well with the locals. The anonymous "Statement of Position" circulated at the conference extolls "the basis and terms of the folk artistic sensibility" and "the employment of new modes of literary expression through oral resources" while excoriating "the plunderers of the new emerging W.I. [West Indian] consciousness."[48] As Sylvia Wynter reportedly put it in her presentation, cultural decolonization is not a racial problem, but a question of "exploiter and exploited," which maps onto the difference between "folk culture versus museum-kultur" (32). The anonymous authors of the "Statement of Position" call for a hostile takeover, or the seizure of metropolitan cultural institutions and the socialization of literary production. Achieving postcolonial cultural autonomy, in their estimation, involves indigenizing literary methods but also curbing the autonomy of the intellectual, who now owes loyalty to a broader constituency.

The instinct to demand unity and to call out other intellectuals from decolonizing areas is on full display in Ngũgĩ's *Decolonising the Mind* (1986), arguably the most bracing anticolonial literary manifesto in English. As if tapping the spirit of the 1955 editorial statement in *Présence Africaine*, Ngũgĩ begins *Decolonising the Mind* by complaining that ethnic and religious distinctions are often blamed for the problems of independence, when in reality "imperialism is still the root cause of many problems in Africa."[49] While his underlying grievance is with imperialist-capitalism and his overarching sympathies with the working peoples of the decolonizing world—the essays gathered here unapologetically combine Marxist and anticolonial rhetorical traditions—he reserves perhaps his most scathing words for the intellectual collaborators, the compradors who write in metropolitan languages. He criticizes Achebe, Es'kia Mphahlele, Gabriel Okara, and Léopold Sédar Senghor not simply for their conscious use, but also for their strategic defense, of European languages as instruments of aesthetic creation. Peasants and workers, meanwhile, have been keeping indigenous languages and traditions alive, and it is to their side the writer should return (23).

Ngũgĩ had been asking questions and making demands such as these for couple of decades. In his coauthored manifesto, "On the Abolition of the English Department" (1968), Ngũgĩ famously asks his Nairobi English colleagues, "Why can't African literature be at the centre [of the curriculum] so that we can view other cultures in relation to it?"[50] As this pithy reflection suggests, Ngũgĩ is less interested in abolishing the study of English and its literatures than he is in reorienting the cultural basis and opening the theoretical premises of literary study: in addition to literature, orature in local languages should be foremost in the new curriculum at a postcolonial university. Part of the reason Ngũgĩ could make these demands in compelling fashion is because, by the late 1960s, he could draw on a substantial body of anticolonial literary theory from the previous fifty years in which vernacular traditions are revalorized. In aligning himself with peasants and workers, or what he calls in *Decolonising the Mind* "the vast democratic and socialistic forces daily inflicting mortal blows to imperialist capitalism" (103), Ngũgĩ borrows heavily from the Marxist revolutionary tradition. On the language question, however, he

deploys a specific brand of nationalism and regionalism to make a more nuanced theoretical point about cultural production: why should African writers
enrich metropolitan languages when they could be contributing to the development of their own tongues and literary canons? African intellectuals should
be working to build up the resources of indigenous languages and literary traditions in much the way Chaucer and Shakespeare built the foundations of
English as a literary language.

Even those late colonial and early postcolonial intellectuals who accept the
usefulness of writing in European languages are apt to link the question of
cultural decolonization to proximity of writer and audience. In "Towards the
Decolonization of African Literature," (1975), extracted from a full-length
book of the same name, the Nigerian "troika" of Chinweizu, Onwuchekwa
Jemie, and Ihechukwu Madubuike take aim at Soyinka and his euromodern-
ist ilk who are "content to scribble exotic marginalia to the literatures of
Europe."[51] Soyinka's poetry is too self-absorbed, too willfully obscure—too
metropolitan, in short—to contribute anything meaningful to the decolonization of African poetry.

Soyinka's response, "Neo-Tarzanism: The Poetics of Psuedo-Tradition," carried in the same issue of *Transition*, which Soyinka himself was editing at the
time, provides a fascinating counterargument on a couple of fronts. First, he
defends his own jagged, experimental, forward-looking verse on the grounds
that it represents contemporary Africa, where airplanes and oil rigs operate
alongside yam harvest festivals, griots, and ancient rites; where metropolitan
languages, creoles and patois, and indigenous languages are spoken alongside
one another. What Chinweizu, Jemie, and Madubuike call traditional poetic
forms—simple, communal, accessible—Soyinka describes as a figment of the
colonial imagination, the sort of nursery-rhyme drivel that European ethnolo-
gists have catalogued as the essence of precolonial, tribal Africa. Soyinka here
mobilizes one version of indigeneity—Africans using all the trappings of the
modern world in their own, unique, unapologetic way—against the tradition-
alist model of an authentic, continuous, precolonial society. Second, Soyinka
concludes the riposte by quoting Trotsky against his implicitly Stalinist detractors. By demanding displays of commitment and authenticity at every turn,
Soyinka explains that his critics deny "selective eclecticism as the right of every
productive being, scientist or artist."[52] African poetry, to become autonomous
and genuinely postcolonial, cannot turn away from the contemporary world,
where modern high life and older folk songs are both part of the ambient
culture. For Soyinka, eclecticism and hybridity reflect a vibrant local scene

that absorbs and adopts many influences; the kind of monoculturalism his critics demand is, in his view, a colonialist (and Stalinist) theory of the arts.

As celebrated book historian Robert Darnton demonstrates in *Censors at Work: How States Shaped Literature*, it is too reductive to characterize censorship—perhaps the most common way of disciplining writers—as merely proscriptive:

> Because complicity, collaboration, and negotiation [between writers, intermediaries, and the state] pervaded the way authors and censors operated, [...] it would be misleading to characterize censorship simply as a contest between creation and oppression. Seen from the inside, and especially from the censor's point of view, censorship can appear to be coextensive with literature.[53]

In *The Literature Police: Apartheid Censorship and its Cultural Consequences*, Peter D. McDonald shows how South Africa's White writers offered only token resistance to the state's draconian censorship system. The argument between Soyinka and his critics adds another wrinkle to Darnton's and McDonald's scholarly studies. When the aesthetic ideas of the cold war and the decolonizing world began to inform one another, as they do in this exchange and many others like it, we see that states are not the only censors, and perhaps not the most influential ones, applying pressure on twentieth-century writers. We should be wary of affixing conventional political labels onto censors and their antagonists: both Soyinka and his critics claim to be speaking from a firmly anticolonial perspective.

Soyinka's response to his fellow Nigerians anticipates Evgeny Dobrenko's extremely perceptive reading of socialist realism as an attempt to turn back the aesthetic clock, to pretend as if metropolitan modernism had never really happened—or better yet, that it happened in western Europe, to its detriment, without contaminating the rest of the world. Although Dobrenko describes socialist realism as utopian, it is not therefore future-oriented: it is an "impossible aesthetic" that "could be defined as postmodernism minus modernism, an aesthetic located in 'minus time.'"[54] African traditionalists, Soyinka reasons, do not want to abolish the printing press, yet they proceed as if the inspiration for writing should be drawn exclusively from oral, autochthonous sources. Even more damaging, from Soyinka's perspective, is that African "pseudo-traditionalism" serves as a form of censorship and aesthetic control. As Dobrenko again says of socialist realism, it is a project designed to produce readers and writing without (individual) writers: "*The transformation of the author into his own censor—herein is the true history of Soviet literature*" (xviii). The act of self-censorship transforms the individual writer into a corporate identity, turning over the creative process to the state and to the readers the state hopes to create: Roland Barthes's funeral dirge for the author sung in a different key.

Lessing too, speaking of Soviet writing in "The Small Personal Voice," calls "the inner censor [...] the enemy" (194). Soyinka expands this formulation, arguing that intellectuals are just as likely as the state to act as censor. Colonial states and their postcolonial successors, like their authoritarian cousins, exert implicit and explicit forms of control over writing. Soyinka reads the arch-traditionalism of Chinweizu, Jemie, and Madubuike as a version of primitivism or auto-exoticization, a lamentable instance of Africans consigning themselves to a cultural "minus time." This view of Africa flourished among Europeans when colonialism itself was "inventing tradition," in Terence Ranger's incisive formulation. Censorship could be perpetrated by state bodies but equally by other intellectuals. For Soyinka, it is worse, in a way, when writers amputate their own intellectual limbs: from autocratic states he imagines nothing less, but writers ought to hold themselves to a higher intellectual standard.

In their pluralist manifesto *Éloge de la créolité* (*In Praise of Creoleness*, 1989), Jean Bernabé, Patrick Chamoiseau, and Raphaël Confiant also insist that censorship and intellectual totalitarianism threaten anticolonial writers as well as their counterparts in the so-called First and Second Worlds. Lingering racial inferiority, on one side, and narrow ethno-nationalism and irredentism, on the other, each put significant pressure on intellectuals in decolonizing situations. Following Soyinka and Édouard Glissant, they embrace the modernity of their situation, reading both Eurocentrism and its putative opposite, racial essentialism, as twin products of a colonial mentality. Retreating into some precolonial fantasy is not a viable option, but neither is a wholesale adoption of metropolitan cultural values. Likewise, they imagine *créolité* as a necessary rejection of cold war binaries, arguing that "full and entire sovereignty of our peoples" can be achieved "without, however, identifying with the different ideologies which have supported this claim to date."[55] They regard *créolité*, by contrast, as a "*nontotalitarian consciousness of a preserved diversity*" (89). Their emphasis on diversity, cultural and ethnic, is generally compatible with the developments in postcolonial theory of this vintage.[56] The significance of their emphasis on the nontotalitarian nature of their political commitments, however, makes sense only if we acknowledge the entanglement of anticolonial and cold war aesthetic theory. Resistance to censorship here figures as an anticolonial gesture, but its logic draws on further resistance to the "different hegemonic [blocs] that share the planet among themselves," locked in competition to shape the development of global literature (116).

On the language question, Bernabé, Chamoiseau, and Confiant work in the space between Achebe's and Ngũgĩ's positions, ending up somewhere closer to Andrade's than to either of them. Following Achebe, they are eager to proclaim that Caribbean people have provincialized or conquered metropolitan tongues, weaponizing language in service of the anticolonial struggle (106–7). On the other hand, in the spirit of Ngũgĩ, they believe that creole languages thrive because of a "fundamental orality" that was nurtured by the region's plantation system (95). Emerging out of the tension of these two positions, the manifesto goes on to affirm that the language of the Caribbean people defeats centralization and standardization by its omnivorous character: "Creoleness is not monolingual. [. . .] Its field is language. Its appetite: all the languages of the world" (108). A cannibalistic culture, now described as a creolized, feeds on all languages.

Their position, like Andrade's, synthesizes heterogeneous elements from the traditions of metropolitan modernism as well as socialist aesthetic theory. From the "Revolution of the Word" manifesto and like-minded documents, we detect elements of revolutionary multilingualism and playful insistence that the language dictators cannot halt change. From socialist aesthetic theories, likewise, the trio believe that cultural sovereignty cannot be divorced from political sovereignty and that the language of art should remain close to the language of the people. Whereas the aesthetic doctrines on either side of the cold war divide had become stale and predictable in the mouths of partisans, anticolonial intellectuals were recombining these stock materials into something they could use. Late colonial and early postcolonial intellectuals are the cold war's aesthetic *bricoleurs*, taking the familiar and often broken pieces of the cold war's artistic debates and fashioning them into new and provocative statements on cultural autonomy.

A simple visual template (Fig. 2.1) might help me summarize the intersection of the aesthetic cold war's two major debates, about literary language and degrees of freedom and responsibility. The vertical axis of this grid represents degrees of aesthetic freedom. The extreme ends of this continuum are theoretical, not practical: no literary forms are free of all outside constraints, just as no forms, even propaganda, are totally controlled by nonliterary interests. From the perspective of anticolonial writers, both high modernist and socialist theories of art had their own distinct claims of autonomy, each viewed with

FIGURE 2.1. Intersection of debates about language choice and aesthetic independence.

legitimate suspicion by neutrals. In any case, many anticolonial writers did not regard utilitarianism as an unambiguous evil, so long as it did not come with unilateral state control of the arts.

The horizontal axis on this chart shows a relationship between approaches to language, or cultural influence more broadly. Some anticolonial writers favor linguistic centralization or monolingualism, in metropolitan or national languages. Other writers believe in linguistic plurality, especially in the vernacular languages. There is no correlation between vertical and horizontal axes in this chart: knowing what a given writer thinks about the need for aesthetic autonomy, for instance, does not allow us to predict how the same writer feels about literary language.

We could plot writers in different quadrants of this chart. Achebe, who defends his use of English and a version of utilitarianism, might appear in the bottom right, where linguistic centralization and an aesthetic pragmatism meet. The PWA manifesto that was eventually ratified by membership, which demands utility of literature and supports the development indigenous vernaculars in writing, would appear somewhere in the bottom left, as might Ngũgĩ and Chinweizu, Jemie, and Madubuike, best known as Soyinka's hostile critics. Andrade's "Cannibalist Manifesto" and the *créolité* treatise would probably fit comfortably in the top left area, favoring a combination of linguistic diversity and aesthetic autonomy. Lessing, who used English exclusively for practical if not ideological reasons, would appear somewhere in the top right quadrant, where commitments to aesthetic autonomy and linguistic centralization overlap. Just as there is no correlation between a given writer's feelings about language and autonomy, there is no clear correlation between a writer's place on this grid and the writer's ideological commitments. Lessing and Ngũgĩ, for instance, both think of themselves as committed to a political left, but they appear on opposite quadrants of this diagram. I do not wish to be too dogmatic about how to position individual writers on this chart. This visual aid is meant to be suggestive, not prescriptive.

As I turn to the book's case studies, it will become more apparent how the aesthetic cold war pulled and pushed anticolonial writers in complicated ways. Cultural diplomacy from the United States and the Soviet Union, as we shall see, promised new types of aesthetic freedom in the decolonizing world, in the form of international literary institutions beyond colonial control. The ironies of this became apparent quickly. Forms of diplomatic support were counterbalanced by measures of surveillance and control of writers. But there were knock-on effects of surveillance, too, as writers found international audiences sympathetic to their plight when they were persecuted by state actors. The unprecedented combination of global literary networks and ideological competition made it difficult for states to muzzle dissident writers. In the next section, I consider the impact of cultural diplomacy on twentieth-century global literature.

Part II

3

Modernism, African Literature, and the Congress for Cultural Freedom

IN JUNE 1962, attendees of the Conference of African Writers of English Expression descended on the campus of Makerere University in Kampala. It was a generation-defining event for anglophone writers, many of whom met one another for the first time at the gathering. Armed with a draft of *Weep Not, Child* (1964), a precocious Ngũgĩ wa Thiong'o buttonholed Chinua Achebe, who was in the process of launching the African Writers Series at Heinemann, leading to Ngũgĩ's international breakthrough.[1] *A Walk in the Night* (1962), by Alex La Guma (invited, but prevented from attending by South African authorities), featured prominently in discussions about encouraging developments in African fiction. Langston Hughes lent his international star power to the event, which was also attended by leading metropolitan publishers, such as André Deutsch, and representatives from up-and-coming African magazines, including *Black Orpheus* (founded 1957, Nigeria) and *Transition* (founded 1961, Uganda). John Pepper Clark-Bekederemo, Bloke Modisane, Lewis Nkosi, Gabriel Okara, Christopher Okigbo, Okot p'Bitek, and Wole Soyinka were among the invited guests. South African exile Ezekiel (later Es'kia) Mphahlele served as lead organizer of the event, and Rajat Neogy, *Transition*'s founding editor, was the local host.

In postcolonial studies, the conference is best known for the debates it stimulated about language, culture, and indigeneity. The conference included a panel organized around the topic, with Nkosi starting discussion by asking the panelists to say whether an identifiable African literature has been born.[2] The organizers asked at least some of the delegates to answer a short exit

FIGURE 3.1. Chinua Achebe (left), Frances Ademola, Theodore Bull, André Deutsch, Arthur Drayton, Dennis Duerden, Bernard Fonlon, Bob Leshoai, and unidentified others at the Makerere conference, June 1962. Image courtesy of Hanna Holborn Gray Special Collections Research Center, University of Chicago Library.

survey, which included the following question: "Are you convinced after the deliberations and doubts of the Conference that there is such a thing that might be termed African literature?" A few replies appeared in *Transition*. Hughes and Modisane replied yes, without a doubt, an African literature now exists. Okigbo, echoing the skeptical response he offered during the panel discussion, responded, "[i]f and when the literature emerges, it will have to divine its own laws for its unity; its own form. Until this happens it appears rather premature to talk of African Literature in terms other than geographical."[3] Implicitly, the question cuts in at least two directions: what qualifies as African, and what counts as literary?

Within a few months, the debate expanded to include the language question. Obiajunwa Wali, also writing in *Transition*, argued that the conference unintentionally demonstrated that African writing in English and other metropolitan languages "is merely a minor appendage in the main stream of European literature," leading only to "sterility, uncreativity, and frustration" for writers emerging from the shadow of imperialism.[4] Arguments and counterarguments reverberated down through the years. Figures such as Achebe and Soyinka adamantly defended their use of imported tongues, insisting that they were doing something creative with the English language, and further arguing that writing in English allowed them to reach national and continental audiences. Ngũgĩ and others countered that writing primarily in European languages extends the cultural subordination of African peoples. Few debates in postcolonial studies have inspired such passion, or such repetition.[5]

Aside from the language debates, the 1962 Makerere conference is known for being one of the many international cultural ventures caught up in the funding scandal of the Congress for Cultural Freedom (CCF). Founded in 1950, the CCF became a leading international arts player by supporting a range of cultural institutions, especially intellectual conferences and serious magazines. The organization started out in western Europe, but its operations soon fanned out to the decolonizing parts of the world. The CCF encountered stubborn resistance in the Indian subcontinent before enjoying somewhat more success in the Middle East, but it carved out a distinct niche in sub-Saharan Africa, where it sponsored several international conferences, pathbreaking magazines (including *Black Orpheus* and *Transition*), radio programming, and cultural centers, such as Mbari in Nigeria and Chemchemi in Kenya. It all came crashing down in 1966–67, when investigative journalists from *Ramparts* magazine and later the *New York Times* broke the story that the CIA had been acting as the CCF's secret financial backer from the very beginning. The Farfield Foundation, the CCF's main patron and a seemingly legitimate nonprofit funder, was merely a front operation for US foreign intelligence, a dummy organization through which the dollars were routed. Although the CCF had always been open about its general ideological position—the CCF manifesto of 1950 identifies "the theory and practice of the totalitarian state" as inimical to freedom of thought—the fact that the organization was covertly directed and funded by the CIA came as a shock to many neutral observers.[6] What could be more hypocritical than an organization touting its intellectual independence being clandestinely bankrolled by a government spy agency? The US and European intellectuals most closely associated with the CCF, such as *Encounter* magazine's founding editors Irving Kristol and Stephen Spender, felt the brunt of the backlash from their peers, but the CCF's African collaborators suffered public rebukes, too. Mphahlele was the CCF's director of African affairs and brainchild of the Makerere conference, and although he had left the organization by 1963, he and many of his fellow African writers spent years trying to live down their involvement, however unwitting, in a CIA scheme.

On the face of it, these two aspects of the Makerere conference—the language debate and the cold war cultural diplomacy scheme—have no obvious connection with one another. Yet the language nativist Wali, without any knowledge of CIA involvement at Makerere, intuitively grasped that international patronage of cultural institutions, autonomy, and language choice were contextually related problems. As he puts it, learning to express themselves in indigenous languages would allow African writers to reach "out to the people [. . .], creating a true culture of the African peoples that would not rely on slogans and propaganda, nor on patronage of doubtful intentions" (14). Following Wali's trail in this chapter, I make the case that the aesthetic controversies that propelled the CCF into being—about the kinds of autonomy secured and attenuated by different models of literary production—lent urgency and immediacy to the disagreements about indigenous language and literary forms. The partisan sponsorship of the CCF, which aligned itself with intellectuals and organizations that valued expressive freedoms, spurred the Makerere delegates to consider the question of autonomy in the context of their own needs and desires. There was, I contend, considerable overlap, but hardly perfect alignment, between the organizational concerns of the CCF and the African intellectuals who attended Makerere and participated in other CCF-sponsored institutions. Although the CCF's African collaborators were not ideologically dogmatic about the cold war, the CCF's projections of intellectual freedom resonated with them. Both the CCF and their African counterparts were pragmatic rather than doctrinaire, finding enough common ground to form a working partnership for nearly a decade.

The aesthetic theories associated with high modernism—especially the flexible notion of autonomy and the question of what counts as literary language and literary form—were the common currency that the CCF and its African collaborators traded in their debates at Makerere and beyond. African intellectuals of this generation exploited the malleability of autonomy, even the contradictory meanings of the term, to shape their ventures during this period. On one hand, a version of aesthetic autonomy could help African writers announce their independence from colonial institutions. For writers with a strong commitment to decolonization, modernist proclamations of intellectual and creative independence held a profound appeal. As they went about setting up indigenous cultural institutions, these African writers would revise the doctrine of aesthetic autonomy to announce their freedom from colonial tutelage. The concept helped this generation of writers draw provisional boundaries around African literature as distinct from metropolitan writing.

On the other hand, autonomy also gave these writers a language through which to negotiate their complicated relationship with state bodies and nationalist movements. The expansive doctrine of aesthetic autonomy, with its ideals of writerly detachment and intellectual objectivity, helped African intellectuals project an image that they could not be bought off or intimidated by agents of the state. Conceptions of intellectual and creative freedom, as used by African writers during the decolonization era, were not strictly apolitical. They could be adapted to assert political independence, so long as these assertions were based in an ethical framework that claimed to transcend vested interests, instrumental politics, and narrowly statist aims.[7]

With surprising frequency, however, African writers and their collaborators also used the idea of aesthetic autonomy to assert the right to be apolitical—in their creative work, at least. At the Makerere conference, the presenters regularly praised literature that was detached and objective, criticizing writers who were too self-conscious about racial discrimination. It was acceptable to broach political themes, the conference presentations seem to suggest, so long as writers do not wallow in anger or pity. A good story or poem ought to retain a posture of disinterest from the situations it depicts. A poet such as Okigbo, who recited his verse at the conference, habitually asserted his right to produce experimental, nonpolitical poetry along high modernist lines. Although Okigbo was willing to die for a political cause, he routinely rejected the notion that literature could have a basis in racial essentialism.[8] In life, he might be a firm believer in the need for Black people to assert their rights. As a poet, however, he believed his work should not observe systems of racial exclusion or separatism in any capacity. If African literature were to assume a distinctive form, as he puts it, some idea of racial difference could not provide a sound basis.

Additionally, modernist ideals of aesthetic autonomy were reinterpreted by African writers to suit the conditions of the cold war. The ideal of autonomy, refashioned to speak to geopolitical circumstances, could permit African intellectuals to reject ideological binaries. Commitments to artistic and political sovereignty were frequently blended in the fabrication of anglophone African cultural institutions of the decolonization era. The doctrine of nonalignment—expressed both politically and artistically—bolstered anticolonial sentiments by insisting on African self-determination in all its forms. Even apolitical art, in a paradoxical formulation, could have some political resonance in that it insists on the right of Africans to determine their aesthetic future without interference from the cold war superpowers, which were prone to evaluate every aesthetic object by its ideological utility. In an interesting twist of literary history, an emerging generation of postcolonial intellectuals from Africa was attracted to the modernist ideals of artistic liberty because these principles could be readily adapted as a rejection of cold war polarities.

This argument implies that African writers of the early 1960s reinterpreted the legacy of interwar modernism to fit the needs of new cultural institutions being founded in the context of decolonization and the cold war. Sometimes, aesthetic autonomy could mean freedom from politics, but in the midst of decolonization and the cold war, it could also mean freedom in politics. At least five different versions of artistic freedom were put into circulation through the institutions examined in this chapter: emancipation from colonialism; independence from the postcolonial nation-state; avoidance of politics in order to foster collaboration among multiple constituencies; freedom from politics altogether as a professional disposition; and ideological nonalignment in the cold war. Rather than see this multiplicity as a disabling contradiction, it makes more sense to regard this as an enabling tension, a bundle of complementary and conflicting ideas that could help a wide array of intellectuals collaborate for a time, suspending or deferring other differences. In suggesting that African writers of this generation reshaped and defended modernist ideals of detachment and aesthetic purity, the chapter also claims that anglophone African writers were some of the most important, and partial, readers of interwar modernism in the postwar period. When the interests of the CCF and their African collaborators diverged, it was largely about the nature of intellectual freedom in the context of the cold war. African writers emerged as the more emphatic defenders of autonomy than their counterparts at the CCF.

The Congress

The CCF was well established in Europe before it began to fund projects in sub-Saharan Africa in the latter half of the 1950s. The vast majority of writing on the CCF, especially Frances Stonor Saunders's well-documented study, tells the story of the scandal, especially the effect on North American and western European intellectual life. Only recently have a handful of scholars begun to trace the global dimensions of the CCF network.[9] Based on my consultation of the archival sources, it seems unlikely that more than a few people operating close to CCF headquarters—and certainly not Mphahlele—were witting participants, to use the lingo of cold war espionage, before the story broke in the press.[10] It is even less likely that CCF collaborators in Africa, such as Ulli Beier, the editor of *Black Orpheus*, or Neogy, the editor of *Transition*, would have known anything before the rest of the world; and more unlikely still that Makerere conference delegates, such as Achebe, Ngũgĩ, or Okigbo would have known anything about CIA involvement. The secretive nature of CIA involvement meant that the CCF could not make explicit political demands of its collaborators. At most, it could try to be selective about the individuals and organizations it supported, but even a cursory scan of the Makerere roster tells us that political leanings of the invitees varied widely.

In functional terms, this meant that protecting the secrecy of the funding source took priority over interfering in the political content of the magazines, conferences, and radio programs supported by the spy agency. Surprisingly, CIA subventions for the arts (in Africa and elsewhere) came with very few strings attached, partly because the operation was covert and the money routed through front organizations, partly because African intellectuals adamantly refused to have their political opinions dictated to them.[11] Protecting the secrecy of the program took precedence over meddling in the political orientation of CCF-sponsored networks. As a result, CCF officers tended to sidestep political confrontations out of concern that they would alienate the very people they hoped to influence, or worse yet, that the source of the funding would be revealed. This form of indirect patronage afforded a generation of African writers more rather than less latitude, both politically and aesthetically, largely because the CIA was so concerned about protecting the secrecy of the program that it could not make any transparent demands on the intellectuals it supported. It consistently backed the idea that emerging African cultural institutions were autonomous of colonialism, of the nation-state, even of cold war ideologies. Peter Benson's book, *"Black Orpheus," "Transition," and Modern Cultural Awakening in Africa*, emphasizes that this unique form of cultural patronage allowed these magazines to develop an indigenous, postcolonial literary culture in Africa; the present chapter suggests that such a culture was open to modernist ideals of detachment and disinterest as a means of carrying out this program.

Following its success with *Encounter* and other periodicals, the CCF was heavily involved with little magazines in Africa, especially *Black Orpheus* and *Transition*.[12] In those cases, CCF operatives identified existing publications that they admired and offered them additional financial support. International conferences were another favored outlet of the CCF network, leading to the

Makerere meeting as well as several other events at Dakar, Fourah Bay, and elsewhere. The CCF also dabbled in radio, establishing the Transcription Centre, which recorded Afrocentric cultural programming in London for broadcast on the continent and in Europe.[13]

I should say here that the CCF never made any pretense about its general political affiliations. Neogy pointed this out to his detractors after the scandal broke: "it would be dishonest of me to say that I now see something sinister in its [*Encounter's*] anti-Communism. It has always been so and one was always aware of it."[14] The CCF consistently supported the independence of speech and thought from state oversight, championing aesthetic autonomy as the embodiment of expressive freedoms and as the antithesis of Soviet authoritarianism. Putting the headquarters of the CCF in Paris bolstered the organization's claim to be a defender of aesthetic freedoms. The city's reputation for tolerance made it a haven for artists of all sorts. But the CCF consistently grounded its claims in the language of autonomy—that is, it attempted to position itself as a protector of intellectual and aesthetic liberties everywhere. Even the United States would be criticized regularly for its expectations of intellectual conformity. For instance, in the pages of *Encounter*, the CCF's Anglo-American magazine, the editors and contributors frequently portrayed themselves as disinterested intellectuals, defenders of aesthetic experimentation, and certainly not as advocates of free market capitalism, which could be hostile to intellectuals. The controversial House Un-American Activities Committee hearings were scarcely less objectionable than Stalin's show trials. The European intellectuals affiliated with the CCF, therefore, tended to depict themselves not as cold warriors per se, but as people who valued dispassionate inquiry and transcendent artistry. Whether or not the CCF was genuine in its repeated affirmations of neutrality is not my interest here. Rather, I hope to document how the CCF's rhetorical commitment to disinterested intellectual inquiry and modernist aesthetics allowed the organization to form productive alliances with African intellectuals who held compatible attitudes about the relationship between art and politics.

In different ways, the major initiatives of the CCF in Africa demonstrate how the language of modernist aesthetics could be adapted to express a version of cold war nonalignment. At the Makerere conference, for instance, most presenters were silent on the dominant political questions of the day, namely decolonization and the cold war. Instead, the participants overwhelmingly focused their attention on matters of literary technique and audience. The archives of the Transcription Centre, the CCF's foray into radio production, show that African intellectuals and their audiences consistently blocked any efforts to introduce pro-US (or anti-Soviet) propaganda into cultural broadcasting. As a result, Transcription Centre productions tended to be confined to literary and musical matters, avoiding stickier issues that were likely to alienate their collaborators. Mbari cofounder and *Black Orpheus* editor, the German expatriate Ulli Beier, called his little magazine a vehicle for "propaganda."[15] But the journal was in the business of promoting Black Atlantic artists of all persuasions, not in defending the United States or free market capitalism. Even more nonsectarian in its approach was Neogy's *Transition*, the underfunded little magazine that grew into an international review. In its early days, it offered the closest thing to a high modernist periodical in 1960s Africa. As the journal matured, its pages began to be dominated by political debates, but it retained its devotion to impartiality. In fact, under the editorship of Neogy, and later of Soyinka, it went out of its way to detach intellectual work from the needs of political parties and nation-states, seeing itself as a unique forum in which intellectuals with conflicting viewpoints could be brought into contact. Studying these cultural institutions as part of a coordinated network shows us how Euro-American modernism—especially the doctrines of aesthetic autonomy and critical disinterest—was reshaped by anglophone Africans to meet the needs of intellectuals in the context of decolonization and the cold war.

The Encounter

Before examining the African cultural institutions in question, it might be instructive to briefly describe the CCF's global network, which has been documented in considerable detail by Saunders, Peter Coleman, Giles Scott-Smith, and Hugh Wilford.[16] Shortly after the conclusion of World War II, the Soviet Union put its sophisticated cultural diplomacy programs in the service of a cold war agenda. It sent writers, dancers, musicians, and artists on well-funded and elaborately staged international goodwill tours, designed to show off the cultural attainments made possible by a workers' state.[17] This was an enlargement and diversification of a tradition that stretched back to the 1920s, when sympathetic foreigners were invited to make the pilgrimage to the Soviet Union. African American and Black Caribbean intellectuals were some of the high-profile invitees during the interwar period.[18] By the end of the 1940s, people in the US State Department and intelligence services became convinced that the United States was losing the propaganda battle. They responded by boosting cultural diplomacy efforts of their own. Some initiatives, such as those overseen by the State Department, were open about the source of sponsorship, as Penny Von Eschen shows in her fascinating study of the jazz tours conducted by Louis Armstrong, Dave Brubeck, and Dizzie Gillespie.[19]

The cultural diplomacy programs developed by the CIA, unlike those from the State Department, were clandestine. Although most intellectuals and institutions associated with the CCF were extremely clear about their political commitments—supporting the arts, critical detachment, and personal liberties while condemning totalitarianism at every opportunity—the people footing the bill at the CIA believed that the programs would be more effective if they appeared spontaneous and free from coercion or direct state oversight. The implied contrast with Soviet cultural diplomacy would be more noticeable if these programs were believed to lack government interference.

In the early days, CCF activities concentrated on western Europe, where it was thought that intellectuals were too sympathetic to Soviet Communism, but affiliates were soon established all over the world. The CCF financed lavish spectacles—such as Nicolas Nabokov's Masterpieces of the Twentieth Century arts festival in Paris (1952)—artistic and musical tours, film screenings, academic gatherings, books—such as Richard Crossman's edited collection, *The God That Failed* (1950)—and, above all, magazines. In retrospect, it may come as a surprise, or seem accidental, that magazines such as *Encounter* were interested in turning modernist aesthetic practices into cold war assets. The earliest issues now feel a bit scattered, as if the editors could not decide what sort of publication they wanted: in some places, it feels like a modernist little magazine, with original poetry and stories and diverse *belles lettres*; elsewhere, it reads as an international affairs quarterly, with extended essays on pressing political issues; and yet at other moments it channels the spirit of its title by serving up quasi-ethnographic travel essays and reportage, bringing the dramas of the decolonizing world to the attention of Anglo-American readers. The first few numbers, for instance, include remnants of and reflections on modernist literary culture, with poems from W. H. Auden, Cecil Day-Lewis, and Edith Sitwell, stories from Christopher Isherwood and Wyndham Lewis, tributes to Dylan Thomas, and extracts from Virginia Woolf's diaries and W. B. Yeats's letters. In the style of an international affairs journal, there are essays by Leslie Fiedler on Julius and Ethel Rosenberg (the couple executed by the United States in 1953 for passing atomic secrets to the Soviets), Mary McCarthy on her flirtation with the Communist Party, and Arthur Koestler on the pro-Soviet intelligentsia in Europe. In its capacity as a publication that would explain the decolonizing world to north Atlantic readers, early issues of *Encounter* include articles and stories on Algeria, British Guiana, Japan, and many on India, the significance of which I consider below.

The statement of editorial policy in the very first issue captures the unstable mix of aesthetic and political values that the journal would try to harness. "Appearing at this time," shortly after the death of Stalin, "*Encounter* seeks to promote no 'line.'" Only a few principles will guide the magazine: the editors "regard literature and the arts as being values in themselves, in need of no ulterior justification; that it should be an international magazine [...] that it should aim, not at the slurring over of differences, but rather at the uninhibited exploration of them."[20] Love of the arts; freedom of expression; diversity of opinion; a spirit of internationalism combined with an appreciation for cultural particularity: it is debatable whether *Encounter* ever met these lofty standards, but these policies became an extremely valuable tool for recruiting intellectual collaborators in the nonaligned world. *Encounter's* investment in modernism, we might say, relied on the notion that aesthetics transcend political interests, reimagining modernist autonomy as the antithesis of cold war binaries (and yet antitotalitarian at the same time). Less than a decade later, *Transition* would use a nearly identical platform to capture the creative energy of a decolonizing continent.

Encounter's debatable claim of cold war neutrality was buttressed by its self-nomination as a curator of the modernist movement.[21] First and most obvious, modernist culture was worth defending precisely because the Soviets were censuring it. The most radical genres of modernism—nonreferential literature, atonal music, and abstract expressionist painting—could be read anachronistically in the cold war context as refusals of orthodoxy, as rejections of party lines. The success of abstract expressionism, because it was dominated by painters based in the United States, was particularly useful in this regard, suggesting that the North American superpower alone was fully capable of offering sanctuary to modernism, salvaged from an exhausted western Europe and shielded from the Communist bloc. Modernist culture becomes valuable as a space for cultural diplomacy because it is supposedly nonideological—and therefore, paradoxically, antitotalitarian. The obvious contradiction of using supposedly nonpolitical modernism as a tool of anti-Stalinism is on display in many CCF-sponsored materials, especially in the editorials of *Encounter*. Giles Scott-Smith calls this the politics of apolitical culture.

A synopsis of Stephen Spender's activities in the 1950s shows how the CCF attempted to use the modernist doctrine of aesthetic autonomy to support its version of "negative liberalism," which involved an attack on Communism without a clear advocacy of capitalist democracies. In *The God That Failed*, Spender and several of his collaborators explain that they are equally critical of Communism and the capitalist nations: Communism on the grounds that it does not respect dissenting viewpoints, liberal democracies on the grounds that they do not pursue social justice. "It is evident to me now that my duty is to state what I support without taking sides," Spender writes in *The God That Failed*. "Neither side," he continues, "in the present alignment of the world, represents what I believe to be the only solution to the world's problems."[22] Louis Fischer, another contributor to the collection, goes a step further, stating that the only viable option is an uncompromising refusal of both sides:

> Some are so obsessed with the crimes of the capitalist world that they remain blind to the crimes and bankruptcy of Bolshevism. Not a few use the defects of the West to divert attention from the horrors of Moscow. My own prescription is: Double Rejection. A free spirit, unfettered by economic bonds or intellectual bias, can turn his back on the evils of both worlds. (223)

The appeal of the CCF agenda—especially for intellectuals in the decolonizing world—relied on this spirit of double rejection, or impartiality. As Fischer declares, it is the responsibility of the writer to work as a "free spirit, unfettered by economic bonds or intellectual bias" (223). Modernist claims of autonomy and cosmopolitanism were central to this self-definition.

Reading Spender's *The Creative Spirit* (1953) as a companion piece to *The God That Failed* helps explain why an attachment to interwar modernism could lead 1950s intellectuals to describe themselves as cold war neutrals or as conscientious objectors. Spender's biographer summarizes the book as a defense of the modernist doctrine of aesthetic autonomy: "In *The Creative Element* Spender clearly expresses his allegiance not to any ideology but to the creative element itself."[23] Spender calls "the great experimenters" of the late nineteenth and early twentieth century—Arthur Rimbaud, Henry James, James Joyce, Franz Kafka, Rainer Maria Rilke—his literary "heroes."[24] Their genius is largely attributable to their "individualist" sensibilities, with a corresponding "rejection of the orthodox" (22). Literary culture, Spender argues, is the antidote to partisan politics. As the CCF began to reach out to writers in the decolonizing parts of the world, the doctrine of modernist autonomy could be used as a basis to recruit intellectuals with no affinity for either of the cold war superpowers. As I argue in *Commonwealth of Letters: British Literary Culture and the Emergence of Postcolonial Aesthetics*, metropolitan writers leaned on the concept of aesthetic autonomy to broker partnerships with late colonial intellectuals during the middle decades of the century. But it is equally apparent, from CCF activities, that modernist aesthetic beliefs were a key part of US cultural diplomacy programs during the early part of the cold war.

Recruiting Africans

From *Encounter*'s earliest days, Michael Josselson, the CIA's operative at CCF headquarters, was determined to make the outlet an international review. With Spender and Kristol taking on the editorial duties, it seemed natural that the magazine would become a cultural symbol of the Anglo-American alliance. But in one of the formative proposals for *Encounter*, the British committee of the CCF said it envisioned a journal international in scope, with special designs on Asian readers.[25] Josselson seized on the idea of attracting south Asian collaborators and subscribers even before the first issue, and he regularly hounded Kristol and Spender to contact prominent Indian and Pakistani intellectuals after *Encounter* was up and running. Spender insisted that the best way to win hearts and minds in Asia would be to produce a magazine that is "excellent on the creative side, excellent on the arts and unchallengably disinterested in politics."[26] Spender frequently complained that the strident tones sounded by Kristol and some of his political contributors would grate on British and Indian intellectuals alike, both of whom were prone to be irked by jingoism and obvious partisanship. Spender's fears would be confirmed in India, at least, where the CCF's proclamations of neutrality were never taken at face value.

By the late 1950s, Spender and Josselson turned their attentions to anglophone Africa, where they hoped for better results than they achieved in India. In 1959, Josselson sent Spender an issue of *Black Orpheus*—a few years before Beier had begun accepting CCF funds—asking Spender to consider devoting space to African poetry in the literary section of forthcoming issues of *Encounter*, later urging Spender to write to Soyinka for ideas.[27] Josselson also asked that poems by Léopold Sédar Senghor be translated and published soon.[28] Shortly thereafter, Spender wrote excitedly to Josselson with the news that the British Council were offering him a trip to South Africa, saying, "I feel that Africa is going to be more and more our preoccupation during the 1960's."[29] Josselson, however, instructed Spender to reject the offer, on the grounds that favoring the apartheid state with an official visit would only jeopardize their plans for African expansion: "The Congress is not interested in South Africa and its only role can be to condemn, in the strongest terms, the present South African regime and its policies." Josselson told Spender to see if the British Council would fund a visit to Ghana, Kenya, Nigeria, and Tanganyika instead.[30]

This exchange on the value of a trip to South Africa says a great deal about the CIA's overall strategy on the continent. It tells us that the United States did not have a consistent policy in Africa—it could condemn the South African government in the context of its cultural diplomacy missions and offer it other forms of support as an anti-Communist ally.[31] This correspondence also reveals that the needs and desires of indigenous intellectuals were one of the primary considerations as the CCF turned to Africa. The CIA did not have its own way with its cultural diplomacy; the existing convictions of African intellectuals, ultimately, determined the broad parameters of CCF strategy on the decolonizing continent.

The Makerere Conference

The Makerere conference was orchestrated by Mphahlele and paid for by the CCF. Conferences with high-profile invitees were one of the favored programs in the CCF repertoire of activities. The Makerere meeting followed on the heels of several conferences in Europe and Asia, but it was the most significant in a string of CCF-sponsored gatherings in Africa over the next five years. Mphahlele, a *Drum* veteran and exiled South African, fresh off the success of *Down Second Avenue* (1959), was hired in 1961 to be the CCF's director of African outreach. Mphahlele came to the CCF through his involvement in Mbari, which had recently joined the CCF network. Mbari, founded in Ibadan in 1961 by Beier, Clark-Bekederemo, Mphahlele, Okigbo, and Soyinka, had begun life as a combination arts center, bar, and restaurant, eventually adding publishing (and a branch in Oshogbo) to its list of sponsored activities. La Guma and Okigbo both published under the Mbari imprint.

The Makerere conference announced the birth of postcolonial African literature in English, and it started off the debate about the appropriateness of imperial languages for use in literary production. Because the subsequent language debates were quite polemical, much of the content of the conference has been long forgotten. The conference proceedings, edited by Mphahlele, reveal that most of the participants were overwhelmingly concerned with matters of literary technique, and secondarily with the precarious state of Africa's cultural institutions.[32] Indigenous arts centers and publishing ventures, such as Mbari, *Black Orpheus*, and the recently launched *Transition*, were greeted enthusiastically by most attendees. Before the language debate really started, in other words, African writers were eagerly building cultural institutions free from imperialist control. Mphahlele, in his press release about the conference, emphasized the need to free African writers from dependence on former colonial powers, and the intervention of the CCF—named as sponsor of Mbari as well as the conference itself—represented a godsend, particularly because the money seemed to support local, nonideological artistic ventures. Animosity toward the departing colonial powers was exploited by the CCF, which described itself as a benevolent supporter of home-grown, autonomous cultural institutions—and therefore as a patron free of the stain of imperialism.

The discussions at the conference show a strong preference for detachment, irony, and universality as the standards worth developing in the literature of independent Africa. Most presenters censured writers who were overly consumed with racialized forms of protest writing—literature should be conscious of its social context, the participants agreed, but it should treat political conflict and racial difference as objectively as possible. Saunders Redding—a US critic invited to the conference because of his CCF connections—approvingly cites the example of James Baldwin, who "stand[s] on his racial foundation" but ultimately makes an "appeal to the whole American audience."[33] For Redding, the test of Baldwin's validity as an artist is his ability to transcend racial and political boundaries. Another keynote speaker, Arthur Drayton, a West Indian literary critic then teaching at Ibadan, made similar claims about the value of Caribbean writing as a viable precedent for the emerging generation of Africans. Against many critics who have complained that Caribbean writers are too parochial, Drayton argues that the best writers are able to turn their sociological treatments of Caribbean societies into universal creative statements: "As long as the novelist in describing the experience of being West Indian can at the same time show that by this very experience he belongs to the stream of humanity, as long as he can universalize, this would seem to be enough on this score."[34] In these presentations, Black writers from the United States and the Caribbean are useful models not because of some crude racial affinity—as the negritude camp was accused of favoring—but because they transcend forms of racial exclusion by producing literature with universal aspirations.

According to Beier and Gerald Moore, the young generation of anglophone African writers had already gone some way toward establishing emotional detachment and objectivity as cardinal virtues of literary production. In commending Clark-Bekederemo's "Night Rain," for instance, Moore claims that the poem captures individual, as opposed to group, consciousness: "Here is no gesture of political or historical protest, no advice, no statement even of the poet's colour or its significance; but a faithful and beautifully-controlled account of individual experience."[35] Beier finds similar things to praise in Dennis Brutus, a highly political South African poet: no one "could accuse him of being self-pitying or even self-centred. On the contrary, . . . [he] manages to stand partly outside the events that [a]ffect him."[36] Even a deeply political writer, such as Brutus, would be requisitioned as an exemplar of detachment and objectivity; lashing out with anger would, it seems, detract from his artistic achievement.

The presence of the flamboyant Okigbo, the young Nigerian poet who would be killed a few years later in the Nigerian civil war, certainly added to the impression that the conference organizers had a deep attachment to modernist aesthetics. Okigbo already had strong links with Mbari and *Black Orpheus*, and after meeting Neogy at the conference, he would be named as the West African editor of *Transition*. In one oft-repeated quip, Okigbo pronounced, "I don't read my poetry to non-poets."[37] He consented, however, to share some of *Limits*—which would appear in *Transition* and later with an Mbari imprint—with the Makerere delegates. Here is the short lyric poem with which *Limits* begins:

> Suddenly becoming talkative
>   like weaverbird
> Summoned at offside of
>   dream remembered
> Between sleep and waking,
> I hang up my egg-shells
> To you of palm grove,
> Upon whose bamboo towers
> Hang, dripping with yesterupwine,
> A tiger mask and nude spear . . .
> Queen of the damp half light,
> I have had my cleansing,
> Emigrant with air-borne nose,
> The he-goat-on-heat.[38]

Written in the early 1960s, published in African little magazines, and later quoted by Achebe as evidence of what African writers are able to accomplish in the English language: given the context, it is difficult to imagine poetry more conspicuously and self-consciously modernist in idiom. We do not know which poems Okigbo recited at Makerere, but this particular poem is typical of the volume. It is a sonnet of sorts, with a meaning that is obscure at best. This sort of poetry, deliberately difficult and willfully apolitical, was designed to provoke his audience, and Okigbo certainly had detractors among his peers and colleagues. Okigbo seems to be engaged in a playful game of one-upmanship with the Makerere delegates, many of whom were calling for detachment, objectivity, and impersonality: if detachment is required of the African writer, Okigbo seems to say, my poetry liberates aesthetic language from the drudgery of prosaic meaning.[39]

From the archival evidence, the CCF was well satisfied with the conference and its proceedings. The meeting was discussed at length through the network's affiliates, especially *Transition* and the Transcription Centre. CCF officers had only one complaint about the conference: press coverage by Nkosi and Dennis Duerden, Transcription Centre director, did not mention the CCF prominently enough as sponsor of the event. In a letter explaining his coverage of the conference, Duerden replied that it was not wise, given the history of imperialism in Africa, to call unnecessary attention to the role of foreign patrons:

> It seems to me that there are two conflicting principles; one is that the Congress will receive much greater credit for its work [. . .] in Africa if it uses its discretion in drawing attention to itself and preserves the image of encouraging work done by Africans for Africans; the other is that it appears that you need publicity in order to finance the projects.
>
> Surely what is required is a balance between the two. Lewis gave the Congress credit in his article on the Makerere Conference and I am sure he would continue to give it credit whenever it is politic to do so.[40]

As a patron, the CCF would be accepted if it supported the development of autonomous literary institutions in Africa—"encouraging work done by Africans for Africans," as Duerden puts it here, or independence from colonial institutions. It would be wrong to construe the conference as an unambiguous defense of modernism or of highly experimental, nonpolitical writing. But it is noticeable how modernist principles of detachment and impartiality dominate the discussions of appropriate literary models. Duerden invokes indigeneity, or that which is autonomously African, as the antidote to cold war sectarianism.

Radio Free Africa

A year or two before the Makerere conference, Josselson and Spender hit upon radio as a possible medium for expanding the CCF's footprint in Africa. During the 1940s and '50s, Spender had been involved in cultural outreach schemes with the BBC's colonial services in India and the West Indies. *Caribbean Voices*, in particular, had been successful enough as a literary serial that Spender must have thought it would serve as a good model for cultural broadcasting in anglophone Africa. In the early 1960s, the CCF approached the BBC's Duerden, knowledgeable about African visual art and himself an artist, to embark on a tour of Africa with the aim of setting up a broadcasting venture. In Kenya, the director of state radio broadcasting told Duerden that he would be happy to meet, but that he wanted to "know, first of all, what exactly is the Congress for Cultural Freedom; it sounds too frightfully Iron Curtain to be true!"[41] This reaction is telling: for many, cultural diplomacy initiatives led by the United States and the Soviets were virtually indistinguishable. In his final report on his 1961 tour, Duerden said it would be imperative that "parallel Congress activities should not create the impression that the Congress has a Cold War stance," envisioning the Transcription Centre as "a sort of club for the promotion of the art of Africa and the study of Africa."[42] By October 1961, Duerden submitted his resignation to the BBC in order to launch the Transcription Centre, to be based in London.

Of all the CIA's activities in Africa, the Transcription Centre was subjected to the most pressure to incorporate anti-Soviet propaganda in its activities. The venture was never on solid financial footing, and Duerden's continual pleas to the CCF for additional support made it especially susceptible on this point. As Gerald Moore tells the story, it is to Duerden's lasting credit that he resisted the temptation to turn the Centre into a propaganda machine.[43] Initially, the CCF were quite satisfied with Duerden's purely literary recordings. John Hunt, a novelist who took over many of Josselson's duties at the CCF, said that Duerden should capitalize on the success of the Makerere conference to publicize the Transcription Centre. Hunt encouraged Duerden to ask Nkosi to write up an article "along the line of 'Africans produce their own Third Program [*sic*] for Africa.' There is a very good story to tell here and I should think that Lewis would do it very well."[44]

Before long, Duerden's backers started urging him to work antitotalitarian messages into his plans. Hunt said that he was reading all the Transcription Centre programming scripts "with great interest," but suggested that Duerden

FIGURE 3.2. Françoise Robinet (left), Dennis Duerden, Gerald Moore, and Langston Hughes at the Makerere conference, June 1962. Image courtesy of Hanna Holborn Gray Special Collections Research Center, University of Chicago Library.

"now give serious thought to the social, economic and political side of the work so that the broadcasts are not exclusively literary." Hunt acknowledged that this "has to be handled with great delicacy," but insisted that Duerden could pull it off.[45] Duerden, for his part, equivocated, stalled, and avoided the question as best he could. When pressed for an answer, he told his funders, in an echo of the first editorial statement in *Encounter*, "Invariably people ask what is this organisation, what line is [it putting] over," recommending that the Transcription Centre stick to cultural broadcasts.[46] Knowing that partisanship would alienate his collaborators and audiences and ruin the Centre's credibility, Duerden tenaciously clung to the resolutely apolitical, modernist-inclined *Third Programme* and *Caribbean Voices* as his models. Interviews with literary personalities, such as Soyinka, Okigbo, and Neogy, were some of the most popular of the Centre's recordings, culminating in the publication of *African Writers Talking*.[47]

When Duerden felt compelled to introduce politics into his work, he insisted strongly that the CCF adopt a nonsectarian line out of respect for his

African collaborators and audiences, few of whom would welcome an anti-Soviet slant. Asked to provide a reader's report on a book manuscript called *Communism in Africa*, which the CCF was considering for publication, Duerden replied firmly that "we should respect the opinions of African neutralists and attempt to assist them to achieve independent ends;" moreover, as Duerden points out, the book's sense that newly independent African nations are up for grabs as part of the cold war struggle resonated uncomfortably with European imperialism.[48] The sort of nonalignment and open-ended intellectual freedom only imagined by Duerden was achieved, rather improbably, by the CCF's African little magazines, especially *Transition*.

A Period of Transition

Before getting involved with *Transition*, the CCF had begun its African subventions with support for *Black Orpheus* and the Nigerian Mbari clubs. Inspired by the 1956 *Présence Africaine* conference in Paris, Beier launched *Black Orpheus* in 1957 with a grant from the Ministry of Education in Nigeria's Western Region. It was only in 1961, as Josselson and Spender were hoping to expand the CCF's African base, that Beier and the magazine joined the network and began receiving modest subventions.

The CCF's backing of *Black Orpheus* established precedents on a couple of different fronts. First, Beier's publication was fastidiously apolitical. As Soyinka later described it, "*Black Orpheus* was literally non-political. It published poetry and plays, it reproduced artworks, the plastic arts, reported on performance arts. Its mission was to link the diaspora culturally with Africa without getting involved in politics."[49] For Beier, this was partly a pragmatic decision: avoiding politics in a divided, ethnically diverse, and rapidly changing West Africa allowed the journal to attract contributors and readers of all stripes from across the diaspora. Serving as a conduit between scattered constituencies was an important part of the magazine's mission, as the first editorial notes: "a great deal of the best African writing is in French or Portuguese or Spanish. *Black Orpheus* tries to break down some of these language barriers by introducing writers from all territories in translation."[50] Avoiding political controversy was crucial to this project of cultural transmission and translation, in Beier's estimation, and the CCF endorsed this strategy when it came aboard. When Beier signed an agreement with Longman to print and distribute the magazine—a deal approved by the CCF—the contract stipulated, "The proprietors guarantee that the non-political character of the work will be retained."[51] Early issues featured English translations of the negritude poets and a report on the Paris conference. The journal would also feature material from the United States and the Caribbean, the literary traditions of which are "highly relevant to Africans" and vice versa (4).

Second, the CCF did not create new magazines in Africa from scratch, as it had done with *Encounter*. Instead, it identified existing periodicals that were compatible with the CCF's general outlook and encouraged those outlets with financial support. In the case of *Black Orpheus*, it seems that the combination of fresh writing, internationalism, and apolitical editorial philosophy fit the bill. The only major requirement for accepting CCF support was agreeing to cross-promotion: *Encounter*, *Black Orpheus*, and *Transition* (and other CCF journals) featured advertisements for one another, adding to the impression that readers were partaking in urbane and cosmopolitan conversation. Contributors also tended to circulate, popping up in magazines or at conferences with the CCF imprimatur.

Like Beier, Neogy began *Transition* without the support of or contact with the CCF. Neogy's first few issues of *Transition* are self-consciously modernist in a way that *Black Orpheus* is not. The title, of course, alludes to the legendary European little magazine published in Paris between the wars. As I discuss in chapter 2, *transition*'s "Revolution of the Word" demands that the literary imagination be "autonomous and unconfined," and that "the literary creator has the right to disintegrate the primal matter of words imposed on him by text-books and dictionaries." It goes on to damn the "plain reader," especially those who would deny the artist "the right to use words of his own fashioning and to disregard existing grammatical and syntactical laws." This influential proclamation of aesthetic autonomy simultaneously projects artistic freedom on a number of different fronts: from politics, from commercial considerations, from the rules of language, and from literal, prosaic forms of meaning. As we shall see from the first few issues of *Transition*, which attracted the attention of the CCF, Neogy envisioned the interwar little magazine as a direct antecedent. For him, at least, there was nothing incompatible or incongruous about using the concept of aesthetic autonomy to launch a new magazine in decolonizing Africa.

Neogy's first literary contribution to the magazine, "7 T ONE = 7 E TON," appears near the beginning of the first issue. It is a short prose-poem, offering a condensed view of the type of literary ambitions Neogy was then nursing: "myriad existences forgotten," begins the piece seemingly in midsentence, "over a tense past and a vocabulary future full of new cooked meanings

7T ONE ≡ 7E TON

by   Rajat   Neogy

myriad existences forgotten over a tense past and a vocabulary future full of new cooked meanings meaning meaning but nothing else. Very where every nothing happens
which is the spitten curse of the image-shadow of the
tired sophisticates — those knowing who wait with
knife and fork and exquisitive table top manners for
the fried egg of love peppered with salt and a shot
tomato.   There, nowhere were pine tree tops which
exhaled and inspired several odours of smelt desires
lust-forgotten in dry leaves of an autumn beak of
bird's hard kiss.   Also granite steps on unposing rocks
slightly naked in the drizzle rain, wet with uxorious
felt and a hat raised to those passing underneath in
the sand of pink avalanches bellied out of the earth
with the rumblings of running round stones in furlined
caps for women with glass eyes and seeing hair.

Also there the juice of a range beyond O in a bottle
with libel on itself.   All so.   Tier after tier of fired
wheels after dead revolution.   In a minute.   An hour.
Ours is the same.   Aim.   am.   I am.   Ham-riders
in porcupine pleasure of standing on end, mushroom-
grown in moist.   Ture was there too.   At the wait
near the wooden flag a blue bus came in an accordion
and pressed holes to cover kilometers.   Bridge-water
rattled like green aces.   And trees stood behind.

Where the man with the feigned hair faced his daily
tooth with broken bread and peroxide fingering holes
of a designing telephone.   Operate.   OBSERVE!
‹Rate of removal was in itself unnecessary but of
course they insisted.   They would.›
And so atomic pictures of X read into newspapers
the final story.

Railway lines sent telegraph messages and veils made
virgins.   Some like sunlight in closed balls.   Others
open their eyes and play with armadillos in lost
swamps.   Mosquito vibrations move mountains and
ants are licked and children dipped into acid.

Serpents glisten like parachute silk with pythons
singing on electric chairs.   Hair-oil is good for the
brain and soap is good for the bones.   Bubbling
advertising the good of man in jungles of sleeping-
sickness.

Go   with the wind, the cock crows everywhere

1

FIGURE 3.3. "7 T ONE = 7 E TON," by Rajat Neogy. From *Transition* magazine #1,
November 1961. Reprinted with permission of Indiana University Press.

meaning meaning but nothing else."[52] The sputtering repetition of "meaning" in this opening line might make the knowing the reader think of a Wallace Stevens poem or a Gertrude Stein piece, or of the original *transition*. Meaning is self-identical; any attempt to attach external referents to this "vocabulary future" would be futile. This sort of tautological wordplay represents an attempt to proclaim the autonomy of poetic language—that poetry can be emancipated from the burden of any prosaic or literal meaning. But as Andrew Goldstone points out, such assertions of autonomy, paradoxically, rely very heavily on contextual cues and audience participation; in this light, we might gloss Neogy's lack of "meaning" as a reference to the tradition of modernist wordplay and its proper performance space, the little magazine.

A few issues later, an article by Robie Macauley on literary periodicals claims that the little magazine was now evolving in exciting ways in decolonizing regions. Macauley, a CIA agent and editor of *The Kenyon Review*—and a participant at the Makerere conference—reports that the modernist magazine has lost much of its vitality in the United States. "On the whole," Macauley reports, "the editors of the little magazines are likely to envy their contemporaries in other countries"—such as Australia, India, the Philippines, and presumably Uganda—"where the intellectual publication may have a little firmer place in the intellectual life of the country as a whole."[53] From this firm national base, however, reviews such as *Black Orpheus* and *Transition* reached a global audience, relatively small in numbers, but nevertheless part of an international community of disinterested intellectuals. For Neogy, modernist magazine culture seemed purpose-built for this task. Its liabilities—insecure funding, erratic publication schedules and distribution channels, and editorial sloppiness—were more than offset by its strengths: Its supposed independence from vested interests made it exceptionally nimble, quick to recognize new talents, allowing Neogy to take substantial risks that more established publications could not afford.

Following Benson's groundbreaking work on *Black Orpheus* and *Transition*, it is tempting to read these little magazines as part of an African literary awakening, creating a system of cultural production that does not rely on networks controlled by metropolitan interests. The CCF's sponsorship of *Transition* and *Black Orpheus* encourages me to shy away from the conclusion that these magazines reached global audiences without the support or approbation of cultural centers in the United States. For something closer to that model, we have to turn to *Lotus* and the Afro-Asian Writers' Association, as I do in the next chapter. But neither do I find fully persuasive Andrew N. Rubin's conclusion that CCF sponsorship of African magazines was a way to "regulate, sanitize, and co-opt the literature of decolonization," or Juliana Spahr's belief that the CIA "manipulated the world republic of letters to be more amenable to [US] political concerns" by promoting "a small number of writers whose concerns they felt overlapped with their own."[54] There is ample evidence in the pages of *Transition* itself that the magazine did not shy away from criticism of the United States and its African allies and proxies. If there was obedience to a party line, it was drawn around aesthetic rather than ideological convictions. Eric Bulson's outstanding work on little magazines, in which he emphasizes the agonistic relationship between modernist, colonial, and postcolonial variants of the form, offers a more reliable guide for my thinking in this chapter, with the caveat that the encounter between Jolas's *transition* and Neogy's *Transition* happened under the auspices of cultural diplomacy programs.[55] For a brief while, at least, the CCF sponsored periodicals in the modernist pattern, which was appealing to Africans precisely because it seemed to affirm the autonomy, and to defend the nonalignment, of intellectual work for nonmetropolitan writers. The form of the little magazine—its willingness to experiment, its presumption of a like-minded audience, and even its haphazardness—created the impression that *Transition* was a space free from orthodoxies and vested interests of any kind.

Unlike many modernist reviews, however, *Transition*—as with *Encounter*—devoted a great deal of space to current affairs and contemporary politics. Neogy's remarkable penchant for stoking controversy by presenting contrasting viewpoints side-by-side—Benson calls it Neogy's "editorial evenhandedness"—seemed to justify the editor's claim that *Transition* promoted a space for detached inquiry (133). And, like Spender, Neogy believed that *Transition*'s political discussions would be successful only if strict editorial disinterestedness were maintained. In practice, this meant that Neogy solicited contributions from people with conflicting viewpoints. The magazine's second issue, largely devoted to discussions of Tanganyika and Julius Nyerere, provides a case in point. Neogy managed to secure an article from Nyerere himself, in which the country's first postcolonial leader defends the one-party state as a modern form of traditional African democracy. An editorial profile on Nyerere later in the issue, however, implies that for all his qualities, the young leader is not inclined to tolerate internal disagreement, noting that Nyerere supported Kwame Nkrumah's decision to imprison dissidents in Ghana. This oblique reply to Nyerere's position becomes more explicit yet later in the issue, as a book review sharply criticizes Nkrumah's one-party state and his willingness to suspend civil liberties. As Benson notes, Neogy was quite opposed to the one-party system in Ghana and Tanzania, but he went out of his way to give its defenders the space to articulate their position in his magazine.

Transition's international aspirations and its willingness to debate, with apparent impartiality, the value of nationalist policies, created the impression that the journal was independent of Africa's dominant, nationalist political movements. When the question of the cold war came up, as it sometimes did, *Transition* claimed to be equally nonpartisan. Bessie Head summarized the impressions of many *Transition* readers in a letter to the editor, included with her subscription order: "To me, at least, *Transition* is a kind of home. It seems to be fighting neither for communism or capitalism."[56] Head's synopsis both describes *Transition*'s editorial detachment and identifies this space as the natural "home" for the African intellectual.

In a letter to his colleagues at *Présence Africaine*, Neogy claims that the little magazine in postcolonial Africa ought to be both aesthetically experimental and politically nonpartisan. He writes that the little magazine must promote "unemotional consideration of a nation's plans and problems," it must show unswerving "integrity and a respect for facts," and it must demonstrate "a fearlessness in the face of unpopularity."[57] As an editor, Neogy himself showed such fearlessness by questioning Milton Obote's rule of Uganda, which landed him in jail, effectively ending his stint as editor of the magazine. But Neogy believed that such independent political thinking ought to be complemented by experimental writing. He insisted that his readers who could appreciate challenging poetry would be better equipped to unravel "the threads of political factionalism." The little magazine "which is actively involved in cultural participation must also by definition be *avant garde*."[58] This editorial philosophy, conjoined with Neogy's ability to attract contributors from all over the continent, had the effect of separating the work of intellectuals from national constituencies. The experimental writing favored by Neogy, with its proclamations of autonomy from literal meaning, could seem to complement affirmations of independence in the political contributions to the magazine. With a certain amount of editorial finesse, *Transition* could sanction both apolitical, experimental modernist writing and explicitly political journalism by claiming that the magazine promotes free intellectual inquiry. Both the literary and political contributions were efforts to define the autonomy of African intellectuals as a joint project between literature and political criticism.

Soyinka's editorial, "The Writer in an African State," appearing just before the CIA funding scandal broke, reflects *Transition*'s attempt to reconcile the

FIGURE 3.4. Neville Rubin (left, foreground), Elizabeth Spio-Garbrah (third from left, identification uncertain), and Wole Soyinka at the Makerere conference, June 1962. Image courtesy of Hanna Holborn Gray Special Collections Research Center, University of Chicago Library.

discourse of aesthetic autonomy with political journalism. Soyinka's main contention is that writers, especially during the rise of dictatorships in Africa, have become too cozy with the state, especially those regimes that insist on documenting the past glories of African civilizations. By the mid-1960s, this kind of anti-imperialist romanticizing was only helping nationalist leaders quash internal resistance. Unthinking portraits of the immemorial African personality standing alone against imperialism had become, in essence, defenses of nationalist projects such as Nkrumah's. Biodun Jeyifo notes that Soyinka spent a good part of his early years railing against worship of the African past.[59] Soyinka calls for writers who have the courage to express "a sensibility and an outlook apart from, and independent of the mass direction."[60] In the pages of *Transition*, where experimental poetry and current affairs pieces sit side-by-side, having the courage to protest against the continent's political leaders seemed to be reinforced by preferences for autonomous, forward-looking literature.

Indigeneity Is Not Enough

Soyinka's early drama combines an interest in modernist aesthetics with a wariness of indigeneity. In fact, one of the big breaks in Soyinka's early career was winning a drama competition sponsored by the CCF and *Encounter*, judged by Achebe, Beier, Mphahlele, and Spender.[61] First prize included public performance during Nigeria's independence celebrations. *A Dance of the Forests* (1960) shows that building the future of Nigeria by resurrecting the past would have potentially disastrous results. In this challenging theatrical piece, which gave Soyinka's critics plenty of ammunition to brand him as elitist, spirits summoned from the past wreak havoc on the modern nation-state before humans futilely try to send them back to the world of the spirits. Autochthonous culture, so often mobilized in the nationalist imagination, becomes zombie culture in Soyinka's hands. Another of Soyinka's early plays, *Kongi's Harvest* (1965), presents a highly aestheticized conflict between a dictator and dissidents in a mythical postcolonial African state resembling Nkrumah's Ghana. There is a five-year development plan, propaganda blaring over public loudspeakers, and preventative detention. In the denouement of the play, the authoritarian ruler attempts to refurbish traditional rites—such as the yam harvest festival—only to have his dissident subjects turn the life-affirming ritual into a scene of protest, a shockingly morbid inversion of the dictator's grandiose dreams.

Although it is widely reported in the scholarly literature that *A Dance of the Forests* was performed at the independence celebrations, Soyinka recalls that the government dropped his play from the official program (*Trumpism* 83–84). The play's coded warning against romanticizing an indigenous past did not win over hard-core nationalists. The play's skepticism about nationalist propaganda was amplified by its victory in a playwriting contest sponsored by a transnational cultural institution. In retrospect, it is fascinating to learn that the CCF orchestrated a literary competition that would give the winner a platform at the official independence celebrations. *Encounter* would run a similar contest in Sierra Leone. The charge that Soyinka was pandering to an elitist, cosmopolitan audience was no doubt bolstered by *Encounter*'s patronage of the event. CCF meddling in the most nationalist of occasions helped create the impression that Soyinka's primary audience existed beyond the boundaries of the nation-state. Soyinka's political detention (discussed in chapter 8) and subsequent exile only amplified the impression that his aesthetic and ethical values could not be contained by the postcolonial nation-state.

Mphahlele's *Down Second Avenue*, published by Faber and Faber two years before he took up his position with the CCF, provides a further example of how anglophone African writers of this generation articulated the relationship between indigeneity and intellectual detachment. Many chapters of the memoir provide ethnographic descriptions drawn from Mphahlele's childhood and young adulthood. Between the ages of five and twelve, Mphahlele lived with his stern paternal grandmother—"not the smiling type," he tells us—in a rural location set aside for Black South Africans.[62] Under her care while his parents struggle to earn a living in the city, Mphahlele learns about the hardships of village life when there is not enough good land to go around. Abruptly, at age twelve his mother collects him and his siblings at Christmas and whisks them off to Pretoria. There, things are different, but no easier. Mphahlele's rich character sketches provide the basis of these chapters on life in the urban slums: his mother, who, like many women, brews beer illicitly to supplement her meager wages; his intrepid aunts, who never back down from a threat; the neighborhood's larger-than-life characters, which include witches, drunks, religious fanatics, petty criminals, and incorrigible busybodies; the memorable schoolmates and the sadistic teachers who do not spare pupils the whip; and of course, the eccentric White families from whom Mphahlele collects weekly washing. These ethnographic portraits give us a tour of interwar Black South Africa. In many respects, these chapters are less concerned with narrating the development of an individual than they are with providing a snapshot of a complex community. Through these sections of the book, which document the particularity of Black life in 1930s Pretoria, *Down Second Avenue* offers something of a cultural stocktaking, an inventory of South African Black life gathered by an insider.

These primarily ethnographic chapters, however, are offset by five short interludes and an epilogue. These sections of the book are markedly different in tone and substance. Whereas most of the chapters are straightforwardly descriptive, these interludes are more introspective and awkward, putting some distance between the autobiographical subject and the culture of which he is a part. "No use trying to put the pieces together. Pieces of my life," he remarks in the second interlude, "They are a jumble" (74–75). Alluding to *The Waste Land*, perhaps, this passage imagines an authorial consciousness that sits uncomfortably with the other sections of the book. In the final interlude, as he struggles to finish writing a short story, he consciously recognizes his separation from the subjects of his work, the subjects that populate the other chapters of the book: "Standing here in a dark little world, viewing them [electric lights of the city] from afar, miles away, you know they are beyond your reach. The more beautiful they look the more distant they appear—or, perhaps, the more distant they are the lovelier they look" (201). Shifting into a second person address, this passage stands at odds with the lively, observant, and relatively easygoing main chapters in the book. Almost never alone in the other chapters, Mphahlele is frequently by himself, brooding, throughout the interludes. If the character sketches emphasize the immersion of the autobiographical subject in the community, these interludes are far more uncertain about the relationship between the intellectual and the culture he claims to know intimately. Mphahlele the writer puts himself at arm's length from the social life he describes elsewhere.

The disparity between the main chapters and the interludes becomes more pronounced when Mphahlele subverts the mode of ethnographic writing he uses throughout much of the book. The penultimate interlude, for example, tells of Mphahlele's teaching job in Basutoland (now Lesotho), having been blacklisted in South Africa. Hiking in the mountains at daybreak, again alone, Mphahlele says, "For one brief moment of rich promise I thought the secret was in the conical hat and the blanket of a Mosuto standing placidly on the edge of a summit at sunrise" (185). Even this flickering description foreshadows his coming discomfort with this train of thought. By the final interlude, he tells us that an urbanized intellectual such as himself can no longer be content with the version of racial or cultural essentialism he imagines in this earlier scene: "your tribal umbilical cord had long, oh so long, been severed and all the talk about Bantu culture and the Black man developing along his own lines was just so much tommy rot" (203). Or as he says argues with more finesse in "The Fabric of African Cultures," it is a mistake to regard "culture as an anthropological thing that belongs in the past."[63] Apartheid-era South Africa, with its pernicious fiction of separate development for different racial groups, makes Mphahlele particularly suspicious of cultural separatism as the way to practice anticolonial writing. *Down Second Avenue* proposes an interesting technical solution to the problem of imagining his community's autonomy without recourse to the language of nativism. The back-and-forth movement between the straightforward ethnographic vignettes and the more hesitant, self-aware interludes generates friction. In his epilogue, Mphahlele reads this friction as a sign of the kinetic energy required to mature as a writer: "In ten years my perspective has changed enormously from escapist writing to protest writing and, I hope, to something of a higher order, which is the ironic meeting between protest and acceptance in their widest terms" (217). Going beyond the "crushing cliché" of the South African situation demands a change of perspective, an ability to move within and against the institutions of cultural difference (218). Mphahlele's ironic detachment in the interludes is a counterpoint of, not the antidote to, the ethnographic storytelling of his other chapters.

There are several observations to be drawn from studying cold war cultural diplomacy and its reliance on modernist aesthetics in the context of anglophone African literature. Simon Gikandi argues "it was primarily—I am tempted to say solely—in the language and structure of modernism that a postcolonial experience came to be articulated and imagined in literary form."[64] If, however, interwar modernism was the major collection of aesthetic practices that gave postcolonial writers their "language and structure," as Gikandi explains, it should be noted that the cold war gave the modernist doctrine of aesthetic autonomy new relevance and new meanings in the 1960s. This is to say that the form of modernism requisitioned by African writers was inflected by ideals of impartiality and detachment. Whatever metropolitan modernism may have been in the 1920s, by the 1950s, non-Communist intellectuals (African, North American, and European) were prone to represent it as an aesthetic philosophy of critical disinterest and freedom from orthodoxy. A different history of European modernism might, in fact, emphasize its forms of political commitment, either to Communism or to fascism—but this is not the message the CCF and its collaborators wanted to spread. This narrative of modernist autonomy, retroactively embedded in the conflicts of the cold war, came to be an incredibly influential account of literary history. The cold war context helps explain why intellectuals such as Neogy, Okigbo, and Soyinka would enthusiastically attach themselves to the legacy of modernism—especially to the form of the little magazine—and also how modernism would become attached to, and dependent upon, the health of literary culture in the decolonizing regions of the world.

Second, it seems clear that modernism's evolution in the middle decades of the century—during which time it came to stand for the antithesis of utilitarian aesthetic theory—was affected by its use in cultural diplomacy programs during the cold war. As the archives show, the desire of the CCF hierarchy to build suitable partnerships in the emerging nation-states was one of the guiding principles of CCF projects, not an afterthought. Modernism's ethos of detachment and its supposed hostility to orthodoxy made it a useful tool for recruiting collaborators among nonaligned intellectuals who were otherwise wary of foreign patronage. This had important consequences for metropolitan British intellectuals as well. In their dealings with intellectuals from Africa, for example, Spender and Duerden were likely to understand the cold war as a conflict that partly defused the tensions created by imperialism. This was not simply a matter of the cold war being a bigger, more all-encompassing kind of struggle than imperialism—though some of that persists—but also a sense that modernist aesthetics possessed newfound relevance as the antithesis of cold war binaries. The scattered proclamations of autonomy found in modernist literature—freedom from financial and political interests above all—were refined and narrowed in the rhetoric of nonalignment. The spirit of "Double Rejection" proposed by the CCF as the proper intellectual disposition of the postwar era resonated with African intellectuals who admired modernist art and steadfastly refused to have their politics dictated to them by outsiders. Shared commitments to anti-totalitarianism only reinforced this connection.

Third, it seems plausible to suggest that the reigning critical emphasis on a stark division between writing inspired by a commitment to indigeneity (Ngũgĩ being the prototype) and eclecticism or cosmopolitanism (Soyinka being the poster child) is vastly overblown. The rough dichotomy has some basis in the literary institutions I have discussed here, but it is worth pointing out that writers supposedly protective of autochthonous forms had various levels of involvement in the cultural networks described in this chapter. It is a mistake, or an exaggeration, to neatly separate the 1960s generation into camps along these implied aesthetic and cultural lines. Moreover, such a split implicitly accepts the binaries many of these writers were anxious to escape or resist. In any event, the aesthetic objects themselves do not always lend themselves to such a tidy interpretation. Mphahlele's *Down Second Avenue* is one example of a text that juxtaposes one strand of modernist writing, featuring the detached intellectual, with the discourse of nativism. Likewise, Ngũgĩ's *A Grain of Wheat* (1967), with its debt to Joseph Conrad's *Under Western Eyes* and its creative use of oral storytelling conventions, consciously blends indigenous and European aesthetic conventions.[65] It makes more sense to argue that indigeneity and cultural eclecticism, like autonomous and utilitarian aesthetic theories, were part of a repertoire of styles and strategies that African writers could bring into different combinations. Within the context of these specific literary institutions, many African writers of the 1960s generation believed that the modernist ideals of detachment and autonomy could adequately reflect a blend of cold war nonalignment, anticolonialism, and independence from the nation-state. From another angle, we could also conclude that the affirmations of experimental modernism by some writers, and their acceptance of patronage from the CCF, does not mean that they were puppets of the United States and its cold war allies. The African writers under discussion here embraced the concept of autonomy to varying degrees because it signaled their desire for independence from the cold war's ideological binaries. The interests of Mphahlele, Okigbo, Neogy, and Soyinka converged with those of the CCF, unstably and unevenly, in the context of specific cultural institutions. It was a fruitful but short-lived collaboration.

Finally, it is evident that the revelation of CIA funding in 1967 left a massive gap, filled enthusiastically by the CCF's main rival in the decolonizing world, the Afro-Asian Writers' Association. As I discuss in the next chapter, many of the African writers who participated in the CCF network had no qualms about working with a Soviet-backed institution when the opportunity presented itself. The CCF, for its part, attempted to reconstitute itself (with no links to the CIA) as the International Association for Cultural Freedom (IACF). The rechristened outfit remained in operation until 1979, financed by "legitimate" nonprofits such as the Ford Foundation, before its members voted to dissolve the organization. *Transition*, damaged not only by the scandal but also by the detention of Neogy, relocated to Ghana, and Soyinka became editor—even changing the name of the magazine to *Ch'indaba* and renouncing IACF support in order to put the funding scandal behind the magazine, which published irregularly until it foundered in the turbulent mid-1970s. The Transcription Centre was eviscerated by the change in fortunes, finally shuttering its operations in 1975, long after its program of activities had dwindled. Of the institutions I have considered in this chapter, *Black Orpheus* was least affected financially as well as politically by the collapse of the CCF, although it too succumbed in the mid-1970s, with a brief revival in 1982. It left *Lotus* as the main international literary player in the region, until it too disbanded during the breakup of the Soviet Union. In the cold war scramble for influence, literary culture is arguably the site on which the Soviet Union left its deepest impression on the decolonizing world.

4

Indigeneity and Internationalism: Soviet Diplomacy and Afro-Asian Literature

THE CONGRESS FOR CULTURAL Freedom was the most important cultural institution in anglophone African literature in the late 1950s and early 1960s, but the Afro-Asian Writers' Association (AAWA) was arguably the most influential postwar network in the development of an anticolonial literary tradition in a fully global context.[1] The first international conference met in Tashkent, Uzbekistan in 1958, a mere two years after the *Présence Africaine* meeting in Paris and four years before the Makerere gathering. The Soviet-sponsored AAWA outlasted its CIA-backed rival network by a couple of decades. After a follow-up conference in Cairo in 1962 and another in Beirut in 1967, the organizers hatched plans to launch an international quarterly, culminating in *Lotus: Afro-Asian Writings* (1968–1991?).[2] Published simultaneously in three languages (Arabic, English, and French), *Lotus* provides a more straightforward instance of cultural diplomacy than the CCF network. Without any subterfuge, Soviet cultural agencies and their Warsaw Pact allies hosted and organized events, arranged for publication and distribution of the magazine in cooperation with their Egyptian counterparts, and took credit, publicly, as a major source of financial backing. Soviet writers, especially from the central Asian nations, shared the conference stage and contributed regularly to *Lotus*, casting the intellectuals of Soviet Asia as the natural allies of their counterparts in the decolonizing world. It will come as no surprise that *Lotus* tends to depict the Soviet Union as having achieved a cultural and social level to which other decolonizing nations might aspire: respect for national minorities and their cultural traditions, higher levels of educational attainment and economic development, gender parity, and generous state patronage for cultural workers. Through the AAWA network, Soviet Asia promised writers in decolonizing nations across two continents a glimpse of the future.[3]

It is tempting to read Tashkent as the neat antithesis of the Makerere gathering, or to regard Youssef El-Sebai's *Lotus*, which published occasional attempts at socialist realism, as an antidote to Rajat Neogy's modernist-inflected *Transition*. Capitalist and socialist aesthetic blocs recruiting intellectuals from decolonizing territories: what else could be the object of cold war cultural diplomacy? But such a neat antithesis, I suggest in the following pages, would vastly underrate the common concerns—political and aesthetic—that animate both the CCF and AAWA networks. We should resist the urge to segregate *Lotus* and *Transition* into stark cold war camps if only because many leading anticolonial writers gladly appeared in both CCF and AAWA venues. Chinua Achebe, Dennis Brutus, Alex La Guma, Es'kia Mphahlele, Bloke Modisane, Cosmo Pieterse, Efua Sutherland, Ngũgĩ wa Thiong'o, Lewis Nkosi, Richard Rive, and Wole Soyinka to name but a few, operated in both networks. Sembène Ousmane, trained in filmmaking in the Soviet Union and AAWA regular, also featured as a guest at CCF events. Tayeb Salih's *Season of Migration to the North*, the publication of which was supported by CCF, later appeared in Russian translation as part of a book series connected with AAWA.[4] La Guma—Lotus Prize winner, who at different times served as Secretary General (head executive) of the AAWA, assistant and later acting editor-in-chief of *Lotus*—transitioned smoothly from his work for CCF-sponsored projects into his influential role at AAWA. Achebe and Ngũgĩ, who were both CCF fixtures, published in *Lotus* and were garlanded with the Lotus Prize in the early years of the award; Ngũgĩ went on to serve on the prize's selection committee. Although the AAWA hierarchy, which was openly critical of US cultural diplomacy, made hay of the spectacular implosion of the CCF, they were by no means censorious of the African and Asian writers who published in such venues or appeared at such conferences.[5] Being part of the CCF setup in no way precluded writers from participating in AAWA ventures and vice versa.

Rather than interpret the Afro-Asian movement through a predetermined set of ideological commitments based on our knowledge of Soviet involvement, this chapter reads for the subtle aesthetic, rather than the obvious political, differences between *Lotus* and competing little magazines such as *Transition*. As in the previous chapter, I contend we will not go far in understanding the *Lotus* project if we simply describe it as a way to capture and redirect anticolonial energies for cold war purposes. The government of the Soviet Union did not control the content of *Lotus* any more tightly than the CIA controlled *Black Orpheus* or *Transition*. The aesthetic particularity of *Lotus* has as much to do with the geography and scope of the AAWA initiative as with any imputed ideological predispositions. Two major material differences between the CCF and AAWA networks help explain both the overlapping aims and the distinctive identities of these organizations: *Lotus*'s distribution networks and stubborn multilingualism.

First, the AAWA attempted to build a global network of anticolonial writers without relying on metropolitan circuits of cultural exchange. London, Paris, and New York were not an integral part of the AAWA's material geography as they were in the CCF system. Instead, the AAWA tried to fashion networks through Alma-Ata, Beirut, Cairo, Colombo, Dakar, Delhi, East Berlin, Luanda, Moscow, Tashkent, and Tunis. It was tough sledding. El-Sebai, Egyptian man-of-letters and *Lotus*'s founding editor, acknowledged that the indifference of booksellers in London and Paris, cities that still maintained control of imperialist trade routes, made it difficult to reach all readers who wanted access to the periodical.[6] But the editorial board persevered, fashioning its own infrastructure when metropolitan channels were closed to them. The difference is not that the AAWA was "socialist" and anticolonial where the CCF was "capitalist" and neo-imperialist: both operated as international patronage networks, relying heavily on soft power, foreign expertise, and financial subventions. Instead, I suggest that the shape of the network grid is telling when we want to account for aesthetic differences. *Lotus* helps show us what anticolonial literature looks like when it does not work through metropolitan patterns of exchange. The middle decades of the twentieth century, as western European imperial systems crumbled and transnational literary institutions incorporated African and Asian writers, represents a distinct phase in the globalization of literary production and consumption. But this was not a market-driven or profit-motivated process. It was determined by cultural diplomacy programs and cold war competition as much as anything related to capitalist or socialist markets for books.

Second, the trilingual scope of *Lotus* makes it an unusually flexible and capacious venue, if also unwieldy and extremely difficult for the editors to produce. The magazine's contributors hail from just about everywhere in Africa and Asia, and even occasional pieces from North American, Latin American, and European writers flash across its pages. Many of the contributions were originally written in languages other than Arabic, English, or French; the editors would rely on existing translations or commission new ones as needed.

Translations could be ad hoc, even sloppy at times.[7] *Lotus* seems to provide a textbook instance of what Rebecca L. Walkowitz calls "born-translated" literature, a form of writing that has no single source or target language but instead begins with the process of translation. There is no original language in which we might read the magazine; it exists simultaneously in three languages, none of which can claim it fully. But neither does *Lotus* develop what we might call a cosmopolitan aesthetic. Despite its staggering multilingualism and global spirit, most of the magazine's content is proudly anticolonial and predominantly nationalist. As one *Lotus* contributor puts it, Soviet Asian literary culture, appearing in many languages, provides an ideal model for writers in decolonizing regions because it is "deeply national in character, but highly international in spirit."[8] Vijay Prashad, describing the Bandung movement, calls it "*internationalist nationalism*," but the phrase could easily apply to *Lotus*.[9] Cultivating regional distinctiveness while emphasizing the international scope and the lengthy timeline of the decolonization process were among the missions of the AAWA.

This presents the taxonomist and literary historian in me with a problem: although *Lotus* is the most international literary magazine I have ever encountered, the overwhelming majority of its short stories, poems, folklore, essays, art, and book reviews are firmly nationalist in orientation. A shorthand description of the magazine's aesthetic might read: nationalist content, internationalist form. In place of a cosmopolitan perspective, *Lotus* provides a framework in which to experience a comparative nationalism, a way for intellectuals in decolonizing nations to compare their situations without sacrificing any claim to cultural uniqueness. Even if *Lotus* does not quite allow us to "forget English," as Aamir Mufti puts it a little mischievously, perhaps studying this unique magazine allows us to put English in its place.

As a consequence, the aesthetic effect of *Lotus*'s heterogeneity is not at all easy to describe. Aside from its multilingualism and cultural particularism, *Lotus* showcases dozens of distinct literary genres. There are lyric poems, mini-epic poems, praise songs, rallying cries, and elegies for heroes slain in battle; prose stories of various lengths, in various styles; extracts from full-length novels, from the boldly experimental (such as Kateb Yacine's *Nedjma*) to the tediously conventional; dialogue from stage and screen and closet drama; diverse literary criticism and intellectual history; book reviews; conference papers; political propaganda (especially on Palestine, southern Africa, and Vietnam); representational and nonrepresentational illustrations; folklore collected by specialists and nonspecialists; a regular art history column, usually written in-house by an assistant editor; and bureaucratic reports on meetings of the AAWA's executive committee.

Although the diversity and quantity of content threaten to turn *Lotus* into a collection of miscellany, attentive readers will not fail to detect an undercurrent of aesthetic unity, a principle of selection. I argue that *Lotus* shows cultural decolonization in action by depicting the uneven temporalities of different regions. Decolonization was not a linear political process, nor were the forms of economic and cultural development associated with decolonization unfolding steadily. It is this sense of experiencing decolonization in real time that the journal's aesthetic consistently strives to reproduce or mimic. The diversity of the magazine's contributions alludes to the diversity and simultaneity of the anticolonial process in a global setting. While some readers were experiencing the first flush of independence, others were still immersed in the struggle, while yet others were well on the way to full political and economic independence. *Lotus* offers a version of decolonization implying different histories, distinct cultures, and varied starting points, but one ultimate destination. *Lotus* proceeds by emphasizing national differences while signifying a common purpose.

Perhaps I can clarify what I mean by describing *Lotus* as an overfull literary magazine—or likening it to an archive or a library in periodical form—of decolonization's uneven temporalities and cultural multiplicity. The arrangement of issues can feel haphazard, seeming to rely on parataxis and juxtaposition, with the result that issues of the magazine tend to accumulate separate pieces rather than coalesce into a coherent whole. As in many repositories, *Lotus* includes a range of materials with different temporal orientations, distinct chronotopes: detailed records of the past, thick descriptions of the present, and plans for the immediate and even distant future. In its art history and folklore sections, which are ongoing special features in the magazine, *Lotus* attempts to recover and document indigenous cultural materials that may be repurposed for a nationalist, anticolonial polity. This move, this reclamation of a distinctive set of aesthetic practices for a usable cultural inventory, is familiar to any reader of late colonial and early postcolonial literature.

Complementing these recordings of folklore and art history are representations of the decolonizing present. The journal's present tense, in a manner of speaking, is registered most clearly in the regular contributions on Palestine, southern Africa, and Vietnam: the places where the decolonization struggle is active and most intense in the magazine's heyday, the 1970s. Sometimes in the form of elegies, sometimes in the form of revolutionary ballads, sometimes in the form of ethnographic short stories, *Lotus* provides a comprehensive survey of the decolonizing present in all its inimitable complexity.

Likewise, *Lotus* does not neglect the future. In a fascinating twist, the future is already observable: all we need to do is transport ourselves to Soviet Asia, where decolonization is, if not complete—there is always room for improvement, even self-criticism—then at least satisfyingly underway.[10] After nationalist revolutions have been secured, the hard work of guaranteeing cultural autonomy begins.

This chapter examines how *Lotus* captures the incomparable temporalities of decolonization by toggling between past, present, and future tenses. Wai Chee Dimock says of the literary history of the United States, "Literature is the home of nonstandard space and time," while Nicolai Volland remarks on "the possibility of productive anachronism" in 1950s Chinese fiction.[11] These qualities are equally evident in Afro-Asian literature as it appears between the covers of *Lotus*, where pride in the past, indignity and determination about the present, and aspirations for the future mingle together in exhilarating combinations—in contrast to the empty, predictable, calendrical temporality of Benedict Anderson's well-cited account of nationalism in *Imagined Communities*. I also lean on the accounts of the Bandung era provided by Leah Feldman, Adom Getachew, Christopher J. Lee, David Scott, and Gary Wilder, each of which teaches us how the visionaries of the anticolonial movement intuitively understood that decolonization presents both political and representational challenges, especially to our understanding of history, development, and progress. Decolonization is not a linear process. Accordingly, *Lotus* combines sprawling accounts of a chaotic present with focused retrievals of the cultural past and hopeful glances at a fully decolonized future. *Lotus* reminds us that that confluence of the cold war and decolonization helped produce an aesthetic movement that relied on complicated temporal juxtapositions and striking geographical contrasts.[12]

Alex La Guma, Communist activist, South African exile, African National Congress representative in Cuba, Lotus Prize winner, and AAWA stalwart, features prominently in my attempt to capture the vitality and singularity of *Lotus*. He was drawn to *Lotus* because of his Communist activism, passed down from his parents. Another mini-biography of La Guma, however, could read very differently if I wanted to emphasize his connections to metropolitan organizations: London-based anti-apartheid activist, CCF regular, and African Writers Series and Mbari author. It is important to observe that La Guma's unwavering political commitments, like so many of the late colonial and early postcolonial writers I consider in this book, did not necessarily limit the kinds of cultural groups with which he worked. I give a special place to La Guma in this chapter not because he preferred Communist politics or socialist realist aesthetics, but precisely because his career encourages us to question the simplicity of these categories as decolonization unfolded amidst the cold war.

His case is particularly interesting because his exploration of the South African situation is crafted in exile, forcing him to communicate his message to an international, almost exclusively non-South African audience. His readership was probably larger in the Soviet Union than in any other book market. With the exception of the censors and those with access to smuggled texts, his South African audience was something he could envision only in a freer future, one he would not live to see. The distinctiveness of multiracial Cape Town and South Africa we encounter in his writing is made, not for mercenary or self-exoticizing export, but for international audiences on both sides of the Iron Curtain. La Guma is a quintessential revolutionary nationalist whose aesthetic life transpired, somewhat paradoxically, in a completely extranational context. If no less a figure than J. M. Coetzee characterizes the exiled South African writers of La Guma's generation as producers of "a kind of émigré literature written by outcasts for foreigners," this chapter seeks to show how South Africa's loss was the world's gain.[13] La Guma's work helps us understand how the cold war and the conditions of his exile frame his approach to anticolonial nationalism.

Industrial Translation

As a student of literature reared in the North American system of higher education, as I am, it is difficult to appreciate how much the literary industry of the Soviet Union and its allies contributed to the emergence of late colonial and postcolonial writing in English, French, Portuguese, Spanish, and other languages. When teaching students about African literature in English, for instance, I usually fall back on the example of Heinemann and its African Writers Series, a publishing venture which has been variously portrayed as a champion of the anticolonial literary movement or as a neocolonial carpetbagger, profiting from the underdevelopment of indigenous cultural institutions.[14] The series spotlights a number of canonical writers, and as a literary institution it offers highly teachable material, providing several ready-made entries into the major debates in postcolonial theory.

Scholarly discussions about world literature have reinforced, rather than dismantled, the debates about metropolitan versus local control over literary institutions first theorized in postcolonial literary criticism. Pascale Casanova's influential account in *The World Republic of Letters* indicates that so-called peripheral writers face a stark choice: either adopt the languages and aesthetic techniques of metropolitan centers or remain defiantly local, wedded to nationalist or regionalist circuits of production and consumption. Franco Moretti, concerned less with literary institutions than the mobility of aesthetic forms, nevertheless concurs that metropolitan practitioners and experts wield a disproportionate influence on the emergence of world literary space. Literary forms, especially the novel, tend to move from dominant to peripheral regions, with content adapted to local conditions.[15] Alternatively, those who regard world literature as a symptom of global capitalism, such as Fredric Jameson and the Warwick Research Collective, are no more enthusiastic about metropolitan domination of the global culture market. World literature of the last century, from this vantage, looks a lot like a part-capitalist, part-neocolonial racket, dominated by Euro-American gatekeepers.[16]

It is difficult to gainsay, categorically, this general perspective. Any account of world literature in the twentieth and twenty-first centuries ought to take account of disparities, of unequal terms of trade, and of pockets of disproportionate influence and deprivation. But by the 1930s, as Katerina Clark, Rossen Djagalov, Steven S. Lee, and Monica Popescu point out, the Soviet Union was already a major player in the global culture game.[17] Paris, London, and New York were not the only centers of aesthetic influence, and this situation persists for much of the century. By 1961, when UNESCO started regularly collecting information on national publishing industries, the Soviet Union was issuing roughly as many books as the United States, United Kingdom, France, and West Germany combined. In terms of literary (as opposed to technical) books, the Soviet Union was on par with the United Kingdom, the global leader in this category, while producing about twenty to thirty percent more than the United States, France, or West Germany. In retrospect, it is easy to chuckle at the Soviet fondness for citing production statistics as evidence of geopolitical prestige—so many tons of wheat, so many thousands of tractors, so many millions of kilowatt hours generated—but book production was one of the major accomplishments of the Soviet state. From the 1950s through the 1980s, the Soviet Union accounted for between fourteen and twenty percent of the world's total annual book production, remaining a major force in literary publishing throughout this period.[18]

Given the number of languages spoken throughout the Soviet Union, it is not a surprise that the Soviet translation industry was one of the world's most robust. Susanna Witt says that the Soviet translation industry "may well be the largest more or less coherent *projects* of translation the world has seen to date."[19] Many books originally published in one Soviet language were translated rapidly into others. Orientalists and other agents of cultural diplomacy played a significant role in the internationalization of Soviet literary culture, bringing non-Soviet authors into the frame. Victor Ramzes, of the Afro-Asian Department of the Foreign Commission of the Union of Soviet Writers, was one of the main midcentury intermediaries, facilitating the translation of anglophone African writers into Russian and other Soviet languages.[20] As Djagalov says in his discussion of Soviet cultural diplomacy, the foreign-language publisher Progress "was a behemoth, publishing close to 2,000 new titles yearly, with a print run approaching 30 million copies and employing close to 1,000 full-time staff, in addition to hundreds of out-of-house translators" (99). The magazine *Inostrannaya literatura* [*Foreign Literature*] provided a major point of entry for non-Soviet writers, with book deals to follow; La Guma's Soviet passage follows this route. Ramzes reports that by the mid-1960s, translations of dozens of African writers were circulating in the Soviet Union, accounting for millions of book printings annually. His 1966 short essay in the CCF magazine *Transition*, of all places, lists a roll call of familiar names as part of the Soviet book market: Achebe, La Guma, Mphahlele, Ngũgĩ, Soyinka, Sutherland, Cyprian Ekwensi, and Gabriel Okara had all amassed a Soviet readership almost simultaneously with their African and metropolitan audiences. It is worth reemphasizing that La Guma started his career in the CCF context—publishing some of his earliest stories in *Black Orpheus*, his first book with Mbari, and continuing with several Transcription Centre projects—before latching onto the AAWA network.

The announcement in *Lotus* of a new Soviet book series about a decade later provides a succinct overview of Soviet interest in Afro-Asian literature. Between 1918 and 1975, Soviet publishers released over four thousand titles by African and Asian writers in the various languages of the Soviet Union, with total print runs of over 165 million copies. Writers from the Indian subcontinent were particularly favored, with over 750 individual titles by more than a hundred different authors, headlined by Rabindranath Tagore, whose Soviet printings ran to an astonishing 5.7 million books.[21] According to UNESCO's 1961 figures, Tagore was the fifth-most translated writer in the world, behind Lenin, Khrushchev, Leo Tolstoy, and Agatha Christie, but just ahead of Shakespeare (377). Soviet interest could move the needle. A new book series, Writers and Scholars of the East, sponsored by the Institute for Oriental Studies of the

USSR's Academy of Sciences, was assuming responsibility for developing literary connections between Soviet readers and Afro-Asian writers. It would issue translations into various Soviet languages of ancient and contemporary figures from all over the two continents. The announcement promises recent work by La Guma, Ngũgĩ, Soyinka, and Agostinho Neto, the Angolan poet and revolutionary. Blanche La Guma, Alex's widow, tells us that his largest audience was probably Soviet, reading him in translation, but his case was hardly unique.[22] His archive contains book contracts calling for publication of his work in Russian, Ukrainian, Hungarian, and several other languages of the Warsaw Pact nations with print runs of 25,000 to 75,000 copies.[23] Audre Lorde, invited to an AAWA meeting in Tashkent in 1976, also noted the Soviet enthusiasm for literature from African American, African, and Asian writers.[24] Put simply, when midcentury African and Asian writers were producing books for international consumption, they were not lured only by the promise of Euro-American readers as scholars of anglophone literature sometimes assume: opportunities to publish with Soviet agencies were a big factor in their reckoning.

Writers' Internationale

The AAWA thus fitted into a more general pattern of cultural diplomacy and a multilingual, multinational Soviet literary culture. Lydia H. Liu cites the AAWA as part of the "The Great Translation Movement" that emerged in the wake of Bandung.[25] The Afro-Asian literary movement traced its intellectual genealogy to the 1934 Union of Soviet Writers conference and the All-India Progressive Writers Association (PWA), both of which were sprawling multilingual projects. As I discuss in chapter 2, Maxim Gorky and Nikolai Bukharin both delivered speeches at the 1934 Congress in which they extol the value of national literatures and emphasize the multilingual nature of Soviet culture. In *Lotus*'s celebration of the sixtieth anniversary of the October Revolution, many of the contributors point to Gorky's address as the start of decolonizing literary institutions on a world scale. In the special issue's introductory essays, Anatoly Sofronov notes that Soviet literature is written and published in some eighty languages, while Nikolai Tikhonov, alluding to Gorky's Congress address, reminds readers "that Soviet literature was from the first a multinational literature."[26] In "What I Learned from Maxim Gorky" from the same issue of *Lotus*, La Guma also channels the spirt of Gorky, arguing that the Russian's respect for the literatures of Soviet Asia and his willingness to portray the lives of people at the margins of society provide a model for writers from places such as South Africa, where the literary tradition had refused to represent many of South Africa's non-White peoples.[27] For subsequent generations of Afro-Asian writers, Gorky's emphasis on the multilingualism of the Soviet project was as important as his theories of socialist realism and interest in proletarian subjects.

With PWA veterans such as Mulk Raj Anand, Faiz Ahmed Faiz, and Sajjad Zaheer as leading participants in the Afro-Asian movement, it is not surprising that *Lotus* contributors point to the PWA alongside the 1934 Moscow Congress as pivotal moments in the decolonization of cultural institutions. In the announcement of Faiz's 1975 Lotus Prize, he is credited as "one of the founder members of the Afro-Asian Writers' Movement."[28] Anand served as *Lotus* editorial board member, Faiz edited the journal for a time after the assassination of El-Sebai, and Zaheer passed away in Alma-Ata while attending the fifth AAWA conference in 1973. *Lotus* regularly names the December 1956 Asian Writers' Conference in Delhi—Anand and Zaheer being two of the organizers— as the inspiration for the Tashkent meeting.[29] At Delhi, the Uzbek poet Zulfiya, later a Lotus Prize winner, acting on behalf of the Soviet delegation, extended an invitation to host a follow-up meeting at Tashkent two years later, with the inclusion of African writers. This offer was subsequently ratified by the AAWA's sibling outfit, the Afro-Asian Peoples' Solidarity Organization (AAPSO), at its inaugural meeting in Cairo at the end of 1957.[30]

The question of precolonial cultural heritage was a thorny issue for the early PWA activists, as it would be in the pages of *Lotus*. Was it worthwhile retrieving and celebrating a precolonial past, or should it be left to one side in favor of the present? The PWA's flexible, pragmatic solution to the problem guided the AAWA approach in subsequent decades. As Anand tells the story, he and M. D. Taseer, another of the London-based PWA manifesto signatories, disagreed from the first about the continuing relevance of India's indigenous artistic traditions. For Anand, it was important to recognize and recover India's heritage, which had been deprecated during the colonial period, but not for the purpose of rote revivalism: "we could only take those things from the past, which have relevance for our own time and put the rest in the library shelves," he says ("Some Reminiscences" 49). His collaborator Taseer was more open to the idea of celebrating the indigenous artistic achievements of precolonial times, if only to remind Indians that they should not unthinkingly mimic European forms. Reverence for autochthonous traditions could be liberating, or so runs the familiar counterargument. Anand remained unconvinced, but he conceded enough to make the PWA manifesto work for both camps.

FIGURE 4.1. Unidentified woman, W.E.B. Du Bois (center), and Mulk Raj Anand at the
Tashkent Conference, 1958. Image courtesy of Department of Special Collections and
University Archives, W.E.B. Du Bois Library, University of Massachusetts Amherst.

The published versions of the PWA manifesto offer something of a compromise position. While acknowledging that there is much of value in classical
literature, the manifesto describes writing of the colonial period as enslaved
to a feudal past, exercising a "rigid formalism" drawn exclusively from classical
sources. Anticipating Mufti's argument that nativist literary movements in the
subcontinent should be regarded less as anticolonial or nationalist and instead
more as variants of Orientalism, the signatories argue that literature ought to

be rescued from the clutches of the "priestly, academic and decadent classes" and returned to the people. This serves an anticolonial agenda, allowing Indian writers to "register the actualities of life, as well as lead us to the future." This patchwork of aesthetic theory and social criticism results in the layered temporalities of the PWA manifesto: a robust classical tradition of which to be justly proud; an extended colonial present, lasting for the better part of two centuries, in which the vestiges of an indigenous tradition limp along, now drained of vitality, used largely to perpetuate the colonial status quo; an unexamined, parallel present, consisting of an amorphous people and their folk practices, currently excluded from literary consideration; and a promising future in which writers will simultaneously claim "to be the inheritors of the best traditions of Indian civilization" while addressing the "basic problems of our existence to-day—the problems of hunger and poverty, social backwardness and political subjection." This amalgam of claiming heritage, while also attending to the exigent needs of the present, will lead inexorably "to the new life" for which writers are striving alongside their fellow Indians.[31] This invocation of multidirectional temporality in the PWA manifesto would become a characteristic feature of the Afro-Asian movement.

Conference Circuit

Similar to other literary institutions I consider in this book, the AAWA began with a conference. Although many Tashkent attendees would subsequently describe the movement as unique and unprecedented, the early participants tended to regard the 1958 meeting as part of a string of similar efforts. In the first editorial in the inaugural issue of *Lotus*, El-Sebai notes that by the mid-1960s Afro-Asian writing had established itself as a global force through international conferences. "The writers of Asia and Africa have made a significant contribution to the treasury of world literature," he observes, citing "the conferences organised by African writers in Paris and Rome and of the literary symposia in Dakar, Freetown and Uganda" as proof of this.[32] Paris and Rome (1956 and 1959) were arranged by the nonaligned *Présence Africaine* group. Freetown (1961 and 1963) and Makerere (1962), by contrast, were hosted by CCF affiliates.[33] Dakar, on one hand, might refer to a CCF meeting held there (1963), while on the other hand it might refer to the First World Festival of Black Arts (1966) held just over a year before the launch of *Lotus*. Other literary and political conferences cited as important reference points for the Afro-Asian literary movement include the 1956 Delhi conference, UNESCO symposia on the cultural effects of colonialism, the Bandung summit, the Non-Aligned Movement, and the AAPSO movement (in which El-Sebai was a leading figure).[34] These represent a wide range of literary-political configurations: some loosely attached to one superpower or the other, some defiantly neutral; some unambiguously political, some primarily literary. Knowing that the AAWA was sponsored by the Soviet Union's literary establishment tells us only the source of most of the money. Ideologically, the movement was more outwardly committed to anticolonial nationalism and autonomy for colonized peoples than it was to the Soviet Union or to the Communist Party. It proudly claimed both socialist and nonsocialist literary movements as its heritage.

In retrospective accounts of the meeting, *Lotus* reports that representatives of thirty-seven Afro-Asian states attended, in addition to nearly two dozen men-of-letters from the United States and Europe; more than two hundred delegates in total.[35] One prominent intellectual in attendance was W.E.B. Du Bois, traveling in the Soviet Union only two years after he announced to the First Black Writers' and Artists' Congress in Paris that the US State Department had denied him a passport (figure 4.1). Anand and Faiz were two of the old hands at Tashkent, joined by a strong Chinese delegation led by Mao Dun and flanked by ambitious youngsters such as the Senegalese novelist and filmmaker Sembène Ousmane, Mozambican poet-revolutionary Marcelino dos Santos, and Indonesian novelist Pramoedya Ananta Toer.

Tashkent was a strategic choice of venue by the organizers. Attendees familiar with either Black Atlantic or Soviet literary history might have recalled that Langston Hughes had spent several months in Soviet Asia in the early 1930s, collecting some of his observations in the little-known *A Negro Looks at Soviet Central Asia* (1934) and the better-known second volume of his autobiography, *I Wonder as I Wander* (1956), as well as a few journalistic essays in US and Soviet periodicals.[36] Hughes, who by the 1960s was doing cultural diplomacy work for the US State Department, says of his visit to central Asia that he wanted to see whether the change from Russian imperialism to Soviet socialism had altered conditions for the indigenous population, whom he regards as fellow Black and Brown peoples. Hughes strives for balance in his account, recognizing that once-ubiquitous racial discrimination, similar to that of the Jim Crow system in the United States, had disappeared almost overnight, but material prosperity was still an aspiration, not a reality. Reports from delegates at the 1958 conference make the 1930s seem like a distant memory: modernized housing, first-class universities and research laboratories, sprawling cooperative cotton farms, and tidy cooperative orchards charmed the

FIGURE 4.2. Sembène Ousmane (center, smoking pipe), Majhemout Diop, and
unidentified others at the Tashkent conference, 1958.

delegates and subsequent AAWA visitors. Not only had racial discrimination
been eradicated, but so had the worst forms of poverty.

Although Tashkent was deemed a success by the organizers, it took a further decade or more for the Afro-Asian movement to evolve into a fully functioning literary institution. At the Cairo meeting in 1962, the group resolved
to produce a collection of poetry, resulting in two volumes of *Afro-Asian
Poems: An Anthology* (1963, 1965). The trilingual propaganda magazine *The
Call* was also envisioned, only for it to be taken over by the Chinese-led Afro-
Asian Writers' Bureau during the Sino-Soviet split of the mid-1960s.[37] The two
anthologies include poetry from twenty-one different nations across the two
continents, including the Soviet Union; a short story collection along similar
lines would follow. The collections are less notable for the quality of the writing included than for the attempt to consolidate an anticolonial literary tradition. Unlike many fledgling literary institutions, which rely on a charismatic
leader to bring something distinctive to the field, *Afro-Asian Poems* are the
result of a bureaucratic process. "Before compiling this book," says editor

FIGURE 4.3. Sembène Ousmane (left), Thu Bon, Ngũgĩ wa Thiong'o celebrating the Lotus Award at the Alma-Ata Conference, 1973. Image courtesy of Sputnik.

Ratne Deshapriya Senanayake, then Secretary-General of the AAWA, "we requested 23 member-countries of the Executive Committee to send in representative material."[38] Representative material, not meritorious or exceptional literary pieces: the choice of adjective tells us a lot about the early objectives of the organization, striving to be inclusive of diverse constituencies. This is one of the earliest tangible records of the Afro-Asian bureaucratic machine that would determine the course of the movement. The AAWA's conferences, edited volumes, house journal, and other enterprises were all governed by committee, not by a maverick impresario. Manifestoes, declarations, and resolutions, of which there are many, were ratified by delegates or their representatives on the executive committee, not issued by small coteries. What the AAWA might have lost in creativity it gained in stability and in member participation, not an insignificant benefit in the context of decolonization and the scarcity of cultural institutions in large parts of Africa and Asia.

The AAWA found its footing in the late 1960s and early 1970s. Between 1967 and 1975, the organization ratified its charter, hosted three major international conferences (Beirut 1967, Delhi 1970, Alma-Ata 1973) and several smaller symposia, began awarding the annual Lotus Prizes, and established the trilingual

FIGURE 4.4. Youssef El-Sebai (left) presenting the Lotus Award to Sembène Ousmane at the Alma-Ata Conference, 1973.

Lotus, appearing quarterly, as one of the top literary magazines on two continents. More than five hundred delegates attended the Alma-Ata gathering.[39] El-Sebai's 1973 conference address distills the major goals of the AAWA. First, he says, the organization is in place to "safeguard our cultural heritage," which will enable the current generation of anticolonial writers to "combine the glory of the past and the newness of the future, particularly in the domain of [...] popular poetry and folk art." Cultural authenticity and self-understanding are key components of the national independence movement in the arts. Documenting autochthonous forms of expression and understanding the richness of contemporary culture will, El-Sebai argues, propel anticolonial literature into a promising future. The AAWA's second goal, however, is rather different than the first: to be as open as possible to "world culture," fashioning an internationalist future in which the "false walls built by imperialist, oppressive and reactionary forces" no longer exist. To this end, the AAWA would rely heavily on cultural exchange programs and translation.[40] By the twenty-fifth anniversary conference, which brought AAWA delegates back to Tashkent, the movement could boast more than sixty national writers' unions as member organizations.[41]

The AAWA thus worked through an alchemical combination of indigeneity and internationalism. It would be easy to regard this as inherently contradictory, as the organization trying to promote nationalist aspirations without sacrificing its claims to international significance. Overemphasizing this latent conflict, however, would make it more difficult to see the particularity of the *Lotus* aesthetic, which I consider in more detail in the following sections of the chapter. The journal's interest in authenticity and cultural particularity become meaningful only in a comparative context. Extroverted nationalism, rather than exclusive or ethnocentric patriotism, best describes it. *Lotus* features not only comparisons across cultures but also across temporal dimensions: retrieving the past and documenting the present allow the magazine's contributors to imagine a future beyond the limits of the colonial world order. This way of imagining alternative futures was a characteristic feature of the Bandung era. It is a potent combination in the pages of the magazine.

The *Lotus* Years

Lotus does not conform to some of the stereotypes of the modernist little magazine. Conventional wisdom tells us that because it was funded by the Soviet Union, it must have been more lavishly supported and the content more tightly controlled than the typical Euro-American *avant-garde* review. It also circulated more widely than many little magazines, with up to 3,500 copies each in English and French, probably fewer in Arabic.[42] But as Eric Bulson points out, we underestimate the flexibility of the form of the little magazine if we remain too hung up on restrictive definitions about editorial practices or circulation numbers. *Lotus*'s layout and design, the paper quality, the length, the price ($2 to $2.50 per issue), the internationalist perspective, the combination of political and literary content: all have clear similarities with other little magazines of the twentieth century. When thumbing through the first fifteen years of *Lotus*, the biggest differences I notice between it and other little magazines are the infrequency (but not absence) of advertisements and the inclusion of the deliberations of the Permanent Bureau (executive committee) of the Afro-Asian movement. The producers of *Lotus* are eager to convince readers that they are part of a cooperative endeavor, a global movement to end the practice of colonialism in its political and cultural forms. *Lotus* showcases the bureaucratic achievement of the AAWA and the capaciousness of the project as much as the brilliance of any particular writer or visionary editor.

In place of an aesthetics of virtuoso particularity, in which the brilliance or uniqueness of individual writers become the focus, *Lotus* relies on the principles of the archive, the collection, or the survey. As the arrangement of *Afro-Asian Poetry* suggests, the contributor's place of origin, in fact, becomes as important as the individuality of the writer. *Lotus* carries on this practice by introducing its contributions with a statement of provenance: "poem from Zambia" or "short story from the Philippines" or "study from Algeria." *Lotus* shows that the tendency to pigeonhole postcolonial writers as representatives from their place of origin is not only a feature of capitalist or metropolitan literary industries.

Cultural inventories, likewise, form a big part of the magazine. Most issues have a special section on a particular country or region: Angola, India, Palestine, Mongolia, South Africa, Soviet Asia, and Vietnam are a few of the places explored in depth through literature. In this respect, *Lotus* is not radically different from *Encounter*, in which special features on decolonizing areas recur. In *Lotus*, however, these efforts are far more systematic, with reports on diverse folklore traditions and art history in every issue. *Lotus* puts national and regional differences on display for inspection and comparison.

Although it goes to considerable lengths to gather material from every corner of Africa and Asia, *Lotus* pays special attention to the decolonizing hotspots of its day: Palestine, southern Africa, and Vietnam. If folklore and art history provide *Lotus* with a past tense, regular features on anticolonial wars and the writers they produce furnish it with a present tense. Poet-warriors and activist-writers are staples of the magazine. Palestinians such as Mahmoud Darwish and Ghassan Kanafani, southern Africans such as dos Santos and Neto, and Vietnamese figures such as Ho Chi Minh provide *Lotus* with the perfect combination of militant politics and up-to-date poetics. The magazine carries nearly annual declarations and resolutions, as well as reports on the wars of decolonization—gleefully celebrating the many successes of the 1970s while remaining steadfast that Palestine and southern Africa would soon be liberated—making it abundantly clear that Afro-Asian writers would not rest comfortably until they had discharged their political as well as their cultural duties. *Lotus*'s present tense, as I have labeled it, is activist, poised to spring into the rhetorical fray when needed.

South Africa, partly because of La Guma's influence and his connections with activists and writers, features in nearly every issue of *Lotus*. The list of the magazine's South African contributors is lengthy, including many who also participated in CCF projects: Peter Abrahams, Breyten Breytenbach, Dennis

Brutus, Basil February, Barry Feinberg, Alfred Hutchinson, Keorapetse Kgos-itsile, A.N.C. Kumalo,[43] Mazisi Kunene, J. Arthur Maimane, Bloke Modisane, Es'kia Mphahlele, Lewis Nkosi, Cosmo Pieterse, and Richard Rive are only some of writers who published with *Lotus*, making it one of the leading international outlets for South African literature in the 1970s. As La Guma points out in one of his own essays, this generation of South African writers sometimes achieved international prominence while remaining virtually unknown to domestic readers because of censorship and banning orders.[44] La Guma was part of the "lost generation" of banned writers of the 1960s and '70s, known far better overseas than at home.

A special section on South Africa in a 1972 issue of *Lotus* provides an instance of how the journal cobbles together an anticolonial aesthetic by alternating between past, present, and future tenses. A report on nineteenth-century folklore, a Feinberg poem, and a Kumalo short story take us on a centuries-long tour of South Africa's non-White heritage. Short stories by February and La Guma walk us through some of the indignities and injustices created by racial discrimination and political oppression in the contemporary moment. A few of the pieces, especially Brutus's poem, "A Wrong Headed Bunch," offer striking combinations of complicated temporal frames in tight spaces:

> [. . .] the bodies of poets will always be
> the anvils on which will be beaten out
> a-new, or afresh, a people's destiny.[45]

In this first stanza, Brutus describes a new destiny hammered out on the anvil of the writer's body. Reminiscent of both *A Portrait of the Artist as a Young Man*'s famous closing metaphor about forging a national conscience, as well as Kamau Brathwaite's reclamation of the Uncle Tom figure as a hammer-swinging blacksmith of racial consciousness in *The Arrivants*, Brutus casts the poet as a figure of both present suffering and future creation. Similar to Brathwaite's poetry, however, Brutus's lyric speaker does not figure the creative act as something radically new or unprecedented:

> —Spirits of the brave
> who have died for knowledge, truth and freedom
> spirits of slave-ancestors knowing the bitter
> price to be free make me strong and brave
> make me too the [bruised] and ready ripened fruit. (158)

This closing stanza reclaims the knowledge of the past and redeems the suffering of the present in the fabrication of a more just future, a fast-forward leap that the poet's vision allows us to glimpse beyond the limits of a blinkered present. These lines do not capture the temporality of decolonization as an unfolding or an even progression; knowledge of the past interrupts the flow of time, while visions of a freer future both sustain and injure the lyric speaker, who must bring news of this destiny to the audience. But the bruising the speaker-poet endures is part of a ripening or maturation, a process that mixes past memories, present resolve, and future knowledge into the messy juxtaposition of temporal collage. The poet's body bears witness to a legacy of abuse in the past, the longings of the present, and the anticipation of the future.[46]

This short Brutus poem, in an assortment of pieces about South Africa, exemplifies the use of nonstandard temporalities in Afro-Asian literature. Only a few years earlier, at the CCF Makerere conference, some of the attendees read Brutus as someone who presents racial injustice evenhandedly, without rancor or bitterness. In that setting, his work transcends the context of South Africa because it is honest without being too particularized or too restricted by its locality. His South African experience, in their view, informs but does not limit cosmopolitan sympathies. In the pages of *Lotus*, Brutus's racial knowledge is also lifted partly out of its South African context and put in the service of a comparative anticolonial nationalism. The CCF-sponsored reading of Brutus relies on an implicit framework of gradualism, of long-term (and slow) decolonization without Soviet tutelage, whereas the version of Brutus appearing in *Lotus* is more jagged and syncopated, reminding the reader that decolonization is not a process that unfolds steadily. While decolonization could be described as a linear process of development in some contexts, *Lotus* consistently avoids presenting national autonomy through the trope of gradual, or separate, development—separate development being a euphemism for apartheid economic policy. It uses the specific example of South Africa to place it in solidarity with a global revolt against colonialism.

If we recall that *Lotus* is the product of extensive collaboration between the Soviet literary establishment and writers across the decolonizing world, it is noteworthy that the Afro-Asian literary movement did not make unthinking use of socialist realism as a kind of prefabricated aesthetic template. Afro-Asian writers, rather, made creative use of socialist aesthetic theory, preferring to emphasize the multilingual and multinational dimensions of the Soviet project. Respect for nationalist aspirations and indigenous cultural traditions were just as important to the AAWA as other features of Soviet literary culture,

FIGURE 4.5. Alex La Guma (left) and Chinghiz Aitmatov at the Alma-Ata Conference, 1973.
Image courtesy of Sputnik.

which nonspecialist scholars have condensed into socialist realism plus ideologically inflexible bureaucratic oversight of creative work. We would be wrong
to conclude that *Lotus* simply offers a tropicalized version of socialist realism
because it relied on Soviet money and expertise. Just as CCF ventures such as
Black Orpheus and *Transition* rework the modernist doctrine of aesthetic autonomy to fit the needs of African intellectuals, so too does *Lotus* reinterpret
the socialist aesthetic models with which it is in closest dialogue. In contrast to
Michael Denning and Joe Cleary, each of whom describes the influence of socialist realism on the literature of decolonization, I suggest the Afro-Asian
movement was more interested in the status of vernacular languages than in
mimicking the literary techniques popular in the Soviet system.[47]

As I turn to La Guma's writing, I use his work as an opportunity for thinking about anticolonial nationalism in a transnational, cold war context: how
anticolonial literature moves when it is not passing through metropolitan
channels of exchange. Although La Guma wrote in English and wrote most
extensively about the South African situation, he was affected by living in exile
for much of his literary life. Although firmly nationalist in his orientation, he
did not write primarily for his South African compatriots, at least not his

contemporaries.[48] Most of his South African readers existed in the future. And although he wrote in exile, for an international audience, he was hardly a self-exoticizing postcolonial mandarin or a disaffected cosmopolitan craving a metropolitan hearing. In other words, he does not fit neatly into the dominant models of postcolonial or global writing in English, which tend to regard an-glophone writing as determined by metropolitan book markets, for better or mostly for worse, and global writers as disengaged from the anticolonial strug-gle. If we acknowledge that Soviet interest in anticolonial writing was a crucial part of the formation of a global literary culture during the twentieth century, our account would look very different indeed.

Into Exile

La Guma's short story, "The Exile," which appears in *Lotus* in 1972, provides a condensed example of how the flexible temporality of the AAWA aesthetic informs the development of an anticolonial South African literature in an in-ternational context. La Guma himself went into lifelong exile in 1966, after spending most of the previous decade in prison or under house arrest. His career was equally determined by the kinds of cultural diplomacy and state discipline that set the course of anticolonial literature for much of the century. The story is set at a country trading post in South Africa, on the border be-tween Orange Free State and the Eastern Cape, in the foothills of the Drak-ensberg mountains near Lesotho (nowhere near La Guma's home turf of Cape Town). The story alternates between the perspective of two men who are barely aware of one another. The first, MacPherson, is the White proprietor of the general store. He nods genially at his Black customers, both the local women and the mounted riders who pass through. He is content with life—he has a stable business, trusted servants, and friendly relations with his Black patrons. He is dimly cognizant of rumors about men running guns southward into the Transkei (one of the nominally independent "bantustans" created by the apartheid regime in 1959) in preparation for a revolution or race war, but "MacPherson had never been bothered, and he never bothered with politics, anyway."[49] Although he sometimes feels bored and lonely, driving occasionally into the nearby town of Aliwal satisfies his social needs. He lives in a bubble of White privilege created by apartheid, barely aware of the political tension all around.

Quite suddenly, the story shifts both tense and perspective. MacPherson, standing on his verandah, sees an older Black man, dressed in the same ragged clothes as his other customers, snoozing in the shade. He wonders what the man could be dreaming about, at which point the story leaps across the color line. We learn that the man dreams of his seeing his dog again. From there, the story spills out in many directions. The dreamer had been exiled from his home and separated from his family for speaking against the government, especially against the separation of South Africans into modernized citizens and tribal subjects, as Mahmood Mamdani describes.[50] A few years earlier, the story's Black protagonist had been relocated hundreds of miles away to a government farm in the Transvaal. Traveling home to see his family without permission, the man would dream, Odysseus-like, of the welcome he would receive from his dog and family after three years apart. From there, after a brief visit, he hopes to continue to Basutoland, or what is now Lesotho, to escape apartheid.

The oddest part of the story is not the use of two main characters or the content of the man's dreams. The strangest part is the narrator's labored use of different verb arrangements, especially a mixed conditional tense. "If he could have dreamt many days into the future, the old man would have dreamt" about being reunited with his family (70). His sons would greet him excitedly, his wife with concern and solicitude; he would lay out his plans for crossing the border. The story presents his dream as it would happen if it could happen, but also makes it clear that it does not happen, in life or even in the man's dream-world. The narrator even reports that the dreamer would dream of the future if he were able to do so: "Now, sleeping in the shade, [. . .] he dreamed, and if he could have dreamt ahead, he would have dreamt that he said to the woman, his wife: 'One day things will be better. The world changes'" (73). The narrator has access to dreams that even the dreamer does not have—dreams about an immediate and distant future for South Africa.

La Guma's weird tenses in "The Exile" are not accidental, calling attention to themselves precisely because the story also uses the simple, conventional past tense to tell chunks of the story. La Guma manipulates tenses to draw distinctions between his two main characters—one White, one Black—and a narrator who has access to the thoughts and desires of them both. The story's White character has no past and, crucially, no distinguishable future. He has immediate needs and desires, mostly relating to his daily comfort. He shows no awareness of how he arrived at his position in life. And the narrator conspicuously refuses to describe him in any future-oriented tense. By contrast, the main Black character from "The Exile," the dreamer, is distinguished from his counterpart in the story not simply by his skin color or his relative poverty, but by his awareness of history and politics: the past and the present. Although he is illiterate, we discover, he knows the history of forced removals and the political opportunities of the moment. But his future is extremely odd, even impossible: the narrator tells us that he would dream of the future if he could do so, but the narrator also emphasizes that he does not, in fact, have the ability to dream weeks and months and years into the future. The future perfect conditional, in a way, is reserved for special use by the narrator. Only the narrator has access to the story's full unfolding.

As this short discussion of "The Exile" demonstrates, I am resistant to reading *Lotus* contributors in general and La Guma in particular as naïve, unthinking exponents of socialist realism. In dialogue with the aesthetic patterns established elsewhere in *Lotus*, La Guma uses striking combinations of past, present, and future to meditate on the effects of colonialism and the aspirations of the anti-apartheid movement in South Africa. In "The Exile," La Guma follows the apartheid system of drawing racial distinctions between people, but these distinctions are related to historical and political effects, not to innate biological differences. La Guma's White character, at least in this story, has no past and possesses no future. His Black character, by contrast, has an acute sense of history despite his illiteracy. It is only the narrator who has access to the dreamer's future. The narrator alone moves without restrictions between past, present, and future. Unlike the two main characters, who are limited in some ways because of their racial classification, the narrator has the freedom to range more widely across temporal divisions. La Guma's narrator has access to a future conditional or subjunctive mood that neither of the main characters fully understands.

La Guma's queer blend of tenses in this minor short story call to mind running tropes in Hannah Arendt's *Between Past and Future*. She calls the essays thought-experiments, creative attempts to describe the experience of living in the present tense in the age of world wars, decolonization, and the cold war. As she puts it, humans exist in their "full actuality" only in the "gap of time between past and future," otherwise known as the present.[51] Most provocative about her account is the contention that both past and future impinge equally on the experience of the present:

This diagonal force [the experience of the present] would in one respect differ from the two forces whose result it is [past and future]. The two antagonistic forces are both unlimited as to their origins, the one coming from an infinite past and the other from an infinite future; but though they have no known beginning, they have a terminal ending, the point at which they clash. [. . .] The diagonal force [the present], whose origin is known, whose direction is determined by past and future, but whose eventual end lies in infinity, is the perfect metaphor for the activity of thought. (12)

Arendt's account of the temporality of thought is germane to my discussion of the *Lotus* aesthetic, especially if we substitute "space of representation" for "activity of thought." The vectors of past and future intersect and terminate at this fulcrum of the present, the only place where ongoing thought and experience may transpire. It is easy to see how her description of the present bears striking resemblance to the way *Lotus* represents the imperfect present tense through the clash of a compromised past and an unlimited future. Immediately noticeable is her willingness to accord both past and future influence on the present: the space of thought or representation is equally determined by circumstances handed down to us and by cognizance of a future we cannot know. The future and past do not cancel one another out—they pressure the present from different angles—but they apply equal force on the space of contemplation. When so many midcentury intellectuals were anticipating nuclear annihilation, Arendt's willingness to give the future its due is notable. Even if Arendt could not share the optimism of the *Lotus* editors, she describes the space of political thought in unexpectedly similar ways.

Critics have sometimes faulted La Guma's writing from exile, claiming that it lacks the freshness and up-to-date feel of *A Walk in the Night*.[52] What many describe as an understandable flaw resulting from La Guma's involuntary absence from South Africa, however, may be read from another perspective as a characteristic feature of anticolonial writing. Many of the most widely read pieces of anticolonial literature move across time in provocative ways: Achebe's and Ngũgĩ's early novels, Kamau Brathwaite's *Arrivants*, W. B. Yeats's poetry, Aimé Césaire's *Notebook*, Wole Soyinka's most famous plays, Jean Rhys's *Wide Sargasso Sea*, and Doris Lessing's *The Golden Notebook* spring to mind readily enough, all refusing the notion that decolonization happens through the regular, predictable experience of time. If La Guma's writing is sometimes stuck in the past, or if it mixes tenses, this may not be a sign of being out of touch with his contemporaries.

La Guma's first major publication, the novella *A Walk in the Night* (1962), though unavailable in South Africa, made an enormous impression on the 1960s generation of African writers from other parts of the continent. Published originally by Nigeria's CCF-affiliated Mbari, the text was distributed to the fiction working group for discussion at the Makerere conference. La Guma was invited to attend, but the South African authorities refused him travel privileges.[53] In a review in the Johannesburg *Post*, Soyinka said that the slim volume "is only ninety pages, but it has achieved what several novels by Africans, three to four times its length are still merely groping towards."[54] The title of the novella alone gives one a sense of being in motion, of inhabiting the present tense fully. The plot largely follows Michael Adonis, a young, working-class man ("Coloured" in the apartheid classification system) from Cape Town's District Six. We meet him just after he has been dismissed from his job for telling off his White supervisor. The narrative follows him as he bounces around Hanover Street, the area's main thoroughfare, nursing his grievances. In one brisk evening, we are treated to a tour of the district's bars and canteens and tenements and brothels; we meet an ample cast of law-abiding slum dwellers, rogues and gangsters, and racist, corrupt police; we become more familiar with District Six's many pious residents and their eccentric neighbors who wander the boulevards late into the night.

The narrative's headlong collision with apartheid policies, however, contrives to stretch the story's ethnographic present tense into the long, uneven timelines of decolonization. The novella's title and epigraph allude to *Hamlet* and hint at how La Guma's narrative bears witness to the inhumanity of the South African system from a distant but anticipated future: "I am thy father's spirit: / Doom'd for a certain term to walk the night, / And for the day confined to fast in fires, / Till the foul crimes done in my days of nature / Are burnt and purged away."[55] The narrative itself takes place in a few hours, giving us a glimpse at how Cape Town's working-class people assert their vitality and individuality against the dehumanizing and deindividualizing effects of endemic poverty and structural racism. La Guma's epigraph, however, slots the narrative's ethnographic present into the longer and uncertain perspective of the liberation struggle: the authorial voice who observes District Six's residents is doomed to walk the night, revenant-like, until the living crimes of the apartheid regime have become the past tense, incinerated and purged. Hamlet's ghostly father gives the narrator a longer view of things, an ability to stand outside the events being depicted until the wrongs of the present are atoned for at some point in the future. This is akin to the way the literature of the African diaspora "addresses itself to an encounter with audiences not yet known or imaginable," in Anthony Reed's words.[56]

The epigraph reappears in the novella's key scene, in which Adonis murders his neighbor, Doughty. Doughty is an apparently harmless, elderly alcoholic, a White man fallen on hard times. He is a former stage actor. He fatefully invites Adonis to share a drink with him, and after some mutual grumbling about their respective difficulties, Doughty says that he and Adonis are both "like Hamlet's father's ghosts." Doughty begins to recite the lines to Adonis, managing to do so with a couple of drunken stumbles, before concluding: "That's us, us, Michael, my boy. Just ghosts, doomed to walk the night. Shakespeare." Adonis will have none of it. A sharp retort of "Bull" comes from the aggrieved young man, who seems to take offense at being likened to a ghost and to an elderly, unemployed White man who lives only in the past (25–26). Adonis then kills Doughty without really meaning to do so.

The reprise of the epigraph produces a different effect at this moment in the narrative. If the epigraph begins the novella by invoking a future in which the crimes of the present will be avenged, the lines at this moment suggest an indefinite postponement either of revolutionary triumph or of racial reconciliation in South Africa. Doughty does not have enough information about Adonis's situation to empathize in a way that Adonis will accept, and Adonis rejects any suggestion that the experiences of a person of color and a White person could have anything in common. There is no sense that the violence Adonis commits against his White neighbor would in any way purge the crimes of apartheid; it is a thoughtless and unintended crime against a pathetic, harmless fellow person. The narrative's ghostly restlessness, then, starts with a moment of mutual incomprehension.

The novella's sense of looking at the unfortunate present from a different, more equitable future is compounded when we realize that District Six, in which this narrative is so embedded, would be dismantled in the decades after the publication of *A Walk in the Night*. Starting in 1966, this historic and multiracial area in which La Guma grew up, close to Cape Town's center, would be legally designated for White habitation, its residents gradually but systematically displaced in a state-sanctioned land grab. With no small degree of irony, much of the area still sits vacant. Alongside Richard Rive's *'Buckingham Palace', District Six* (1986), *A Walk in the Night* became the most lasting testament to this multiracial community. As Grant Farred discusses in the context of Rive's fiction, it is possible to read *A Walk in the Night* as a kind of politically charged, anticipatory elegy, leading to regular symbolic returns and memorials in the years to come.[57] In yet another curious temporal distortion, the narrative's energetic presentism mutates into a kind of historicism, an archival deposit in the record of the long anticolonial struggle. The text participates fully in the kind of record-keeping practiced by today's District Six Museum, where the writings of La Guma and other South Africans adorn the walls. Perhaps

because *A Walk in the Night* was forced from the beginning to circulate trans-
nationally, not as a national or regional literary artifact, it shares some of the
aesthetic qualities I have documented in *Lotus*, especially its mixture of heterogeneous temporalities and in the taking of cultural inventories.

La Guma's third full-length book, *The Stone Country* (1967), and his sixth,
Time of the Butcherbird (1979), each stretch and distort the narrative present in
curious ways. *The Stone Country* comes closest to observing the features of socialist realism that La Guma is sometimes thought to practice. As in *A Walk in
the Night*, La Guma's prefatory remarks to *The Stone Country* set the agenda:
"Dedicated to the daily average of 70,351 prisoners in South African gaols in
1964."[58] In this ethnographic novel, South Africa becomes notable for its community of convicts. It is the story of an ever-fluctuating group, a statistical ag-
gregate, united only by finding themselves on the wrong side of the penal system. The text makes little distinction between political prisoners, such as the
main protagonist, George Adams, and common criminals, such as the Casbah
Kid whom he befriends. *The Stone Country* offers, as with many stories of incarceration, a story of waiting and patience and the feeling of being isolated from
the events taking place outside, what Christopher J. Lee calls in another context
La Guma's poetics of quarantine.[59] The novel's elongated present tense carries
with it the sensation of being suspended or stalled. There is a hint that Adams
will politicize a few of his fellow inmates and perhaps an empathetic guard, but
the narrative is far more invested in conveying the experience of being ma-
rooned in prison than in the coming revolution. In this novel, at least, the moment of decolonization or revolutionary action is postponed indefinitely.

Time of the Butcherbird is arguably La Guma's most conventional novel, at
least in terms of the plot and its narrative architecture. It offers a reading of the
long timelines of the anticolonial movement. The butcherbird is an animal that
kills insects and hangs them on branches for later consumption; it is commonly regarded as a hunter of pests, thereby ridding the community of un-
wanted elements. Revolutionaries are human incarnations of this avian preda-
tor. Revolution is now, but the story concludes without a clear resolution:
ongoing resistance is certain, but victory less so.

Set in a small, dusty, Afrikaner *dorp* during a drought, the narrative inter-
weaves three distinct storylines. The first narrative tells of Edgar Stopes, a
White, English-speaking South African traveling salesman who is stuck in town
for a few days, waiting for his automobile to be mended. The second narrative
is drawn straight from the apartheid drawer: a mining company and the local
Afrikaners are annexing some adjacent communal lands and relocating the

Black villagers, who debate whether or not to resist eviction. The third narrative follows Shilling Murile, a Black man who grew up in the village and returned after a stint in prison, determined to avenge his brother's death at the hands of a local Afrikaner farmer. The three distinct narratives converge in the novel's climactic scenes.

We know the end of the land theft story from the very beginning of the novel. In the text's opening paragraph, before the narrator introduces a character or establishes a setting, readers confront a group of dispossessed people, abandoned on barren ground with tents and a few possessions. Nearby, a rusty tank collects brackish water from a sluggish well. Anonymous children cry, someone curses the Karoo's sandy earth, but then a song breaks out, soon joined by all: "At least one could sing in this wretched and deserted land."[60] No individual characters, no action, no plot to speak of, but already resilience in the face of adversity: thus the narrative begins where the plot ends.[61]

If the conclusion or moral of the story precedes the telling of the story itself, perhaps this is because the novel's other plotlines refuse the temporality of the present in deference to both the past and the future. Stopes, the traveling salesman, feels stranded among hostile foreigners, the local Afrikaners, who are themselves stuck in a prolonged drought. Immobility is an existential condition for him: his career has stalled; he has become estranged from his wife whom he once loved, a woman who now hopes secretly that her husband would die, as he does in the climax, leaving her an insurance settlement; and he thinks, stubbornly and against all outward signs, that some unforeseen event will improve his fortunes. The novel's Afrikaners also refuse to look squarely at the present. Praying for rain, they alternate between looking to other times: backward toward the lost cause, their armed resistance to British imperialism, which they memorialize everywhere, and covetously forward to the nearby land they plan to steal and the mineral wealth it holds. The novel underscores their moral paralysis by having them studiously avoid the predicaments of the present.

Time of the Butcherbird's revenge narrative, centered on Shilling Murile, likewise evacuates the present of its moral content. A prominent local farmer had killed the main character's brother about a decade before the main story begins. During the dispute, Murile had injured one of the farmer's party; Murile received a sentence of ten years' hard labor, while the White farmer was let off with a fine because the manslaughter had been provoked, supposedly, by the victim. During his incarceration, Murile learns to bide his time: "[b]ad things" happened to him behind bars, he admits to an old villager upon his return, "[b]ut one learns to wait, to remember. [. . .] It is better to remember and to wait, rather than to talk. In that place [prison] one got into big trouble through talking too much, so one just waited" (20). Imprisonment delivers the lessons of patience, silence, endurance, and memory, the deferral of the present so that the injustices of the past and the retribution of the future may assume their proper place in the story's moral order. In a reversal of sorts, Murile's avoidance of talk threatens to cancel out or refuse the reparative function of narrative itself. Telling story after story of apartheid injustice—in La Guma's case, almost exclusively to international audiences—is a weak substitute for political action. If so many anticolonial novels bear witness to trauma and in-justice, as Nicole M. Rizzuto points out in *Insurgent Testimonies: Witnessing Colonial Trauma in Modern and Anglophone Literature*, *Time of the Butcherbird* testifies ambivalently to the place of storytelling as a form of revolutionary praxis. South Africa's political situation, like Murile's revenge narrative, remains stuck between temporalities, grieving a past that will not rest quietly and await-ing a time of revolutionary action that never seems to arrive soon enough.

A key moment in the revenge plot happens when Murile visits his brother's grave, presumably for the first time. To this point in the text, readers do not really know his full story, only that he has returned home to avenge his brother's murder. Murile chews his cud at the cemetery, ruminating on the meaning of his brother's death:

> I will do this some thing [take revenge], he thought and rolled the bitter-ness in his mouth as if it was something to relish. Hatred sat behind the bleak eyes and watched through the obscuring brown panes; hatred was a friend to be given shelter, nurtured and petted as the old-time diviners, petted the avenging rhingals; hatred crouched like a patient leopard, wait-ing, but alive with the coursing blood of bitter memory. He was at one with the graves, the battered headboards with doom peeling off them: Death lay at his feet and waited to be aroused. (66)

Murile, the avenger, is an undead subject. He is at one with the graves, dwelling in and through death, animated not by life and its possibilities, but by griev-ance. Only his longstanding grudge is fully alive: his hatred is a friend to be given hospitality or a stalking carnivore waiting calmly for its prey. Death feeds his meager appetite for life. Once avenged, he swears he will have to have noth-ing more to do with the community of the living.

Many observers regard La Guma as practicing a form of committed, realist fiction, whether influenced by journalism, Soviet writing, or otherwise.

Coetzee, already mentioned as one of La Guma's toughest critics, says that he "is the inheritor of the worst excesses of realism" (358). Abdul JanMohamed, in one of the more sympathetic readings of La Guma, describes his writing as "simple and succinct, and his novels are short and terse—they lack the digressions and embellishments born of luxury and plenitude."[62] Succinct La Guma's novels may be, but I do not think the blanket category of realism fully captures how La Guma's anticolonial nationalism operates in a global literary context necessitated by his banning in South Africa and made possible by his participation in Afro-Asian networks.

My perspective is more in line with La Guma's biographer, Roger Field, who reads La Guma's short fiction as formally anarchic, borrowing from both socialist realism and modernism, and Monica Popescu, who notes La Guma's propensity to mix temporalities.[63] I attribute much of this disorder to an anticolonial aesthetic that labors in the uneven temporalities of South African decolonization. The past and the future loom incredibly large in La Guma's work, but the present tense, even in a novella such as *A Walk in the Night*, is continually harassed and harried by a history that refuses to stay in the past and a future that presses relentlessly on the current moment. The present is either too long—the promise of a better, decolonized horizon cannot arrive quickly enough—or it vanishes before our eyes, diverted into past and future tenses. La Guma's version of the colonial past will only be redeemed in a future he cannot fully apprehend, at least in his fictional oeuvre. The future is only dimly realized in his fiction, as *Time of the Butcherbird* implies. After personal revenge, the novel shows us ongoing communal resistance, stretching indefinitely into the future. For a better understanding of how La Guma represents a postcolonial future, I close this chapter with a brief turn to his travel writing in *A Soviet Journey* (1978), originally commissioned and published by the Soviet firm Progress Publishers.

It is something of a paradox to claim that La Guma and many of his *Lotus* contemporaries envisioned the postcolonial future for Africans and Asians not through speculative or science fiction, but through nonfiction travel writing. Christopher J. Lee's outstanding work on La Guma helps us understand how La Guma negotiated the relationship between his political activism and his writerly imagination. As Lee documents in his substantial introduction to a new edition of *A Soviet Journey*, the travel writing marks a departure from his fictional persona: "*A Soviet Journey* exhibits in contrast a robust vision of the future—a dreamworld—through [. . .] celebratory portrayals of Soviet development written in a frequently exuberant tone" (29). If colonialism in South

Africa means racial discrimination, poverty, and disenfranchisement, Soviet Asia imbues La Guma with a sense of optimism.

Following Langston Hughes but with increased emphasis, La Guma insists that racial discrimination and foreign domination are a thing of the past in the Soviet republics. When a group of curious medical professionals inquire about health care in South Africa, La Guma has a hard time conveying his experience, but not for want of trying: "Most Soviets I have met find racial discrimination difficult to comprehend, and it usually takes a lot of explanation. Those who were victims of the Nazis have a better understanding" (195). The same goes for colonialism: Soviet Asians do not really understand the concept, La Guma reports, unless they are old enough to have experienced tsarist domination of the region. Although most non-Soviets assume that Russia exerts an imperialist influence within the federation, La Guma insists nothing could be further from reality: from 1921, the Soviet system took upon itself the task of helping the Asian republics "create their own courts of law, administration, organs of government operating in their native languages [. . .]; develop their own press, schools, theatrical activities, cultural and educational institutions in their own native languages" (132). But the cultivation of linguistic and cultural differences should not be confused with isolationism or cultural chauvinism: increasing cultural exchange within and beyond the Soviet states was part of the project. In short, La Guma affirms that the Soviet system encourages indigenous social life and language in the Asian republics.

In material terms, however, La Guma depicts the Soviet state as far more interventionist among those he calls, self-consciously, the "once backward peoples" of the federation (83). Industrialization was just as significant as collectivization in these economically deprived regions, as La Guma describes it: increasing productive capacity as urgent a mission as sharing wealth equitably. As a result, economic development was terrifically swift in Soviet Asia, the rate of which outpaced that of Russia and the industrialized world for much of the century. La Guma is besotted by this aspect of the Soviet Asian experiment as he tours bountiful cooperative farms and orchards, massive infrastructure projects (dams and roads and electrification grids), state-of-the-art research laboratories, and shiny university campuses. The unique combination of cultural and material development—the simultaneous renaissance of indigenous languages and the improvement of economic conditions—makes La Guma wonder if the anticolonial movement could learn more than just ideological slogans from the socialist project.

Reading *A Soviet Journey* with the advantage of hindsight, it would be comparatively easy to be angered by La Guma's starry-eyed wonderment. Undoubtedly, there is much that La Guma overlooks or ignores in his reports on the Soviet system: as an exile and former political prisoner himself, he could not have been ignorant of the harassment of dissidents in the Soviet Union and the ongoing repression of subaltern peoples. I do not wish to explain away or apologize for La Guma's wide blind spots in this travelogue. But I regard his enthusiasm for the Soviet model as a culmination of his aesthetic preferences as much as it is an expression of his political commitments. The Soviet Union represents to La Guma a place where intellectual exchange across national boundaries happens without metropolitan domination. During a tour of Siberia, the editor of a regional magazine announces, the "literary industrialization" of the hinterlands has commenced: "we shall have our own local literature, based on local material, but equal to the all-Union literature in importance and quality" (208–9). Right after this meeting, as he wanders back to his hotel, La Guma discovers a copy of his own novel, *In the Fog of Seasons' End*, at one of the local booksellers (209). La Guma's Soviet experience allowed him to imagine a South African literary future, one in which antiapartheid writers could take their place on bookstore shelves.

With too much credulity in the things he saw and not enough skepticism for the things he did not see on his Soviet travels, La Guma fully believed that Soviet literary culture had fostered respect for indigenous cultures in the pursuit of international intellectual exchange. Although the AAWA functioned as an anticolonial literary institution in a global context—supporting Palestinian, southern African, and Vietnamese resistance—it also was complicit in Russia's cultural domination of Soviet Asia. This reminds us that cultural forms of anticolonialism, especially in the cold war context, are rarely pure or totally unambiguous. In *On the Postcolony*, Achille Mbembe describes the turn of the twenty-first century as the *"time of entanglement,"* but a consideration of La Guma's case suggests that this representation of temporality has a longer history (16). La Guma's distortions of Soviet Asia are underwritten by an imagined future that awaits postcolonial South Africa. Development, including the development of the literary and cultural industries, without metropolitan domination: this is the vision of the future that La Guma's writing provides for the colonial regions of Africa and Asia. It is a future he would not live to see.

5

A Failure of Diplomacy: Placing Eileen Chang in Global Literary History

THE PREVIOUS two chapters document how the aesthetic cold war opened unique opportunities for cultural diplomacy, allowing large states to influence aesthetic practices in the decolonizing world by creating a new system of world-literary space. Although Soviet- and US-led networks competed with one another, they used similar techniques (sponsoring conferences, magazines, radio features, prizes, and book publications) and drew upon an overlapping pool of talent. In a sense, then, the leading cold war protagonists collaboratively rewrote the rules of the literary field by drafting producers and consumers of texts into a global arena of competition, related to but distinct from the world republic of letters described by Pascale Casanova and the global system of cultural prizes considered by James F. English.

I have argued against the common assumption that the cold war's leading states dictated terms to writers from decolonizing areas. In both the CCF and AAWA networks, writers from the decolonizing world had a good deal of latitude to pursue the most promising lines of development for their work, partly through their astute manipulation of competing forces. But even if the United States and the Soviet Union did not fully control the circulation of late colonial and early postcolonial literature in a global context, these large states most certainly shaped how intellectuals interacted with one another and with their global readers. For Alex La Guma, who was denied a national audience, connections with the CCF and AAWA networks were not the perquisites of a deracinated cosmopolitanism, but a professional necessity: without access to global distribution systems, he could count the South African censors as his most attentive readers.

The bilingual Chinese/English writer Eileen Chang (or Zhang Ailing) was another midcentury figure who, for many years, was denied a national audience for political reasons. After a glittering start in Shanghai in the 1940s, her opportunities in China became limited, first by her wartime association with the Japanese puppet regime, and second by the victory of the Chinese Communist Party in the civil war (1945–49). She responded by seeking audiences beyond mainland China. Being fluent in two international languages, she was capable of envisioning readers among the large Chinese diaspora as well as among readers of English fiction the world over. Leaving the mainland in the early 1950s, first for Hong Kong and later for the United States, Chang soon teamed up with the United States Information Agency (USIA), the cultural diplomacy offshoot of the US State Department. She started with translation assignments, rendering Ernest Hemingway, Henry James, and Walt Whitman into Chinese. Before long, USIA provided support for her own fictional work, especially her two novels from the 1950s, *The Rice-Sprout Song* (*Yangge*, 1954) and *Naked Earth* (*Chidi zhilian*, 1956). With an abundance of talent and an influential patron, Chang was poised to become a leading international figure, seemingly destined to be mentioned alongside Chinua Achebe and Derek Walcott as the most widely recognized writers from decolonizing areas.

Her timing, it would appear, could not have been better. Intellectual exchange between China and the United States surged during the interwar years and peaked, in somewhat different forms, in the immediate postwar period. From the 1930s through the 1960s, there was a notable uptick in China–US literary traffic, including the runaway success of Pearl S. Buck's fiction, especially *The Good Earth* (1931), which found admirers among anglophone and sinophone communities. Cultural exchange was uncharacteristically reciprocal in the interwar years, with Chinese figures such as Lin Yutang and Lao She impacting US literary culture while Buck was influencing developments in sinophone circles, as Richard Jean So documents in *Transpacific Community: America, China, and the Rise and Fall of a Cultural Network*.[1] By the time Chang started her career in the 1940s, things looked promising for her. There were existing forms of bilateral cultural exchange, and she was a precocious talent who was comfortable in two international languages. By the 1950s, as Christina Klein points out in *Cold War Orientalism: Asia in the Middlebrow Imagination, 1945–1961*, the United States might have offered an ideal literary refuge for Chang, whose interest in so-called women's issues and domestic fiction would be sure to resonate with middlebrow audiences primed to accept Asian themes.[2] She simply needed to keep writing, play the professional game, and hope that political gridlock would not interfere with her ambitions.

It did not work out that way. After such a promising start in Shanghai, Chang kept writing in the United States, but increasingly without hope of recognition. There are a variety of reasons for this, several of which I discuss in the following pages. Chance was perhaps the most important variable of all; Chang's status as a woman and her quirky feminism; her reclusiveness as she aged; her reluctance to link up with the emerging creative writing program in the United States; her obsessive returns to the same material, which she reworked in both languages to the point of imaginative exhaustion; and her uncertainty about what it means to be authentically Chinese all played a part in her professional struggles. But I do not want to manufacture one singular or definitive explanation of why Chang did not experience the kind of critical or commercial success in her prime that she would enjoy from the 1980s forward, as the cold war approached its closing chapters (if not the end of Communist Party rule in China). The meddling of large states in the global literary field did not, in many cases, lead to recognition and success for writers from the decolonizing parts of the world. Reading *Encounter* and *Lotus* cover-to-cover makes this abundantly clear: a few names stand out, while most contributors to these venues have been totally forgotten by literary history. Likewise, writers who earned the wrath of one cold war state often found sympathetic audiences elsewhere. Neither state sponsorship nor state discipline fully determined the career prospects of cold war intellectuals.

This chapter turns to Chang's case to describe the limits of soft power in shaping the field of global literature during the cold war. Very often, the evaluative judgments reached in the literary field were indifferent to state manipulation. Many of the most significant writers from the decolonizing world participated in cold war cultural diplomacy programs, but even greater numbers of those who worked with state agencies fell by the wayside. Although many existing studies of the arts in the cold war would have us believe that such backing led, almost inevitably, to sanctioned forms of global recognition— Serge Guilbaut, Andrew N. Rubin, Frances Stonor Saunders, and Hugh Wilford provide a few of the most gripping and thoroughly documented conspiracy narratives—the actual record shows us a high rate of failure. Scores of talented writers, Chang among them, were not able to leverage state patronage into critical or commercial success. Her work with USIA made it impossible for Chang to keep an audience in mainland China, yet it could hardly guarantee her a favorable hearing in North America and elsewhere. For writers from the decolonizing world, collaborating with the cold war's main antagonists was risky. It could be parlayed into lasting status, as in the case of Wole Soyinka, or it could lead to a purgatorial exile, cut off from national audiences without securing a place in the wider literary world. In Chang's particular example, it was the work of a few dedicated literary critics from the Chinese diaspora—and certainly not her audiences in English—that resuscitated her career, first in Chinese and later in English.

Chang's case also demonstrates how skillful nonaligned writers could move between different ideological camps without thereby making enormous aesthetic compromises. As I argue in the following pages, Chang's signature literary techniques—what she describes as a pervading mood of desolation and the formal device of equivocal contrast—are ever-present as she moves from pro-Fascist to pro-Chinese Communist to US-backed anti-Communist literary networks. Chang's most loyal readers tend to describe her as consciously resisting propaganda and ideological manipulation despite her involvement with cultural diplomacy programs; her fiercest critics, meanwhile, suggest that she sacrificed her credibility as an artist by using her talents for propagandistic, subliterary purposes. This chapter describes Chang neither as ideologically uncontaminated nor as a political sellout. She was a knowing participant in cultural diplomacy programs, and yet her aesthetic principles survived her liaisons with competing diplomacy initiatives. Her work shows someone whose distinctive literary style is best described as an aesthetics of nonalignment. As she adapted her work down through the years, moving between Chinese and English and between different ideological blocs, her core aesthetic principles remained surprisingly constant despite her appeals to different audiences. This consistency, I want to suggest, is not that of a politically autonomous or nonideological writer, but that of a cagey operator whose belief in equivocal contrast—in something other than stark binaries—allowed her to adapt to different political pressures and ideological expectations without reinventing herself as a writer.

Ambitious, Bilingual, Precocious

Chang worked between two languages from the very start of her career. One of her earliest published pieces, the autobiographical essay "What a Life! What a Girl's Life," appeared in English in the *Shanghai Evening Post* when its author was still a teenager. She reworked the essay in Chinese as "Whispers," which she included in the collection *Written on Water* (*Liuyan*, 1945). The essay offers some autobiographical revelations. Chang's cosmopolitan mother left her daughter in the care of her opium-smoking ex-husband and his new wife while she toured western Europe with her ex-husband's sister. But the interest of literary historians might be piqued by her confident allusions to Lao She and Lin Yutang, both prominent figures known for their work abroad. Chang says that she dreamed of learning the art of animation "as a means of introducing Chinese painting to the United States," where she hoped "to make an even bigger splash than Lin Yutang."[3] Lao She was a favorite of Chang's from the 1930s for his depictions of Chinese émigrés in London, but he became best known overseas for *Rickshaw Boy*, translated with the help of the US State Department, which became a Book of the Month Club selection and cracked the top five of the *New York Times* Best Seller list in 1945. Even before she had established a name for herself in the local literary scene, Chang nurtured hopes of an international readership. As she says in a preface to her first collection of short stories, *Romances* (*Chuanqi*, 1944), she was overeager to become famous by her pen: "I have to hurry: faster, faster, or it'll be too late!"[4] Appealing to Shanghai's readers in two languages, rather than one, might enable her to reach beyond the confines of her city and nation. These were not idle fantasies, as it turned out, although Chang's bilingual career would not be free of complications.

Chang's literary practices emerged in stark contrast to the two major examples she might have followed, that of the internationalist Buck, on the one hand, and that of the major nationalist writers of the May Fourth New Culture Movement (1919–30) and the League of Left-Wing Writers (1930–36), featuring figures such as Lu Xun, Mao Dun, and Ding Ling.[5] The kind of liberal humanism and cultural relativism on display in *The Good Earth*[6] was no more appealing to Chang than Lu Xun's brand of vernacular nationalism.[7] Working against the kind of national allegory associated with figures such as Lu Xun, who took great trouble to document China's social and political ills, Chang presents a China in snatches and fragments and equivocal contrasts. Rather than particularizing Chinese culture, Chang writes with a determination to show Chinese culture to outsiders yet with a sneaking suspicion that no such thing as Chinese culture or China can be described, except at an angle or through a detour. As Chang herself remarks in a letter to her critical champion, C. T. Hsia, "I always have a hunch, for those who love China, the China they love is exactly the China I intend to disavow."[8]

In contrast to Buck, Chang presents a China marred by all kinds of social vices and political ills: concubinage and the subordination of women in family life; opium addiction; corruption; European and Japanese imperialism; feudalism; and later Communism, to name a few. Whereas *The Good Earth* shows us an enterprising peasant who becomes wealthy through a combination of hard work and good fortune, Chang shows us a cast of characters whose development is stunted by an oppressive environment. Chang's heterodox anticolonialism dodges the cultural particularities of a more straightforward nationalism while chafing against the hopeful internationalism offered in Buck's fiction. Rey Chow's observation about the national question in Chinese literature is instructive on this point: "In the writing of fiction, this relationship [between intellectuals and 'the people' or the nation] always presents itself as a question rather than a solution."[9] Anticolonial without being a committed nationalist, cosmopolitan yet exhibiting a skeptical anti-humanism: this is how I describe the tangle of Chang's aesthetic and ideological commitments. Her crisscrossing movements between Chinese and English accentuate her tendency to negate and double back.

Equivocal Contrast

A few examples from her early stories and essays will help me illustrate Chang's particular version of aesthetic nonalignment, her attempt to write between nationalist and internationalist movements in the context of the aesthetic cold war. She describes her favored technique of equivocal contrast in "Writing of One's Own" and elsewhere as way of avoiding stereotypes about Chinese culture. As she matured, equivocal contrast would allow her to present the cold war's ideological blocs in terms other than irreconcilable difference. Unlike classical literary forms, such as epic and tragedy, which represent good and evil, love and hate, or truth and falsehood as eternally clashing forces, Chang presents more subtle forms of contrast "as a means of writing the truth beneath the hypocrisy of modern people." Because "[t]here are very few people after all, who are either extremely perverse or extremely enlightened," equivocal contrast allows Chang to imagine characters bristling with ambivalence and contradictions (*Written on Water* 19, 17). Rejecting both allegory and caricature, Chang prefers equivocal contrast because it permits her to be indirect, to hedge, creating individual characters who are neither this nor that but unpredictable combinations of different traits. Chang's early stories feature "weak and ordinary people" because they "can serve more accurately than heroes as a measure of the times" (17).

Equivocal contrast gives Chang an extremely flexible procedure for representing both heterosexual coupling and the relationship between individuals
and the nation. Couples, for her, are never perfectly matched; the same is true
of the relationship between individuals and the nation called China. To translate Chang's favored practices into the language of the aesthetic cold war, we
might say that her writing tacks between autonomy and utilitarianism, dwelling on the fundamental conflict between individual desire and group consciousness. "Aloeswood Incense: The First Brazier" opens with the young
protagonist, Weilong, as she approaches her wealthy aunt's home in Hong
Kong to ask for help with her school fees. Weilong's aunt, a socialite who mixes
with the upper crust of Cantonese and British society, has decorated her man-
sion with an amalgam of foreign and indigenous articles:

> The furniture and the arrangement were basically Western, touched up with
> some unexceptionable Chinese bric-a-brac. [...] These Oriental touches
> had been put there, it was clear, for the benefit of foreigners. The English
> come from so far to see China—one has to give them something of China
> to see. But this was China as Westerners imagine it: exquisite, illogical, very
> entertaining. (8)

Over the course of the story, it becomes obvious that Weilong's aunt is happy
to play on stereotypes, entertaining and flirting with Hong Kong's Europeans
in exchange for social status. Whatever she may be, striving to be authentically
Chinese is not one of her objectives. She knows, her servants know, Weilong
knows, the narrator knows, and even her British guests, we suspect, know that
this is all for show: this is China only as a foreigner could imagine it, or as a
Chinese person who wants to flatter a foreigner would interpret it.

The narrator immediately establishes an equivocal contrast between Weilong and her self-exoticizing aunt. Rather than depict Weilong as somehow
authentically Chinese, the narrator tells us that Weilong's self-presentation is
difficult to categorize. It does not fit the model in which authentic and inauthentic China appear in direct conflict. As she approaches the house,

> Weilong glanced at her reflection in the glass doors—she too was a touch
> of typically colonial Oriental color. She wore the special uniform [of her
> school]: a dark blue starched cotton tunic that reached to her knees, over
> narrow trousers, all in the late Qing style. Decking out coeds in the manner
> of Boxer-era courtesans—that was only one of the ways that the Hong

Kong of the day tried to please European and American tourists. But Wei-long, like any girl, sought to be stylish, and she wore a small knitted vest on top of the tunic. Under that little vest, the tunic stretched down a long way—the effect, in the end, was unclassifiable. (8–9)

It is a subtle, deft touch, providing a simple description of the young protagonist's attire. But in this quick maneuver, Chang uses her favored technique of equivocal contrast to illustrate an important difference between Weilong and her aunt, and in so doing she encourages the reader to think about what it means to be authentically and inauthentically Chinese. Our protagonist is not, the narrator observes wryly, an authentic Chinese counterpoint to her aunt's artful and knowing display of an essentialized Chinese chic. Instead, Weilong presents herself in a way that even our narrator cannot quite pin down. She modifies the school uniform that would make her resemble a Boxer-era courtesan without fully making it into something authentically Chinese, whatever that might be. If this is rebellion against imperialist fantasies, it is not open but passive resistance of some kind. It is perhaps a protest against racist and imperialist stereotypes, but it cannot be described as a clear expression of nationalist sympathies.

"Love in a Fallen City," likewise, uses the genre of romantic comedy and the technique of equivocal contrast to apply pressure to the concepts of authenticity and indigeneity. In this story, the main protagonist, Bai Liusu, a divorcée approaching thirty, plots her escape from her awful birth family, to which she has returned after the collapse of her marriage. They are a declining Shanghainese clan, not unlike Chang's, having frittered away most of their inheritance. The narrator describes them as a family living in the past, so much that they refuse to observe the newfangled practice of daylight savings: when everyone's else's clock says eleven, theirs remains stuck at ten.

Liusu's chance comes when a wealthy overseas Chinese man, Fan Liu-yuan, is set up with one of Liusu's nieces. Liusu ruthlessly pursues him for herself, attracting his attention to the fury of her family. During their courtship, it comes out that Fan, who has spent most of his life outside of China, regards Liusu as a "real Chinese girl," approvingly. When Liusu hears this summary of her charms, she laughs it off, saying merely that she is "old-fashioned," wondering if a "modern man" such as Fan could really accept an unworldly woman as a wife. Fan parries the accusation in turn: when she says modern, what she really means is Europeanized, and while he admits that he is "not a real Chinese," he is learning to become Chinese, humorously noting that a foreigner such as himself "who's become Chinese also becomes reactionary, more reactionary than even an old-fashioned scholar from the dynastic era" (135–36). It is difficult to tell exactly what Fan thinks it means to be an authentically Chinese person. Liusu fails to meet the "reactionary" caricature on at least a couple of counts: she is no believer in filial deference, and as a woman she is open with her romantic preferences. She does not defer to men, to her elders, or to her family. Being Chinese is something desirable from Fan's perspective—he seeks it for himself and in a potential mate—but it is difficult to tell precisely what he might mean by the idea. Chang's early stories do this frequently: when a character identifies a person or a cultural practice as authentically and unmistakably Chinese, Chang uses an arch narrator, contextual clues, or another character to question this assertion of authenticity.

Desolation

In addition to equivocal contrast, Chang's early fiction relies on what she calls a mood of "desolation." Her use of the term provides a textbook example of the anticipation of violence endemic to the middle decades of the century, as Paul K. Saint-Amour documents in *Tense Future: Modernism, Total War, Encyclopedic Form*. In her preface to the second printing of *Romances*, Chang's first short story collection, she describes her push to become famous as a race against the destructiveness of the times:

> Even if I could wait [to achieve fame by writing], our whole era is being pushed onward, is breaking apart already, with greater destruction still coming. Our entire civilization—with all its magnificence, and its insignificance—will someday belong to the past. If the word I use most often is "desolate," it's because I feel, in the back of my mind, this staggering threat. (*Love in a Fallen City* 1)

It is a fascinating passage written by someone who elsewhere contradicts herself by saying that "[t]here is no war and no revolution in my works" (*Written on Water* 18). The sense of desolation that pervades her writing, as she describes it above, would seem to be all about war and revolution, about the feeling that everything we know in the present is on the verge of being swept away in a cataclysm. It is also a sign of Chang's anti-humanist instincts. She remains skeptical of the idea that human beings are anything more than the playthings of fate, or that human beings are capable of fashioning durable bonds of understanding and sympathy. There is no bond of love, familial or sexual, free from profound misunderstanding, even mistrust.

In addition to conveying this premonition of doom, Chang's use of desolation carries with it some formal consequences for her fiction. Desolation, she says, provides an open-ended aesthetic solution to the problem of narrative conclusions. Tragedy, she says in "Writing of One's Own," offers "a kind of closure." The tragic fall and catharsis leave us with a clear resolution. Desolation, by contrast, "is a form of revelation" (17). Chang reads the mood of desolation as a way to represent the perseverance that ordinary people display as they cope with bad luck and the unforeseen consequences of their own decisions. Because her stories feature unexceptionable people who are not involved in life-and-death struggles, her stories end, but they do not reach a climax in the way that tragic form dictates. Desolation, therefore, is more inconclusive than its tragic cousin. Her stories end, sometimes in remarkable ways, but they do not provide a sense of closure or finality. The idea of open-ended or revelatory conclusions, as I will discuss later in this chapter, gave Chang remarkable flexibility when she began to adapt her work to meet different political pressures.[10] Chang's thoughts on tragedy find an unlikely corollary in the writing of C.L.R. James, whose thoughts on classical literary forms I consider in chapter 7.

We find one of the best examples of Chang's desolate, inconclusive endings in "Love in a Fallen City." Liusu, the protagonist, spends much of her courtship with Fan in trying to obtain a commitment of marriage before she agrees to consummate the relationship. Fan, for his part, spends much of their courtship pressuring Liusu to begin a sexual relationship before a promise of marriage as a way to prove her love for him. Liusu, loathed by her family and without financial resources of her own, gives ground first. But before Chang reveals the full consequences of her protagonist's gamble, a *deus ex machina* intervenes: the Japanese invade Hong Kong, where the couple have reconvened after a period of separation. "Hong Kong's defeat had brought Liusu victory," the crafty narrator reports. Liusu and Fan publish their wedding banns even as the bombs fall around them. Lest we think this wedding marks the joyful conclusion of a conventional romantic comedy, the narrator divides our attention equally between the war and the newlyweds. "But in this unreasonable world," the passage continues, "who can distinguish cause from effect? Did a great city fall so that she could be vindicated?" (167).

Chang's use of this technical solution to the problem of narrative closure is worth considering in the context of midcentury fiction. A range of critics have thought extensively about the relationship between narrative form and large-scale conflict.[11] In contrast to many of her midcentury peers, who were preoccupied with endings, finality, and systems of narrative containment as a way to tell stories of contemporary life, Chang uses endings to reveal what she regards as the patchwork nature of existence, the contingent and equivocal ways that the lives of ordinary people transpire against the backdrop of mass destruction. What started as an ingenious technical solution to the problem of endings, however, became something of a curse for Chang in her later career. As she moved back and forth between languages, she also returned again and again to the same basic stories, resulting in a kind of creative paralysis. The kinds of inconclusiveness she so prized as a young writer served her cruelly in the long run.

Pen for Hire

Although Chang is regarded by many of her admirers as a nonpolitical writer who happened to write in an ideologically charged environment, this conveys at best a partial truth. As more recent scholarship has demonstrated, Chang had dealings with a variety of political interest groups from the beginning of her career. Chang began publishing her work shortly after the Japanese invasion of China in 1937. Several of her early English-language essays appeared in Klaus Mehnert's magazine, *The XXth Century*, which was an identifiably pro-Axis periodical based in Shanghai.[12] She had a brief, unhappy marriage to Hu Lancheng, who held a government position in the collaborationist regime installed by the Japanese; after the war and the breakdown of their marriage, he fled to Japan, a traitor. In the years of the civil war and the immediate aftermath, Chang temporarily reconciled herself to the kind of writing that would be acceptable to the Communist authorities. She serialized *Eighteen Springs* (*Shiba chun*) in 1950–51 and *Little Ai* (*Xiao'ai*) in 1951–52, described as pro-Communist novels by David Der-wei Wang and Chang translator Karen S. Kingsbury, and she attended the inaugural Writers' and Artists' Conference arranged by the Party in 1950 Shanghai.[13] Perry Link, who provides an introduction to *Naked Earth*, offers an unconfirmed report that Chang turned down offers of lavish sinecures from the Communists.[14] By the time she connected with USIA in Hong Kong in 1952, she was hardly a political innocent, even if few of her early stories and essays display obvious signs of ideological commitment.

Chang's career arc is interesting, if not unique, for writers from decolonizing areas. She was ideologically flexible enough that she could work with a

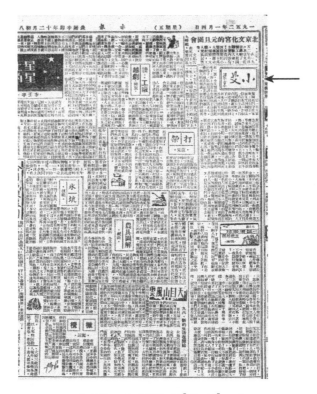

FIGURE 5.1. Installment of *Little Ai* [*Xiao'ai*], under pen name
Liang Jing. *Yibao* newspaper (Shanghai), 4 January 1952.

variety of political groups. Her various collaborators, including the Chinese
Communist Party and USIA, did not necessarily blacklist Chang because she
was politically contaminated by earlier collaborations. USIA, for instance, did
not believe that Chang's past connections would prevent her from doing useful work for their purposes. Rather than condemn Chang for her engagements
with state interests or make the counterargument that her work ultimately
transcends those unfortunate, worldly entanglements, I propose trying to understand the role of cultural diplomacy in her aesthetic development.

What were USIA's designs? The US Department of State's cultural diplomacy programs, out of which USIA grew, tended to be relatively transparent about the nature of their work, although they sometimes downplayed
or completely suppressed their involvement in particular ventures.[15] Penny
Von Eschen's research on State Department jazz tours shows how the US

government brought African American musical icons, such as Louis Armstrong, to decolonizing regions in an attempt to counteract the Achilles' heel of cold war foreign policy, domestic racism. Acknowledging public sponsorship was an important part of State Department strategy: a progressive national government was trying its best to defeat lingering pockets of discrimination back home. The message did not always convince the skeptics and neutrals, as Von Eschen's and Mary L. Dudziak's research on the question confirms.[16] The Soviet Union made sure that reports about Jim Crow stayed in front of audiences in decolonizing areas, and sometimes even the jazz ambassadors themselves could be openly critical of racism in the United States. In addition to musicians, the US government sent art exhibitions, athletes, dance troupes, and writers on tour; it staffed and stocked hundreds of Information Centers, libraries, and reading rooms all over the world; it produced original television content, documentary films, and especially radio programs, with Voice of America.[17]

As Greg Barnhisel demonstrates, above all else the State Department and USIA believed that books were the most efficacious medium for cultural diplomacy. Although books tended to reach a small, literate minority in most decolonizing regions, policy makers believed this privileged group exerted a disproportionate influence on public opinion. Fetishizing the book was also an attempt to rival the Soviet publishing juggernaut, as discussed in the previous chapter.[18] In the postwar years, the United States devised a number of programs to compete with the Soviets in the global book market, blending private and public sponsorship in various book production and dissemination schemes. It commissioned individual writers for particular projects as well as paying for translations of US writers into other languages. It also subsidized publishers in English and other languages, guaranteed book sales, and underwrote international distribution costs for titles requested by staff at embassies, consulates, Information Centers, and reading rooms.[19]

In southeast Asia, the US State Department and USIA hoped to tilt the political field away from Communism by facilitating translation and cultural exchange programs. In one of the earliest efforts, the State Department commissioned an unauthorized translation of Lao She's novel, *Rickshaw* [*Luòtuo Xiángzi*], even creating a special edition for US armed forces, before then inviting him on a lecture tour of the United States in the late 1940s (So *Transpacific* 178–207). Once it was clear that the Communist Party had consolidated its political supremacy in China, the United States mounted a campaign to influence other nations in the region. In the early 1950s, the State Department and USIA recruited Jade Snow Wong and other Chinese Americans to publish books on their cross-cultural experiences, to undertake lecture tours in southeast Asia, to create content for Voice of America, and to serve as general goodwill ambassadors for the United States.[20] Thus, Chang was one of a cohort of intellectuals who enjoyed official sanction from the US government. To adapt Josephine Nock-Hee Park's language, USIA built an institutional mechanism for recruiting and integrating the "friendly" into the cold war's intellectual circuits. Friendlies were Asian collaborators who could "shield her friends [the US] from the charge of neocolonialism, even though her very existence perpetually belies such attempts."[21]

Chang's main contact at USIA was Richard M. McCarthy, who has an interesting story of his own. After working for the State Department in Beijing during the civil war and witnessing the transition to Communist rule firsthand, he transferred to Hong Kong as an information officer, and later as Public Affairs Officer, from 1950–56. He worked on the China Reporting Program, which he describes as being responsible for "producing material in English and other languages for worldwide consumption about what was happening on the China mainland."[22] In other words, McCarthy was one of the principal figures disseminating anti-Communist propaganda related to China during the early years of the People's Republic.

In addition to liaising with press outlets, McCarthy's office developed original content in several different media, from radio and television to periodicals and bound books. The bimonthly magazine *World Today* [*Jinri shijie*], distributed throughout the diaspora, was one of their success stories. It was in his capacity as a propagandist that McCarthy met Chang. She started in the translation program, which under McCarthy's leadership was producing up to sixty books a year, before releasing *The Rice-Sprout Song* and *Naked Earth* with help from USIA (McCarthy interview). Mei-Hsiang Wang suggests that *Naked Earth* was commissioned by USIA, which supplied the outline for the novel.[23] Scraps of information suggest that Chang kept up her contact with McCarthy and USIA even after she moved to the United States and he left Hong Kong for other postings.[24] Chang also continued her work with Voice of America after leaving Hong Kong.[25]

In the first half of 1954, the Chinese-language version of *The Rice-Sprout Song* appeared in *World Today* in thirteen regular installments (see figures 5.2, 5.3, and 5.4). The magazine was produced and distributed by USIA's Hong Kong office with McCarthy's guidance. The magazine's sponsors were quite open about their geopolitical affiliations, as the English-language memos sent

秧歌 (連載)

張愛玲

第一章

一到這小鎮上，第一先看見長長的一排茅厠。都是迎面一個木板照壁，架在大石頭上，半遮着裏面背對背的兩個坑位。接連不斷的十幾個小茅棚，裏面一個人也沒有。但是有時候一陣風吹過來，微微發出臭氣。下午的陽光淡淡地晒在屋頂上白蒼蒼的茅草上。

走過這一排茅厠，就是店舖。一排白色的小店，上面黑鬱鬱地矗立着一座大山，山頭上又現出兩抹淡青的遠山。

極窄的一條石子路，對街攔着一道碎石矮牆，牆外望出去什麼也沒有，因爲外面就是陡地削落下去的危坡。過了街，把店裏走出一個女人，捧着個大紅磁臉盆，過了街，一盆髒水往矮牆外面一倒。不知道爲什麼，這舉動使人驚駭，像是把一盆污水潑出天涯海角，世界的盡頭。

差不多每一片店裏都有一個殺氣騰騰的老板娘坐在櫃枱上，齊眉戴着一頂粉紫絨線帽，左耳邊更綴着一顆孔雀藍大絨毬——也不知道這樣的打扮是什麼時候興出來的，倒有點像戲台上武生扮的綠林大盜，使遇往行人看了很感到不安。

有一片吃食店，賣的是小蘇餅與黑芝蔴捧糖。這兩項之外，櫃枱上還堆着兩疊白紙小包，看不是什麼一類的東西。有人來買了一包，當場就拆開來吃，想必是黑芝蔴捧糖了。——不過也許仍舊是蘇餅。

另一片店擺着一刀一刀的草紙堆積如山，靠門卻懸空釘着個小玻璃櫃，裏面陳列着牙膏牙粉。牙粉的紙袋與髮夾的紙板上都印有五彩明星照片，李麗華，周曼華，周璇，一個個都對着空空的街道倩笑着。不知道怎麼，更增加了那荒凉之感。

幾隻瘦雞在街上走，小心地舉起一隻脚來，小心地踏在那一顆顆嵌在黑泥裏的小圓石子上。賣的又是黑芝蔴捧糖。

不論是鄉下，是城裏，永遠少不了有這麼一片香燭店，彙寶燈籠，一簇簇的紅蠟燭，高掛在屋梁上，嫋嫋地垂下來。隔壁的一片佛堂裏，四壁蕭然，只放着一張方桌，一個小女孩坐在桌子跟前，用機器捲製「土香烟」。那機器捲是個綠漆的小洋鐵盒子，大概本來是一隻洋油桶，裝了一隻柄，霍霍搖着。她用着臉觀着眼向他望着，忽然高興地叫了起來，「咦，這不是荷生哥麼？你們家兩位老人家都好？荷生哥好呀？你四嬸好？」

那小販起初怔住了，但隨即想起來，她是他們隔壁鍾家親戚，彷彿曾經見過兩面。那個子生得矮，臉型很短，抄下巴，臉色晒成深赭紅，像風乾的山芋片一樣，紅而皺，向外捲着，穿着補了又補的藍布大褂。她載着舊式的尖頂黑帽匼，眯縫着眼睛，彷彿太陽照在臉上，說話總是咪着眼笑，彷彿隔着大片田野。

「你這位大嫂，難得到鎭上來的吧？」這小販問她。

「噯，我今天是陪我姪女兒來的，」老嫗人大聲喊着。「那孩子可憐，爹娘都沒有了，就一個哥哥。他們兩口子今天到區上去登記。那孩子明天出嫁，嫁到鄰村。今天到區上去登記。嫂嫂上城去幫人家去了，家裏就是一個哥哥。他們兩口子今天都要到的。我們這遍人太少了不像城裏人多，今天他們都要了來了。」她仰着臉覷着他望着他笑，「噯呀，我只好也跟了來，怎麼會碰着你！我剛纔來正在那邊路亭裏歇脚，看他們周家的人來了沒有。不要我們比他們先到，顯得新娘子太性急了不好。」

「來了來了！我瞅見幾個周家的人坐在區公所的台階上。我得要走了，去把新娘子領來。讓人家老等着也不好。你也不要老站在這裏說話，就搁了生意。」

FIGURE 5.2. First installment of *The Rice-Sprout Song* in the USIA magazine *World Today* [*Jinri shijie*], 1954.

FOREIGN SERVICE OPERATION MEMORANDUM

TO: USIA, Washington   January 13, 1954

FROM: USIS, Hong Kong

SUBJECT: IPS: "World Today" No. 44, dated January 1, 1954

Transmitted herewith are 15 copies of issue No. 44 of World Today
dated January 1, 1954. The contents are as follows:

Cover: Christopher Wei
Inside front cover: Servant of the people (five pictures)

Page 1.   Editorial — a New Year message to our readers.

Page 2 & 3. Chinese Communists facing grave crisis — an article on the
             shortage of oil and food supplies in Red China, also on the
             new government bonds issued by the Chinese Communists.

Page 4.   The U.S. Court of claims — An article explaining the organiza-
             tion and operations of this unique U.S. court where individuals
             or business organizations may sue to recover damages if and when
             they believe they have suffered injustice as a result of Govern-
             ment action. One picture.

Page 5, 6 & 7. "Who Distorted "Ni Huan-chi" — a feature story exposing
             Communist distortion of a best-seller about a conscientious school
             teacher.

Page 8 & 9. Ten big events of 1953 (picture story).

Page 10 & 11. The worker under the Soviet Regime — an article discussing
             what the thirty-six years' of Communist dictatorship have brought
             to the Russian workers in contrast to the promises made by
             Communist leaders during the Russian Revolution. (Four pictures)

Page 12.   Motion picture. On Miss Li Mei, promising and talented Chinese
             movie star.

Page 13.   Anti-Communist folk songs, part 2, continued from previous issue.

Page 14 & 15. Searching oil under the snow — a story on men searching for
             oil in Canada. (Four pictures)

Page 16.   My musical life, part 2 by Walter Damrosch.

Page 17.   Movie review.

Page 18.   Atomic energy for peace — An article on the peaceful use of
             atomic energy, present stage and future. (Four pictures)

Page 19.   What Nonsense — On contradictory statements made in the Communist
             press.

FIGURE 5.3. USIA memo distributed with *World Today* [*Jinri shijie*], 1954, page 1.

Page 20 & 21. "Our smelling power". -- a science feature on human smelling
system.
Four short science items, two pictures.

Page 22, 23, 24 & 25. "Rice Sprout Song" -- first installment of an anti-
Communist novel by Aileen Chang, one of the most outstanding
novelists in China.

Page 26. A trip to the Sun-Moon Lake -- an article on the author's recent
trip to the famous summer resort in Taiwan. One pic.

Page 27. General Chiang Chin-kuo's recent tour to the U.S. -- A reproduction
of the questions put to the eldest son of Generalissimo Chiang
Kai-shek and his answers during an interview with the VOA on
November 13, 1953. One pic.

Page 28 & 29. Student essays -- Six essays contributed student readers of WT.

Page 30, 31 & 32. Pen-pal columns and letters to editor.

Inside back cover: Electricity goes to the countryside. Five pictures.
Back cover: Good wishes and a calendar of 1954.

Distribution is as follows:

Hong Kong	16,525 copies	Manila	4,000	copies
Taipei	35,000 "	Singapore	3,000	"
Kuala Lumpur	7,000 "	Djakarta	6,500	"
Surabaya	500 "	Medan	3,000	"
Rangoon	3,000 "	Hanoi	2,000	"
Saigon	15,000 "	Bangkok	3,000	"
Pusan	500 "	Penang	500	"
Lima	200 "	Havana	150	"
São Paulo	100 "	Kingston	25	"

USIS:AWH:CTCross:vt

Enclosures: 15 copies (USIA send 6 copies to IFI/F, 5 copies to IPS)
cc: SEA Posts (with 2 copies WT)

UNCLASSIFIED

FIGURE 5.4. USIA memo distributed with *World Today* [*Jinri shijie*], 1954, page 2.

with the magazines make readily apparent. Several articles in the first 1954 issue depict the dreariness of life under Communist rule, and a regular column—"What Nonsense"—reports "contradictory statements made in the Communist press."[26] Other issues of the magazine offer features on life and popular culture in the United States, as well as reports on US industrial strength and military technology. According to the figures here, USIA produced about one hundred thousand copies for distribution throughout the world, with most destined for readers in the Chinese diaspora. Archival records suggest that printing numbers may have reached one hundred fifty thousand.[27] The memo announcing *The Rice-Sprout Song* describes Chang's contribution as the "first installment of an anti-Communist novel" by "one of the most outstanding novelists in China" (2). There is nothing particularly subtle about the propaganda in these pages.

McCarthy's influence on the world of arts and letters extended well beyond his stay in Hong Kong, which ended in 1956. As So and Eric Bennett have demonstrated, McCarthy played a role in starting the International Writing Program at Iowa, the global counterpart of the Iowa Writers' Workshop. Dozens of writers from Taiwan, South Korea, Japan, and other parts of Asia were trained there. McCarthy studied literature at Iowa and remained close to one of the instructors, Paul Engle, who was directing the MFA program in the early 1940s. In letters to Engle, McCarthy talked up southeast Asian writers he admired (including Engle's future spouse and program codirector, Nieh Hua-ling) and mooted collaborative book projects. McCarthy also supplemented Engle's fundraising efforts by helping secure grants from the Asia Foundation (a CIA-controlled institution), which complemented grants from the Rockefeller and Farfield foundations, both active players in the aesthetic cold war.[28] McCarthy proposed that Chang teach at the International Writing Program, but she refused, fearing a loss of privacy in a small midwestern town.[29] Mark McGurl labels postwar US literary culture "the program era," but if we pan back from the North American frame we might think of this as the cultural diplomacy era. Paul Nadal and Kalyan Nadiminti have shown how the US creative writing system has welcomed global south writers into the fold.[30] Chang's near-miss suggests that the MFA system within the United States was interpenetrated by the cultural diplomacy network internationally: a period not only when US universities and market-driven capitalism made demands on global south writers, but also when powerful states solicited their opinions, used their influence, and tried to secure their loyalties. These inducements were complemented, as I discuss in the next section of the book, by coercive measures.

With her new status as a friendly, Chang earned some critical acclaim for *The Rice-Sprout Song*, but only modest sales, and it would prove to be her high-water point in the US literary marketplace during her lifetime. Despite some level of USIA support for *Naked Earth*, she could not interest a publisher in the United States for the novel, settling for an English-language release in Hong Kong instead. She failed to find a US publisher for any of her subsequent long-format fiction during her lifetime: *Pink Tears* remains unpublished; *The Book of Change* and *The Fall of the Pagoda* appeared posthumously in English; and for *The Rouge of the North*, she found a second-tier British publisher, Cassell.

Hungry Years, or Desolation Part 2

There is some disagreement about whether Chang wrote *The Rice-Sprout Song* in English first and then translated it into Chinese or vice versa.[31] Either way, it appeared almost simultaneously in Chinese and English, being published by Charles Scribner's Sons in the United States. I think it makes sense to treat *The Rice-Sprout Song* as a sign of creative continuity, not radical change, given Chang's penchant for shuttling continuously between English and Chinese and her willingness to work with a full range of political interest groups. For Chang's fiercest critics, *The Rice-Sprout Song* and *Naked Earth* are novels tainted by Chang's acceptance of partisan sponsorship. For Chang enthusiasts, these novels represent a nonpartisan, humanist protest against the cruelty of authoritarian regimes.

This chapter stakes out a different position. Chang carried ideological nonalignment and a skeptical anti-humanism from her wartime writing through her collaborations with the USIA and beyond. Her reliance on equivocal contrast and desolation persists during her career in exile. If in the 1940s she considers authentic and inauthentic versions of Chinese culture not to be in stark opposition, in the 1950s her work shows Communism and anti-Communism to be impossible to disentangle. Although ideologues would have us believe that one must choose sides, Chang finds that stories and therefore political commitments continually intermingle, making it difficult to keep one's categories firm and entirely separate. Chang's preference for equivocal contrast and desolation became handy techniques as she wrote for different constituencies.

The Rice-Sprout Song tracks a peasant family in southern China as they adjust to life during the Communist Party's implementation of land reform. The novel is partly a response to *The Sun Shines over the Sanggan River* (1948), by

Ding Ling, the Stalin Prize winner who based her novel on actual fieldwork in rural areas. Chang's novel invites comparison to *The Good Earth*, too, especially in its depiction of agricultural land tenure. Chang had a bit of firsthand exposure to rural areas, but mostly she relied on sketchy news items and the reports of defectors to furnish her depiction of food shortages and the Party's consolidation of power in agricultural districts. She even defended the factual accuracy of her fictional accounts by adding prefaces to both *The Rice-Sprout Song* and *Naked Earth*, saying of the former story that it was inspired by the public self-criticism of a Party cadre.[32] Of the latter novel, her preface insists it is based on "real people and their true stories" (xiii). Chang was prescient even if some guesswork was involved: famines during the Great Leap Forward (1958–62) were widespread, resulting in millions of deaths.

The plot centers on a married couple, Gold Root and Moon Scent. Gold Root is a peasant who now owns a field for tilling and sowing, thanks to land reform. He cannot read, but he is immensely proud of the official documents attesting his ownership of the land. He has been decorated as a model worker. His spouse, Moon Scent, returns to the village after a few years working as a domestic servant in Shanghai. She comes home because she believes the Party's propaganda that conditions are improving rapidly in the rural districts, only to be horrified to find that shortages have worsened in her absence. Local Party functionaries have exacerbated the problem in a bid to impress their own superiors, levying a stream of "voluntary" taxes on the people to fund the war effort in Korea. On top of that, informers eavesdrop on every conversation. As conditions worsen, Gold Root and some of the other villagers raid the government granary in search of provisions. He dies of a wound inflicted by security forces during the riot, and Moon Scent kills herself while trying to burn down the storehouse in revenge. It is a grim conclusion to a desolate story.

The novel slips, perhaps in a deceptively easy manner, into the shape of anti-Communist propaganda. Land reform leads to famine and deprivation; Communism relies on authoritarian methods that encourage friends and family members to inform on one another; revolutionary economic and political reform cannot be accomplished without heaping more misery on the people in whose name reforms are carried out. But a patient reading of the novel's subplots reveals that the narrative is not nearly so unequivocal about political allegiances. Similar to Chang's earlier fiction, *The Rice-Sprout Song*'s storylines do not quite stay in place.

At a key moment in the novel, when Gold Root's extended family are slaughtering a pig to cover their contribution to a government food drive, they think back to the period of Japanese occupation. The Communists controlled the region for a while, but they withdrew, leaving the "Peace Army of the puppet government" to occupy the area (129). Periodically, the forces stormed local villages, looking for provisions, male conscripts, and women for sexual exploitation. During one such expedition, the family vainly tried to hide its young people and its lone pig, only for the pig and a young man, Gold Root's cousin, to be requisitioned. The cousin is never heard from again. Thinking back on this episode, the boy's parents wonder if he is still alive, against all odds. First, they worry that he might have been conscripted in the Kuomintang army after the defeat of the Japanese: "If he is still alive he might be fighting for the other side," against the Communist Party, the boy's father remarks ominously. This would be terrible, for the whole family could be branded as traitors. But the mother notes it is just as likely that he had been captured by Communist forces, becoming a soldier in the "Liberation Army." This would entitle the family to special consideration (140). This brief recollection threatens to turn the novel's main anti-Communist storyline inside-out. The Communists do not come off particularly well here, or in the novel as a whole, but neither do any of the alternatives. Japanese imperialists, the anti-Communist Kuomintang, and the Communists themselves are virtually interchangeable as far as these people are concerned.

The novel's main subplot also presents a story of woe and desolation with uncertain ideological coordinates. It involves Comrade Ku, a filmmaker whom the Party sends to the countryside to conduct research for his next project. Ku is a clear proxy for the author. He is tasked with finding an uplifting and ideologically correct narrative with enough tension to sustain a feature-length film. He boards with the extended family of the main characters so as to experience their life. He dispels his hunger and boredom with clandestine visits to town, where he can eat something that offers more sustenance than the ubiquitous thin rice gruel. Finding an idea for a film seems next to impossible in this deprived outpost, until the villagers riot and Moon Scent burns down the granary. Suddenly, their uprising provides the providential raw material for a film, if only he can find the right historical setting and the proper political signposts. Initially, he contemplates moving back the story a few years in time, having the villagers rebel against oppressive landlords, with Communists saving the day. Upon reflection, however, he decides this will not do. The Party issued a directive that stories should not dwell unnecessarily on past struggles but should instead glorify future triumphs. With this in mind, he suppresses the bit about the peasant uprising, turning the saboteur into a former landlord and current Kuomintang secret agent. The Communists step in to save the day, catching the arsonist and quelling the fire before it does much damage to "the people's" grain.

For a work of ostensible propaganda, *The Rice-Sprout Song*'s mood of desolation and its reliance on equivocal contrast suggest that little has changed with the triumph of Communist forces in China. Their principles and policies are to be deplored, to be sure, but there is no suggestion that conditions are measurably worse than those experienced under Japanese imperialism or under the US-backed Kuomintang of the Republican era. Stories with interchangeable villains do not allow for simple, expedient political interpretations. Even Chang's delicate character portraits are unexpectedly complicated for a text designed to vilify the Communists. While the narrative mainly generates sympathy for the starving villagers, Chang cannot help wondering if the local Party boss also suffers throughout the ordeal. After turning the police loose on the protesters, the story's main villain admits, "We have failed. We have had to shoot at our people" (146). Although this moment of introspection does not redeem him in the eyes of the reader, he finally admits some culpability and ponders the nature of the relationship between the Party and its nominal supporters. Similar to her writing on authenticity and the national question, Chang here entertains doubts that even steadfast Party members can be orthodox in all circumstances.

Just as in "Love in a Fallen City," *The Rice-Sprout Song* turns something resembling the proverbial act of God—a surprise attack or a famine culminating in an uprising—into a kind of accidental windfall for a bystander, in this case the filmmaker, Ku. He is at best an accomplice after the fact; he does not participate in putting down the riot, and there is no way he could have foreseen how it might benefit him. Additionally, we know that Communist propaganda materials inspired Chang in her depiction of the Ku subplot, as she notes in her preface to the first English edition of the novel:

> One cold afternoon in the public library in Communist Shanghai, while I was looking through a magazine called *People's Literature,* I came across the confession of a young writer. He had said he had been a government worker in a small town in north China during the spring famine of 1950. When the hungry townspeople got desperate enough to attack the public granary, the local militia had to open fire on the mob. But they kept on trying to steal the grain and the shooting went on all day.[33]

At the time of the insurrection, the writer of this testimonial (much like Ku and even the local Party boss), had great sympathy for the hungry townspeople. By the time the story is printed, however, the writer has recanted, learning the error of his ways, returning his trust to the wisdom of the Party. Chang reports this confession "made a deep impression on me, weighing on my mind until it merged with other things I know of" (vi). Chang tells us *The Rice-Sprout Song* is inspired directly by propaganda stories. The caveat is that endings are prone to rearrangement: Chang turns the confessional, pro-Party impetus of the original story inside-out, showing us the narrative flexibility of propaganda stories.[34] Rather than showing how different these two stories are, Chang's testimony tells us how closely these two narratives resemble one another.

David Der-wei Wang reads the Ku subplot as an allegory about Chang's own uncomfortable position as an anti-Communist hack, highlighting the vulnerability of all writers in the cold war: "She nevertheless managed to work out her own version of anti-Communist literature, a version that has unexpected depths but may not be welcome to the propaganda machine" (*Monster That Is History* 137). Wang preserves Chang's integrity and aesthetic independence by suggesting that her clever version of anti-Communism protests against cold war states that demand propaganda or ideologically approved material from writers. Perry Link, in his introduction to *Naked Earth*, says it with greater emphasis: "It is far-fetched to imagine that the [USIA] distorted Chang's writing" (xii).

I think Wang and Link are correct about Chang's writing not being marred by state sponsorship, but for the wrong reasons. I suggest that Chang's use of equivocal contrast and desolation might lead us to interpret Ku's lucky break as Chang's presumptive lucky break, too. Chang understands the position of Ku, and of the Chinese propaganda writer who inspired this story, because she understands how propaganda could provide writers with opportunities that might not be readily available under other conditions. Writing at the pleasure of large states created limitations as well as new possibilities. Chang was undeniably concerned about the fate of China under Communist Party rule, but she was not afraid to seize the opportunity with USIA to write anti-Communist propaganda in order to reach new readers. Communist rule in China was in some way Chang's opening to an international audience. Instead of reading cultural diplomacy and state-sponsored writing as a function of maleficent political pressures that Chang tried to resist and undermine as best she could, we could admit that cultural diplomacy initiatives created rich ironies that she exploited with her favored literary techniques. On this point, I am in broad sympathy with Mark Wollaeger's main claim in *Modernism, Media, and Propaganda: British Narrative from 1900–1945*, that twentieth-century fiction and propaganda are secret sharers, learning from and influencing one another in contradictory ways. Chang was a writer who grasped the nature of cultural diplomacy and knew how to cultivate its potential before she was recruited to work for USIA.

Double Agents, or Equivocal Contrast Part 2

The spy character hatches from a stray seed in the mind of Ku, the Communist filmmaker in *The Rice-Sprout Song*, growing and blossoming in *Naked Earth* and "Lust, Caution" ["*Se, jie*"] (1979). *Naked Earth* tells a story of the making of a double agent. The protagonist, Liu, is a young cadre who sours on the Party after volunteering for work on land reform. Mistakes and bad luck lead him to the front lines of the Korean War as a propagandist, drilling Chinese soldiers on matters of doctrine. After being wounded and captured by the United Nations forces, he initially tells them he would rather not be repatriated. After some contemplation, however, he goes back on his choice, freely deciding to return to China when given the chance:

> What waited for him at the end of the truck ride through the truce zone and past the Communist lives, he wondered. It would undoubtedly be unpleasant. There would be interrogations and he'd have to write confessions and he'd be punished. [. . .]
>
> But he would survive the punishment. And he would be able to march in the parades and shout the slogans again—he'd shout louder than anybody else. They'd never completely trust him again, of course, but he'd work hard at any job they gave him, study the books, join the campaigns, help to hunt down the saboteurs and counter-revolutionaries when they told him to.
>
> And all the while he'd keep hidden the slow flame of hatred. He'd wait— he was in no hurry now. Ten years, twenty years; his chance would come. As long as one man like him remained alive and out of jail, the men who ruled China would never be safe. They're afraid, too, he thought, afraid of the people they rule by fear. (311)

Liu commits to life as a covert agent without anyone coercing him. He works for no one but himself. He does not need to rely on other parties for help and he does not need to communicate with any organization about his progress.

Liu believes he has the discipline to pull off the deception because he was once a zealous Party member. This passage is reminiscent of *1984*'s Winston Smith, the Party functionary who fancies himself the last man alive because he thinks for himself, even if he cannot act on those thoughts. Smith's nemesis, O'Brien, is also a double agent, and more effective than Smith because he can be a loyal Party operative and an anti-Party rebel at the same time, without any outward signs of strain. *Naked Earth* closes with Liu resolving to bide his time, intuiting that the regime will never rest easy knowing that the kindling of dissent may burst into flames at unpredictable moments. But as with other Chang stories, this conclusion lacks finality. There is ample time for the double agent to switch allegiances, which is precisely what happens in "Lust, Caution."

The short story that became "Lust, Caution," which Chang wrote in Chinese, began life in English as "The Spyring, or, Ch'ing K'ê!, Ch'ing K'ê!" (n.d.). The manuscript indicates that Chang sent the story to McCarthy, her USIA handler, although I have not happened upon any record of "The Spyring" appearing in print during Chang's lifetime (see figure 5.5).[35] The story takes readers back to the days of the Japanese occupation, when the Kuomintang were recruiting agents to infiltrate the puppet government. A young woman (Shahlu Li in "The Spyring" and Wang Chia-chih in "Lust, Caution") becomes the mistress of a traitor, a man who is highly placed in the collaborationist regime. Her job is to win his confidence and then lead him into an ambush. At the very last moment, when the trap is about to snap shut, the undercover agent blurts out a warning to the target, who narrowly escapes. The narrator does not tell us why she balks at the final hurdle. She wonders if she has fallen in love with him (she cannot decide); another possibility is that he buys her loyalties, unwittingly, by purchasing an expensive piece of jewelry for her. Now alerted to the danger, he rounds up the plotters, including her, and has them all executed that very evening.

There are a few notable features in Chang's portrayal of double agents in "The Spyring" and "Lust, Caution." Explaining why the assassination target has his lover killed even though she saved his life by betraying the plot, the narrator concludes that double agents are prone to ideological vacillation:

Since the war began there had been this saying, "*T'eh wu pu fung chia*, special agents are all one family," because they could switch sides with ease. ("The Spyring" 18)

    He could have kept her on. He had heard or read somewhere that all spies are brothers; that spies can feel a loyalty to one another stronger than the causes that divide them. ("Lust, Caution" 52)

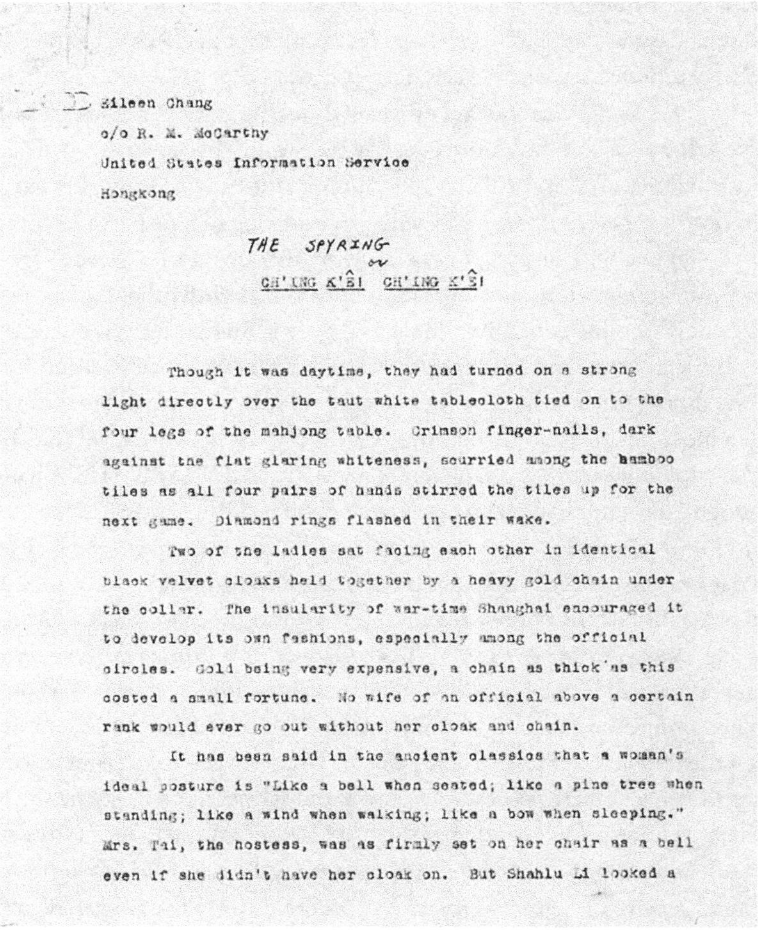

Eileen Chang
c/o R. M. McCarthy
United States Information Service
Hongkong

THE SPYRING
or
CH'ING K'ÊI CH'ING K'ÊI

Though it was daytime, they had turned on a strong light directly over the taut white tablecloth tied on to the four legs of the mahjong table. Crimson finger-nails, dark against the flat glaring whiteness, scurried among the bamboo tiles as all four pairs of hands stirred the tiles up for the next game. Diamond rings flashed in their wake.

Two of the ladies sat facing each other in identical black velvet cloaks held together by a heavy gold chain under the collar. The insularity of war-time Shanghai encouraged it to develop its own fashions, especially among the official circles. Gold being very expensive, a chain as thick as this costed a small fortune. No wife of an official above a certain rank would ever go out without her cloak and chain.

It has been said in the ancient classics that a woman's ideal posture is "Like a bell when seated; like a pine tree when standing; like a wind when walking; like a bow when sleeping." Mrs. Tai, the hostess, was as firmly set on her chair as a bell even if she didn't have her cloak on. But Shahlu Li looked a

FIGURE 5.5. First manuscript page of "The Spyring." Full typescript available at http://www.zonaeuropa.com/culture/c20081005_1.htm. © Roland Soong and Elaine Soong through Crown Publishing Company, Ltd.

The assassination target toys briefly with the idea keeping her on as a lover or even as an agent, now more firmly in his control, but he congratulates himself for being too clever and too pragmatic to let his feelings of gratitude and amorousness interfere with his instinct for self-preservation. Chang's anti-humanist impulses are perfect for representing life in totalitarian environments, where only fools trust other people. The assassination plot's target further rationalizes his decision to have her killed, thinking that is why she fell for him in the first place: "She must have hated him at the end. But real men have to be ruth-less. She wouldn't have loved him if he'd been the sentimental type" ("Lust, Caution" 53). Ang Lee's film adaptation (2007) drives home this point even more emphatically than the story. Chia-chih develops complicated feelings, if not love, for the intended target because he is compromised by his work as a collaborator, just as she is compromised by her work as an agent. She comes to appreciate how it feels to be used as the instrument of a political cause.

There is nothing particularly unusual about Chang's suggestion that double agents lack constant loyalties. Or, to put a finer point on it, the passage from "Lust, Caution" admits that spies have ideological beliefs and causes, but their fellow feeling creates yet stronger bonds. As Erin G. Carlston and Allan Hep-burn each discuss in their studies of spy fiction, the theme of espionage allows writers to show how citizenship, sexuality, and political affiliations shape mod-ern forms of subjectivity. In keeping with her earlier fiction, Chang presents loyalty and disloyalty in other than stark contrast. The protagonist's under-standings of loyalty and disloyalty in "Lust, Caution" cannot be disaggregated from one another. To be authentic or true to herself, she must recognize that her feelings are divided. Chang suggests in these stories that we can learn our true feelings only by crisscrossing the ideological lines created by the national question and the cold war.[36] Staying firmly on one side or another only means being inauthentic, being a caricature. Roughly, this process is what Tina Chen calls "impersonation" and "double agency" in Asian American literature.[37] For Chang, I think the practice of adaptation better explains how crossing ideo-logical and linguistic boundaries are analogous processes, and it is with these ideas that I close the chapter.

Adaptation or Translation?

After seeking refuge in the United States, Chang continued to write steadily, even if her rate of publication slowed. A longtime film enthusiast, she com-posed scripts for and consulted on various movie projects for a Hong Kong studio, as well as doing translations and various odd jobs, including work for Voice of America. But she spent much of her time revising and adapting and rehabilitating stories she had already written in other forms. *The Golden Cangue* [*Jinsuo ji*] (1943), which appeared originally in Chinese, became a decades-long companion: she translated it into English; she expanded it and revamped it in English as *Pink Tears*, a manuscript for which she would never find a publisher; she rewrote the story again, in two languages, serialized as

Yuannu in Hong Kong and Taiwan and appearing as a stand-alone novel in English, *The Rouge of the North* (1967). In her letters, Chang reports that Knopf rejected *Pink Tears* in 1957 because its depiction of Republican-era China was so dreary that it creates the unintended effect of turning Communists into saviors.[38] One basic narrative template—a beautiful woman marries up the social ladder, only to be so bitterly disappointed by her situation that she becomes a termagant—with at least five distinct versions in two different languages. Her lightly fictionalized autobiographies provided another space for incessant tinkering. *The Fall of the Pagoda*, *The Book of Change*, both in English, and *Little Reunions* [*Xiao tuanyuan*], in Chinese, are all part of a sprawling exercise in life-writing, employing a simple narrative scaffolding that allows for endless variation as she changed character names and timelines, added and deleted individual scenes, and switched languages. As with *Pink Tears*, Chang never found a publisher for *The Fall of the Pagoda* and *The Book of Change* during her lifetime, despite enlisting McCarthy's help to place her manuscript.

Although my approach to Chang is informed by debates about literary translation, I do not think translation is quite the right umbrella concept for describing Chang's repetitions as she matured.[39] Chang filled her quota of translation work, but it frustrated her. She complained that political circumstances had further "restricted" the "Western view of China," leading her to conclude that neither anglophone nor sinophone readers had moved much beyond the stereotypes that were prevalent in the early part of the century.[40] The bilingualism of her original fiction, however, cannot be captured fully by the nominal idea of translation. Bilingual adaptation is a better way to describe it. These texts bear a family resemblance, but they are not simple renderings of a unique source text in a target language. The narrative recycling in these late texts is a different manifestation of Chang's early fascination with ambiguity and equivocal contrast: these are texts in constant motion, under threat of erasure and rearrangement, refusing to be pinned down in any one form or language. Her fascination with movement and patchwork remains operative in these various adaptations, but instead of looking forward to an uncertain future, the mature Chang increasingly looks back to a dark past, displaying a gothic streak in novels such as *The Rouge of the North*. After *Naked Earth*, she mostly avoids any representation of Communism in China in her fictional work. In her early stories, we should recall, Chang refused to give in to the pressure to portray China as exotic and illogical. In her later fiction, she similarly refuses to bow to the expectation that she write anti-Communist fiction, returning instead to memories of the Republican era. But even as the overarching message in her late fiction becomes more unvarying, the form of her fiction goes through a series of variations.

This proliferation of forms had both aesthetic and political consequences for Chang's career in the larger context of decolonization and the cold war. This becomes evident in a comparison of *Eighteen Springs* [*Shiba chun*] (1950) and *Half a Lifelong Romance* [*Bansheng yuan*] (1969). Both novels were published in Chinese: the former on the mainland just after the establishment of the People's Republic of China, the latter intended for overseas readers. *Eighteen Springs* originally appeared during Chang's short Communist phase; the novel was serialized in one of Shanghai's Party-approved venues, *Yibao* (not to be confused with *Wen Yibao*). With *Half a Lifelong Romance*, Chang revised *Eighteen Springs* after nearly twenty years. In the interval, of course, she had worked for USIA as a friendly and, just as significant, she had become disillusioned with writing for anglophone audiences. *Half a Lifelong Romance* appeared with Chang's Taiwanese publisher, Crown Press, mainly for readers in the diaspora, as it would not circulate in the People's Republic.

Chang's second version implements aesthetic and political changes on the original, mostly to the closing chapters. *Eighteen Springs* covers a span of eighteen years and ends with the main characters attending a political rally after the Communist victory. Additionally, *Eighteen Springs* brings narrative closure by permitting its star-crossed lovers to find fulfillment in their personal lives. With *Half a Lifelong Romance*, Chang retains much of *Eighteen Springs*, making two major changes: shortening the timeline to fourteen years (thus concluding in 1945 rather than 1949, which wraps up the story before the civil war) and having the major characters remain frustrated in their search for true love. The arc of the plot has the story break off before the Communists come to power, thereby allowing Chang to sidestep any questions about how the outcome of the civil war might affect her major characters.

Like so many of Chang's readers outside mainland China, her translator tells us that the later, non-Communist version of the novel ought to be considered the "authorized" version, in which Chang deliberately suppresses references to major political developments "in order to keep its emphasis on the personal, the psychological and the sensory" elements of the story.[41] Throughout this chapter, I have questioned this approach to Chang's complicated political entanglements. Chang's revisions show that she expected somewhat different reactions from different reading constituencies, but it also demonstrates that she believed she could satisfy those expectations by repackaging virtually the same story with a few crucial adjustments, by keeping the conclusion of the narrative open, not closed. Changing the conclusion is entirely consistent with her use of an aesthetics of equivocation, in which stories end without the finality of tragedy. Rather than read Chang as a nonpolitical writer dragged into political matters against her will, we might come to a better understanding of her dilemmas and choices by thinking of her as a figure who knowingly engaged with cultural diplomacy only to be disappointed by the results, at least during her lifetime. Both versions of the novel belong unquestionably to Chang; neither version is more authentic than the other. Regarding her as ideologically aloof by choice, forced into politics only by circumstances, attempts to measure her career against a modernist standard that is not flexible enough to apply here. If Chang achieved a degree of autonomy through her work, it came through her conscious engagement with cultural diplomacy, not through her repudiation or avoidance of political matters. Her refusal to continue writing anti-Communist propaganda was not simply an outward sign of her inward political inclination, but instead a clear indication of her disappointment with her reception by anglophone audiences. Treating her with due critical sympathy and respect means reckoning with her conscription in the aesthetic cold war, realizing that her work with state agencies limited her room for political maneuver but enhanced her professional mobility. Her flight from China ultimately led to global forms of recognition, even if she did not live to enjoy them.

Finally, we might admit that Chang would be virtually expunged from the record of both Chinese and English literary traditions were it not for the efforts of a small band of readers in the diaspora, especially the influential critic C. T. Hsia, Chang's unstinting champion. For those readers who ascribe near-omnipotence to large states, Chang's case reminds us that neither the United States nor China unilaterally determined how Chang's work would circulate in a global context. Yet neither should we read Chang as a singular writer who resisted state involvement in literature whenever and wherever she could. Chang was a willing participant in diplomacy schemes, even if she was skeptical about their ability to make Chinese culture legible to outsiders.

As I turn to state surveillance and discipline of writers in the next section of the book, I argue that cultural diplomacy programs were counterbalanced by various coercive measures. The most important fact about this period is that virtually all states routinely collected information on writers. Liberal democracies, colonial and postcolonial states (from reactionary to reasonably progressive regimes), and Communist governments took special care to note what writers were doing and saying. As in the case of Chang, I will suggest that the containment/resistance model takes us only so far if we hope to understand how the actions of states impacted the emergence of a global literary field. Writers actively resisted state control of their work, to be sure, but they also responded in creative and unexpected ways to the experience of being monitored and punished.

Part III

6

The Activist *Manquée,* or How Doris Lessing Became an Experimental Writer

IN THE SPRING OF 1956, Doris Lessing, then living in London, visited Southern and Northern Rhodesia, or what is now Zimbabwe and Zambia. She spent much of her childhood and early adulthood in Southern Rhodesia. She left for London at thirty, in 1949, with only a book manuscript, a small pot of money, and one of her children. By the time she visited Rhodesia seven years later, she was an established writer, having published *The Grass is Singing* (1950) to approving reviews. She recorded her experience of returning to central Africa in *Going Home* (1957), illustrated by a travelling companion, Paul Hogarth. Lessing and Hogarth were both British Communist Party (CPGB) members at the time, although Lessing would leave the Party just as she was finishing the book, during the mass exodus of 1956–57. Royalties from Soviet translations of her work helped defray costs for the trip, but she appended a few hasty paragraphs as the book was going to press to say that she had been disillusioned by the Soviet clampdown in Hungary late in that year. She allowed her membership to lapse and became increasingly vocal in her criticisms of the Party.

Going Home provides a journalistic account of Lessing's trip. She spends a good deal of time describing the idiocies and hypocrisies of the color bar, Southern Rhodesia's version of apartheid. She uses her travelogue to attack the Central African Federation, a short-lived, last-ditch effort to stave off decolonization through economic and political union between Nyasaland (now Malawi), Northern Rhodesia, and Southern Rhodesia. Lessing also describes her interactions with a wide range of local notables, from colonial officers and entrepreneurs to White and Black political activists. On a more personal note, the book has strong undertones of an *apologia pro vita sua*: a defense of her pursuit of the life of the mind and her choice to leave behind the slog of progressive politics. As she says, not without regret, "I am an agitator *manquée*." Although she talks of sorely missing the incessant routine of study groups, demonstrations, and meetings in dim, smoky back rooms, she had by then determined "that a writer should not become involved in day-to-day politics."[1] Thereafter, Lessing participated in dozens of progressive movements with donations of time, money, and moral support throughout her life, but she continued to assert the need for creative autonomy in her intellectual life.

Aside from the genres of travel writing and the apologia, *Going Home* leans on the conventions of spy fiction. Admittedly, to call *Going Home* a recognizable instance of spy fiction may be stretching the point: there are no double-agents, moles, betrayals, daring escapes, coded messages, or honey traps. Instead, it is the kind of spy story written by indignant political dissidents who suffer harassment from police agents. In the following passages, Lessing offers a humorous vignette about the experience of being tailed by a plainclothes officer while she and Hogarth traveled through the Rhodesian backcountry. Moments after stopping at a roadside shack so that she can stretch her legs and Hogarth sketch the ubiquitous ads for soft drinks,

> a big car came up along the road the way we had come very fast and stopped with a screaming of brakes, just behind our car. The man in it immediately got out; but he did not buy Coca-Cola. He stood for a moment, looking at the number-plate of our car; then remained standing on the road, looking suspiciously at Paul [Hogarth], who was sitting on his stool drawing, and suspiciously at me. (221)

There are no other White faces for miles around, no other passing vehicles, and the agent makes no attempt to conceal his intentions. Lessing had been seeing his type throughout the trip, so much that she could sense them before she could see them. "But what could the C.I.D. [Criminal Investigation Department] be doing here?" she wonders (221). Are Lessing and Hogarth likely to turn a couple of curious children who have gathered to watch the White strangers buy refreshments into bloodthirsty revolutionaries? Lessing shapes the material into the form of an exasperated joke:

> I think Governments should employ mercenaries for this sort of work; true believers are a bad policy; for there are countries where one can pick out the political police streets away by their look of disgusted and irritated

hatred. This man walked up and down the road for half an hour, looking at
Paul, looking at me, as if he would like to wring both our necks if only there
was a law to permit it. When [. . .] we had got into our car, the man got into
his car. We drove off, but he remained sitting in his car looking after us, and
did not follow us again, though we were driving slowly now, on purpose so
that he should catch us up. (222)

Lessing's brush with the political police works better as farce than as nail-
biting suspense. Lessing and Hogarth know they are being watched and, at
least in this encounter, make no effort to conceal the fact that they know. The
special agent huffs and puffs in irritation, not so much at being caught out, but
at the law that prevents him from committing violence against them. This is
an intelligence operation in a White-dominated, Black-majority colony: White
agent and White dissident eyeing one another with aggravation on one side
and indignation on the other, only for the pair to meet some time later, by
chance, in the bar of the hotel or at a party hosted by a mutual acquaintance.

Given this set piece, it will come as no surprise to learn that Lessing's MI5
file includes a great deal of correspondence between the intelligence services
in metropolitan Britain and colonial territories, including South Africa, Rhodesia, Kenya, even Australia and Zanzibar. From the late 1940s through the
early 1960s, spies were vetting Lessing's travel permits, reading her mail, tapping her phone calls, tracking her movements and visitors, questioning her
acquaintances, peeping at her diaries, and, naturally, reading her publications
and clipping her reviews. Agents watched her in England and when she traveled.
When we recall that Lessing was one of thousands of people under observation,
we might conclude that MI5's network was surprisingly efficient in collecting,
cross-referencing, and disseminating data to agents working around the
world. But we should not then assume that Lessing, or others like her, were
unaware of this attention. Either through sloppiness or with the intent to
intimidate, the state's political police let Lessing know she was under regular
observation.

Lessing is not known for her gripping spy thrillers, but in this chapter I will
suggest that her ongoing encounters with the political police left a sizable imprint on her writing of the 1950s, '60s, and '70s. Two related claims will help
me measure the extent to which surveillance influenced her literary practices.
First, as with Claudia Jones and C.L.R. James, the political police and their
bureaucratic collaborators worked hard to steer Lessing away from colonial
regions and toward metropolitan Britain. The underlying rationale is not hard

to summarize. In southern and central Africa, the intelligence services classified Lessing as a zealot who might foment an insurrection among the oppressed majority. This assumption was wrong, in that Lessing and her fellow White activists had precious little contact with revolutionary Africans, who were scared off by security agents, but this paranoid view persisted. In England, by contrast, she would be easily absorbed as another harmless eccentric. If MI5 and Special Branch had a negative impact on Lessing's writing, it was by making it difficult for her to travel freely. This is especially apparent in *The Golden Notebook* (1962), in which the main character struggles to describe her African experiences. The intelligence services impeded Lessing's ability to move through colonial regions. It impacted her writing about Africa in particular, as *Going Home*, *The Golden Notebook*, and the *Children of Violence* series show.

The second claim is more counterintuitive. Although the political police constrained Lessing's physical movements, they also helped unlock her creative impulses. As Lessing experimented compulsively with form and genre during the 1950s, '60s, and '70s—especially as she flitted between the conventional, realist *bildungsroman*, the experimental fiction of *The Golden Notebook*, and the apocalyptic science fiction of her later career—the international surveillance network came to serve as her model for the revolutionary potential of human consciousness. In the early installments of *Children of Violence*, the state's agents are little more than a nuisance, showing up as quiet observers at political meetings. In *The Golden Notebook*, surveillance systems begin to feature in the form of special psychic powers that unusual, disturbed, or disabled humans may possess. By *The Four-Gated City* (1969), however, the final installment of *Children of Violence*, the spy network provides the imaginative infrastructure for human solidarity in the face of nuclear catastrophe. The human beings who survive the disaster are led by those who have paranormal or visionary powers, especially telepathy. The ability to listen to the thoughts or perceive the feelings of others—to spy—with or without their consent, across unfathomable distances, becomes the primary way humans share information after the collapse of the cold war's international system. A network of intelligent perception transcends barriers of culture, language, and geography. Shorn of political blocs and the straitjacket of social institutions, Lessing's postapocalyptic people cultivate the extrasensory powers that conventional society had coerced them to repress. Seeing distant things, foreseeing future events, communicating with other species, and listening to the thoughts of far-flung people become invaluable skills in this future world.

Home Is Where the Police Are

It is instructive to compare MI5's treatment of anticolonial intellectuals to the FBI's treatment of figures such as James and Jones, who were jailed, prosecuted, and deported from the United States, as I discuss in the next chapter. The British political police exerted much less overt pressure on Lessing, James, and Jones than did the FBI on Black dissidents in the United States. We know that MI5 kept tabs on James and Lessing at various points in time, and the intelligence agency must have compiled a dossier on Jones, although my searches for it have been fruitless. But enhanced scrutiny in the British system did not lead to detentions or prosecutions, as FBI surveillance did for James and Jones, whose dossiers include plans for arrest and prosecutive summaries almost from the beginning. Rather, MI5 preferred to keep Lessing and other anticolonial intellectuals close to London and away from the colonies. This arrangement suited both officials in Rhodesia and South Africa, who campaigned actively to keep agitators out of their areas, and metropolitan agencies, it would seem, who were more preoccupied about collecting information and less worried about the threat of insurrection. As I discuss in the case of Lessing, the political police impacted her primarily by restricting her travel and by letting her know that she was person of interest.

It is equally instructive to compare MI5's treatment of anticolonial intellectuals to their treatment of other metropolitan writers who came to their attention, such as Stephen Spender. James Smith's compelling study of the topic, *British Writers and MI5 Surveillance, 1930–1960*, observes that the British political police had less tangible influence as outright censor or bully than as patron of formerly wayward artists. Spender's stint as editor of *Encounter* was probably facilitated by British intelligence. Other progressive figures such as Cecil Day-Lewis and George Orwell, both surveillance targets, later became useful cogs in the cold war propaganda machine. Smith describes this prostate turn, in which the dissident writers of the 1930s became apologists of the 1940s and '50s, concluding, "it now appears clear that, for many [intellectuals], periods of service with sensitive agencies smoothed the path back into the flock" (157). Co-opting skeptical writers became one of the British state's most effective tactics of containment.

The case, however, is different for anticolonial intellectuals such as Lessing. There was no rapprochement between Lessing and government agencies. Despite her anti-Communist turn, she never made peace with the political establishment and was never recruited by it to serve as an apologist or cultural diplomat. The same is true of James and Jones. The oft-noted tendency of Auden-generation intellectuals to be recuperated during the 1950s simply does not apply to staunchly anticolonial figures, of whatever racial background. James and Jones were not reconciled to the British state not simply because they were Black, but because they remained firmly anticolonial in their views. Neither did Lessing's Whiteness facilitate a mutually beneficial arrangement with the state when her anti-Communist views became pronounced.

Triangulating Lessing's intelligence dossier, her private correspondence, and her published work of the 1940s and '50s offers a composite view of an intellectual whose antiracist commitments led her to the Communist Party but whose aesthetic commitments led her to affirm a spirited nonalignment. Although Lessing and several of her associates in 1940s Rhodesia were sympathetic to communist ideas, there was no functioning Communist Party at that time in the colony. She was a member of many small activist groups in the 1940s, especially during the war, but she did not officially join the Party until she lived in London, in 1951 or 1952. Her membership would last about five years. As a writer, however, she was never much of a Party enthusiast, refusing to leaven her creative work with ideological doctrine. In an interesting twist, the intelligence agencies who watched her were equally exercised by her work as a writer—in which she was liable to criticize British imperialism and racial discrimination in the colonies—as they were by her manifestly political activities on behalf of the Communist Party, which waxed and waned with circumstances and opportunities. Lessing describes herself as a failed activist, but it was her writing, which she always imagined as independent from the cold war's ideological conflict, that continued to raise questions even after her political activities subsided.

Lessing's intelligence file opens in 1943 and trails off in the early 1960s.[2] If there is a clear biographical outline that emerges through the dossier's hundreds of pages, it is that Lessing harbored significant reservations about the Communist Party, but about racism she was implacable and unwavering. Through 1951, there are several exchanges about Lessing between the Central African Security Liaison Officer, the Director General of MI5, and the metropolitan Special Branch (the domestic political police). These early documents describe Lessing as a possible Party member and likely sympathizer who has not done anything to merit special concern. Only in 1951, when a review of *The Grass Is Singing* appeared in the *Daily Worker*, did MI5 take much notice of her activities. By 1952, MI5 described her Party membership as "doubtful" to their counterparts in the Central African office, but went on to claim that "[h]er

FIGURE 6.1. Doris Lessing's Communist Party registration card, 1955, from MI5 dossier.
Image courtesy of the National Archives of the United Kingdom.

Rhodesian background has brought out in her a deep hatred of the colour bar
which has now reached the point of fanaticism."[3] An MI6 report culled from
the same period, written because Lessing was part of a delegation of writers
visiting the Soviet Union, reaches similar conclusions, rating Party membership as unlikely but regarding her views on racism to be "irresponsible" to the
point of saying "everything black is wonderful and that all men and all things
white are vicious."[4] As late as 1955, MI5 were still ascertaining the status of
Lessing's Party membership, reporting to the Central African office that "a
delicate and reliable source" had confirmed that she joined back in 1952.[5] During her trip to Rhodesia in 1956, agents on the ground concluded that during
meetings with African political leaders, Lessing "professed to Communist
Party membership without trying to push the Party line."[6] By 1962, when the
political police were confident that Lessing had broken with the Party, they
continued to categorize her as a person with "extreme left wing views" as an
"avowed opponent of racial discrimination."[7] About Lessing's political beliefs,

at least, the intelligence network was pretty close to the mark. Lessing's enthusiasm for the Party ebbed and flowed during this period, but her stance on racism and British imperialism remained steadfast.

Lessing's file lies dormant for long stretches, springing to life when she traveled internationally or when she published something. The reports on her trip to Rhodesia in 1956 provide some of the most fascinating moments in her dossier. Of course, there is the fairly routine material we would anticipate in police reports: notes about her travel arrangements, the people whom she contacted, descriptions of her belongings, her communications, and notes on her demeanor. But there are also traces of the cat-and-mouse games that are staples of espionage fiction. In a request issued from MI5 Head Office, the authorities in Kenya were directed to sneak a glimpse of Lessing's diary during her return flight through Nairobi. Kenyan agents could not fulfill this order, reporting, "On the plane from Livingstone they [Lessing and Hogarth] were seen to be busy writing all the time, but covered up the pages when anyone passed by."[8] In another set of notes, someone at MI5 asks agents at London Airport to "have a look at the note book which Mrs. LESSING is carrying and get it copied," but only if this can be done without arousing her suspicions. It goes on to warn that Lessing is "an extremely irritated woman" because of all the attention she has received, concluding that "[i]f she has the slightest cause to suspect her belongings are being unreasonably interfered with, she will give the maximum trouble possible for all concerned; the least we can expect is a question in the House [of Commons]."[9] All parties concerned seemed to be in on the secret. As Cristina Vatulescu reminds us in *Police Aesthetics: Literature, Film, and the Secret Police in Soviet Times*, calling the political police a "secret" state agency in totalitarian contexts is oxymoronic, since they continually advertised their extent of their reach and the strength of their grasp.[10] Everyone who was anyone had a file. This was true of the Soviet system, but it also has some bearing on colonial situations, especially in Rhodesia and South Africa, where White dissidents were easy to follow.

Knowing that she was being monitored throughout her trip, Lessing occasionally took steps to throw her pursuers off the scent, or so it seemed to the people assigned to track her movements. Perhaps she was having a bit of fun. In a report to the Prime Minister's Private Secretary, the Rhodesian director of security admits that his agents temporarily lost touch with Lessing and Hogarth in or around Salisbury (now Harare): the pair "are taking a great deal of evasive action and abnormal security precautions to shake off surveillance." As a result, the plainclothes agents assigned to the case "have lost track of them

but hope to pick them up later in the day." The
head of security goes on to plead for more resources: "The difficulties of keeping these very
alert people under surveillance emphasises the
need for a properly equipped Special Branch.
Moreover, even though the C.I.D. are in reasonable touch with the movements of these people it
is not really known what mischief they are up to."[11]
When Lessing was not dodging agents, she occasionally liked to test their mettle by confronting
them directly. Lessing knew there was a good
chance she would be denied entry to South Africa
if she attempted to enter the country—in fact, although she was on the prohibited immigrant list
in Rhodesia, too, she was let in, probably because
the intelligence agencies hoped to learn some-

FIGURE 6.2. Doris Lessing's
passport photo circa 1950s,
from MI5 dossier. Image
courtesy of the National
Archives of the United
Kingdom.

thing from her trip—but she decided to book a flight south anyway. As soon
as she landed at Jan Smuts airport, she reports knowing that "every person in
it is a member of the Special Branch of the police, down to the girl selling ciga-
rettes" (*Going Home* 98). Forcibly returned to Rhodesia on the next flight, she
dispatched a telegram to the Reuters news agency. Hogarth, however, was
admitted, one sign that the local security services were much more concerned
with Lessing than with her travel partner.[12]

There is no evidence that Lessing was directly or indirectly censored, put
on an industry blacklist, pressured to testify in anti-Communist hearings, or
otherwise targeted as were many intellectuals during the high points of the
cold war. The major effects she suffered include restrictions on travel, particularly to central and southern Africa, and the kind of quotidian stress that
comes with knowing that one's actions, communications, and movements are
being monitored. As she says in the second volume of her autobiography, her
every brush with "the famous British secret services—and they have always
been slight—has had this flavour of the farcical, the surreal."[13] She knew the
political police were opening her mail even in London, for instance, but she
claimed it had little effect on her activities. By comparing her situation to more
spectacular forms of political repression during this period, I do not wish to
downplay its effects on Lessing or other intellectuals who suffered a similar
fate. In Lessing's case, I think we can observe the impact of this treatment in
her writing about Africa. In *Going Home*, the dents are like gaping potholes on

the surface of the text. Lessing writes angrily and ironically about the experience of being under regular surveillance. In an epilogue written eleven years later, Lessing says coolly that she "was far too heated by the end of that trip; but being chased around by the C.I.D. and then forbidden entry to the country you were bred in, does arouse emotions the reasonable mind finds an impediment" (299). With hindsight, however, she says she does not regret a moment of it, especially of her belief in the rightness of progressive principles. "[T]he most valuable citizens any country can possess are the troublemakers," those belonging to "ginger-groups" and the defenders of hopeless causes, such as holding the idea of racial equality as a White person in a colonial outpost (316). She reasons that being harassed by the security apparatus of a racist state means she must have been doing something right.

The Golden Notebook, by contrast, records the effects of punitive travel restrictions obliquely. Readers of the notoriously complex novel will recall that Lessing's main character and probable narrator, Anna Wulf, has a biography not unlike Lessing's: published novelist, experience living in central Africa, time in and out of the Communist Party, a divorced woman with a child who has moved to London. Unlike Lessing, however, Anna suffers writer's block. The primary manifestation of this blockage is suggested by the complex form of the novel. "There is a skeleton, or frame, called *Free Women*," in Lessing's own words, "which is a conventional short novel, about 60,000 words long." This frame narrative, however, is broken up with a series of notebooks, appearing in regular order: "Black, Red, Yellow, and Blue," each bracketed by a section of *Free Women*, before the introduction of a new diary, the golden notebook, followed by the end of the frame narrative.[14] The proliferating notebooks are a symptom of Anna's creative paralysis. She cannot bring the various parts of her creative life together, so she segregates them: black for Africa; red for politics; yellow for a life-writing novel; blue for self-analysis, mental exploration, and factual details of her life. Lessing routinely complained that her readers latched on to one section or another, not bothering to relate the parts to the whole.

At risk of repeating this schoolboy error, I am most concerned with the black notebook here, in which Anna records her thoughts about Africa. My point is straightforward: Anna's creative block takes the raw material of a travel ban and turns it into an existential and epistemological crisis. At the end of the first installment of the black notebook, after narrating her wartime experiences in Rhodesia (lightly fictionalized from Lessing's biography), Anna complains that she cannot find the right tone to record these events:

I read this [material] over today, for this first time since I wrote it. It's full
of nostalgia, every word loaded with it, although at the time I wrote it I
thought I was being "objective." Nostalgia for what? I don't know. Because
I'd rather die than have to live through any of that again. And the "Anna" of
that time is like an enemy, or like an old friend one has known too well and
doesn't want to see. (145)

As an artist, Anna finds the problem of narrating her colonial experiences
impossible to solve. Her writing introduces a nostalgia she claims not to feel,
or so she concludes when she rereads her work. The person she describes is
an old and intimate friend turned enemy: watching her own movements and
making a report on them is a painful exercise.

Other fragments of the black notebook strike the same chord in different
keys. In the second installment, Anna entertains proposals that she adapt her
Rhodesian novel, *Frontiers of War*, for television or cinema; she balks at the
thought, not only because she is snooty about these media, but also because
the producers wish to radically change her treatment of the color bar. She rejects their ideas summarily. The third section of the black notebook introduces
a parody of an atmospheric "African" story, "Blood on the Banana Leaves,"
which includes all the overblown stereotypes about a timeless African village.
The story is a bad joke, an attempt to poke fun at racist, colonialist myths that
ends up reinforcing them. In the fourth and final fragment from the black
notebook, Anna's plan to continue using it as a writing diary devolves. Instead,
there are newspaper clippings on "violence, death, rioting, hatred, in some part
of Africa" during the mid-1950s (501). There is only a single paragraph in Anna's own hand, saying that the black notebook is to be closed permanently. If
she were to describe the black notebook's contents, she "would say it was
about total sterility." Besides, she is no longer able to remember how her
friends looked, what they said, or how they acted. "It's all gone," she sums up
her recollections (502). The black notebook takes physical immobility and
turns it into an imaginative impasse. Lessing's inability to travel freely in Africa
is transmuted into Anna's failure to represent her experiences of the region.

Lessing's private correspondence and her fiction also give us some clues
about how the security apparatus misunderstood Lessing's political intentions
and exaggerated her influence. In the intelligence dossier, the state's agents are
convinced that Rhodesia's Black majority is incapable of creating effective
leaders out of their own ranks. With ingrained racism, the political police believed that Lessing and other White troublemakers would suddenly mobilize

huge groups of otherwise docile Africans. A report on Lessing's 1956 visit to
Rhodesia from the Central African security chief says that she "made well over
half a hundred contacts during the time she was in Salisbury," many among
educated Africans. It goes on to speculate that "LESSING was trying to form
a 'cell' amongst these African leaders," although the reliability of the information is in some doubt.[15] Other reports in the dossier assume or conjecture that
Lessing's views and presence would be immediately accepted by disgruntled
Africans, presumably because she was White.

This kind of thinking was well off target. During the war, when Lessing and
her small band of White activists tried to establish firm contact with Black
people who cared about politics, they were thwarted at every turn. In her letters
to "Smithie" [Leonard Smith], Lessing expresses skepticism about ongoing
efforts of a small band of White Communists to force their vision of revolution
on Africans: "If we have learnt nothing else, we have learnt that trying to impose
communism from above is a waste of time." Although the local White press
drone on and on about the influence of the Communist Party, Lessing marvels
at how little their ideas resonate with the indigenous population. Even a couple
of industrial strikes by railway workers, she reports, were events the White
Communists had to watch from afar:

> According to the newspapers, this [strike in 1947] was organised by us; in
> actual fact, it was run and organised by the natives themselves, and a
> damned good job they made of it too. There is a big strike on now again
> [1948]. I dont [sic] know anything about it, except for what I read in the
> papers, for although once again we are supposed to be responsible, in actual
> fact we havnt [sic] had anything to do with it.[16]

According to Lessing's report, White progressives could only watch in admiration or frustration as Black Rhodesians went about the business of political
mobilization. But the spies who watched Lessing were not immune to the
common prejudices of their context. Although they assumed, correctly, that
Rhodesia's Black subjects were discontent with their lot, they took it as an
article of faith that organizational skills were exclusively European traits. In a
perverse twist, the colonial government and intelligence agents could only
attribute disciplined industrial action to a White-led, Communist conspiracy,
failing to credit Black Africans with their own limited forms of political agency.

In *The Golden Notebook*, there is an air of total futility about the prospect of
a cross-racial progressive alliance. Virtually every meeting of the small, White
action group is about "how to draw the African masses into militant action."

The group's political line is simple: Black workers and White workers need to act cooperatively to challenge the status quo. With a White working class unwilling to give up their racial privileges and a Black working class that does not trust its White counterpart, the resulting situation "of what ought to happen, must happen in fact, because it was the first principle that the proletariat was to lead the way to freedom, was not reflected anywhere in reality" (85–86). It is roughly the same, with even greater detail, in the middle installments of *Children of Violence*: the protagonist, Martha Quest, is drawn to Communists and socialists because they are the only White people to oppose the color bar, but because they are utterly isolated from Black political activities, they struggle fruitlessly.[17] Their few Black contacts are probably police agents, anyway. The actions of the security apparatus only reinforced this kind of racial segregation. By recruiting informers among the Black population, and by warning any Black person who met White radicals that they would face repercussions, most Black people were wary of Lessing and her associates. Lessing had far greater freedom to meet with anticolonial intellectuals in London, where Special Branch and MI5 noted her contacts with Black African activists as well as figures such as Cheddi Jagan, leader of Guyana's People's Progressive Party.[18] As a political activist, Lessing's influence on the anticolonial movement was negligible.

The particularities of this situation mean that Lessing had far more political clout as a writer—despite refusing any suggestion that she use her fiction for propaganda purposes. Her letters from the late 1940s are more or less resigned to some version of Communism as a political necessity, but she was convinced from the beginning that the Communist Party was trying to push the aesthetic genie back into the bottle by force rather than cunning. As early as 1945, she reports to Smith that she is "off the party line badly" but remains "prepared to continue to work for the party wherever I am provided I dont [sic] have to worship blindly at all their shrines."[19] In another long letter to Smith in 1947, Lessing tries to explain why Communists "should understand that the creation of works of art are so hazardous, difficult and obscure, that there should be no fetters whatsoever on their artists. [. . .] But dont [sic] misunderstand me [. . .] I have no hopes whatsoever that communist parties will be so tolerant."[20] As she announces plans for her migration to England in a letter to John Whitehorn, she pledges to stay out of the Party when she arrives: "I shall not join the party in England. Shall remain a fellow traveller. It's no good joining the party when I can't endure half the things they do."[21] She changed her mind, of course, becoming a member a little over two years after arrival. And her correspondence with members of the Soviet literary establishment, begun after her visit, gives the impression of someone who willingly and enthusiastically joined the Party.[22]

Things changed quickly after the Soviet invasion of Hungary. On the back side of a stint in the Communist Party's writers' group, Lessing told E. P. Thompson that the events of 1956 provided something of a relief: "I feel as if I've been let out of a prison."[23] Trying to reconcile her literary practices with her political affiliations had become tricky. As Matthew Taunton points out in a recent essay, Lessing had serious doubts about the Party's attitude toward writers yet joined anyway. She was well versed in the Party's uncompromising stance on art. Throughout this period, she struggled to hack a way out of this creative thicket. Longstanding resistance to aesthetic doctrine, Taunton says, encouraged Lessing "to circumvent the Cold War opposition between realism and modernism" by asserting "a place for artistic autonomy" against Party doctrine.[24]

Alongside the Communist Party, the global British spy network is an underappreciated witness to Lessing's creative development, especially as she tried to navigate between a socialist aesthetic theory, to which she felt some ideological affinity but artistic antipathy, and a metropolitan experimental literary tradition she admired but hoped to move beyond (Marcel Proust being, probably, the writer she adored most of all). Undermining her political activities and restricting her travel, the political police kept track of her written work throughout this process. When she published a novel or premiered a play, they were sure to add the reviews to her file. This service to literary history continued for about five years after she left the Party. Figure 6.3, for instance, is an intercepted letter about Lessing's involvement at a Campaign for Nuclear Disarmament event.

The details of the image are not easy to understand out of the context of the intelligence dossier. The letter itself is a reply to a request for information about the Campaign for Nuclear Disarmament, intercepted by MI5. What catches the eye are the handwritten notes. The notes are the numbers of the MI5 files for each of the people named in the letter as campaign supporters, most of them writers of one sort or another. J. B. Priestley and his spouse and collaborator Jacquetta Hawkes, C. P. Snow, John Braine, Arnold Wesker, Alan Sillitoe, Iris Murdoch, John Wain, Shelagh Delaney, Cecil Day-Lewis: a diverse cross section of British writers active in the early 1960s. As writers, these figures have very little in common other than the attention they received from the political police. If Lessing's case is typical, we can infer that a copy of this

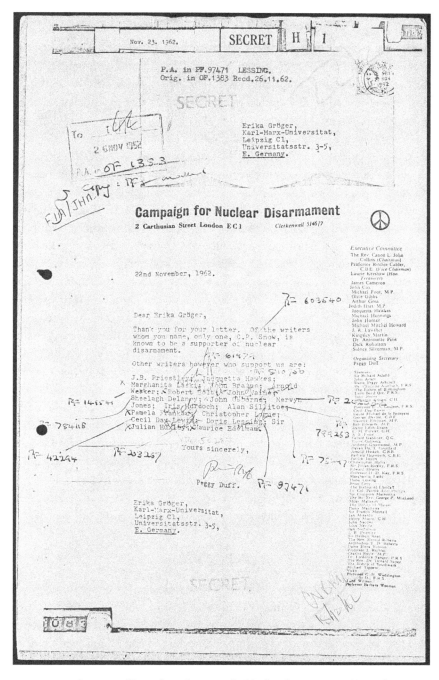

FIGURE 6.3. Intercepted letter from Campaign for Nuclear Disarmament, November 1962, with handwritten cross-references to intelligence file numbers of Lessing and other writers in attendance. Image courtesy of the National Archives of the United Kingdom.

letter made its way into the files of each of those listed here.[25] From the evidence gathered in Lessing's dossier, we learn that the conjunction of the cold war and decolonization brought intellectuals newfound scrutiny from the political police. Writers mattered to the state in a way that would be difficult to fathom in the current climate.

Despite being a target of an active, intercontinental monitoring program, Lessing did not turn to what Richard Hofstadter famously called the paranoid style or the conspiracy narrative common to some postwar writers, notably Orwell, Muriel Spark, and Thomas Pynchon. Lessing felt the presence of the political police in her life, acknowledging it frankly in her writing. But she was also a committed anticolonial thinker who believed that authoritarian measures were part of the normal functioning of imperialist powers. Unlike some of her peers who regarded the existence of domestic spy networks as comparatively new, and as an outrage against liberal democratic principles, Lessing understood this to be one of the predictable and longstanding effects of imperialist controls. The cold war may have increased the range and sophistication of intelligence operations in Britain and its sphere of influence, but Lessing understood that recruiting informants and gathering intelligence had been part of subjugating unruly populations for decades. Perhaps because of this difference in outlook and experience, Lessing began to see the spy network not only as an imminent threat to progressive activities, but also as a model for human development in the nuclear age. Circumventing or outmaneuvering the political police would require ordinary humans to become more like spies. As she turned from the realist *bildungsroman* of the first four installments of *Children of Violence* to experimental fiction in *The Golden Notebook* and then to science fiction, Lessing began to reconceive intelligence work as a set of sensory powers that could be put in service of human survival.

Oedipal Spy

In *The Golden Notebook*, the character Tommy most resembles an intelligence agent. Tommy appears primarily in the *Free Women* sections, or what Lessing calls the conventional frame narrative of the novel. Elsewhere, I have likened the *Free Women* sections to a parody of domestic fiction.[26] Using ordered, restrained prose written from the perspective of a third-person narrator, these sections describe the life of Anna (the main character), Anna's friend Molly, and Molly's complicated family, consisting of her son, Tommy, her ex-husband, Richard, and Richard's second wife, Marion. Tommy, in his late teens and early

twenties, lives with his mother, Molly, for most of *Free Women*.[27] Tommy tends
to get lost in scholarly discussions of what is, by any measure, a long and complicated novel. When noticed, he is typically regraded as an ominous character, a young man who worries his parents and frightens Anna.

Yet Tommy's life, even more so than Anna's, provides the major plot points
of *Free Women*. The adults fret about Tommy, but for different reasons. Richard, a wealthy business executive, thinks his son is drifting, aimlessly, wishing
Tommy would take a position in his company. Molly, by contrast, supports her
son's self-exploration but harbors concerns about his depression and anxiety.
Anna, for her part, believes Tommy judges those of her generation for their
lack of direction and loss of firm convictions (set in the late 1950s, *Free Women*
shows the devastating effect of 1956 on old Party members such as Molly and
Anna). Tommy, Anna thinks, is unrealistic about his parents' generation, expecting them to stand firm on their principles even as their world disintegrates
around them.

Tommy's suicide attempt, at the end of "Free Women: 2," changes the entire
shape of *The Golden Notebook*'s narrative skeleton. He shoots himself with a
revolver, but survives. He nearly makes a full recovery but loses his sight permanently. In one of the earliest scenes of the novel, Anna, with a premonition
of what would come later, compares him to a blind man: "once she had sat
opposite a blind man on the train [. . .] and so had his eyes been, like Tommy's
even when he was looking at someone: as if turned inwards on himself" (33).
Tommy's likeness to the blind, even before his self-inflicted wound, represents
for Anna a deficiency, his willful inability to see or understand other people.
He has the selfishness, the self-absorption, and often the certitude of the
young. He cannot understand another person's point of view, least of all Anna's. This irritates her.

Only a few hours before his suicide attempt, Tommy and Anna have a
showdown. He demands to examine her notebooks—the four notebooks or
diaries she keeps—none of which she permits other people to read. In the
midst of an edgy discussion in her flat, Tommy walks over to her notebooks
and picks them up, looking them over skeptically. She longs to forbid him from
touching them, but an inexplicable force checks her: "She could not endure
that anyone should see those notebooks and yet she felt that Tommy had a
right to see them: but she could not have explained why" (253). For some
reason, Tommy has a hold over her. The ensuing scene has all the qualities of
a fractious and lengthy interrogation, full of bluster and accusations on his side
and defensiveness on hers. Her suspected crime: failing as a writer.[28]

Tommy begins by asking Anna the question on every reader's mind: why does she keep four notebooks, instead of one? A feeble defense of "I don't know" is all Anna can muster. Tommy presses her for a response, insisting there must be a reason and she must know it. One notebook would be a disorganized "scramble," "a mess," she offers by way of explanation (254). Tommy rejects this idea, replying that messes ought to be permissible in a writer's diary. She should accept the disorder of her life and times instead of trying to straighten up things. Anna realizes she is falling apart under the intense scrutiny of her best friend's son: "She wanted to laugh, to cry, even to scream; she wanted to hurt some object by taking hold of it and shaking and shaking until—this object was of course Tommy" (254). After a brief interruption, the line of questioning resumes. Increasingly frustrated by her vague and unsatisfactory answers, Tommy lashes out: "'Why aren't you honest with me Anna?' This last phrase he positively shrieked at her; his face was distorted" (260). Anna continues to wilt under his gaze, "terribly exposed, [...] remembering the intimacy of what she had written" in the notebooks about Tommy and others (260).

Doggedly, Tommy continues the questioning about her notebooks, asking why she writes things in different kinds of handwriting, or why she grants certain kinds of observations importance and downgrades the significance of other things by striking through the prose. Again, she says she does not know, and again Tommy insists on finding a better answer. Pressed, Anna admits that she suppresses and marginalizes "mad flashes" and violent fantasies by placing these in brackets and sometimes crossing them out altogether, while notes about doing the shopping and cooking meals for her daughter are written in solid, measured script that sticks to the page (261). Anna reasons that the events of her daily life are real and therefore true in some way, while her "mad flashes" are temporary psychological lapses, part of her bundle of neuroses, totally unconnected to the humdrum world of domestic chores. Again, Tommy rejects her flimsy reasoning. Anna loathes conventional people, such as Tommy's father, but these notebooks show her desire for a tidy world to be just as strong as any bourgeois fantasy of comfort and social order. She claims to want to experiment, to open herself to all forms of knowledge and experience, but the way she arranges the notebooks shows this to be a complacent lie. "If things are a chaos, then that's what they are," Tommy insists; dividing herself and her writing into careful compartments—censoring herself, in other words—is another example of self-deception (262). In a spirited moment, Anna accuses Tommy of snooping in her flat, reading her notebooks when she goes on errands. By this point, alert readers will think back to

Tommy's introduction to the narrative, when he eavesdrops on a conversation between the main characters before properly walking onstage (31). Tommy unapologetically concedes that he lets himself into her flat and reads the notebooks in her absence. Like the intelligence agencies, he assumes he has the right to see anything he deems materially relevant. The interrogation concludes only when Anna offers a "small self-accusatory smile on her face," which placates her questioner, who nods with "a sort of malicious triumph" (264). Shortly after this exchange, Tommy almost kills himself.

There are a couple of noteworthy features of this interaction. It is one of a handful of moments in which *The Golden Notebook* makes a forthright attempt to explain the text's unconventional form. Although this scene has the hallmarks of an interrogation by the secret police—in generic terms, it would not feel remotely out of place in *Darkness at Noon* or *1984*—it pursues a line of questioning about aesthetic structure. For her questioner, the diaries do not encode some self-incriminating fantasy of revolution or resistance. The diaries do not record seditious thoughts or disclose a secret network of contacts. Instead, as Tommy correctly intuits, these jumbled notebooks are all about the problem of how to tell a complicated story. They are about censorship and self-censorship. Politics dance around the edges of the exchange, but Anna's interrogator is mainly preoccupied with her unwillingness to experiment with her writing as she experiments with her life. Outwardly, she preaches nonconformity and free thinking, but aesthetically she sticks to old-fashioned, utterly conventional ways of ordering her material. Secretly, Anna wonders if Tommy is correct, which is why she increasingly regards her successful novel, *Frontiers of War*, as an artistic failure: she now finds the book too staid. It is the political police, or their stand-in Tommy, who forces the matter of aesthetic form out into the open. Even though Anna thinks Tommy of average intelligence, he understands the novel's formal successes and failures better than most readers. As an interrogator, he does not make the mistake of reading for plot: when everyone is dishonest, it is the form of the exculpatory narrative that will reveal the hidden truth of the matter.

Additionally, the structure of the interrogation scene ought to heighten our awareness of the ironical nature of the content. Tommy, playing the role of the political police, accuses Anna of censoring herself. Anna's crime, as it were, is playing it too safe as a writer, sticking too close to some sort of objective reality, which Tommy regards as a bourgeois myth. With respect to the blue notebook especially, in which she records materials about her psychoanalytic sessions, Tommy accuses her of suppressing the terrifying things she feels and overrepresenting mundane events with no emotional content. Aesthetically, she has renounced the kind of free thinking she and Molly have been preaching to Tommy all his life. For her part, Anna puts up a token defense against these charges. Writing needs form, even if life does not, she seems to protest. In a switch that defies all the conventional wisdom of the cold war, it is the writer who begs for stricter oversight of aesthetic forms—censorship, we might say—and the interrogator who insists that such restraints place artificial limits on expressive freedoms. This might seem a curious reversal, but as I have argued in chapter 2, anticolonial writers were some of the toughest censors of the cold war period, importing the logic of state control of the arts into debates about authenticity and national form. What I call the aesthetic cold war included not only the standoff between aesthetic autonomy and aesthetic utilitarianism, but also the debates about cultural authenticity and hybridity. These debates shaded into one another, as Tommy's interrogation reveals. Tommy, I wager here, gets the better of his exchange with Anna, and the rest of the novel bears out this reading. In the red notebook, Anna complains extensively about self-censorship in the Communist Party, while in the black notebook, as I have already considered, she worries about her inability to represent her experiences in Africa. Tommy likewise regards the blue notebook as a failure of the imagination, and Anna reaches the same conclusions after being confronted by him. At just about the time when she and Tommy have their exchange, she condemns her work in the blue notebook: "So all that is a failure too. The blue notebook, which I had expected to be the most truthful of the notebooks, is worse than any of them" (448). When we finally reach the golden notebook, the new diary that replaces the four we have been reading, Anna seems to agree that prescribed aesthetic forms limit her. She increasingly forgoes the comfort of segregating her experiences into separate notebooks, resolving that the value of aesthetic hybridity is worth the risk of formal chaos. In *The Golden Notebook*, the intelligence agent liberates the writer from censorship, not the other way around. As we know from her thoughts in "The Small Personal Voice," Lessing argues that the aesthetic realm should not abide by the cold war's labels and formal categories, which seek only to limit the creativity of writers.

Tommy's role as a spy does not end with his suicide attempt. After recovering in the hospital, he returns to his mother's home. He seems more at peace with himself. He strikes up an odd relationship with his stepmother, his father's neglected second wife, Marion. Now blind, Tommy develops a powerful "sixth sense," aware not only of the presence but of the thoughts and intentions of the people around him (360). Before the accident, Anna would drop by Molly's house on the thinnest of pretexts, just to socialize; after the accident, Anna's visits become infrequent, and she stops calling on the telephone altogether because Tommy acts as an uninvited participant, answering questions posed to Molly about him before the sentences are even finished. Molly feels tormented by her disabled son, who knows where she is, what she is doing, and what she thinks before she herself does: "'I could scream with irritation,'" Molly reports. "'And the thing is, I have to leave the room because I know quite well *he* knows I'm feeling like that and . . .' She stopped herself. Then she made herself go on, defiantly: 'He enjoys it'" (362). Anna, too, feels threatened by Tommy, but she reckons it is something very different from the kind of bullying he did before his accident. "No, he's not mad," she thinks to herself, "but he's turned into something else, something new . . ." (386). Her thoughts trailing off, she cannot quite articulate what is different about his condition. The probing questions and hysterical accusations are gone, replaced by a deep knowledge of other people's movements, thoughts, even desires. He no longer needs to interrogate people because he collects information continuously. Tommy's new powers, Anna vaguely realizes, are ones of intelligent perception. The physical injuries he has sustained have made something new out of him, or broken his form, to use the language of the novel itself.

If we think about *Free Women* with Tommy as a leading character, we can read his story as an Oedipal drama played slantwise. Tommy does not yearn for carnal knowledge of his mother, or even his mother's friend. Instead, peeking at Anna's notebooks reveals to him something he cannot bear to see. He and Anna remain haunted by the image of him poring over her diaries. He wants, not a sexual knowledge, but instead to know whether Anna has the courage and honesty to put her political beliefs into aesthetic practice. He concludes that she does not, and this seems to disturb him greatly for reasons we never fully understand. Unlike Oedipus, however, Tommy does not experience a tragic fall. The form of his story, like his body, is broken apart and recombined into something new and strange. Molly concludes, paradoxically, that the young man is "all in one piece for the first time in his life," the incident making him whole, rather than deformed (362). If anything happens to him, it is a kind of confirmation or intensification of what was there before. Instead of a tragic purge, there is a diagonal thrust, an evolutionary development along an unforeseen track. Before his injuries, he actively seeks knowledge of Anna's literary activities by rummaging through her things and by questioning her. He wants her to confess her crimes and shortcomings as an artist and as an ex-Communist; he suspects things, but he demands confirmation from her. After blinding himself, he no longer feels the need to pursue this type of knowledge: he senses these things, or intuits them, without recourse to the normal methods of surveillance and questioning. He is a spy who no longer needs to snoop around or to interrogate suspects.

Thinking about *Free Women* from Tommy's perspective also forces into view Lessing's fascination with people regarded by conventional medicine as physically and emotionally disabled or sick. Anna both dreads and wishes to emulate this young man whom she believes has mutilated himself. After his injuries, he opens himself to impressions and experiences that he could not readily perceive in his former state. There is something patronizing and ableist about this—Anna's perspective seems to rely on the old-fashioned notion that blind people are able to develop an almost superhuman sense of hearing or smell to compensate for their lack of vision—but in another respect Lessing seems eager to pursue the idea that most people learn to ignore their intuitions and inborn extrasensory powers because they rely too heavily on reason and their five primary senses. Tommy learns or cultivates a skill that all of us possess, in other words. Ato Quayson's category of "aesthetic nervousness" aptly describes Tommy's place in *Free Women*'s narrative.[29] Anna is troubled by him, obsessed with him, and cares for him all at the same time. More important, this disabled character temporarily occupies the center of a narrative that does not seem to be about him, if most of the critical readings of the novel are to be believed. He forces Anna to think in new ways about her writing. As Tobin Siebers argues, disability became "a unique resource discovered by modern art and then embraced by it as one of its defining concepts."[30] *The Golden Notebook* combines this "disability aesthetics" with a belief that the political police were influencing the development of literature during the cold war.

Space Fiction

Lessing's interest in what she called space fiction, or what might be called speculative fiction nowadays, has been difficult for literary historians to satisfactorily explain. For many fans of *The Golden Notebook*, this turn was hard to countenance. But as Michael Trask shows in *Ideal Minds: Raising Consciousness in the Antisocial Seventies*, the barrier between the literature of ideas (which is how I would categorize *The Golden Notebook*) and science fiction was quite porous in and around the 1970s. Trask argues that both the literature of ideas and science fiction pursued compatible and mutually reinforcing techniques for describing subjectivity, developing a theory of personhood that relies on the supposedly limitless powers of cognition and the possibility of enlarging and enhancing human consciousness. In comparing science fiction novelist Philip K. Dick and highborn poet James Merrill, for instance, Trask shows how the latter's masterpiece *The Changing Light at Sandover* presents "supernatural entities" who enjoy "unlimited access to everyone's thoughts"—similar to the characters populating Dick's fiction.[31] Not only heightened thinking, but paranormal forms of perception, became a prominent way of aestheticizing the possible development of human species-potential in the 1970s. Likewise, in *The African Novel of Ideas: Philosophy and Individualism in the Age of Global Writing*, Jeanne-Marie Jackson observes that the novel of ideas depends in part on expanding the space for individual thought: such novels grant ideas and consciousness "a force and even an ontology of their own by a turn to narrative designs that advance individual integrity, as against porosity or dissolution."[32] Lessing's experiments in speculative fiction take this injunction about strengthening rather than winnowing subjectivity literally. With these insights, we are in a better position to see how Lessing's generic promiscuity fits into a broader web of literary movements of the postwar years. Add to this Lessing's pronounced anticolonialism, her longstanding interest in psychoanalysis and Sufism, and the experience of being a target of state surveillance, and it becomes a little easier to regard Lessing's swerve into science fiction as less a tangential dead-end and more a widening of her creative options.

Taken as a group, the novels of the *Children of Violence* series are part of a lengthy but recognizable *bildungsroman*, so much so that Lessing herself was a bit defensive about their putatively realist form. In the afterword to *The Four-Gated City*, Lessing describes the series as "what the Germans call a *Bildungsroman*," as if the loan word had not made much headway into English. "This kind of novel has been out of fashion for some time," she reports, but we should not therefore conclude "that there is anything wrong" with this type of fiction (655). The series conforms roughly to the template of the colonial coming-of-age narrative identified by Jed Esty in *Unseasonable Youth: Modernism, Colonialism, and the Fiction of Development*: a main character who feels hopelessly stuck, or ruthlessly stranded, between the rigid temporal logic of capitalist development and the messy social geographies of colonial difference. By the fifth and final novel of the series, however, the narrative of *bildung* starts to go strange. *The Four-Gated City* takes us beyond a recognizable cold war present into a postapocalyptic future in which small bands of humans survive in far-flung habitable zones. Lacking modern communications infrastructure, these groups stay in loose contact with one another through telepathy and other senses unrecognized by modern science. To put this in another way, the narrative problem of development, one of the key concepts in the *bildungsroman*, shifts from the material to the psychological plane.[33]

The Four-Gated City begins by transporting Martha Quest from central Africa, where she spends the first four volumes of *Children of Violence*, to the London of the 1950s. The atmosphere is tense and the mood dour: rationing continues five years after the end of the war, bomb damage remains visible everywhere, and the cold war has begun, rife with rumors of espionage programs and treason. Martha takes a job working for Mark Coldridge, an industrialist and part-time novelist. One of Mark's brothers, by coincidence, is a Cambridge physicist who leaks scientific secrets to the Soviet Union and then defects. Martha's employer and eventual lover, Mark, who refuses to denounce his brother, becomes a target of the security apparatus. First, the agents sent to talk to him ask politely about his brother's acquaintances; then, they pose more persistent questions about Mark's political affiliations; and finally they hint that Mark himself might provide a valuable service if he were "prepared to become an agent for Britain, whether a member of the Communist Party or not." At this, point, Lessing encourages us to have a laugh at this imaginary Englishman's expense. He is outraged by the insinuation that he could provide information on family or friends. The arch narrator momentarily steps back from the action:

> There is a certain kind of Englishman who, on learning that his country (like every other) employs spies; or (like every other) taps telephones, opens letters and keeps dossiers on its citizens; or (like every other) employs policemen who take bribes, beat up suspects, plant information, etc.—has a nervous breakdown. In extreme cases, such a man goes into a monastery, or suffers a sudden conversion to whatever is available. (181–82)

Mark's breakdown includes a brief fling with Communist ideas, but eventually he affirms his nonalignment: neither organized Communism nor Britain's blend of capitalism and imperialism are the way forward. His allegorical novel, *A City in the Desert*, becomes a guidebook for how to imagine a better, simpler world beyond the cold war's ideological standoff. A poor man's Albert Camus, Coldridge becomes a reluctant guru for various British nonconformists who are looking for a way to resist the state's increasingly authoritarian measures.

Just when the novel appears as if it will use the same basic narrative patterns as the first four texts in *Children of Violence* (Martha's next youthful infatuation leading to rebellion and then to a more sober wisdom), the novel suddenly veers onto an altogether different path. Midway through the story, Martha begins to hear the inner voices of the people around her. The feelings of Mark, Mark's family, and Martha's friends start to invade her consciousness. Confused, then alarmed when she realizes what is happening, she resists the urge to use this new power: "At first she tried not to [listen to the thoughts of others]. Good heavens, it wasn't far off eavesdropping" (370). Within a few days, however, she realizes that Mark's estranged wife, Lynda, has been battling to manage strong telepathic powers her whole life. In and out of mental institutions, her mind clouded by powerful drugs, Lynda has been telling Martha of her condition for years, but Martha simply could not understand her. When it finally clicks with Martha, the pair become inseparable, Martha honing her new skills under the guidance of an experienced mentor:

> Martha was certainly a radio: so was Lynda. Martha was a television set, only, unlike a television set, not bound by time. She was a camera: you could take pictures of any object or person with your eyes, and bring it out afterwards to examine it—that is, depending on how you had concentrated when you looked at it. What else? (501)

Reminiscent of Christopher Isherwood's *Goodbye to Berlin* and Dziga Vertov's *Man with a Movie Camera*, Lessing's protagonist imagines herself as a telepathic machine and information storage device, able to receive words, images, and ideas transmitted by other people. Mark Goble's observation that modernist writers claimed the powers of media technologies as their own is certainly relevant when we try to make sense of this passage, as is Marshall McLuhan's foundational recognition that as new media extend the communicative powers of people, these new media also change, fundamentally, the people using them. Martha's sensory powers, like television and radio and photography, change her, make her into a different kind of person. But as the later sections of *The Four-Gated City* suggest, the cold war relationship between writing and other media is not simply a two-way process. A third factor, the intelligence network, shapes how Lessing represents the relationship between expanded consciousness and media technologies.

As Martha sharpens her telepathic talents over the latter half of the novel, we learn that another member of her social circle is wandering along the same tracks. Mark Coldridge's business partner, Jimmy Wood, it turns out, is a science fiction writer, enthusiastic researcher in occult knowledge, and cybernetic genius all rolled into one. For about a decade, the polymath Jimmy had been experimenting with machines that could enhance the sensory powers of humans. Scouring old manuscripts about witchcraft, alchemy, and other forms of esoteric knowledge, Jimmy is on the verge of a breakthrough in developing "a machine, or device, for stimulating, artificially, the capacities of telepathy, 'second sight,' etc." (532). He graduates from testing the machines on animals to testing them on people. The British government provides clandestine support for this work, and we learn that the Soviets are conducting experiments in the same field. The possibilities for improving intelligence work and military efficiency are beyond the wildest dreams of the cold war's main antagonists. The only difficulty: Jimmy's machines, rudimentary as they are, tend to destroy the minds of the people on whom they are used. To perfect these ESP devices, Jimmy and his government backers need an inexhaustible supply of humans whose sacrifice to scientific progress will not raise a cry of protest. Like the Nazis, they turn to mental hospitals and asylums.

In other words, Jimmy and Martha are drawn into a different sort of cold war arms race. Extrasensory powers, rather than bigger, more destructive nuclear devices, are the goal. Martha develops her extrasensory powers as a part of her self-cultivation. Although she is idealistic and progressive in her politics, she has no idea, at least at this point, that such powers may come in handy as tools of resistance. She does it because she wants to learn more about herself. Jimmy, on the other hand, is the ultimate mad scientist who lacks any sort of conscience or ethical awareness. He is by no means an evil person—the text consistently describes him as affable and kind to others—but his pure, disinterested pursuit of knowledge does not permit him to examine the ethical consequences of his research. He naively, improbably believes that his discoveries will benefit the human race, regardless of how his experiments are conducted or how his findings will be utilized.

The main narrative ends at this point, in about 1969, right when the novel is first published. There is an element of suspense: will Martha's discoveries enable the progressive political movement to harness telepathy and other recondite senses to create a force powerful enough to challenge oppressive national governments, or will the leading cold war states use secretive research into the paranormal to tighten the security apparatus and bring the last refuseniks to heel? A few appendices, some written from thirty years in the future (roughly the year 2000), give us some clues about how this battle of wills between militarized states and dissident telepaths was resolved. Around 1970, we are told, things became openly authoritarian in metropolitan Britain, a "vast interlocking systems of spies and counterspies," where private letters were "opened, telephones tapped, dossiers proliferated" (622–23). Against them, a scattered band of hippie-like dropouts, including Martha, begin to imagine "the possible dent in this structure made by a group of people with ordinary telepathic powers" (623). The realization that "a significant proportion of the population had various kinds of extrasensory powers—not as a theoretical possibility but as a fact"—convinces them that if "human beings themselves were growing [. . .] powers which could make all this machinery useless, out of date, obsolete," humanity itself might be preserved in some form (622–23). Only a better, more efficient network of intelligence, wielded by ordinary people, can outmaneuver the political police and their surveillance network. At some point during the 1970s there is a nuclear holocaust—whether by a series of accidental leaks or through open warfare it is difficult to tell— making huge swathes of the earth's surface uninhabitable. Widespread radiation accelerates the development of ESP among children born after the disaster.

Nuclear fallout splits the cold war world asunder. Functionaries of the old national governments retreat to underground bunkers to wait out the nuclear winter. Nonconformist groups such as Martha's, meanwhile, find relatively habitable places (such as the west coast of Ireland, where prevailing winds carry the most intense radiation away from them) where they can reconstruct a simple life of hunting and gathering. They have intermittent telepathic contact with other small human settlements scattered across the globe. In Martha's community, none of the children born since the disaster have developed physical deformities, but most of them have second sight or second hearing, and occasionally both. In her group, the seven children with both second sight and hearing are revered by the community:

Well, what distinguishes them from the others [those with no ESP or only one or type]? There's nothing you can measure or count, but we all feel it, and particularly the other children. For one thing, they are grown up— no, not physically of course, but mentally, emotionally. One talks to them as if they were adult—no, not that; one talks to them as if they are superior to us . . . which they are. They all carry with them a gentle strong authority. They don't have to be shielded from the knowledge of what the human race is in this century—they know it. I don't know how they know it. It is as if—can I put it like this?—they are beings who include that history in themselves and who have transcended it. They include us in a comprehension we can't begin to imagine. These seven children are our—but we have no word for it. The nearest to it is that they are our guardians. They guard us. (647)

These children, physically fit and healthy by all observable measures, have begun a new chapter in evolutionary history. By developing human consciousness, these children have become more-than-human. Even the adults see themselves as inferior to these special children. They exceed familiar forms of humanity in their sensory powers, of course, but they also "include" human history in themselves and somehow "transcend" it. These children are charting a new path of development. Development of the material or economic world—along capitalist or Communist lines in a cold war context—has led to nuclear disaster. Development in *The Four-Gated City*'s postapocalyptic world will be psychic and evolutionary, involving an enlargement of the sensory organs. This turn of the story resembles what David T. Mitchell and Sharon L. Snyder call "narrative prosthesis:" formal devices "that expand options for depicting disability experiences."[34]

These superhuman children, of course, have brought the powers of the surveillance network—reading thoughts, understanding feelings, interpreting motives, forecasting events—into the fold of consciousness itself. Martha describes them as the guardians of this community, superior to the old version of humans in every way that matters. They guard, watch, and forecast without government backing, military budgets, or technological gadgets.

If the concluding sections of *The Four-Gated City* help us see connections between different aspects of Lessing's career, as she shuttled between realist *bildungsroman*, the novel of ideas, and speculative or science fiction, the novel also gives us tools for understanding how the aesthetic disagreements of the cold war were reformulated by anticolonial writers. The acting censor was not always and not only the state. The aesthetic choice offered by the major cold war antagonists was for Lessing a losing proposition. Breaking the form of the novel led her to push beyond the fictional boundaries demarcating personhood. Of all the writers considered in this book, Lessing is probably the one most influenced by the political doctrines of the Communist Party (Alex La Guma being the other obvious candidate) and most repelled by socialist aesthetic theory.

Likewise, politically progressive futures imagined by midcentury writers were not always and not only determined by the world's material and social limits. Thinking beyond the polarities of the cold war could involve a kind of generic impulsiveness and restlessness that pressured the forms fiction might take. Lessing's fiction discards the conventions of representing consciousness found in both socialist writing and in experimental high modernism. She takes this process a further step in *Canopus in Argos: Archives*, her next fictional series. For instance, in the first installment, *Shikasta: Re: Colonised Planet 5* (1979), the basic narrative of the *Children of Violence* series becomes only one brief segment of an intergalactic race to colonize the planets.[35] Observed from the perspective of a more advanced alien species, major events of the twentieth century, such as decolonization and the cold war, become short but interesting narrative digressions in a story of immense duration and interplanetary scope. What surprises most, perhaps, is her reliance on the intelligence network as her model of how consciousness or sentience will evolve. In contrast to *1984*, which regards state surveillance as the ultimate tool of oppression and control, *The Four-Gated City* concludes that only by mimicking the powers of the political police will ordinary humans reclaim some measure of independence and freedom. *Shikasta* suggests that higher forms of consciousness, likewise, will be based on advanced powers of observation and communication. Lessing proposes to decolonize the mind, to borrow Ngũgĩ's apt phrase, rather literally, through acts of evolutionary development that cannot be anticipated or controlled by large states.

7

Caribbean Intellectuals and National Culture: C.L.R. James and Claudia Jones

IN JUNE 1957, two FBI special agents knocked on the door of Audre Lorde, an aspiring poet in her mid-twenties studying library sciences at Hunter College in New York City. The FBI had opened a file on Lorde a few years earlier, in 1954, during her studies and travels in Mexico, where she met several expatriates already under surveillance. As Lorde reports in her biomythography, *Zami: A New Spelling of My Name* (1982), the progressive enclave was welcoming but cautious of newcomers, knowing full well that the FBI had informants in place.[1] The 1954 FBI report from Mexico states that although Lorde herself disavowed the Party, she leaves "the impression of following the Party line in conversation."[2] For the next few years, her file is pretty thin, only flagging her subscription to the *Daily Worker*. Yet something about her and her associates held the FBI's attention, for in 1957 they wanted to talk with her directly, not summoning her with a threat of prosecution, but instead making a proposition that she provide information about her acquaintances. In *Zami*, Lorde says that the FBI had come to ask her about some of her friends as early as 1952, but she refused to provide much information (121–22). The FBI file tells a story that differs in the details but not the essentials. In the 1957 report, Lorde invited the special agents into her home and "was friendly during the interview, but would not cooperate with the FBI to the extent of informing on her friends. She stated she was never a member of the CP and wondered why the FBI was interested in her for this work."[3] If you listen hard enough, you can hear E. M. Forster somewhere in the background cheering this news, the fellow queer writer who would rather betray nation than friend.

More than twenty-five years later, Lorde would write "Grenada Revisited: An Interim Report" (1983), in which she excoriates the United States government for invading the Caribbean island and overthrowing the People's Revolutionary Government, all in the name of defeating international Communism. Lorde took the invasion personally: although born and raised in the United States, her mother was Grenadian and her father was probably Barbadian, although Grenada is also cited by many as his place of birth. As she reports in her essay, she visited Grenada for the first time less than a year before the 1979 regime change, which replaced a "wasteful, corrupt, and United States sanctioned" government with a progressive, independent leadership which improved education, expanded social services, and reduced unemployment in its short tenure.[4] The US government insisted that the island needed to be purged of Communist infiltration, especially of hard-to-find Cuban agents, but as Lorde points out, this flexing of imperialist muscles has a long history in the Caribbean: "This short, undeclared, and cynical war against Grenada is not a new direction for american [*sic*] foreign policy. It is merely a blatant example of a 160-year-old course of action called the Monroe Doctrine. [. . .] Thirty-eight such invasions occurred prior to 1917 before the Soviet Union even existed" (181). Anti-Communist rhetoric merely provides cover for US imperialism, which preferred weak client states to independent, self-reliant neighbors. While the US government deemed the People's Revolutionary Government a Communist front, Lorde reads it as the cornerstone of an independent, nonaligned Caribbean nation and as a sovereign Black republic: "In addition to being a demonstration to the Caribbean community of what will happen to any country that dares to assume responsibility for its own destiny, the invasion of Grenada also serves as a naked warning to thirty million African-americans. Watch your step. We did it to them down there and we will not hesitate to do it to you" (184). Lorde reinterprets official statements of anti-Communist intent as the paternalistic jingo of US imperialism supported by a deeper pattern of White supremacy.

Returning to the middle decades of the twentieth century, when the FBI first watched and then courted Lorde, this chapter wonders how fraught encounters between the US political police and Caribbean intellectuals influenced the evolution of anticolonial thought as the struggles of the 1930s morphed into the cold war. I follow William Maxwell's observation that "*the FBI helped to define the twentieth-century Black Atlantic, both blocking and forcing its flows*" (*F.B. Eyes* 179). Carole Boyce Davies and Mary Helen Washington also guide my handling of intelligence files.[5] As Lorde's writing and comparatively slender dossier show us, awareness of the political police as a force of repression and cooptation helped shape African American letters throughout much of the twentieth century. Maxwell and Washington point out that the FBI and the US State Department actively managed the movement of African American intellectuals during this period, restricting some from travel abroad while keeping others safe distances from the United States. This had a direct impact on the most important nonaligned gathering of Black Atlantic intellectuals, the 1956 *Présence Africaine* meeting, which was attended by James Baldwin and Richard Wright, but from which W.E.B. Du Bois was barred. Du Bois's letter of salutation to the conferees reported that any Black attendees from the United States had the tacit approval of the government, or at least some departments within it. Du Bois was not altogether wrong: Baldwin and Wright both had connections to the CCF and Wright to the State Department, which means that they were being watched closely, too, as Maxwell demonstrates.[6]

The political police made comparable efforts to track the movements of the Caribbean diaspora, members of which spent time in the United States and participated in African American literary circles. In Lorde's case, I suggest that her brush with the intelligence services, which must have made her cognizant that her movements were being scrutinized even as she was offered a chance to collaborate, increased her awareness of her roots in the Caribbean and the political significance of this connection in the context of the cold war. First, her staunch defense of the People's Revolutionary Government as an autonomous, nonaligned, progressive expression of Grenadian self-determination— as opposed to another Caribbean beachhead for international Communism— replays the personal drama of surveillance and collaboration at the level of international politics. Her insistence that Grenada be allowed to manage its own affairs without being coerced or bribed by US imperialism or Soviet internationalism follows analogically from her individual experience of being recruited to inform on her acquaintances. The tendency to regard anticolonial nationalism as the only viable expression of autonomy for colonized peoples reflects a belief that neither of the cold war superpowers could fully appreciate or respect the desires of colonized people. Second, Lorde's interest in drawing direct lines of connection between US imperialism and the continuing oppression of African Americans shows a heightened sensitivity to the strength and durability of US hegemony. She regards the cold war United States, with its political police and its fondness for toppling independent governments, as merely the latest chapter in a long-running story about the subordination of Black people in the Americas.

The FBI's approach of Lorde in 1957 came during a period of surveillance and repression of Caribbean activists and intellectuals under the guise of anti-Communism. The two main subjects of this chapter, C.L.R. James and Claudia Jones, were monitored by the FBI throughout the 1940s and deported from the United States on political grounds in the 1950s. Although James and Jones were both from Trinidad, and both spent large chunks of the 1940s in New York City engaged in radical political causes before being detained on Ellis Island, they were political opponents before leaving the United States. Jones was a proverbial card-carrying Party member, at least from the late 1930s to the mid-1950s, emerging as its leading expert on the special exploitation of African American women. Meanwhile, James was a revolutionary socialist, but he was an unstinting critic of Stalinism and therefore on the Party's blacklist. James describes the mutual animosity between himself and the Party coming to a head during his confinement at Ellis Island, where he was bundled into a cell with a band of Stalinists: "[T]he Communists knew me personally as their open and avowed enemy. I had written or translated books against them, which had been published in England, in France, and the United States. They knew me well and [. . . t]he reader of this book will not need to be told how deep in me is the revulsion from everything they stand for."[7] Although the US government tossed them into the same camp of subversives, James and Jones believed fervently that they were on opposite sides of the barricades throughout the 1940s.

The shared experience of being spied upon, incarcerated, and deported from the United States, however, softened the potential for mistrust between them by the time they had washed ashore in London. They both became strong advocates of national autonomy in the Caribbean, subtly but meaningfully drifting away from their support for international socialist revolution as the best remedy for lingering European and growing US imperialism in the region. In the 1930s, James and Jones, using different approaches on account of their political affiliations, tended to see the struggle for racial justice in the Caribbean and southern United States as part of an international, revolutionary, and broadly socialist movement. James's research on Black uprisings and Jones's study of African American women's experience make that clear enough. Without ever definitively renouncing their shared interest in socialist revolution, however, by the 1950s the pair were more inclined to emphasize the cultural and political singularity of the Caribbean. Both James and Jones turned to the cultural particularity of the Caribbean as a place of refuge from the cold war's ideological partisanship. Partly because the US government refused to recognize the differences between them as legitimate—James's plea that he be granted US citizenship because he was a rabid anti-Communist was firmly rejected—and partly because the Communist Party of Great Britain failed to regard Jones as a useful asset, the duo found less of ideological substance to divide them by the mid-1950s. Although they did not become close associates, they moved in overlapping circles and lent their support to the same causes in London.

The respective prosecutions of James and Jones brought them together in yet another unexpected way: as intellectuals and as writers. The surveillance files amassed on each of them, and the prosecution cases against them, continually emphasize the importance of their published words, over and against their concrete political deeds. James recalls that when he appealed to the US Immigration and Naturalization Service (INS) to remain in the country, the department's letter of rejection mainly listed the titles of his publications, as if they alone were enough to deport him. The FBI files on Jones quote from her written work at great length, almost to the exclusion of other materials. Again, Maxwell provides useful guidance here, noting that the Bureau often took African American writers more seriously, as writers, than just about anyone else. In the case of a scattered group of Caribbean intellectuals, however, the selective but attentive readership of the political police had the unintended consequence of creating new tactical alliances out of old animosities. The experience of being monitored through a combination of misplaced US patriotism, aggressive racial profiling, overzealous anti-Communism, and rabid fear of intellectuals brought James and Jones together, as thinkers and writers, under the broad banner of anticolonial nationalism. The political police sometimes deflected rival streams into the same Black Atlantic channels.

In noting that James and Jones became more supportive of national self-determination and cold war nonalignment during the 1950s, and less clearly identified with international socialist revolution, I am situating them in the broader context of the anticolonial movement during this period. This involves a significant revision of Paul Gilroy's Black Atlantic paradigm, which hinges on the incompatibility of national culture and internationalism. By contrast, this chapter contends that many intellectuals of the Caribbean and African diaspora pressed for cooperative, nonaligned forms of national culture in the spirit of Bandung.

James and Jones were part of a cohort of scattered Caribbean intellectuals who recognized the potency and salience of national aspirations. Jan Carew, Aimé Césaire, Frantz Fanon, George Padmore, and Sylvia Wynter are part of this story, too, supporting inclusive nationalist movements during the 1950s. Fanon's widely cited essay, "On National Culture," originally delivered at the second *Présence Africaine* conference in Rome (1959), makes the most passionate and succinct case for national autonomy as the fullest expression of the anticolonial movement: "We believe the conscious, organized struggle undertaken by a colonized people in order to restore national sovereignty constitutes the greatest cultural manifestation that exists" (178). Fanon, who incidentally and not altogether improbably believed he was being watched by CIA operatives, states that the project of cultural autonomy and national political sovereignty are inseparable. There are many reasons for this shift of emphasis, including US aggression in the region, the inconstancy (or cynical opportunism) of Soviet support for decolonization, the articulation of cooperative nationalism at the Bandung meeting, the hopes and frustrations stoked by the West Indian Federation and its spectacular collapse, the "departmentalization" of Guadeloupe and Martinique, the Cuban Revolution, and the tangible success of nonaligned movements around the world. To this short list I add the experiences of the Caribbean intellectuals who lived in the United States, with its conformist atmosphere and coercive pressures. The ordeal of being spied upon and disciplined as part of this global war of position made a small but noteworthy contribution to the development of an anticolonial national culture in the Caribbean. Through their travels in the United States especially, Caribbean intellectuals learned to appreciate the limited objectives of national sovereignty as a cultural and political project. To state the matter more bluntly: diaspora facilitates a desire for national culture under certain conditions. The cold war's centrifugal forces produced centripetal aspirations among the Caribbean's scattered intellectuals.

Intersectionality

Jones was an early proponent of intersectional social analysis before it came to be theorized as such. This quality of her thought comes across most clearly in her research on African American women who work in domestic service, conducted for the Communist Party USA (CPUSA) in the 1930s and '40s. In "An End to the Neglect of the Problems of the Negro Woman!" (1949), Jones considers the special difficulties borne by working-class women of color. The pamphlet duly notes the statistics from the Department of Labor, which show that a higher percentage of African American women seek paid employment than White women, and for far lower wages, congregating especially in the informal labor market. She calls this the "super-exploitation" of African American women.[8] The vulnerability of African American men contributes directly to this situation, leaving women to make up the pay gap in Black families. Jones moves on to discuss racial chauvinism and the myths created by White supremacy: the common belief that Black women do not have technical skills or professional ambitions; that they prefer the deeply offensive "mammy" role assigned to them by White society; that they are difficult to unionize because they often work in casual occupations. By contrast, Jones argues that African American women are in leadership positions in many of the community organizations to which they belong, making them proto-militants. She calls on the Party to properly organize this segment of the working class before the Trotskyites and social democrats do so.

Although the pamphlet reproduces much of the familiar Party jargon from the period, it differs from standard Communist fare of its moment. By identifying the super-exploitation of African American women, as I have already suggested, Jones was pushing the Party to recognize that the labor movement could be a diverse assemblage, not a one-size-fits-all political movement. Jones was leagues ahead of the pack in this regard. She reserves some of her most severe criticisms for the Party itself, which has been painfully slow to recognize the untapped potential of African American women for the labor movement. The pamphlet begins on this very note:

> This neglect has too long permeated the ranks of the labor movement generally, of Left-progressives, and also of the Communist Party. The most serious assessment of these shortcomings by progressives, especially by Marxist-Leninists, is vitally necessary if we are to help accelerate this development and integrate Negro women in the progressive and labor movement and in our own Party. (3)

Although Jones was among the inner circle of the CPUSA throughout the 1940s, she was hardly a blind follower who avoided self-criticism. Much of the booklet continues in this vein. Jones closes by saying that "progressives must acquire political consciousness as regards her [African American women's] special oppressed status" (19). It was not a plea the CPUSA hierarchy ever seriously entertained, and within a few years the fallout from Stalin's reign would further thin the ranks of an organization already ravaged by anti-Communist persecution. But if her status as an Afro-Caribbean woman made her something of an anomaly in the context of the United States, it was utterly foreign to the British wing of the Party, which never accommodated her talents.

Person of Interest, Part 1

The FBI amassed a hefty file on Jones, coming to over one thousand pages, of which some eight hundred are now available through Freedom of Information Act requests. As Washington says, the FBI tended to be "[f]ar more enterprising and thorough than most literary historians," and this is certainly evident in the Jones dossier (126). The file opens in February 1942.[9] Jones came to the attention of the Bureau through the Party's newspaper, the *Daily Worker*, which announced her leading role in the Young Communist League. Almost all the information drawn from this first report is culled from her appearances in newspapers, starting as early as 1937. At this point, the special agent who opened the file knew little about her, except her name or alias, rough age, putative race, and how she is mentioned in the print sources.[10] This report includes only a rumor about her place of birth: she is "said to have been born" in Virginia, although it is not clear who says this. It would be another four years and seventy or eighty pages of documentation before the agents working on her file concluded that she was probably born in Trinidad in 1915, coming to the United States in 1924 to join her parents, and nearly another year before they were certain about the matter.[11]

The reliance on periodical reading increases, dramatically, as the pages of the Jones file accumulate. For instance, the lengthiest report from the early part of the file, coming to twenty pages, is virtually all quoted material taken from articles and pamphlets mentioning or written by Jones.[12] The first section of the report establishes her position in the Party by combing through the Young Communist League *Review* and *Spotlight*, its successor, which Jones edited. The report's second section takes up the question of Jones's knowledge of the revolutionary aims of the Party, documenting this by quoting a six-page extract from an article by Jones that appeared in *Political Affairs*, the Party's monthly magazine. The agent preparing the report felt this material was insufficiently conclusive as a sign of Jones's revolutionary intent, so the report adds more than a dozen further passages attributed to Jones, drawn mostly from the *Daily Worker* between 1935 and 1947. The report also includes a tiny amount of information from operatives and informants who witnessed her at rallies and public events, but the overwhelming mass of evidence captured here is written material.[13]

A few years later, probably in 1951, the first "prosecutive summary" assembled by a special agent appears in her dossier.[14] Jones, along with more than a dozen others, was charged with violation of the 1918 Smith Act, which limited speech or teachings critical of the government. As in the detailed reports from early in the files, the FBI's prosecutive overview, which would be redrafted and expanded as her case progressed, is a piece of extensive research, relying less on confidential informants, wiretaps, surveillance photographs, or other methods of spycraft than on the skills of archivists and librarians.[15] It is 111 pages in length with forty exhibits. The prosecution's star witnesses, it turns out, are the head librarian of the New York Public Library and the Librarian of Congress, who would be called upon to furnish all the exhibits and most of the expert testimony.[16] The exhibits are all choice selections from periodicals, mostly the *Daily Worker*.[17] A list of informants, with names redacted, is included in the first version but disappears in a later draft, making it clear that the political police regarded her case primarily as a matter of literary interpretation.[18] The desire to protect informants, undoubtedly, encouraged the FBI to shield them from public scrutiny whenever possible, although prosecutors did not always heed this recommendation: when Jones was brought to court, a few informants did take the stand. The FBI file, however, is hardly the stuff of cloak-and-dagger espionage or even courtroom denunciations. If the cold war is often remembered for spygames, elaborately choreographed show trials, and public hearings, the less dramatic but most effective harassment of dissident intellectuals happened when the political police recruited the help of librarians.

After serving over nine months in prison with several of her codefendants, most notably her close friend Elizabeth Gurley Flynn, Jones was deported.[19] Technically, she arranged to leave the United States voluntarily in order to avoid a standing deportation order. Rather than go to Trinidad, then a British colony, she arranged to go to the United Kingdom. We have every reason to believe that the FBI and State Department supplied information to their counterparts in the British government, encouraging them to steer her away from the Caribbean. Her FBI file contains a report that the British consulate visited her in prison about her travel documents. The consulate reportedly told Jones that she would not be barred from Trinidad, but "the British Government did not welcome her return."[20] The FBI's legal attaché in London continued to provide sporadic reports after she arrived in London, and it is likely, although not certain, that the FBI and MI5 shared information about Jones

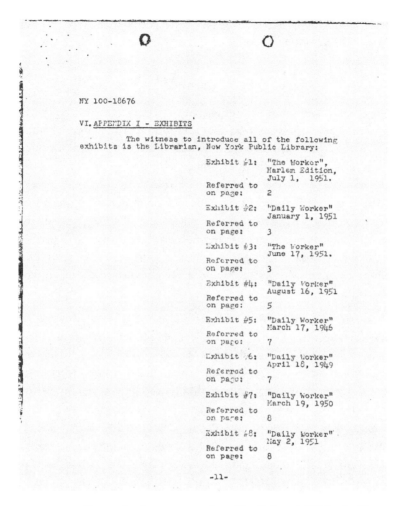

FIGURE 7.1. Prosecutive Summary, 1951, from Claudia Jones's FBI dossier. The witness for the prosecution was head librarian of the New York Public Library.

through the 1960s.[21] James also reports that he "once caught a glimpse in a United States Immigration Office of a file of papers two or three inches thick dealing with my activities in England" during the 1930s (*Mariners* 154), a dossier that is now available for public inspection, at least in part. The deflection of Jones away from Trinidad and toward metropolitan Britain, it is worth underlining, was at least partly determined by the British state. In an interesting twist, the expansion of Jones's knowledge of the Caribbean diaspora led her to become more dedicated to the project of developing the national culture of the West Indies from overseas.

Gazetteer and Carnival Impresario

As her biographers report, Jones was not embraced warmly by the British wing of the Party when she settled in London.[22] As a divorced woman, as a Black, colonial person, and as a commanding orator—with a North American accent to top it off—who had been critical of the Party for assigning Black women subordinate roles in the struggle, the relationship was never likely to be straightforward. Her perspective on imperialism was not shared by her comrades in the British Communist Party (CPGB), and she was not afraid to confront them with her opinions. While attending the twentieth-fifth Party Congress in 1957, she delivered a statement calling on members to renounce imperialist attitudes and make alliances with the anticolonial movements:

> If, therefore, in my first Party Congress, I, in turn address you on the theme of greater solidarity with the struggles of colonial peoples, and with the coloured workers and peoples in Britain, you will understand that it stems from the first-hand experience and confidence that this Party of ours, the British Communist Party, has within its capacity to make this turn—a needed turn. [. . .] It is not a very wise tactic to seek to allay disquiet, uneasiness and dissatisfaction [of colonial subjects] by telling those whose experience has taught them otherwise, that they are foolish, or to dub them as backward. [. . .] The backward peoples of China and the backward people of Czarist Russia were the first to throw off the old regimes [. . .] while the technically advanced peoples of Western bourgeois democratic tradition are still steeped in the mire of backward imperialist ideology. And now India is following suit. The anti-imperialist struggle of the backward, mind you, Afro-Asian nations, from Egypt to Ghana, are today leading the progressive anti-imperialist ideological struggle. [. . .] Let us learn a few things from these so-called backward people. [. . .] In their new world historic unity of Bandung [. . .] they will know how to defend themselves against the threat of a new imperialism—they will not be in any mood to substitute new masters for old.[23]

For a first-time delegate, Jones was shockingly direct with her comrades, on whom she calls to abandon their racist presumptions. White Communists ought to learn from the nationalist struggles in Africa and Asia, which have accomplished far more than metropolitan Communists. Black and Brown peoples provide models for advanced revolutionaries and self-aware proletariats, while their western European counterparts lag behind: it is the metropolitans who operate with a "backward imperialist ideology." She calls on the Party to make a "needed turn" towards solidarity with Black metropolitan workers and colonial subjects. This emphasis clearly builds on her experiences with the CPUSA, which she believed did not do enough to bring African American women into the fold. Although Jones received some general support for her position, she left the conference believing that the CPGB was saddled with imperialist baggage it could not shake off easily.[24]

While Jones never publicly renounced the Party, even as droves tendered resignations in 1956, she increasingly dedicated herself to serving the Caribbean diaspora. In 1958, shortly before the violent confrontations in Notting Hill, London, and Nottingham (in which young White men attacked people of African descent), she began the monthly newspaper the *West Indian Gazette*, later renamed the *West Indian Gazette and Afro-Asian Caribbean News*. In 1959, following the suggestion of an audience member at a community meeting, she helped organize the first Carnival celebration in London.[25] It was to these endeavors she devoted most of her remaining energies.

In metropolitan Britain, Jones is probably best known not as a Communist dissident but as Carnival visionary and as the founding editor of the *Gazette*. Unlike some of the state-sponsored, international periodicals I consider in previous chapters, the *Gazette* was a scrappy, locally distributed affair, appearing somewhat irregularly because of financial difficulties. It had no regular sponsor, certainly not the Party; Jones seemed to keep it afloat with erratic support from friends and a bit of advertising revenue, which was patchy at best.[26] Jones could afford to compensate neither her contributors nor herself, yet she used her extensive network to cover the important events of the decolonization process. Amy Ashwood Garvey and Paul Robeson were among the influential friends who helped her secure interviews and audiences with leading political figures of the day, such as Jomo Kenyatta, Norman Manley, and Martin Luther King Jr. In addition to political affairs, the *Gazette* kept abreast of cultural developments, with reviews of the latest publications from Black Atlantic writers. Several Windrush Generation novelists were contributors and collaborators.

The first issue of the *Gazette* clearly announces the paper's support for the decolonization struggle around the world and for West Indian Federation in

FIGURE 7.2. Claudia Jones reading the *West Indian Gazette*. Image courtesy of
New York Public Library.

particular. "West Indies Federation" (March 1958) outlines the paper's position on the move towards national autonomy:

> We affirm, like other great African and Asian peoples, our spirits too have
> caught the contagion of national independence. And that nothing less than
> that achievement will satisfy us.
>   The *West Indian Gazette* supports Federation. In common with the vast
> body of West Indian opinion, we see this step as a first, halting but unfailing
> new step towards national independence for the Federation and a complete
> self-government for its units.[27]

After her deportation from the United States, Jones's political orientation did
not change entirely. She remained a supporter of the causes she had espoused
during her years as a Party organizer. But she strikes a different note after she
moved to England, reflected in the *Gazette*'s coverage of Algeria, the Congo,
Cuba, Ghana, Kenya, South Africa, and the West Indian Federation. In each
of these situations, Jones declared herself and her constituency to be on the
side of national liberation struggles.[28] The Bandung-inspired inclusion of
"Afro-Asian and Caribbean News" on the masthead may have been suggested

RETHINKING NATIONAL CULTURE   193

by her collaborator and romantic partner, Abhimanyu Manchanda, an Indian Communist, but it was certainly consistent with the paper's political outlook. Strong nationalist movements in the colonial world, whether aligned with international Communism or not, earned her backing. As this editorial from the first issue of the newspaper shows us, Jones did not see the movement for national autonomy in the Caribbean as antithetical to Black Atlantic, transnational solidarity, but instead as complementary poles of the decolonization struggle.[29]

Similar to the more celebrated Caribbean intellectuals Fanon and James, Jones believed that political autonomy for individual nations could be enhanced by cultural activities. Although few of her comrades in the CPGB showed interest in the popular entertainments of working-class people as a means of political mobilization, Jones believed that celebrations of Caribbean culture would augment the quest for political sovereignty. To this end, she became the driving force behind the first Caribbean Carnival celebration in London, in the winter of 1959. Her efforts were extraordinarily successful, given the limited resources with which she worked. For five years running, until her death, she was one of the main organizers. BBC television broadcast live from at least the first two events. The committee convinced leading musical and literary personalities to participate: the calypso star Mighty Sparrow was the main attraction in 1962, while diverse writers and theater personalities, such as Jan Carew, Joan Littlewood, George Lamming, John Osborne, Andrew Salkey, Sam Selvon, and Sylvia Wynter judged talent and beauty contests (Schwarz 274–75). After a one-year hiatus in honor of her death, the Carnival celebration gradually evolved into an outdoor event at the end-of-summer bank holiday, now reportedly the largest street fair in western Europe.

The souvenir guide to the first Carnival event includes a short essay from Jones, "A People's Art Is the Genesis of their Freedom." The provocative title signals the political intent of the gathering. If that were lost on some of the participants, Jones declares that this community showpiece should be regarded as a determined response to the events in Notting Hill and Nottingham, "binding West Indians in the United Kingdom together as never before" to ensure "that such happenings should not recur."[30] She goes on to reinforce the sentiments of her title:

> If then, our Caribbean Carnival has evoked the wholehearted response from the peoples [. . .] in the new West Indies Federation, this is itself testament to the role of the arts in bringing people together for common aims

and to its fusing of the cultural, spiritual, as well as political and economic interests of West Indians in the UK and at home.

A pride in being West Indian is undoubtedly at the root of this unity; a pride that has its origin in the drama of nascent nationhood. (166)

Jones believes the "drama of nascent nationhood" will be performed on Carnival stages as well as through political movements. The West Indian Federation is the political manifestation of a cultural particularity, with the establishment of the former securing the autonomy of the latter. Jones here advocates nationhood as a cultural condition and as a political project: a non-exclusive nationhood, in full sympathy with other expressions of national culture, but nationhood nonetheless. In *Beyond a Boundary* (1963), James famously makes a comparable case for the importance of cricket in developing West Indian national culture.

My presentation of Jones lingers on the national question in order to clarify the status of internationalism in the context of the aesthetic cold war. Gilroy's *The Black Atlantic* is unambiguous in declaring that the intellectual tradition he studies is fundamentally incompatible with expressions of national culture (he is particularly critical of British cultural studies and African American studies): "In opposition to [. . .] nationalist or ethnically absolute approaches, I want to develop the suggestion that cultural historians could take the Atlantic as one single, complex unit of analysis in their discussions of the modern world and use it to produce an explicitly transnational and intercultural perspective" (15). Brent Hayes Edwards makes a similar point, with more finesse, when he writes, "black internationalism is not a supplement to revolutionary nationalism, the 'next level' of anticolonial agitation. On the contrary, black radicalism necessarily emerges through boundary crossing—black radicalism *is* an internationalization."[31] Michelle Ann Stephens, along the same lines, studies the creation of a "global vision of the race that superseded and transcended black nationalist discourses" in the first half of the twentieth century.[32] Davies, in her groundbreaking work on Jones, emphasizes her transnational, diasporic experiences—which makes her a "deportable subject" in her formulation.

My position in this chapter is deeply indebted to, and broadly sympathetic with, these readings of the Black Atlantic and anticolonial movements as international in character and operations. Jones's experience of diaspora—conditioned in no small part by the actions of the political police and her expulsion from the United States—shaped her belief in the value of the West Indian Federation as an articulation of political sovereignty and cultural unity. In emphasizing the internationalist dimensions of Bandung-era Black radicals, however, the Black Atlantic model sometimes underestimates the extent to which international dispersal produced longing for national culture through the channels of diaspora. Such visions of national culture were not exclusive and reactionary, as Gilroy would have it, but cooperative and progressive, at least in their ideal articulation. For Jones, as for Fanon, James, and Padmore, securing national autonomy built a solid foundation for international collaboration, while boundary-crossing experiences facilitated a desire for national autonomy. National culture and internationalism are not oppositional terms for most Bandung-era intellectuals.

As I turn to James, it will become clear that his move from international revolutionary of the 1930s and '40s to national politician of the 1950s and '60s— he led a spirited campaign for the West Indian Federation while serving as secretary of the Federal Labour Party—involves a subtle reorientation rather than a *volte face*. James held strong views on the importance of West Indian independence before he began his engagement with Marxist theory—he makes the case for autonomy in *The Life of Captain Cipriani: An Account of the British Government in the West Indies* (1932) and its abridged version, *The Case for West-Indian Self Government* (1933)—and he continued to nurture hopes for international revolutionary working-class movements long after the collapse of the West Indian Federation. Like Jones, James argued that the so-called backward peoples of the colonial world were actually part of a militant *avant-garde*, far in advance of their metropolitan counterparts of the time. Tracking James's career through the midcentury allows us to see how the experience of living in, then being deported from, the United States influenced his intellectual development, particularly visible in his reading of important literary texts, such as Herman Melville's *Moby-Dick*, and key historical periods, such as the great revolutionary era. By the early 1960s, James was less prone to treating the cold war as an intractable situation in which intellectuals had no part to play. Unlike his metropolitan counterparts, who often regarded the cold war as a political standoff over which they had little influence, his experiences encouraged him to rewrite the script of postwar deadlock as anticolonial opportunity.

Person of Interest, Part 2

James first arrived in the United States in 1938, shortly after the appearance of *The Black Jacobins: Toussaint L'Ouverture and the San Domingo Revolution*. He only intended to stay a few months as part of a Socialist Workers Party lecture tour, but with the outbreak of war, and falling in love with Constance Webb, he stayed fifteen years. He was already an established figure in Trotskyite circles, having published studies of revolutionary movements, including *World Revolution, 1917–1936: The Rise and Fall of the Communist International* (1937) and *A History of Negro Revolt* (1938). As Robert A. Hill and biographer Paul Buhle point out, James was active in a few radical micro-organizations that splintered from the Socialist Workers Party, such as the Johnson-Forest Tendency (James's alias was J. R. Johnson).[33]

Although MI5 started collecting information on him in 1936 and continued gathering reports from the United States into the war, James escaped notice of the FBI for perhaps six years after entry to the United States. It appears that INS, the main residency and border-security arm of the US government at the time, instigated monitoring and disciplinary action against James at the request of the FBI.[34] One of the earliest documents in the FBI file, dated 22 July 1947, reports that James had overstayed his visa (which expired 18 August 1939) and that INS had plans to deport him.[35] As his legal representatives later complained, INS first informed him that his legal problems were for visa infractions, only later admitting that James was being targeted for political reasons. The memo states that "extensive investigation was conducted [by INS] to locate JAMES between the years of 1940 and 1945 with negative results." James was hardly working underground during this time; he divorced, married, received papers for military service (but was not called up), and remained active in political circles. He eventually surrendered to authorities in December 1947, although he had been worried about deportation from his early years in the United States.[36] For James and his defenders, this timeline is meaningful. Although he was accused of violating both the McCarran Internal Security Act of 1950 (requiring Communist organizations to register with the government) and the McCarran-Walter Immigration and Nationality Act of 1952 (making it easier to exclude subversive aliens), ultimately leading to deportation, he was first arrested well before these acts became law. His defense team argued, unsuccessfully, that James was convicted of acts that were not criminal at the time he committed them, a view shared by a number of James scholars.[37]

As in the case of Jones, James was incarcerated and then deported largely on the basis of his publications and speeches. The FBI file states that James is "head of a faction in the Workers Party known as the Johnson faction [. . .]. Subject has written several books on Marxist subjects."[38] The report detailing James's early interviews with INS indicates that he was questioned primarily about his work as a writer and orator.[39] When the matter went to court, the government based its case on the danger posed by James as a writer and as an activist, in that order of importance. The court filings in James v. Shaughnessy summarize the deportation hearings conducted by INS in 1949–50. Quoting

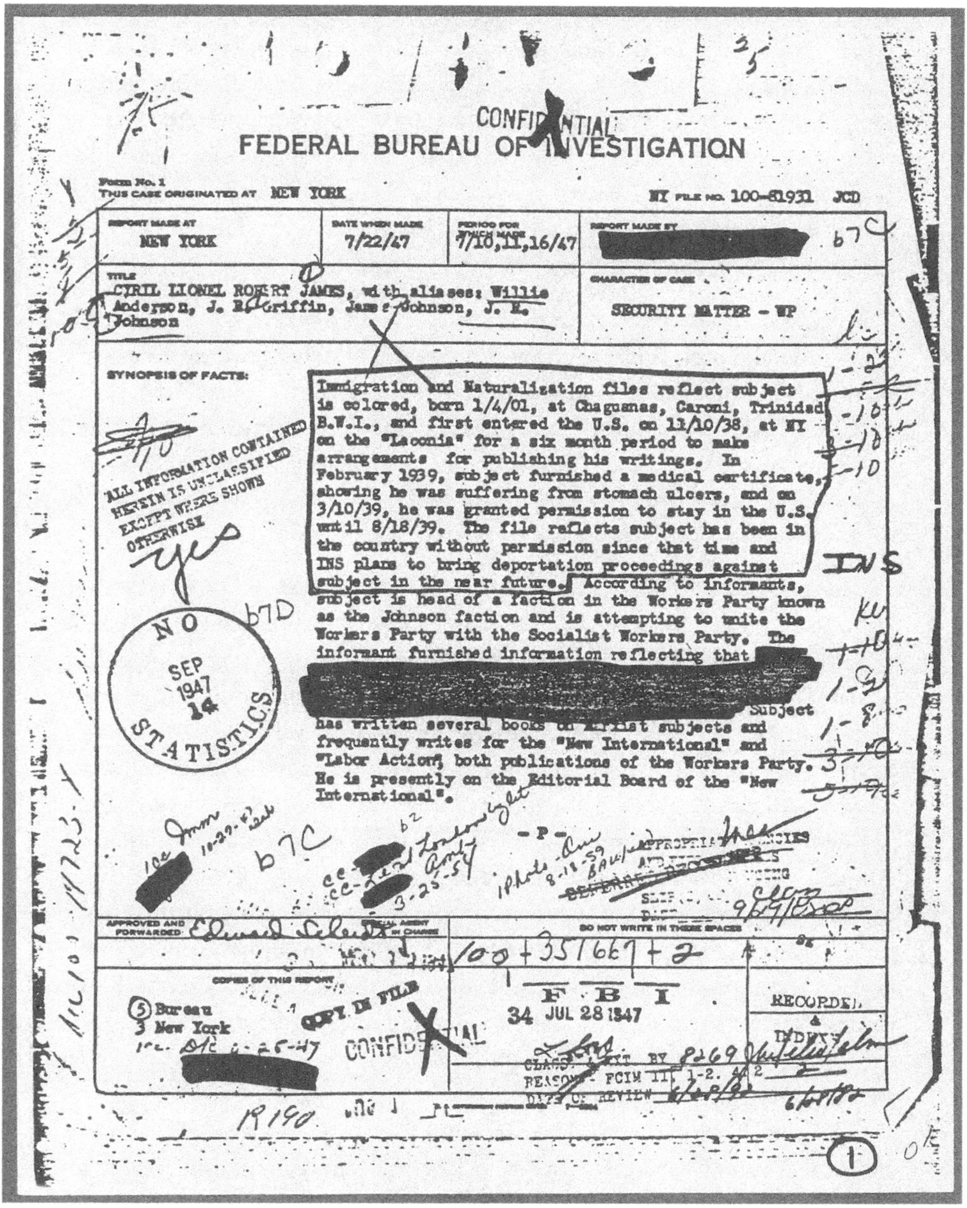

CONFIDENTIAL

FEDERAL BUREAU OF INVESTIGATION

Form No. 1
THIS CASE ORIGINATED AT NEW YORK

NY FILE NO. 100-81931 JCD

REPORT MADE AT	DATE WHEN MADE	PERIOD FOR WHICH MADE	REPORT MADE BY
NEW YORK	7/22/47	7/10,11,16/47	[redacted] b7C

TITLE	CHARACTER OF CASE
CYRIL LIONEL ROBERT JAMES, with aliases: Willie Anderson, J. R. Griffin, James Johnson, J. R. Johnson	SECURITY MATTER - WP

SYNOPSIS OF FACTS:

Immigration and Naturalization files reflect subject is colored, born 1/4/01, at Chaguanas, Caroni, Trinidad B.W.I., and first entered the U.S. on 11/10/38, at NY on the "Laconia" for a six month period to make arrangements for publishing his writings. In February 1939, subject furnished a medical certificate, showing he was suffering from stomach ulcers, and on 3/10/39, he was granted permission to stay in the U.S. until 8/18/39. The file reflects subject has been in the country without permission since that time and INS plans to bring deportation proceedings against subject in the near future. According to informants, subject is head of a faction in the Workers Party known as the Johnson faction and is attempting to unite the Workers Party with the Socialist Workers Party. The informant furnished information reflecting that [redacted] Subject has written several books on Marxist subjects and frequently writes for the "New International" and "Labor Action", both publications of the Workers Party. He is presently on the Editorial Board of the "New International".

- P -

ALL INFORMATION CONTAINED HEREIN IS UNCLASSIFIED EXCEPT WHERE SHOWN OTHERWISE

NO SEP 1947 14 STATISTICS

b7D

INS

b7C

APPROVED AND FORWARDED: Edward Scheidt SPECIAL AGENT IN CHARGE

DO NOT WRITE IN THESE SPACES

100-351667-2

COPIES OF THIS REPORT

5 Bureau
3 New York

COPY IN FILE

CONFIDENTIAL

F B I
34 JUL 28 1947

RECORDED & INDEXED

FIGURE 7.3. One of the earliest documents in C.L.R. James's FBI dossier, dated 22 July 1947. Image courtesy of Columbia University Rare Book and Manuscript Library.

extensively from *World Revolution*, the INS cites James's study (and sharp criticism) of international Communism as evidence of his unfitness for residency and citizenship in the United States. Although his legal team countered that James's political beliefs had shifted in the intervening years, thereby seeming to concede the point that he might have been a revolutionary socialist at one time, although never a Party member, the INS appeals board opined that "it is highly doubtful that there has been any basic change."[40] INS lawyers went one step further when challenged by James in court:

> [James's representatives] claim that respondent is not an actionist, merely a writer and philosopher. It is our impression that the world revolutionary movement has been founded and led by writers—Engles [*sic*], Marx, Lenin, Stalin, and others. The books the respondent admits to have written or worked on are 1. *"World Revolution"* [. . .] 2. *A History of Negro Revolution from 1700 to 1937* [*sic*] [. . .] 4. *"Black Jacobins"* [. . .] 5. A work not yet published at the time of the hearings on Herman Melville.[41]

In *Mariners*, James reiterates the ludicrousness of the case to his readers: "The Trotskyist group I was associated with never at any time exceeded 35 people. It quite often was less than half that number. I was then as I am now, essentially a writer" (154–55). It is an interesting reversal, thrown up by the odd circumstances of the cold war: the state rates the impact of radical writers more highly than do writers themselves, explaining perhaps why the state patronized some and made life miserable for others. If cold war jockeying offered writers from the decolonizing world unprecedented opportunities to reach new audiences through superpower patronage and transnational networks, it also made them vulnerable to new kinds of state oversight and discipline. But it is difficult to predict the cold war political sympathies of a writer simply by knowing information about patrons and persecutors. Of the figures I consider in this book, James was one of the most vociferous defenders of the United States, its popular culture, and its liberal political traditions, and yet he was one of the most persecuted by the political police.

To a certain extent, James's observation that he was a member of a fringe political group was shared by the state, despite its unwillingness to acknowledge this in court proceedings. In one FBI memo, a confidential informant describes James as a "powerful speaker who is extremely intelligent and well read and who far out-shadows any other personality he has come into contact with during his association with either the Workers Party or the SWP [Socialist Workers Party]."[42] The MI5 dossier concurs, describing him as a lecturer

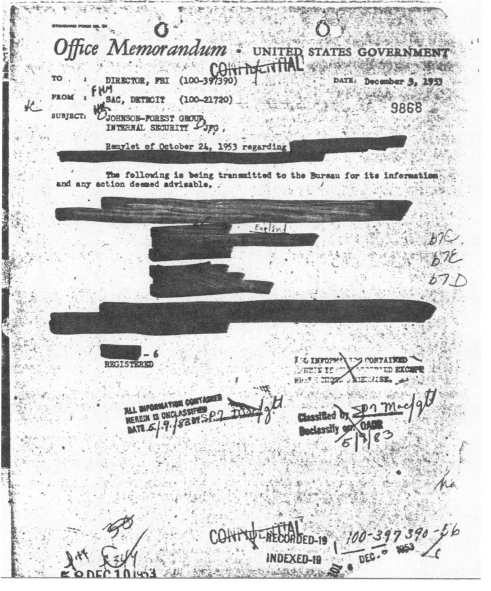

S.B. No. 5. (Flimsy). Copied to PF 206636 PORT OF PLYMOUTH. 907/21/5 COPY

SPECIAL REPORT.

METROPOLITAN POLICE (Special Branch)

ENCL_____

14 JUL 1953   11th day of ____ July, ____ 19 5 3.

TO_____

T

REF Arrived here to-day as a deportee on the s.s. 'Italia' from United States:-

DEPORTEE.
Cyril Lionel
Robert JAMES.

REFERENCE TO
PAPERS.
No trace C.R.O.

Cyril Lionel Robert JAMES, born Trinidad, West Indies on 4.1.1901; travelling on Deportation Emergency Certificate No. 61/53 issued at British Consulate, New York on 29.6.53. This bears a fairly good photograph of him (he is in fact fatter in the face) and will be forwarded to Home Office in due course by the Immigration Officer. Previously travelled on British Passport No. 27270 issued Trinidad 22.2.1932. Reason for deportation given as "Visitor remained longer".

This man claimed to be a lecturer and author and to have been in the United States for the past 15 years. A specimen publicity card showing that he lectured at The Institute of Arts and Sciences, Columbia University is submitted herewith. The photograph thereon is a good one. He is shown as being a noted British author and educated in England; to have lectured at many universities in the U.S. and to be the author of "Minty Alley", "Black Jacobins", "Toussaint l'Ouverture", and "Mariners, Renegades and Castaways". Before going to the United States he said he had lived in this country for some years and at one time had reported for the Manchester Guardian and The Glasgow Herald.

M.P.-48-36908/15M. c135 (2)   572/11/B   He was in possession of 1,600 U.S. dollars and said

FIGURE 7.5. C.L.R. James's MI5 dossier springs back to life after his deportation from the United States in 1953. Page 1 of this report includes details of his stay in the US and his ocean crossing. Image courtesy of the National Archives of the United Kingdom.

who "exhibited considerable facility of speech."[43] James was the standout performer in an otherwise weak, bickering ensemble. Another FBI memo, written long after James had been deported, summarizes one of his pamphlets as "difficult to comprehend by an individual not well acquainted with the writings of Marx, Lenin and Trotsky."[44] The tiny size of the ever-shifting political factions with which James worked in the 1940s and '50s alerts us to one important difference between his file and that of Jones, loyal Party member: there is so much redacted material from confidential informants in James's dossier that a reader leaves with the impression that the FBI had more undercover infiltrators than there were uncompromised militants. As an FBI report on James's deportation hearings claims, his testimony is contradicted by "various informants [who] have furnished information" to the Bureau.[45] In later reports on James and the Socialist Workers Party and its various offshoots, there is so

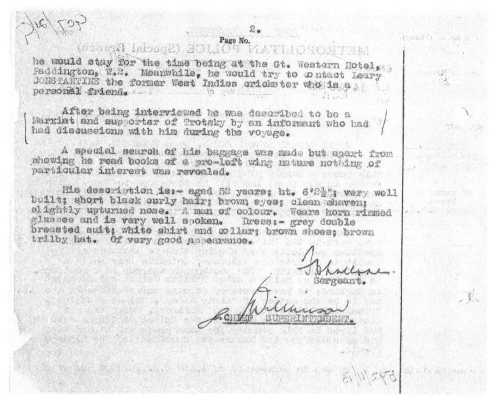

he would stay for the time being at the Gt. Western Hotel,
Paddington, W.2. Meanwhile, he would try to contact Leary
CONSTANTINE the former West Indies cricketer who is a
personal friend.

After being interviewed he was described to be a
Marxist and supporter of Trotsky by an informant who had
had discussions with him during the voyage.

A special search of his baggage was made but apart from
showing he read books of a pro-left wing nature nothing of
particular interest was revealed.

His description is:- aged 52 years; ht. 6'2½"; very well
built; short black curly hair; brown eyes; clean shaven;
slightly upturned nose. A man of colour. Wears horn rimmed
glasses and is very well spoken. Dress:- grey double
breasted suit; white shirt and collar; brown shoes; brown
trilby hat. Of very good appearance.

Sergeant.

CHIEF SUPERINTENDENT.

FIGURE 7.6. C.L.R. James's MI5 dossier springs back to life after his deportation from the
United States in 1953. Page 2 of this report includes information from an agent about his
ocean crossing. Image courtesy of the National Archives of the United Kingdom.

much information withheld that is it difficult not to imagine swarms of informants competing for the same juicy bits of information, probably reporting
more often on other confidential informants than on genuine FBI targets.[46]

Reading the FBI and MI5 files alongside one another provides glimpses of
how these security services collaborated, but also how their methods and attitudes differed. Various documents show officers from different agencies sharing information about James's appearance, past associations, present contacts,
and future plans. When James was deported from the United States in July 1953,
the MI5 file springs back into life after a period of relative inactivity; there is
even a short statement from an informant who chatted with James during his
voyage across the Atlantic on the SS Italia, noting James's Marxist ideas and
Trotskyite commitments (see figures 7.5 and 7.6). Despite these convergences
in the files, there are significant differences, too. Whereas the FBI dossier

makes a case for arresting and deporting James from the very beginning and hazards ludicrous claims about his activities (such as being instrumental in organizing the so-called Mau Mau uprising in Kenya),[47] the MI5 file shows an agency more content to track James's movements and correspondence, especially outgoing letters to associates such as Padmore.

Although the FBI's case against James strikes me as racist and reactionary, I do not wish to imply that the political police are simply unfaithful or sloppy readers of his work. James of the 1930s was a revolutionary socialist, even if he was more high-flying theorist than rank-and-file soldier. His reading of the anonymous slaves that led a successful revolt in Haiti gives us a sense of how his brand of revolutionary socialism impacted his understanding of historical events:

> The slaves worked on the land, and, like revolutionary peasants everywhere, they aimed at the extermination of their oppressors. But working and living together in gangs of hundreds on the huge sugar-factories which covered the North Plain, they were closer to a modern proletariat than any group of workers in existence at the time, and the rising was, therefore, a thoroughly prepared and organised mass movement.[48]

Writing in the late 1930s, James's heroes are proto-socialist revolutionaries. The slaves who emancipated themselves are militants who wish for "the extermination of their oppressors." I will return to this important passage, which appears in both *A History of Negro Revolt* and *The Black Jacobins*, a few more times in this chapter, but for the moment I emphasize its continuity with revolutionary socialist thought of the interwar moment. James reads the only successful slave revolt in the new world as a proto-socialist revolution. Although these excerpts do not make it into the parts of the police file that I reviewed, nothing in this passage would have diminished the FBI's case against James. We may recall that James defended himself against the political police not by denying his revolutionary socialism of the 1930s, but by saying that his views had evolved and changed. Some scholars have read this as a form of capitulation to the anti-Communism of the US government, but I would like to take James seriously here, arguing that his views evolved meaningfully as political circumstances changed.[49]

Space of Modernity

By rendering Haiti's victorious slaves as a proto-socialist revolutionaries, James is also taking a subtle dig at fellow progressives who did not accord Black and colonial peoples a significant place in revolutionary theory. James emphasizes the self-consciousness of the slaves. Rather than depict them as politically backward or as unthinking, accidental revolutionaries, James figures them as more modern and organized than any working-class group of their moment. He inserts these revolutionary men and women into the narrative frame of modernity.

In *Conscripts of Modernity: The Tragedy of Colonial Enlightenment*, David Scott shows us the political significance of this shift in perspective by examining the differences between the 1938 and 1963 versions of *The Black Jacobins*. Scott's reading of the revised text notes James's substitution of revolutionary Romance with postcolonial tragedy, a change of generic codes that seems appropriate for narrating the disappointments of the postcolonial age, which included the collapse of the Federation. In James's words, he imagines the revolution as "one of the great epics of revolutionary struggle and achievement" (ix; following James's own words, I amend Scott's attribution of genre, substituting "epic" for "Romance"). By the time he revised the text in the early 1960s, it had become clear to James that the era of national sovereignty, with its many disappointments and missed chances, required a different set of narrative conventions. To paraphrase Karl Marx of *The Eighteenth Brumaire of Louis Bonaparte*, revolution plays as tragedy the first time around, the second time as farce. James, bending this tragedy–farce progression, writes his history of the first successful slave revolt and war of independence the first time as proto-socialist epic. In revisions, he casts it as national tragedy.

Many things changed between the 1930s and the 1960s, of course, but most pressing was the global dimension of the cold war, which created both unprecedented opportunities and unexpected dilemmas for colonial peoples. It led James to idealize the late colonial intellectual as an ideological go-between, tacking nimbly between competing, irreconcilable forces. Rather than depicting the ideal colonial writer as a staunch, uncompromising partisan, James increasingly saw the role of the Black Atlantic intellectual as a cunning strategist, versed in evaluating character. Starting in the 1950s, James began to refigure the history of anticolonial struggle as a rejection of cold war binaries. Intellectuals, he believed, could play a crucial part in this process by theorizing not only the narrative trajectory but also the key characters of revolutionary situations.

The Black Jacobins: Toussaint L'Ouverture and the San Domingo Revolution, as the subtitle tells us, presents a history of the revolution through the life of its now-celebrated leader. Right at the outset, James makes the case for evaluating the first successful slave revolt and war of independence through the accomplishments of Toussaint, who, "with the single exception of Bonaparte himself," is the most gifted individual of his age. James pegs the fate of the revolution to the biography of its epic hero, building his narrative around the "record of his achievements and his political personality" (x).

Yet it would be a gross oversimplification to read *The Black Jacobins* as mere hagiography, an attribution the revolution's victories (the culmination of which Toussaint did not live to see) to its longtime leader alone. Immediately after testifying to Toussaint's greatness, James echoes Marx, claiming "Toussaint did not make the revolution. It was the revolution that made Toussaint. And even that is not the whole truth" (x). In this chiasmus, James distills his thinking about the biographical mode and its utility for writing history. For political biography to be effective, it cannot lose sight of the social contexts in which the main subject acts. James's Toussaint is the great visionary only when he represents the desires of his people, as in his declaration to the French Directory that slavery would not be restored to the island. At the height of his powers, in James's estimation, Toussaint was able to channel the needs of his comrades through his pronouncements, giving his affirmations "a strength and a single-mindedness rare in the great documents of the time" (198). In a moving passage, James compares this letter of Toussaint to the great democratic pronouncements of Pericles, Tom Paine, Thomas Jefferson, and Marx and Engels, outdoing them all when we factor his humble beginnings into the analysis.

Likewise, when Toussaint stumbles and falls, James tells us it is because the revolutionary masses have moved in front of their erstwhile leader, who makes the grave error of the moderate, trying to defend limited gains "when face to face with a revolutionary struggle" (300). By sometimes casting Toussaint as the primary embodiment of the revolution, and then at other moments as an important but ultimately dispensable part of a mass movement, James figures the anonymous revolutionary foot soldiers and their leader as narrative counterweights, working in tandem. When his constituents cower in fear at the arrival of some new foe, the responsibility falls to Toussaint to raise their hopes by articulating their true ambitions; when Toussaint doubts his own abilities or the revolution's chances, his followers haul him up with their selfless devotion to the cause. It is only when the two forces become imbalanced, when the invisible cord joining Toussaint and his revolutionary followers frays and finally severs, that Toussaint begins his ultimate descent, cut loose from the machinery of the narrative.

By joining Toussaint and the former slaves of the island in this kind of reciprocal relationship, James writes a revisionist history of the Haitian revolution, casting revolutionary struggle into epic form.[50] In retrospect, however, it is also possible to read *The Black Jacobins* as a sidelong intervention in the great literary debates of the interwar period through the use of the biographical mode. The pitched contest between the aesthetics of individual autonomy, on one side, and utilitarianism, on the other, informs the basic narrative parameters of the text. Over the course of his career, James rejected a whole collection of tropes associated with what is now recognized as literary modernism, especially what he saw as the narcissistic examination of individual subjectivity found in many experimental novels and lyric poems of the era. With *Mariners, Renegades and Castaways: The Story of Herman Melville and the World We Live in* (1953), as I discuss below, his thoughts on the question are even more explicit. In *The Black Jacobins*, this hostility toward representations of the autonomous subject is most apparent in his treatment of Toussaint: when the revolutionary masses no longer need him, when he falls out of step with the march to freedom, they desert him without ceremony, correctly perceiving him as an obstacle in their path. There is no autonomous subject in James's narrative, only individuals who make choices in circumstances not of their own choosing.

It is equally notable that James rejects a narrative steeped in historical or social determinism, or what I might describe as an extreme form of utilitarianism. James writes that Toussaint is of and for the revolution—which is to say that the narrative form of his life, especially his primary attribute of greatness, is realized only within the revolutionary movement he at first hesitated to join—and yet Toussaint is the movement's most complex and representative character, a concentration of revolutionary forces in one discrete individual. Writing the story of the revolution as an epic, James loads his protagonist with tremendous symbolic freight, allowing him to stand with, and stand in for, a mass revolutionary movement. James's narrative scrupulously avoids vulgar Marxist social determinism, on one side, and the liberal doctrine of autonomous individuals, on the other.

A brief detour by way of Georg Lukács's *The Theory of the Novel* (1916) may help us understand how pegging biographical form to a revolutionary epic resonates with the aesthetic debates of the interwar years, and also why James's status as a colonial intellectual makes his particular interventions telling. If James were simply writing as a Black Atlantic comparatist, as he does in *A History of Negro Revolt*, or as Trotskyite political theorist, as he does in *World Revolution*, we might be left with a very different sort of book, one without the imperative of squeezing revolutionary conflicts into literary frames. The narrative structure of *The Black Jacobins* makes a little more sense if we know James's overlapping work as a novelist and literary critic, efforts that immersed him in the aesthetic conflicts of the 1930s.

In *Theory of the Novel*, Lukács warns against modernist experiments in fiction, particularly against portrayals of the lonely individual, which simply hold up a mirror to "a world gone out of joint."[51] Lukács contrasts modernist depictions of autonomous, interiorized subjectivity with epic heroes (epic, of course, being the literary antecedent of the novel) and later with the protagonists of the realist novel. His description of the epic hero is precisely the model on which James depicts Toussaint in *The Black Jacobins*:

> When the world is internally homogenous, men do not differ qualitatively from one another; there are of course heroes and villains, pious men and criminals, but even the greatest hero is only a head taller than the mass of his fellows, and the wise man's dignified words are heard even by the most foolish. The autonomous life of interiority is possible and necessary only when the distinctions between men have made an unbridgeable chasm [...]. [T]he epic hero, as bearer of his destiny, is not lonely, for this destiny connects him by indissoluble threads to the community whose fate is crystallised in his own. (66–67)

The descriptions of Toussaint's role in the revolution put into practice the theory of epic form offered here by Lukács. Similar to the epic hero described by Lukács, Toussaint steps on stage virtually unannounced—his childhood and adolescence being of no real consequence—and exits when he is no longer required, swept out of the way by a cast of characters who no longer have need of his leadership. I do not know if James read Lukács carefully, or merely if he had arrived at a similar position by way of a shared interest in Hegelian philosophy. Moreover, both Lukács and James attempt to establish room for a narrative theory that avoids the extremities of the fragmented psyche, as found in modernist writing, and of the denuded psychological landscape of socialist realism. The biographical form, postulated in similar ways by Lukács and James, offers a something of a hedge against these equally unsatisfying alternatives, a way of honoring the individuality of revolutionary heroes without succumbing to the modernist cult of personality or erasing individual agents from the revolutionary cause.

The key difference between Lukács and James on this matter is that the latter critic, at least in the 1930s, seems convinced that there is yet space for the epic hero—a figure banished from the modern world in *Theory of the Novel*—in Black Atlantic narratives. For Lukács, the modern world is too politically complex and socially differentiated to support this sort of relationship between an epic hero and other members of a given society. By contrast, *The Black Jacobins* implies that this type of relationship obtained in revolutionary Haiti, not because the society was primitive, but precisely because its people were thoroughly and unmistakably subjects of the modern world. As I discuss at the start of this section, James depicts the slaves of San Domingo as "closer to a modern proletariat than any group of workers in existence at the time." James supports an epic hero in his narrative not because he depicts West Indian culture as primitive, but because people who live in such a situation are not shielded from the worst effects of industrial capitalism, or what is now commonly referred to as combined and uneven development, as the Warwick Research Collective suggests. There is no separation of outlook between Toussaint and the revolutionary masses because they have experienced the full effects of modernity. Although more than a century stood between the author and his epic protagonist, James would imply throughout *The Black Jacobins* that the relationship between metropole and colony had not changed all that dramatically during that time, even if slavery had been legally abolished in the Caribbean. Being at the rump end of the world economic system allowed colonial peoples to perceive the workings of modernity much more clearly than metropolitan subjects, who are in the main cosseted from the vicissitudes of uneven development.[52]

This subtle difference between James and Lukács on the geographical coordinates, rather than the temporal unfolding, of modernity is far more evident in retrospect than it would have been to contemporaneous observers. This is partly because the cold war made the split between international Communism and liberal democracy seem wider, both in political and aesthetic terms, as the chaos of World War II settled into the cold war. Whereas industrialized regions tended to experience the cold war as a prolonged stalemate, the global south experienced civil wars, proxy wars, and wars of liberation by the dozens.[53] At around the time *The Black Jacobins* was originally published, James departed for the United States, expecting to spend only a few months there but instead staying over a decade. It was during this extended residence in the United States that the latent differences between the international revolutionary and the defender of national culture become more apparent in his writing.

The Choice of Modernity

Written largely during his detention at Ellis Island, *Mariners* represents the symbolic culmination of his first stay in the United States. As a piece of literary criticism, the book is a bit of a curiosity. Some have knocked it for being unfaithful to Melville's work, especially *Moby-Dick*. I am less preoccupied with defending James's objectivity as an historian and critic than I am with suggesting how *The Black Jacobins* and *Mariners* illustrate some of the key preoccupations of colonial intellectuals as the revolutionary hopes of 1930s adjusted in the ideological climate of the 1950s. *Mariners* demonstrates that James was no less a revolutionary, and by no means less an internationalist, as he assessed the impact of the cold war on decolonization projects. Rather than be disappointed or disillusioned by the failures of international Communism—as happened with many metropolitan writers—James became cautiously optimistic that the cold war offered unprecedented opportunities for colonial peoples. In contrast to many western European fellow travelers of the 1930s, some of whom by the 1950s had become rabid anti-Communists, colonial intellectuals such as James—who had been disillusioned by Communist equivocation on the colonial issue well before the war—would find the international political situation of the 1950s more open to ambiguity and more hospitable to anticolonial projects.

First, it is worth pausing to note that *Mariners* recognizes that anticolonial movements would have to contend with the United States and the Soviet Union, not simply with the imperial powers of western Europe. While giving a brief personal history, James reports that he had been in Great Britain only for a few years "before I came to the conclusion that European civilisation as it then existed was doomed, an opinion which I have never changed and am not likely to change" (154). It is a cheeky, stray comment, but it is one that many students of British and postcolonial literature have been slow to recognize as symptomatic: as far back as the 1930s, and certainly in the 1950s, many anticolonial intellectuals were far less preoccupied with lingering forms of European imperialism than they were concerned about how a new balance of geopolitical power could affect their situation. Would the decline of western Europe unleash a new system of imperialism, with an elaborate network of client states, puppet governments, military alliances, and aid packages, or would the destabilization of Europe allow colonial territories better opportunities for self-determination? *Mariners* and James's voluminous notes toward *American Civilization* (published posthumously) both attempt to answer this basic question. Western Europe's faltering hold on its empires no longer preoccupied this particular strategist.

Second, we must note that James of the early 1950s is, if possible, even more hostile to modernist writing than his younger self. In a long digression, James compares *Moby-Dick* favorably to the literature of the twentieth century, which lacks vision and fortitude in his estimation: "*The Waste Land, Journey to the End of the Night, Darkness at Noon, Farewell to Arms, The Counterfeiters, In Remembrance of Things Past*," he bemoans, provide little more than "a catalogue of misery or self-centered hopelessness" (113). These kinds of texts are written by and for a small group of snobby bohemians, most of them narcissistically obsessed with their own failings. The intellectual who does not take the time to become acquainted with "the anonymous but unfailing humanity of the renegades and castaways" cannot understand the complexity of the modern world (114). The political weakness of western Europe was being reflected in its decaying literary culture. Experimental modernism, obsessed with portraying the vicissitudes of individual consciousness, represents the aesthetic dead end of capitalist crisis.

Third, although *Mariners* is arguably less indebted to the genre of biography than *The Black Jacobins*, the book's principal method operates through the concept of character types or personalities. James's interest in character types, similar to his use of biographical narrative forms to write political history, represents an attempt to escape the aesthetic strictures of the cold war. He reads Ahab as a totalitarian, the debut of a new personality onto the world-literary stage. Ahab revolts against industrial capitalism, but not for the establishment of a more equitable distribution of work and benefits. The officers aboard the *Pequod* are his bureaucratic subordinates, the men he can bully and bribe. Melville draws the real distinction between the dictatorial Ahab and the egalitarian crew, a largely anonymous group James says would have been "the real heroes" of the book if Melville had not been afraid of criticism from his peers (18). They are not simply workers, James notes, but representatives of all the subjugated peoples of the world: "They are a pack of ragamuffins picked up at random from all parts of the earth. [Melville] tells us that in 1851, while white American officers provided the brains, not one in two of the thousands of men in the fishery, in the army, in the navy and the engineering forces employed in the construction of American canals and railroads were American" (18).

Mariners thus censures the hypersubjectivity prevalent in modernism and subtly amends the stock narrative materials prevalent in socialist realism. These shadow protagonists, the men of the crew, provide an objective glimpse of uneven development in practice aboard the ship. Ideologically, the members of the crew are unformed and immature—they never revolt, James notes, as a politically self-aware proletariat might. More important than their group political awareness is their appearance as a character type in the novel. Their manifest difference from Ahab puts the text's theory of uneven development in motion, animating the plot not through direct narrative conflict (the conflict is Ahab against the whale, or Ahab against the natural order of things) but through personality contrast. In a revealing aside, James tells us that he did not see the significance of this stark contrast until the cold war had alerted him to the new geopolitical situation:

> The three American officers [of the *Pequod*] represent the competent technological knowledge, brains and leadership. The harpooners and the crew are the ordinary people of the whole world. The writer of this book confesses frankly that it is only since the end of World War II, that the emergence of the people of the Far East and of Africa into the daily headlines, the spread of Russian totalitarianism, the emergence of America as a power in every quarter of the globe, it is only this that has enabled him to see the range, the power and the boldness of Melville. (19)

The fact that the crew hail from the subjugated regions of the world is important for James's purposes. Seeing the crew as a character type, with an array of cultural differences between them yet sharing in their attitude to work and leisure, allows the reader to perceive their structural position in a world-economic system. James seems to admire Melville's choice that the crew does not revolt: their existence as a character type, with distinct attributes, is more meaningful than showing us political consciousness among them, thereby telling us where socialist realism has gone awry. If James of the late 1930s was keen to turn colonial peoples into proto-socialist revolutionaries, by the mid-1950s he seems more inclined to admire them for their lack of revolutionary acumen.

I am particularly struck by James's admission that he could not understand the full relevance of the crew's diverse composition until after World War II, when the outlines of the cold war and the maturity of the anticolonial movements had become manifest. The unique contribution of *Mariners* is not its reading of Ahab as a totalitarian—other critics of this generation were making similar claims—but instead the contention that social relations on the boat miniaturize the geography of modernity, the spatial dimensions of uneven development. The conjunction of the cold war and the growth of anticolonial movements encouraged James to understand the independence struggle as something other than righting the imbalances between metropolitan and colonial spaces. The contest between cold war blocs presented colonial subjects with a different set of problems and choices. If western European imperialism tended to reify the metropolitan–colonial relationship, making colonial space appear as a backward version of the metropolitan core, the cold war disturbed that theory by offering divergent models for development. James implies that we can understand the crew differently not because they are mere victims of tyranny, but because they refuse to be seduced by ideological sophistry. The members of the crew are politically savvy and ideologically unaffiliated, even if they do not revolt in Melville's account. The castaways on Ellis Island are the same—clear-eyed and disillusioned but smarter than most.

Although both Ahab and the crew represent new character types, James spends a disproportionate amount of space discussing Ishmael, whom James reads as the prototypical modern intellectual. Ishmael's problem, according to James, is his vacillation between Ahab's visionary powers and the crew's displays of solidarity and earthy wisdom. James reads Ishmael as the only character in *Moby-Dick* who faces a genuine choice:

> But if Ishmael, the intellectual, is so strongly attracted to the man of action, equally strong on him is the attraction of the crew. That in fact is what makes him modern. He must decide. (42)

It is a telling choice of words: Ishmael is modern because his affinities are divided, swinging between Ahab, the individual who would bend others to his will, and the collective identity of the crew, who cannot quite be forced into the shape Ahab wishes (at least in James's account of the novel). Ishmael's temporal frame of reference, his participation in the space of modernity, James links in some way to his indecisiveness, or to his ability to see the problems of the *Pequod* from mutually incompatible perspectives. His status as a modern subject is determined by this choice, by his wavering between autonomous individuality and utilitarianism. James faults Ishmael, as he faults most western European and North American intellectuals, for refusing to cast his lot with the men of the crew. But his description of Ishmael's burden as the definition of modernity is a cold war judgment. Being encouraged or forced to choose camps, especially in the shared context of anticolonial movements, is the part of Ishmael's dilemma James figures as his very own.

The description of Ishmael's equivocation in *Mariners* comes as a dress rehearsal for the description of Toussaint's crisis in *The Black Jacobins*—that is, in the revised 1963 version of the text. Scott's nuanced reading of *The Black*

Jacobins emphasizes the tragic dimensions of Toussaint's conundrum. Scott reads the choice between freedom without France (and without the ideals of the French Enlightenment) and subjugation within the French system as a choice from within modernity; James's Toussaint is a tragic figure because he cannot reconcile the discourses of enlightenment and practical freedom. Scott takes this dilemma to be the central paradox of modernity, especially in decolonizing regions of the world. It is worth emphasizing that James did not revise *The Black Jacobins* extensively between 1938 and 1963, except to append an epilogue and insert perhaps a dozen paragraphs on the specifically tragic nature of Toussaint's fall, on which Scott's delicate reading hinges. By the early 1960s, James had changed his thinking about Toussaint ever so subtly—which is to say that James was thinking differently about the prospects of self-determination for colonial peoples—making the story less epic and more tragic in its dimensions. Knowing this about the genetic evolution of *The Black Jacobins*, the depiction of Ishmael as a specifically modern character, and as a product of a cold war order, suggests that *Mariners* marks a pivot in James's thinking over the middle decades of the century.

Returning for a moment to the work of Lukács may give us better access to the aesthetic and critical context through which we can track James's evolution. In *The Historical Novel* (1936/7), Lukács reiterates his assertion that epic heroes are only a head taller than their counterparts, but he spends his critical energies on the emergence of a new character type in great historical fiction: the mediocre hero, the individual who has the ability to move with relative ease between contending social groups, or warring factions—between what Raymond Williams might call residual and emergent forces. Here is how Lukács describes the key figure or character type of Sir Walter Scott's fiction:

> Scott always chooses as his principal figures such as may, through character and fortune, enter into human contact with both camps. The appropriate fortunes of such a mediocre hero, who sides passionately with neither of the warring camps in the great crisis of his time can provide a link of this kind without forcing the composition.[54]

The mediocre hero, in Lukács's view, provides a flexible aesthetic solution to the problem of representing totality: with this socially mobile and ideologically nonaligned character who is yet fully plausible, Scott nudges his readers away from the tragic mode (which turns social crisis into individualized drama; the bourgeois approach to conflict) and toward a form of realism capable of understanding the logic of historical change. In a slightly different manner than in *Theory of the Novel*, Lukács warns us to avoid the formulaic pitfalls of socialist realism—which tends to prioritize the growth of militancy for revolutionary or proto-revolutionary groups—and also to avoid the privileging of individual consciousness at the expense of rich social contexts, or what Lukács calls totality.

In *Mariners*, James harnesses the main thrust of Lukács in *The Historical Novel* but redirects the point of attack ever so slightly. Ishmael, for James, is a mediocre go-between, a character who secretly identifies with the men of the crew yet finds Ahab's determination too compelling to resist. In the final section of *Mariners*, formerly suppressed but restored to the text in a 2001 version edited by Donald E. Pease, James makes a nuanced comparison between himself, as a colonial intellectual, and Ishmael. Similar to *Moby-Dick*'s betwixt narrator, James is on familiar terms with the great contending camps of his day, the Communists and the defenders of liberal democracy. His stay at Ellis Island makes him peculiarly intimate with both sides. Unlike Ishmael, however, his extraordinary situation does not cause James to waver in his commitments. Although he admires the tenacity and ingenuity of the Communists, he is never tempted join their ranks; and although the experience of pleading his case for US citizenship makes him a more passionate defender of civil liberties and legal protections, he reaches the conclusion that the leading nation-states of the cold war have compromised their moral mandate in their fight against perceived external threats. The colonial intellectual, James implies, is in a unique position to coolly assess the accomplishments and demerits of two antithetical political models. Unlike Ishmael, who ultimately founders from his indecision, James accepts the challenge of understanding, yet remaining uncommitted to, both sides.

To translate the dynamics of the text into slightly more theoretical terms, the final section of *Mariners* confronts two major problems, one political, the other aesthetic, both concerning the status of colonial peoples in the cold war. Politically, James defines the conundrum as a choice between two equally unappealing models: rapid economic development (along the lines of the five-year plan) without legitimate democracy, or nominal democratic rule and national independence for colonial territories in the broader context of uneven development. For James, this represents a trap, a false choice. Colonial peoples, he reckons, are in the best position to see this situation for what it is. As he tells the story, his fellow detainees at Ellis Island, renegades and castaways from the world over, have no faith in the cold war's ideological standoff: they will fight for either side, if necessary, provided the result is a lasting peace with genuine self-determination for the subjugated peoples of the world. The United States, with its "venomous anti-alien policy," gives the Communists more than enough ammunition in the battle for hearts and minds (154). Jim Crow, the so-called Achilles' heel of US foreign policy, does nothing to win over people in decolonizing areas. If colonial people were not so canny and cosmopolitan, he argues, they could easily be swayed by Communist propaganda on these points.

Aesthetically, the text explores the space between the psychological dynamism of high modernism and the cultivation of political responsibility implicit in socialist realism. In a final salvo against a deracinated modernism, James says he is "familiar enough with what the European intellectuals call culture, which they claim they must preserve against American vulgarity." These intellectuals are, he asserts, "greater enemies of the American people than I am" (159). In *Mariners*, through lengthy explorations of character types, James at once steers away from the interior poverty of socialist realism while simultaneously rejecting modernism's avoidance of what Lukács calls totality. But the translation of literary into political values is not as straightforward as this short passage might suggest. Substituting an unreflective egalitarianism for the elitism of modernism does not make one a genuine democrat in James's book: the telling contribution is how the artist and critic represent not only the temporalities, but also the geographies, of modernity.

The unique conclusion to *Mariners*, in which James records his own experiences at Ellis Island and outlines his plea for US citizenship, functions as a space for pushing the formal boundaries of literary criticism. Unlike the vast majority of literary scholars, who strive for impersonality and objectivity in their critical work, James insists that his autobiography forms an essential component of the story he tells about the cold war and decolonization through a reading of Melville's fiction. His original preface gives us a sense of why he includes the concluding chapter in his account:

> A great part of this book was written on Ellis Island while I was being detained by the Department of Immigration. The Island, like Melville's *Pequod*, is a miniature of all the nations of the world and all sections of society. My experience of it and the circumstances attending my stay there have so deepened my understanding of Melville, and so profoundly influenced the form the book has taken, that an account of this has seemed to me not only a natural but a necessary conclusion. (175)

A conclusion at once "natural" and "necessary" is how James describes his closing pages, in which he details his legal battle against deportation. It is natural in that it helps explain what Melville's catalogue of cosmopolitan outcasts tells us about the midcentury moment; it is urgent and necessary in that its form attempts to capture how the geography of uneven development—or what Lukács might call totality—might be figured in the practice of literary criticism. This testimonial turn refuses the protocols of a more restrictive formalist interpretation—which grants the object of criticism a degree of autonomy by respecting its internal rules of composition—and also rejects the principle that criticism ought to be utterly subservient to political causes, a tool in service of an ideological agenda.

National Revolutions

As I discuss at various points in this chapter, Scott's *Conscripts of Modernity* offers a remarkable, comparative analysis of the 1938 and 1963 editions of *The Black Jacobins*, suggesting that James retroactively elevates the status of tragedy in his telling of the Haitian revolution, partly to acknowledge the disappointments of decolonization without abandoning the project altogether. As Scott points out, James's alterations are nowhere more evident than in his appendix, "From Toussaint L'Ouverture to Fidel Castro." If James wrote the first edition in England, where he could use his imagination to hear "most clearly and insistently the booming of Franco's heavy artillery, the rattle of Stalin's firing squads and the fierce shrill turmoil of the revolutionary movement striving for clarity and influence," the 1963 appendix calls our attention to a different context, one in which the early promise of the Haitian revolution is being redeemed in the anticolonial movement (xi).

Although the 1963 revisions make *The Black Jacobins* more reliant on tragedy, we should not conclude that James had become despondent about political action. He begins the appendix by stating that Toussaint is tied to Castro, but not "because both led revolutions." Instead, James explains, it is because both men were connected to significant mass movements that "are peculiarly West Indian, the product of a peculiar origin and a peculiar history" (391). While the first edition of *The Black Jacobins* as well as *The History of Negro Revolt* liken the revolutionary peasants to their oppressed counterparts across the world, James here emphasizes the idiosyncratic, national qualities of the Haitian and Cuban uprisings. This interpretive gesture, in which James downplays their revolutionary connection and plays up the uniqueness of their regional identity, becomes a bit less surprising if we recall how the experiences of the 1950s affected Caribbean intellectuals such as James and Jones. Already in *Mariners* we can detect James refashioning proletarian revolutions as expressions of national culture, or what he calls "a peculiar origin and a peculiar history" in his appendix to *The Black Jacobins*. By 1963, Toussaint becomes the "first and greatest of West Indians," the man who is there at the birth of a new social identity (418). The revolution in Cuba, likewise, he reads not as another chapter in the imperialist script, in which first the western European nations, and then later the United States and the Soviet Union, scramble for influence and territory, but instead as "the ultimate stage of a Caribbean quest for national identity" (391). In an act of critical nonalignment, James offers a different political genealogy of the Cuban revolution. People in the decolonizing world are uniquely positioned to comprehend this new geopolitical order.

The appendix makes it equally clear that West Indian intellectuals learned how to understand themselves as West Indians only by going abroad, often literally and in some cases only figuratively. Colonialism had systematically encouraged intellectuals to look down on local culture. It was only when Caribbean intellectuals learned more about the diaspora—by going to the United States, to metropolitan Britain, and especially to Africa itself—that they learned to appreciate their deep attachment to their natal culture. "The first step to freedom was to go abroad," writes James in the appendix. *"Before they could begin to see themselves as a free and independent people they had to clear from minds the stigma that anything African was inherently inferior and degraded. The road to West Indian national identity lay through Africa"* (402). He names Césaire, Padmore, and Marcus Garvey as a few of the figures who made real and symbolic voyages throughout the diaspora. The ordering of this progression is telling, going against the grain of much research on the Black Atlantic. The journey out leads to knowledge of home and newfound enthusiasm for national culture. There is no mistaking the cosmopolitan, internationalist significance of James's vision. West Indian intellectuals learned many things by following and in some cases participating in the national liberation projects in Africa. But in James's view, this international experience produces a special kind of local knowledge. James, Jones, and other Caribbean intellectuals of the midcentury learned to appreciate the value of national culture through the painful but productive experience of exile, facilitated in unlikely ways by their encounters with the political police.

8

Notes from Prison: Individual Testimony Meets Collective Resistance

WRITING ABOUT INCARCERATION came into its own during the second half of the twentieth century, when literary genres associated with imprisonment spiked in frequency and underwent rapid development as the stories of the Nazi concentration camps, Soviet gulags, US internment programs, and prisoner-of-war facilities spread to mass audiences in the midcentury. Fictional accounts of political detentions, such as Arthur Koestler's *Darkness at Noon* (1941), George Orwell's *1984* (1949), and Alexander Solzhenitsyn's *One Day in the Life of Ivan Denisovich* (1962), worked in tandem with non-fictional memoirs, such as Primo Levi's *If This Is a Man* (1947) and Eugenia Ginzburg's *Journey into the Whirlwind* (1967). What has long existed as an intermittent form of writing became something of a literary staple during and after World War II.

As students of the anticolonial movements know, large numbers of activists from Africa and Asia were political prisoners during the midcentury years, often working their experiences into literary form. Dennis Brutus, Faiz Ahmed Faiz, C.L.R. James, Claudia Jones, Alex La Guma, Rajat Neogy, Ngũgĩ wa Thiong'o, Wole Soyinka, and Sajjad Zaheer each spent time behind bars, and most of them wrote in detail about their experiences. Pramoedya Ananta Toer, the great Indonesian novelist, composed his celebrated *Buru Quartet* in the eponymous penal colony without the benefit of writing materials, at least for several years—he recited the material to other prisoners before he was granted the use of paper.[1] Even after his release, Pramoedya's publications were banned in his native Indonesia, meaning his primary audiences were international.

World War II, the cold war, and decolonization created new, global audiences for a literature of human rights.[2]

In their testimonies about unjust detention, these texts bear the signs of what Mark Greif calls "the age of the crisis of man," when the concept of humanism seemed up for grabs.[3] Anticipating Greif's language, Achille Mbembe calls these literary practices "*meaningful human expressions*," succinctly joining together the language of humanism with a description of the expressive capabilities of people in decolonizing situations (*On the Postcolony* 6). The literature of decolonization fully immersed itself in midcentury debates about the status of the human as a holder of individual rights and a bearer of collective responsibilities. Without glossing over the differences between European, African, and Asian accounts of political detention, this chapter will recognize some of the representational affinities between them by suggesting that the idea of human rights brought intellectuals from metropolitan and decolonizing parts of the world into closer contact. Elaborating the humanist tradition outlined in *Darkness at Noon, If This is a Man*, and *1984*—Orwell's working title for the novel was *The Last Man in Europe*—writers from decolonizing areas extended and criticized the discussion of what it means to be human, and to practice writing, in a cold war context. In telling stories about detention, these narratives muse on the relationship between the status of the individual, the act of writing, and the nature of collective struggle.

Scholars tend to treat prison writing from Africa and Asia as a form of anticolonial resistance. Barbara Harlow's influential work in *Resistance Literature* and *Barred: Women, Writing, and Political Detention* set the course for such a reading. As Harlow writes about jailed women writers of the anticolonial movements, "[t]heir personal itineraries, which have taken them through struggle, [. . .] are attested to in their own narratives as part of a historical agenda, a collective enterprise."[4] This echoes her argument in *Resistance Literature*, in which she insists on the "the collective strategies of political resistance" that distinguish anticolonial prison writing from other related genres.[5] Harlow reads the typical prison memoir as a continuation of the struggle by other means: a statement of solidarity, not an individual speech act.[6] The Malawian poet and linguist Jack Mapanje, himself a detainee and author of a remarkable memoir, regards prison writing as the result of historical continuity, noting that the "variants of colonial legislation" limiting free speech and right of assembly "were never substantially revised" after independence in many postcolonial nations.[7] Ngũgĩ makes the same point at the start of his prison memoir, saying that his detention ought to be put "in the context of the historical attempts, from colonial times to the present, by a foreign imperialist bourgeoisie, in alliance with its local Kenyan representatives, to turn Kenyans into slaves." Against these imperialist and neo-imperialist forces, Ngũgĩ applauds the "struggles of the Kenyan people" as they resist the imposition of cultural, economic, and political bondage.[8]

Although there are compelling reasons to read prison writing from decolonizing parts of the world as the enunciation of a collective struggle, this chapter also notes how this genre evolved as it became closely associated with non-governmental organizations (NGOs), especially International PEN.[9] NGOs such as PEN, which collaborated with Amnesty International, Human Rights Watch, and even the Congress for Cultural Freedom on some of the cases discussed in this chapter, are not part of an identifiable, anticolonial network, although they have sometimes aligned themselves with particular anticolonial spokespeople. Instead, these outfits are part of the cold war's tangled cultural diplomacy and human rights programs, which emphasized the need to protect individual civil liberties—especially but not only freedom of speech and dissent—and de-emphasized how collective struggles, such as decolonization and self-determination, fit into the human rights paradigm.[10] During the interwar period, the liberal democracies used human rights discourse to forestall independence for colonies and to limit the sovereignty of independent African nations, even as they used it to challenge fascism and totalitarianism. In the postwar era, human rights organizations such as PEN often found themselves at odds with the Soviet cultural bureaucracy over its treatment of dissenting intellectuals. Most important, from the 1970s forward, the international movement for human rights increasingly defended individual rights against the actions of coercive states, whether in Africa, Asia, or the Warsaw Pact nations, although late colonial and postcolonial writers, as we shall see, had no qualms about balancing individual freedom against collective responsibility.[11] Rallying around imprisoned writers from the Communist bloc and from decolonizing regions became one of PEN's major activities.

Postcolonial prison writing thus pulls readers in two directions at once. On one side, these memoirs describe the shared struggles of decolonizing peoples. On the other side, these memoirs seek to protect individual freedoms against coercive states. These texts intermingle expressions of solidarity with defenses of individual rights. Rather than resolve this nascent tension, I read this strain of human rights literature as part of a cultural proxy war, in which arguments between the cold war superpowers are expanded and pursued through conversations about the decolonizing parts of the world. The consequences of this process were contradictory. The expansion of the cold war's human rights debates through PEN and other NGOs brought postcolonial prison writing into the fold of an international but highly unequal system, emphasizing the individuality of rights-holding subjects without recognizing the claims of subordinated groups. Just as often, however, these texts signal their allegiance to forms of solidarity, with memoirists insisting that their stories are broadly representative, not particular. We put ourselves in the best position to appreciate these texts, I argue in the following pages, when we see how they work at the switch point between a flagging Bandung spirit of collective anticolonial resistance and an emerging post-cold war system dominated more clearly by the United States and its allies. Toggling between solidarity and the articulation of individual rights, or between aesthetic models of utilitarianism and autonomy, these narratives show how cold war legacies inform both the individualist logic of global human rights discourse and the collectivist impulses of an increasingly embattled anticolonial project. Arguments about human rights pursued through cultural organizations in the First and Second Worlds were restaged in the expressive laboratories of Africa and Asia, where the difference between self-determination for groups and civil rights for individuals had to negotiate the legacy of imperialism.

As I discuss in my considerations of five African memoirs—Ngũgĩ's *Detained*, Ruth First's *117 Days* (1965), Soyinka's *The Man Died* (1972), Nawal El Saadawi's *Memoirs from the Women's Prison* (1983), and Mapanje's *And Crocodiles Are Hungry at Night* (2011)—the genres of prison writing bear the marks of tension between cooperative resistance to colonialism and the implied individualism of human rights discourse from the 1970s forward. Koestler's relationship with PEN and the CCF and his well-known novel *Darkness at Noon* offer something of a template for the ensuing discussions. Koestler's message about defending brave individuals against totalitarian states, which appealed greatly to PEN in the 1930s and early 1940s, resonated with the organization's longstanding commitment to freedom of speech. By the 1960s, PEN expanded its advocacy of intellectual freedoms to include persecuted writers from the decolonizing world. But even a cursory reading of *Darkness at Noon* shows it to be a novel equally concerned with collective struggle, a variant of the aesthetic utilitarianism I have been describing throughout this book. Emulating some of Koestler's narrative strategies in *Darkness at Noon* helped postcolonial prison memoirists to carry over, or smuggle in, explicit messages of solidarity.

Poets, Essayists, Novelists

PEN, originally an acronym for Poets, Essayists, Novelists, was founded in London in 1921. According to the society's short online history, it is one of the oldest NGOs and human rights campaigners in the world.[12] John Galsworthy, the association's first president, helped define PEN's mission by articulating three core principles, later enshrined in the PEN Charter: defending free expression; increasing opportunities for international exchange between writers; and maintaining the nonpolitical character of the organization by insisting that national affiliates admit writers of any political persuasion.[13]

PEN's nonpolitical character would be tested repeatedly during the mid-century decades. During H. G. Wells's stint as president from 1933–36, PEN expelled the German branch, which refused to distance itself from Nazi anti-Semitism and book-burning. Ernst Toller's passionate support for writers targeted by fascist regimes at the 1933 meeting in Dubrovnik and the 1934 meeting in Edinburgh helped consolidate the organization's commitment to defending free speech against totalitarian governments.[14] In 1937, Koestler became one of PEN's first public relations success stories. Then a Communist Party member, Koestler had been imprisoned and sentenced to death in fascist-controlled areas of Spain, where he was nominally on duty as a journalist. In coordination with international press syndicates and even the British government, PEN lobbied General Franco to pardon Koestler.[15] Wells also tried to intervene in Federico García Lorca's case, but the appeal came too late. The Koestler campaign, however, succeeded, allowing him to resettle in England. It would begin Koestler's long collaboration with PEN. His case defined the gameplan for PEN Writers in Prison campaigns of the postwar period.

Koestler featured prominently in PEN activities throughout the 1940s. During the war and its aftermath, he was a regular PEN speaker, giving talks, participating on roundtables, and chairing sessions.[16] In an address in 1946, he told a PEN audience that the organization had saved his life a second time, during the war in Paris, by offering him a place to hide when he was wanted by the police.[17] With Aldous Huxley and John Dos Passos, Koestler launched the Fund for Intellectual Freedom, which supported writers exiled "by the action of totalitarian governments." In 1952, he turned over this fund to PEN, under whose direction it merged with the Writers in Exile program, becoming the Fund for Exiled Writers.[18] The program helped Russian émigré and Nobel winner Ivan Bunin, and it would rush to the aid of Hungarian intellectuals fleeing the Soviet crackdown of 1956.[19]

Despite forming a productive working relationship, Koestler and the PEN hierarchy did not see eye to eye on the usefulness of a nonpolitical organization protecting freedom of expression in the context of the cold war. Koestler believed in taking an uncompromising stand against the Soviet system, while PEN preferred to defend intellectual freedoms yet keep the organization non-sectarian. Even as PEN contemplated an appeal to Franco on Koestler's behalf, the executive committee debated whether a public campaign of this sort would compromise the organization's nonpolitical character. In the end, the pro-Koestler faction within the executive won the day, but not without debate and abstentions from those who were not convinced.

PEN's stance on Soviet Communism was equally ambivalent. On one hand, the executive committee had for decades encouraged the Soviet authorities to establish a local PEN branch, with the only stipulation that non-Communist writers be allowed to join.[20] The parties nearly struck a deal during World War II, but the Soviets would not agree to the provisions in the PEN Charter, staying out until the late 1980s. Branches existed in several Warsaw Pact nations, although these went dormant for lengthy periods.[21] The goal, from PEN's perspective, was to keep the hope of real dialogue alive. Against this sentiment, however, PEN felt compelled to censure Soviet actions in Hungary in 1956, helping intellectuals who fled through the exiled writers' initiative that Koestler had founded. By the late 1950s and early 1960s, PEN international secretary David Carver and Alexei Surkov, during and after the latter's term as head of the Union of Soviet Writers, clashed swords over Boris Pasternak (Surkov, incidentally, served as Doris Lessing's official host when she was part of the first delegation of western European intellectuals to visit the Soviet Union after the end of the war).[22] In 1958, Pasternak was pressured to refuse the Nobel Prize. It later emerged that Olga Ivinskaya, Pasternak's longtime mistress, and her daughter had been imprisoned shortly after his death, in retribution for the publication of *Doctor Zhivago* (1957) abroad, after the denial of clearance at home.[23] In short, PEN's attitude to the Soviet literary establishment was inconsistent.

PEN and the CCF began working together in the 1950s. Koestler and the Italian writer Ignazio Silone helped coordinate activities. As far back as 1948, as plans for the CCF were brewing, Melvin Lasky appealed to PEN members for contributions to *Der Monat*, the US-backed West Berlin periodical that would serve as the blueprint for the CCF periodicals program. As Lasky puts it in his notice in *PEN News*, "*DER MONAT* is activated by the very same ideals which have found expression in the P.E.N. Charter."[24] Through Lasky, PEN and the CCF would collaborate on protests during the Pasternak affair. Koestler, by then no longer a PEN member, went even further in his attacks on the Soviet regime.[25] As Koestler distanced himself from PEN and became more active in the CCF network, Marion Bieber, John Hunt, and Robie Macauley, all part of the CCF setup, became points of contact in the 1950s and '60s. Hunt was a PEN member and on good terms with international secretary Carver, putting him in position to influence the direction of PEN. As Frances Stonor Saunders tells the story, Hunt took advantage of this connection to infiltrate PEN, using it to distribute *Encounter*, install personnel in key positions, and support PEN with financial disbursements.[26]

The Soviet cultural apparatus took notice of growing collaboration between the CCF and PEN. In 1964, PEN's old sparring partner Surkov published a blistering attack on the NGO, accusing it of being little more than the pawn of imperialist, reactionary forces. Naturally, this provoked a lengthy rebuttal from Carver. In the exchange, recorded in the March 1964 PEN executive committee minutes, Surkov describes the CCF as a propaganda outfit filled with "second-raters, such as out-of-work Trotskyites, turncoats from Communist parties, renegades of every description, and suchlike rabble."[27] A partisan description, obviously, but not inaccurate on all counts: the CCF was stocked with ex-Communist Party members, as *The God That Failed* illustrates. Surkov accuses PEN, described as a "one-time respectable international writers' organization," of now doing the CCF's dirty work (1). The editorial goes on to castigate it for sheltering émigré writers from socialist countries. Hypocritically, Surkov contends, PEN condemns legitimate Soviet censure of reactionary writers, such as Pasternak, while staying silent about progressive writers persecuted "by fascist dictators in Europe or Latin America" (3). Carver's response points out that PEN, for some three decades, had been trying to bring Soviet writers into the PEN fold, with no tangible progress. Carver also defends PEN's reputation of aiding writers persecuted by fascist states. As for the CCF link, Carver merely says that the organization does not need PEN's protection, "for it can very well look after itself."[28]

The point of this short overview of the PEN–Koestler–CCF connection is to note how PEN, against its stated purpose of remaining nonpolitical, became mired in the partisan conflicts of the aesthetic cold war. For this it can hardly be faulted, given its stated aims. More important, perhaps, is to see how easily PEN's criticisms of fascism could be refitted as blanket arguments against state involvement in the arts, especially as practiced in the Soviet bloc. Although Koestler privately warned the CCF's Michael Josselson that PEN preferred constructive engagement to open confrontation with the Soviet cultural apparatus, PEN's movement from antifascism to anti-Communism resembled Koestler's personal journey.[29] Later, this kind of ideological flexibility would morph into criticisms of autocratic rule in postcolonial states.[30]

As an NGO promoting the interests of writers, different courses were available to PEN. It might have concluded that state involvement in literature should be balanced against state support of the arts. But it did not adopt this approach: PEN clung to freedom of expression as an absolute value without also insisting that states have an obligation to support literary production (and with it, the idea that writers may owe some duty to the state). This is what Isaiah Berlin describes as "negative" as opposed to "positive" liberty: negative freedoms involve freedom from restrictions, whereas positive freedoms necessitate active support of and constructive participation in activities deemed to be social goods. This support usually comes from a state or other collective. Free speech is an example of a negative freedom. State support for the arts as a social good, on the other hand, might be regarded as a positive freedom. PEN's embrace of negative liberty implicitly encourages writers to see themselves as individuals in two distinct ways: as individuals whose opinions are in need of protection from repressive states, and also as individuals whose work stands or falls on its own merits. The state is not a potential resource, only a threat to intellectual freedoms. PEN's stance leaves no room for the idea of aesthetic utilitarianism in which many late colonial and postcolonial writers were invested.

The Koestler Effect

As I discuss later in this chapter, the PEN campaign to liberate Koestler from death row provided the model for PEN's Writers in Prison program. His writing, too, especially *Darkness at Noon*, develops some formal principles that were utilized by prison memoirists later in the century. Although it is a work of fiction rather than a strict exercise in life-writing, *Darkness at Noon* uses two specific formal devices that would be developed in prison memoirs from decolonizing regions.[31] First, the novel makes extensive use of analepsis, whereby the main character, Rubashov, connects past events to current conditions. As he sits in his cell, awaiting interrogation and certain death, he thinks about the choices he made, the people he compromised, the questionable principles by which he lived as a revolutionary. Through these narrative flashbacks, Rubashov's experience as a political prisoner becomes saturated with the past, both through personal recollections and through the history of the revolution. Second, *Darkness at Noon* recognizes what the Party calls the "grammatical fiction," or the first-person singular, as the proper basis of intellectual freedom.[32] Although the text employs a third-person narrator, it proposes that Rubashov's intellectual qualities give him enough autonomy, even on death row, to understand, to explain, and at times to resist the workings of totalitarianism. These techniques pull the narrative in two different directions, emphasizing on one hand the typicality of the protagonist and on the other hand his unique individuality. Through this mechanism, the novel stages a debate between the principles of individual freedom and collective responsibility.

At first, the flashbacks in *Darkness at Noon* appear as a simple narrative device, providing psychological depth and backstory. Rubashov was a leading revolutionary figure who becomes ethically tainted through his participation in the state's network of agents, spies, and functionaries. He betrayed comrades, friends, and lovers when the movement asked him or pressured him to do so. He may not be guilty of conspiring against the state, the offense of which he is formally accused, but he is an accessory to all the revolution's major crimes. His arrest causes him to question his participation in the revolution:

> His past was the movement, the Party; present and future, too, belonged to the Party, were inseparably bound up with its fate; but his past was identical with it. And it was this past that was suddenly put in question. (58)

In keeping with the dictates of the revolutionary state, which insists that the "individual was nothing, the Party was all" (82), Rubashov believes he has no individuality, no distance between himself and the movement, at least until his arrest. The flashbacks, therefore, shape the narrative in two distinct ways. First, the flashbacks, like all such devices, break the temporal progression of the narrative. The narrative moves us backward and forward in time, rearranging the order in which distinct events are represented. Second, these flashbacks confirm that Rubashov is one of many who participated in the revolution, betrayed comrades in the name of the struggle, and were ultimately betrayed by their former allies. Finding himself now on the wrong side of state terror, Rubashov regards his earlier forms of commitment with regret. Rubashov has changed, but the movement has not, in essence. It merely casts him aside, as he has done to many others. His story differs in particular details, but not in its general outline.

Whereas the flashbacks tend to emphasize the representativeness or typicality of the main character, the narrative's selective use of the "grammatical fiction," or the first-person singular, accomplishes quite the opposite effect. Rubashov becomes an individual in these moments. Peculiarly, Rubashov is most individuated when he puts himself in other people's position, seeing the world from their perspective, at least temporarily. This becomes evident when he lodges his first protest at the conditions in his cell. Instead of self-righteous indignation, Rubashov sees the situation through his jailer's eyes:

> he fell once more under the familiar and fatal constraint to put himself in the position of his opponent, and to see the scene through the other's eyes. There he sat, this man Rubashov, on the bunk—small, bearded, arrogant [. . .]. Of course, this man Rubashov had his merits and a great past; but it was one thing to see him on the platform at a congress and another, on a palliasse in a cell. So that is the legendary Rubashov, thought Rubashov in the name of the officer with the expressionless eyes. Screams for his breakfast like a schoolboy and isn't even ashamed. Cell not cleaned up. Holes in his sock. Querulous intellectual. (22)

Rubashov's status as a querulous, hair-splitting intellectual is somehow connected to the ability to see things from other people's point of view. Being an intellectual, in other words, means refusing to accept doctrine without question. Later, during the official interrogations, Rubashov falls into the same pattern of thought, putting himself in the position of his examining prosecutor:

> The old compulsion to think through the minds of others had again taken hold of him; he sat in Ivanov's [his interrogator's] place and saw himself through Ivanov's eyes, in the position of the accused [. . .]. He saw this degraded Rubashov [. . .] and he understood the mixture of tenderness and contempt with which Ivanov had treated him. (111)

The other major characters in the novel (including the young Rubashov, in many scenes) are monologic, clinging fast to one set of beliefs and one ruthless code of conduct. The Rubashov of the present tense, by contrast, is dialogic, at least in his best moments. Rubashov establishes some distance between himself and the state—some measure of particularity and intellectual autonomy—by insisting on the need to view himself and the world from the perspective of other people. Rubashov's capacity to resist the state relies on this mental exercise. Physically, there is little space for autonomous action. He is in a high security prison, after all. Only with his mind can he fashion some distance between himself and his tormentors. Paradoxically, he does this not by emphasizing the uniqueness of his perspective—he knows full well that countless others have faced similar trials—but by practicing a curious kind of empathy, a willingness to admit the non-exclusiveness of his position.

In sum, *Darkness at Noon* uses two formal devices that resurface often in postwar variants of prison writing. In the text's depiction of the relationship between the past and present, the novel relies on flashbacks to historicize and contextualize. Analepsis tends to de-emphasize the individuality of the protagonist, who is caught up in vast historical processes and political forces. He is one of many such victims of circumstance. As Lyndsey Stonebridge puts it, this type of writing is "a means of excavating the mind in transit between different modes of political and historical belonging" (20). When Ngūgī says that his imprisonment is simply one episode in the long anticolonial struggle, analepsis is the basic formal device he will use to make this claim, much like Koestler. But *Darkness at Noon* also features a countervailing technique that becomes a staple in postwar prison memoirs. In the novel's selective use of the first-person singular, the narrative carves out a space of particularity for the protagonist by emphasizing his intellectual autonomy within the space of the prison. In contrast to the state's agents, Rubashov has the ability to recognize the perspective of others, even enemies. His individuality depends, in some measure, on his intellectual adroitness.

Last, it is important to emphasize the ideological flexibility of Koestler's narrative. This ideological flexibility is based in autobiographical details. Koestler borrows from his experience as a political prisoner in fascist Spain—when he was a Communist—to craft a novel about the experience of being a political prisoner in a Stalinist state (although the Soviet Union is never identified explicitly). Reminiscent of Eileen Chang's writing, this tendency to see all oppressive regimes as similar, or as interchangeable *dramatis personae* of a scripted confrontation, features prominently in prison memoirs written after the war. In African writing, especially, it has the tendency to minimize the difference between the cold war's ideological blocs when decolonization is at stake.

PEN Power

Much as Koestler served as a conduit between PEN and CCF in the early 1950s, Soyinka did the same in the 1960s. PEN set up the Writers in Prison committee in 1960, and Soyinka's imprisonment later in the decade led to the committee's first high-profile international campaign. As I discuss in chapter 3, Soyinka was one of the CCF's favorite African writers, which included a close working relationship with Dennis Duerden, director of the Transcription

Centre. At the urging of the CCF and with expenses paid by the Farfield Foundation, the CIA front organization, Soyinka attended the 1965 PEN meeting to help elect Arthur Miller, the CCF's preferred candidate, to the PEN presidency.[33] When Soyinka was arrested a few months later for holding up a Nigerian radio station at gunpoint and broadcasting a message critical of the regime, the CCF network sprang into action to defend him. Bruce King, scholar of postcolonial literature who was then teaching at Ibadan, appealed to the CCF's Melvin Lasky for help: "It seems to me as much should be done for Soyinka as, say, for any writer in trouble with the authorities behind the Iron Curtain."[34] Duerden organized a letter campaign that included members of the CCF network, including *Transition*, Alfred Kazin, Robert Lowell, and Lionel Trilling.[35] Duerden instructed the locally based Walter Schwarz, a reporter for the Manchester *Guardian* and Soyinka's friend, "to retain the best defence counsel available in Nigeria to defend Wole Soyinka and that the Congress for Cultural Freedom will meet the cost."[36] This time, at least, the CCF campaign could claim victory: Soyinka was charged with specific crimes in a timely manner and acquitted in a court of law.

By 1967, when Soyinka was detained again in the early stages of the Nigerian civil war, the CCF was in turmoil due to the revelations about CIA funding. Nevertheless, the Transcription Centre's Duerden was on hand to act as a liaison between the CCF, Soyinka's family, and PEN, who took the lead in the Soyinka campaign this time around. Before his arrest, Soyinka went into hiding after receiving warnings from "friendly officers" of an army assassination plot. He reassured acquaintances he was alive through Duerden.[37] In November 1967, when the Writers in Prison Committee sent Peter Elstob, a writer and PEN staffer who had fought and been imprisoned in Spain, to Lagos on a fact-finding mission, it fell to Duerden to brief his PEN counterpart before the trip. Elstob was dispatched to learn more about Soyinka's detention, telling the Nigerian authorities that PEN has sent him "to enquire into the circumstances of WS's imprisonment, the state of his health, his safety and to enquire when he was going to stand trial." PEN is a "responsible organisation," he emphasized to them, saying that it would not "lend [its] weight to a world-wide protest" before knowing the basic facts of the case.[38]

Duerden provided Elstob with a list of Nigerian contacts who might prove helpful, but the document would cause Elstob some trouble as he departed Nigeria. At the airport, security demanded to see all his papers. When Elstob refused, repeatedly, to share his correspondence, his examiners threatened him with "other methods" if he persisted.[39] Conceding defeat, Elstob was questioned at length about the contacts on the list supplied by Duerden, and security forced him to hand over letters that Soyinka's wife wrote to Duerden, which Elstob was carrying out of the country. Elstob managed to destroy parts of his PEN report before turning over the documents; he worried that off-the-record comments by officials sympathetic to Soyinka might land them in hot water. Although Elstob found little hard evidence of anything during his trip—officials dodged his questions and refused him access to Soyinka—his own experiences confirmed the alarmist reports coming from Soyinka's camp. PEN would proceed.

With the help of the CCF, PEN launched a protest letter campaign and organized demonstrations in front of Nigerian diplomatic buildings. Duerden arranged a letter of protest to *The Times*, signed by prominent literary figures such as Doris Lessing, V. S. Naipaul, Harold Pinter, Kenneth Tynan, John Wain, Arnold Wesker, and Angus Wilson.[40] Organizing letters of protest and well-timed demonstrations in front of embassies became part of PEN's standard playbook. These basic publicity tactics would be used in later campaigns involving Ngũgĩ, El Saadawi, Mapanje, Salman Rushdie, and Ken Saro-Wiwa. Increasingly, from the 1960s, literature became an important venue in which conflicts over human rights were staged. As the Koestler case reminds us, the template for these debates was created in the context of Europe's ideological wars. As this rhetorical contest shifted to the treatment of writers from the global south, some of the debates that characterized the aesthetic cold war—especially about the role of the state in literary production—were transported into discussions about human rights in the decolonizing world.

Who Are You, Again?

Each of the prison memoirs I discuss in this chapter reflects the campaigns conducted by writers themselves and their international collaborators. South African journalist and activist Ruth First was an important part of the anti-apartheid movement both before and after her detention in 1963. Published in exile, *117 Days* was a key instrument in her own work to publicize the criminality of the apartheid state. The BBC adapted it as a documentary, with First herself playing the lead role. El Saadawi's and Ngũgĩ's narratives both make matter-of-fact references to the international campaigners who lobbied the Egyptian and Kenyan governments, respectively, for their freedom. Soyinka's participation in the movement for his release, in keeping with his personality, forms part of a cat-and-mouse game with the authorities. Despite former

Mbari colleague J. P. Clark-Bekederemo representing the government's position, going so far as to make use of appearances before PEN audiences to argue that Soyinka deserved his imprisonment, Soyinka feels confident he won the public relations battle.[41] Even the superintendent of his prison tells Soyinka that his detention was an enormous mistake (285). The ability of these memoirists to participate in the international campaigns waged on their behalf, despite being imprisoned, marks one obvious difference between their narratives and *Darkness at Noon*. Although Koestler narrowly escaped execution in Franco's Spain partly as a result of international pressure, this biographical feature does not intrude on his major novel about political detainees.

And Crocodiles Are Hungry at Night carries a deep structural imprint left by Mapanje's relationship with PEN. The narrative is bookended by a simple question, posed to Mapanje by the chief of Malawi's political police: "Who are you?"[42] Asked this blunt question at the start of his confinement as part of his prison intake, it confuses detainee and reader alike. It is close to, but meaningfully different than, "what is your name (date of birth, home address, and so on)?" The security officer explains that he does not know why Hastings Banda, Malawi's dictator, has signed the warrant for Mapanje's indefinite detention. Mapanje is not known to the special branch, in other words, when he is taken into custody. If this claim of ignorance is credible, it means that the order came from another wing of the government—probably from one of Banda's cronies, Mapanje reckons. Of course, Mapanje does not really know how to answer this loaded question about his identity, but it serves as an imaginative prompt for the book itself. The intervening pages delicately unpack the layers of his story through the device of this existential inquiry. Head of the university's English department; linguist and poet of international stature but frustrated that he faces censorship at home; devoted family man; lapsed Roman Catholic; contacts at the BBC and at metropolitan universities from his PhD studies in England; friendly with people connected to international human rights organizations; private loathing of Banda's regime but guarded in his public comments; proud of Malawi's rich culture, especially its oral and folk traditions; genuinely unsure what might have led to his arbitrary detention; courageous and cunning in equal measures when circumstances demand: these are a few of the things we learn about Mapanje over the course of the story, as if we are watching his life unfold at the prompting of the security apparatus.

We ride the narrative swells and troughs as news of the international campaign spills over the prison's defenses. Upon arrival in Mikuyu prison, the warders sequester Mapanje, denying him all external communication. Although

FIGURE 8.1. Harold Pinter (foreground) reading Jack Mapanje's poetry at a PEN protest in front of the Malawi High Commission, London, 1987. Photograph by Frank Martin. Image courtesy of *Guardian*/eyevine/Redux.

news of his arrest becomes public knowledge quickly, even filtering to most prisoners—the BBC World Service broadcast the news by the following day after receiving information through one of Mapanje's friends, an Irish priest— Mapanje initially remains unaware of the news, cut off from the world outside and even from most other detainees.

Unbeknownst to him, his fellow prisoners in another cell block wage a campaign of their own: to have Mapanje transferred to their wing of the facility, where he can "record everyone's story and send it abroad to human rights activists" (103). It works. Released from quarantine to a more populated wing of Mikuyu, Mapanje becomes record-keeper and spokesperson, representing the privations of the group to a global network of protestors. Flashes of collective joy occur when we learn that protests from abroad draw an angry written response from Banda himself, who is rattled by the negative publicity. Moments of despair, likewise, transpire when the prison guard who ferries messages to the outside world is nearly exposed, or when rumors of pending releases turn out to be unfounded. The response to the book's fundamental question—who are you?—gradually unfurls as imprisonment reveals new sides of Mapanje's character.

Some of the most remarkable moments of the narrative occur as Mapanje exchanges secret correspondence, through his warder-courier, with leaders of the campaign for his release. One incoming missive includes a poem by David Constantine, written to honor the dissident Soviet poet Irina Ratushinskaya. It inspires Mapanje to write his own poem in reply:

> What cheer distant voices must bring
> Another poet crackling in the Russian
> Winters of icicle cells, I imagine. [. . .]
> What fresh blood flushes
> When an unexpected poem arrives,
> What fire, what energy
> Inflames these fragile bones!
> Indeed we have the verses in common,
> The detention camps
> The laws against poems. (248–49)

The form of Mapanje's memoir is briefly given over to a kind of international chain letter, combining prose and poetry, what he calls "verses in common." Tracing the relay backwards, Mapanje the poet is heartened by the efforts of campaigners who have taken an interest in his cause, who in turn think he may be buoyed by verses written by a British poet in honor of an exiled Soviet poet and former political prisoner, who must in turn have been inspired by "distant voices" that reached her as she shivered in her "icicle cells." Metropolitan British, Soviet Russian, and Malawian poets share, in his words, "detention camps / The laws against poems." As the memoir reveals to us more about who Mapanje is, it does so by tracing a kind of transnational circuit of contact that draws dissident writers, human rights activists, and international readers into a thick exchange.

More than three-and-a-half years after his arrest, when at last Mapanje is being released, the Malawian security chief repeats the question, who are you? Again, the question throws the author off-balance. His interrogator elaborates:

> Dr Mapanje, what I mean is we've imprisoned tens of thousands of people in this country, some more distinguished than yourself, but we've never had the same amount of trouble as we've had over your case. People who supported you came from unexpected corners of the globe. That's why I ask who you are. And your answer will not change the position of your release: I am only enquiring for my own information, to enlighten my police force

and myself. You see, Dr Mapanje, there were so many versions of the causes of your imprisonment, in the university and outside it, that my staff were surprised and often confused. We still do not know what happened to you in the university or who reported you to the H.E. [Banda]. So, tell me, who are you? (364)

For the political police, the international campaign to release Mapanje is a *deus ex machina*, an unexpected, inexplicable foreign intervention into the plot. Mapanje's readers and his supporters more broadly, however, have been conscripted into the story already. None of this is news: it is part of the author's story, who he is. By now, we know a welter of details, especially of the PEN-organized protests featuring Ngũgĩ, Soyinka, Susan Sontag, Harold Pinter, and Nuruddin Farah. Who Mapanje is—as a narrative construction—cannot be answered without some understanding of his life as a prisoner of conscience who could help orchestrate an international pressure campaign on the behalf of himself and Malawi's political detainees.

Flashbacks

The prison memoirs I consider in this chapter each use a specific literary device, analepsis, or flashback, to connect the narrative of imprisonment with more general stories of oppression. These breaks in narrative progress show how personal situations reflect wider social conditions. Mapanje's narrative is typical. Naturally, he speculates about what events may have led to his arrest because he is neither charged with a specific criminal offense nor given a fixed term of detention. He also ruminates on his life as an academic and poet in a place where freedom of expression does not exist, a problem endemic in 1980s Malawi.

In contrast, *The Man Died* contains some of the most striking flashbacks in the genre, arguably out of character for Soyinka. When chained by his captors, he reports "that never until this moment did [...] self-definition become so clear." Uncharacteristically, he says that the starkness of this realization comes from a racial memory: the experience of being fettered "does not stand alone, most especially as a black man. [...] Surely it cannot be a strictly personal experience" (39). Although Soyinka in other contexts tends to downplay racial affinity as a basis of collective spirit, here he seems to emphasize his connection with the diaspora, putting his individual plight in the historical context of the slave trade.[43] His working title for the book was *A Slow Lynching* (12). It is only later that Soyinka reminds himself that his oppressors, too, are Black men. He is neither a slave being marched to auction nor a convict in a "chain-gang in South Alabama or Johannesburg" but a Black Nigerian being arbitrarily detained by fellow Black Nigerians in an independent, postcolonial state (39). Even the most individualist of writers is prone to appeal to the collective in life-writing about imprisonment.

In *Detained*, Ngũgĩ makes such extensive use of historical flashbacks that he willfully subordinates his own experiences of jail for long stretches of the narrative. In his preface, he says that he tries to see his loss of freedom "not as a personal affair" (xi). The ensuing text is as good as his word, especially in the first half of the narrative, much of which he gives over to historical analysis. Simon Gikandi argues that this bestows the text with a moral authority, allowing Ngũgĩ to "allegorize his own experiences and turn them into fables of the class struggle."[44] Research for an aborted book, on the culture of Kenya's White settlers during the colonial period, furnishes the raw material for a full chapter. Colonialism produced a culture of vice and luxury among Europeans and offered an "aesthetic of submission and blind obedience" to the conquered peoples (42). In moments such as these, Ngũgĩ and Soyinka sound very similar about the history of racial subordination in colonial contexts.

A chapter on detention without trial traces its continuous use in Kenya from the colonial to the postcolonial period, the great irony being that Jomo Kenyatta suffered from and then systematically exploited this security measure on either side of Kenyan independence. Further sections place the author in the history of the resistance movement, especially the Land and Freedom uprising in which his elder brother participated. Their resistance songs and poems, as well as J. M. Kariuki's prison memoir, *Mau Mau Detainee* (1963), form Kenya's anticolonial literary tradition into which Ngũgĩ inserts his own life-writing.[45] "Detention could not break him," Ngũgĩ writes proudly of Kariuki before glumly recalling that assassins would kill the patriot years later, in the postcolonial period. "A colonial affair . . . a neo-colonial affair . . . what's the difference?" (96), wonders Ngũgĩ, who argues at great length that very little of substance changed when the British departed and turned over the reins of government to an indigenous "comprador bourgeoisie" in thrall to "foreign economic interests" (56). In these passages, at least, Ngũgĩ sounds like an African Rubashov, pacing his cell for hours, desperately trying to figure out how the nationalist movement made a wrong turn.

Ruth First's use of narrative flashbacks in *117 Days* provides one of the most innovative examples of the device in the prison memoir mini-canon. In First's case, it might better be described as a narrative sideswipe: rather than tell of personal details from pre-detention life or relate chunks of South African history, she fashions cameos from the lives of colleagues in the anti-apartheid struggle. Most of First's narrative uses a straightforward first-person voice, divulging, in chronological order, the major events of her detention. The moment of her arrest, her experiences during solitary confinement, her few contacts with family, and her cagey showdowns with interrogators: these are all narrated in chronological order in no-nonsense prose. First casts herself as something of a flawed foot-soldier in the movement. She does not incriminate herself or others under the pressure of solitary confinement and indefinite detention, but she attempts suicide in a moment of despair. She lists many of her heroes in the movement, but she is very modest about her own efficacy as an activist. Her main story of detention is compelling precisely because it is not exceptional. She does not fashion herself as heroine or White savior of the movement.

She punctuates her personal story with italicized passages that tell of others who have struggled against and suffered at the hands of the apartheid state—what I call the sideswipes in *117 Days*. The first such vignette tells of a daring prison break that happens, by coincidence, only a few hours after First is taken into custody at Marshall Square prison. Four prominent activists on ninety-day detention orders—the same as First—hatch a plan to escape. They succeed, with the connivance of a White police officer, making it out of South Africa despite a nationwide search. It is an enormously morale-boosting event in the anti-apartheid movement. First tells their story with obvious vicarious pleasure, the details of which she could reassemble from her own network and from press reports. The four escapees' path to exile is notably different than First's. She waits out detention, wracked by doubts, before leaving on an exit visa. As a White woman (albeit married to Joe Slovo, also a major figure in the movement), and as someone not directly implicated in acts of sabotage, she takes a different path to exile. Eventually, South African agents would assassinate her.

Other sideswipes in *117 Days* are not nearly so uplifting. Dennis Brutus makes his own courageous escape attempt just outside Marshall Square prison. Brutus, a talented athlete, simply runs for it while his captors are preoccupied. He does not succeed: one of his police escorts shoots him in the back. Although Brutus survives his injuries, he is sentenced to hard labor on Robben Island, where he was serving time when *117 Days* was written. But Brutus's capture is less demoralizing than Looksmart Solwandle Ngudle's heartrending story, relayed in another of First's italicized passages. Ngudle is an African

National Congress activist, also picked up on a ninety-day detention order. Less than three weeks after his arrest, however, he dies in custody. The police devise a program of physical and psychological torture to extract information, eventually killing him. His mother, learning of his arrest and death at the same time, begins the process of claiming his remains and discovering his fate. With the help of lawyers, her efforts lead to a public inquest that establishes some of the details of the state's interrogation methods. The outcome of the hearings offers cold comfort for Ngudle's family—officially, the court rules that he hanged himself in his cell—but the process does get some facts about the South African justice system on record. The contrast with First's experience is obvious.

Formally, *117 Days* tinkers with the conventions of the detention memoir to perform a cross-referencing inventory of the anti-apartheid movement. First does not use conventional flashbacks to do this, as Koestler and Mapanje do. Instead, she borrows contemporary vignettes from comrades in the anti-apartheid movement to contextualize her part in the broader struggle. This has the effect of mitigating the uniqueness of her own story, which becomes typical, even lacking in drama in comparison to these more spectacular instances of oppression and resistance. Although her own situation occupies the bulk of the word count, her unexceptional, matter-of-fact narrative throws these shorter interruptions into sharp relief. As a White South African, and perhaps as a woman in a male-dominated movement, First subordinates her own story of hardship to a collective endeavor. Compared to Ngũgĩ, for instance, her narrative is far more self-effacing about her own contributions to the struggle.

Grammatical Fictions

Although these examples of life-writing use flashbacks and similar techniques to place their authors in the context of broader struggles, these texts also show a countervailing tendency to emphasize the autonomy and intellectual freedom of the writer. This is evident in Mapanje's text, in which the existential question "who are you?" determines the shape of the narrative. Prison only seems to sharpen the appetite for individuality in life-writing. On this point, *Memoirs from the Women's Prison* is probably the most emphatic of the bunch. Many prison memoirs describe the experience of solitary confinement as a form of torture. Ruth First, for instance, follows Koestler's lead in describing isolation as a method for breaking prisoners who refuse to confess, repent, and implicate others. Soyinka includes long hallucinatory passages describing the effects of being denied social contact. For El Saadawi, ever the contrarian, prison involves torture by enforced proximity to others in communal cells. "Since childhood, I've had a passion for solitude," she tells us, but once in the women's prison, ambient noise assaults her.[46] Incessant quarrels of fellow prisoners, persistent wails of newborns (kept with mothers to suckle), recitations of scripture from pious cellmates, and verbal abuse from wardens leave her with little space for quiet contemplation. "I had imagined prison to be solitude and total silence," a sort of involuntary writer's retreat, but the realities of incarceration do not so much as preserve the privacy of the toilet (128). She lobbies for solitary confinement, but prison authorities deny the request.

Memoirs from the Women's Prison thus imagines the life of the mind as a special calling, an activity that helps define our humanity yet demands some measure of independence and solitude. Defiantly, El Saadawi contrasts herself with writers who collaborate with the state. She recalls with scorn how one unnamed eminent Egyptian writer describes himself as little more than a state functionary (it could easily be Youssef El-Sebai, *Lotus* editor and Minister of Culture):

> "I am only a civil servant . . ." [an unnamed colleague tells El Saadawi] The writer is a civil servant . . . the thinker is a civil servant . . . the philosopher is a civil servant . . . thus, we have no writers, thinkers, or philosophers. What is the difference between the Internal Security officer who is a civil servant and the writer who is a civil servant? Both carry out orders. Neither wants to lose the monthly salary, or the position. (123)

El Saadawi proudly says she prefers her "place here on the ground, in the dust" to that of the salaried functionary who is "bound by the fetters of his position" (123). In her view, better the chains that remind Soyinka of the middle passage than the ties that bind the intellectual to state interests. Convinced that she has landed in prison because of the things she writes and publishes in the oppositional press, in favor of democracy and free expression (like so many others, she is never formally charged with a crime), she declares, "The pen is the most valuable thing in my life. My words on paper are more valuable to me that my life itself. More valuable than my children, more than my husband, more than my freedom" (116).

Writing as I do from the security of an academic position, it would be easy but lazy to conclude that El Saadawi overplays her hand when she rates the value of her pen higher than freedom, family, and life itself. It is more telling to read this kind of statement as typical and credible for its context rather than hyperbolic. The circumstances of the aesthetic cold war, as I have described it, sometimes made the debate between autonomous expression and state involvement in writing seem like an urgent choice between intellectual freedom and intellectual servitude. For writers from the decolonizing world, however, this choice between autonomy and state oversight of cultural production does not correspond to a simple choice between alternatives. El Saadawi was imprisoned by a rabidly anti-Communist regime; the Egyptian press, subservient to the government, smeared her by describing her as the agent of a Soviet plot (186). El Saadawi protests by saying, "My reputation as a nationalist is worth my life to me" (187). Being a devoted nationalist—but not in the pay of the state—and being an autonomous intellectual are equally important to her.

Detained follows the same general line of thought. Ngũgĩ's state tormentors paint him as a follower of "godless communism," but he consistently describes himself as a patriotic Kenyan who believes in social justice for the people (61). Ruth First, of course, as a member of the South African Communist Party before it was banned, was persecuted along with many other activists on this basis alone. The same is true of Mapanje and Soyinka, both imprisoned by fanatically anti-Communist dictators. In the decolonizing world, anti-Communism was the pretext many states used to lock up dissident intellectuals. When organizations such as PEN aligned themselves with writers in the decolonizing world, they were in effect resisting the efforts of the US state and their proxies to suppress Communism in decolonizing areas. The global propaganda battle against Soviet totalitarianism led human rights activists to be sharply critical of anti-Communist regimes in the decolonizing world. Organizations such as PEN developed in contradictory ways, serving both as instruments of the US hegemony in their anti-Communist campaigns and as critics of US client states in the decolonizing world.

And Crocodiles Are Hungry at Night repeatedly draws our attention to the terms of the conflict between intellectual activity and state prerogatives. Mapanje wonders at length if his poetry and his work as a linguist, neither of which is political in nature, contributed to his detention. His reasoning goes something like this: any project that brings credit to an individual Malawian threatens to upstage the dictator himself. Mapanje speculates whether the publication of his first collection of poetry while he was abroad in the early 1980s, studying for his PhD in London, contributed to his persecution:

> In other African countries the publication of the book would have been good reason for celebration. But no-one cared that *Of Chameleons and Gods*

was the first book of poems from a Malawian to appear in the then famous Heinemann African Writers' Series. Or that the book put my country, my university and me on the literary map of the continent. This was thought to be the kind of "showing off" that did not impress those in power. I was not surprised, therefore, when I received stern admonition from relatives, colleagues and friends that the poems had displeased "people in authority" back home, and that I had to be careful what I said or wrote, which countries I visited and what I did while I read for my doctorate degree. (89)

The poems are not critical of Malawian society or its government. In fact, Mapanje points out that his writing is influenced by Malawi's oral culture, "which the verse was trying to preserve" (107). Mere publication of his work abroad—where it was not subject to the Malawian censorship board—appears to have displeased those in power at home. Mapanje's situation reprises the Pasternak affair, but in this instance, it is a fanatically anti-Communist regime that pressures the writer to conform or face the consequences. A few years later, when Mapanje seeks permission to license a Malawian edition of the volume, he confirms this supposition firsthand through interactions with the censorship office. Although the members of the board offer largely positive reports on the content and quality of the poetry, the censorship board's chief protests that Mapanje should have submitted his work for their approval before publishing it overseas. There is no official protocol about this, just an unwritten rule that Malawians should not put their own literary talents above state oversight of culture. Mapanje's drama recalls the Pasternak affair, with the crucial difference that an anti-Communist regime plays the role of tyrant.

Mapanje speculates that his work as a linguist only enhances his local reputation for self-aggrandizement. Chair of the regional linguistics association of southern Africa at the time of his detention, Mapanje was involved in research projects collecting data on "stories, riddles, proverbs, songs, chants, and other interesting" bits of Malawi's vibrant oral culture (132). Building an inventory of vernacular culture brings Mapanje a certain amount of regional and international notice. Once in prison, he again wonders if this work, which might have brought positive external attention to indigenous cultural resources, is counted against him. His research on local languages might have threatened the state's official guardianship of national culture. Ngũgĩ tells a very similar tale in *Detained*, surmising he was imprisoned because he "was involved in the writing of a play in the Gĩkũyũ language, *Ngaahika Ndeenda*, and in its performance by a group of workers and peasants" from his home district (174). Like

Mapanje, Ngũgĩ presumes (he is never convicted of a criminal offense) that he is detained because his efforts to restore the dignity and resilience of vernacular culture are not welcomed by the authorities. Both writers believe they were jailed for their independent work on vernacular language, thereby rivalling the state as custodians of national customs. As El Saadawi frames it, the duty of the writer is to defend national culture against authoritarian states.[47]

The Man Died provides one of the most complicated reckonings of state power, national culture, and the role of the writer in representing this relationship. As the memoir's title indicates, this is a book about the status of humanism in the context of spreading authoritarianism: "The man dies in all who keep silent in the face of tyranny" (13). This pronouncement becomes a standard reference point for others working in the genre. To be human in the face of tyranny means to resist by speaking, communicating, representing, and writing if at all possible.

In the course of his substantial criticisms of state power and the actions of the Federal Government during the civil war, Soyinka concludes that ethnicity, language, even shared values or culture cannot provide the basis of national identity. In a chapter on the genocidal attacks on Nigeria's Igbo people, the cause of Biafra's secession, Soyinka concludes that "there is only one common definition for a people and a nation—a unit of humanity bound together by a common ideology" (183). It is a fascinating statement. Why does he stress ideology here? Conventional wisdom suggests that most anticolonial writers define national identity through common culture, language, history, or political institutions—not as a shared ideology. *The Man Died* otherwise testifies to the importance of humanism, individuality, and literature as tools for resisting dictatorships. Rejecting ethnicity or language as the basis of national identity is consistent enough with Soyinka's other commitments; it makes sense. But to affirm that only shared ideology leads to workable national cultures seems out of step with his other thoughts on this question. His major intervention in *The Man Died*, as I understand it, is that rigid beliefs lead to bigotry and tyranny. He often compares the Nigerian state to the Third Reich: Did not the Nazis, after all, have a shared ideology, albeit one based in racial superiority? What sort of acceptable shared ideology might galvanize a national culture Soyinka does not specify.

The passage substantiates his statement about ideology by posing two contrasting examples of how such a national identity might be won or lost. First, he quotes several lines of poetry by August von Platen, a nineteenth-century German poet and orientalist. Soyinka explains that Platen's lines reflect his pessimistic moods, when he fears that the wrong kind of national culture is all that Nigeria possesses:

> And those who hate evil in the depth of their heart
> Will be driven from homeland, when evil
> Comes to be worshipped by a nation of slaves
> Far wiser to renounce such a country. (183)

Better to go into exile than to allow the prejudices and hatreds of one's countrymen to infect oneself. So far, this sounds more like the Soyinka his readers have come to know from his other publications. Soyinka would himself go into exile after his release. These lines provide a negative example, an individual protest against the kind of ideology that turns national culture ugly.

In his more "euphoric moments," Soyinka says, he turns to lines he attributes to Fidel Castro. Castro, he suggests, offers a constructive ideology of nationhood:

> Esta tierra
> Este aire
> Esto cielo
> Son los nuestros
> Defenderemos
> This earth is ours
> And the air
> And the sky
> We will defend them (183; Soyinka's translation)

Soyinka glosses this brief description of a national ideology as elective and collective, neither driven by ethnocentrism nor imposed by state interests. "It is better to believe in people than in nations," he explains earlier in the chapter (175). The individual becomes a part of Soyinka's national group by affinity of outlook, not by birth or by conscription. This national spirit must share a "vision beyond lines drawn by masters from a colonial past" (183). In Nigeria, of course, colonialism helped produce the mess by drawing arbitrary national boundaries and by pitting ethnic groups against one another.

Soyinka's description of a workable national culture as shared ideology remains enigmatic to me. Out of context, the negative and positive examples, drawn from Platen and Castro, leave too much undeclared. If we know a bit more about how Platen's verse resonated in this period, however, we can fill some of the ideological gaps. Platen's poetry appeared in the CCF's *Encounter* magazine about a decade before the publication of *The Man Died*. The December 1962 issue carried a selection of Thomas Mann's correspondence. The final installment is an open letter from Mann to the arts section of *Neue Zürcher Zeitung*, the Swiss German-language newspaper. In this 1936 letter from exile, which apparently contributed to the Nazis stripping him of his German citizenship, Mann is openly critical of anti-Semitism. He believes that the totalitarian regime will permanently damage German literature and culture. Mann closes the letter by quoting poetry from Platen—some of the very lines Soyinka quotes in *The Man Died*.[48] Soyinka, however, does not fully attribute these verses, neither mentioning that they appeared in one of Mann's letters from exile nor explaining that they were subsequently published in *Encounter*.

With this information, we are in a slightly better position to understand some of the ramifications of Soyinka's claim that shared, elective ideology can create national culture. First, Soyinka's version of ideology is by implication nonaligned. By putting Platen's and Castro's ruminations on national culture beside one another, Soyinka suggests that the intellectual ought to be intellectually well-traveled, finding inspiration from various sources. Writers who cannot gather useful ideas from different camps limit themselves. Partisanship cripples intellectual activity. Writers from the decolonizing world are best positioned to understand this. Soyinka's repurposing of Platen through Mann follows the basic trajectory of PEN itself, which pivots from antifascism to anti-Communism and later defends imprisoned writers in decolonizing areas.

Second, we might speculate that Soyinka's thick citational practices prefigure those that appear decades later in Mapanje's memoir, *And Crocodiles Are Hungry at Night*. As I discuss earlier in the chapter, Mapanje writes a poem as part of his correspondence with the PEN campaign, inspired by Russian dissident Irina Ratushinskaya and British poet David Constantine. Soyinka's borrowings from Castro and Platen are not part of his own letters to the outside world from within prison. Instead, he lifts the Platen lines from letters by the German exile Mann. Mann quotes Platen to help explain turning his back on Nazi Germany. From there, the citations and cross-references pile up: Platen, through Mann, through the pages of the CCF's *Encounter* magazine, through the PEN campaign, and then through Soyinka's prison memoir, which puts this chain of transmission in direct juxtaposition with Castro's words. The Castro citation, by comparison, reverses the flow of exile, as he returned from banishment to lead a nationalist revolution. Soyinka's version of nonaligned humanism, then, does not reject ideology, but welcomes it, relying on it for new intellectual combinations.

Like Soyinka in *The Man Died*, Frantz Fanon closes *The Wretched of the Earth* by arguing that ideological nonalignment leads to a rejuvenated humanism, fit for a decolonized world. In Europe, Fanon says, "we are witnessing a stasis," a continent paralyzed by the cold war's ideological standoff. Only in the "Third World," Fanon suggests, are we in a position to "reexamine the question of man," to "start over a new history of man" (237–38). Fanon insists that this new humanism ought to learn from the mistakes of the cold war's antagonists, but it must chart a new path, unencumbered by the failures that have come before it. Soyinka's criticisms and tentative defenses of a national culture rooted in humanism luxuriate in the same kind of ideological promiscuity. *The Man Died* fashions a grammatical fiction, a first person, by stitching together a disparate set of fragments. The human being lives rather than dies, we might riff on Soyinka's title, when writing allows us to make creative use of ideology, instead of cowering before it or protesting, futilely, against it. Ideology, in Soyinka's hands, is not the antithesis of intellectual work, but the faithful servant of intellectual work. Hacks misuse ideology; legitimate intellectuals make it serve their needs, nonexclusively.

Collectively, these prison memoirs rehearse, in pointed forms, arguments about the function of literature in the context of decolonization and the aesthetic cold war. What are the means of securing intellectual autonomy in the context of a global ideological conflict? Should writers decolonize cultural production by pushing language in horizontal directions or by consolidating it along a vertical axis? Should writers collaborate with international cultural diplomacy programs to support the decolonization of literary institutions, or should writers simply ask to be left alone? Prison writing from the postcolonial moment shows us that writers became jealous of the nation-state's claim to preserve national culture, arguing instead that vernacular literature is opposed to state interests. In their very forms, I suggest, these notes from prison inscribe the ideological conflicts of the aesthetic cold war being waged on a global field. As Jini Kim Watson says in her research on PEN conferences in Asia, "the core liberal principle of 'freedom of expression' becomes recoded, challenged, and retheorized" when we reflect on how the conjunction of decolonization and the cold war affected PEN's nonpolitical commitments in decolonizing regions.[49]

The ruminations in these memoirs also allow us to trace the fault lines that the aesthetic cold war opened on the literature of human rights. In *The Last Utopia*, Samuel Moyn describes anticolonialism as something opposed to (not consistent with) human rights in the second half of the twentieth century: "[H]uman rights entered global rhetoric in a kind of hydraulic relationship with self-determination: to the extent the one appeared, and progressed, the other declined, or even disappeared" (88). As both Antony Anghie and

Joseph R. Slaughter point out, Moyn's perspective depends too much on a metropolitan outlook if we recognize that self-determination, as a fundamental human right, is the major premise of the Bandung movement. Crystal Parikh complements these criticisms of Moyn by arguing that US writers of color align themselves with "decolonization, socialist, and other political struggles in the global South" when they mobilize the language of human rights in their work.[50] Adom Getachew offers yet another angle to consider when she demonstrates how European states used the notion of human rights to limit or encumber sovereignty in decolonizing parts of the world. The foregoing chapter reads prison memoirs as an important site of struggle, suggesting that international debates about human rights can be extricated neither from the cold war nor the decolonization movement. Reading this as an either-or proposition—either (individual) human rights or collective self-determination; either superpower rivalry or decolonization—underestimates the extent to which human rights organizations such as PEN served contradictory political purposes, working on behalf of US interests in the context of anti-Communism and then as an implicit critic of US interests when it publicized how proxy states and anti-Communist allies intimidated dissidents, especially writers.

With their allusions to ongoing collective struggle against colonialism and neocolonialism, these texts emphasize their commitment to the Bandung project of nonalignment through collective resistance. Even the most individualist of writers, such as El Saadawi and Soyinka, use their texts to articulate forms of solidarity with oppressed groups. But the participation of this literature in human rights networks also gestures toward the individualist ethos that would prevail in the post-cold war geopolitical order. As Moyn says in answer to some of his critics, the human rights project, which largely seeks to protect individuals against autocratic states, has fashioned its objectives to fit within the global neoliberal economic order: "the age of human rights, while a good one for some of the worst off, has mainly been a golden age for the rich" (*Not Enough* 5). The human rights project rallies to the defense of autonomous individuality more unambiguously at the end of the cold war, whereas these prison memoirs move between individual freedom and collective responsibility without signs of strain. Prison literature from the decolonizing parts of the world sits at this historical crossroads, where powerful states abandoned large-scale intervention in the literary field in favor of a capitalist marketplace for books and ideas, prizing individual autonomy at the expense of collective responsibility.

Conclusion

MY INTEREST IN THE RELATIONSHIP between the literature of decolonization and the cold war began over a decade ago, in 2010. At the time, I was working on a different project, mostly about twentieth-century cultural institutions that brought writers from Africa, metropolitan Britain, and the Caribbean into close contact. Bob Taylor, one of the many remarkable archivists at the Harry Ransom Center at the University of Texas, told me about their holdings from the Transcription Centre, which was founded by Dennis Duerden, an ex-BBC radio producer who specialized in African art and music. As someone studying transatlantic literary culture, had I ever heard of it? Did I know that the CIA bankrolled a scheme to record and distribute radio programs on African literature and culture? My ignorance of the venture was total. I started digging into the papers that very afternoon and I have not stopped. There are more relevant archival materials than one person could possibly digest.

When I started this archival work, I held only vague notions of how the cold war and decolonization might be related in aesthetic terms. These geopolitical events happened at the same time, but I had never seriously considered how writing about them as one process might force me to understand intellectual and literary history in different ways. I knew that figures such as Aimé Césaire and Doris Lessing had been Communist Party members, quitting like so many others in the aftermath of 1956. I knew that the Congress for Cultural Freedom had been a big scandal in western Europe, but I had no more than a dim recollection that it sponsored a couple of magazines in Africa. Even more vaguely, I knew that the Soviet literary establishment had sponsored the highly influential *Lotus*, but I had never looked at an issue of the magazine. I had not read so much as a good secondhand description of it. The magazine was not easy to find, then or now. Likewise, I was aware that MI5 had collected information on Lessing and that C.L.R. James had been deported from the United States.

How these bits of knowledge might be connected I had no idea. Along with many literary scholars, I continued to read the literature of decolonization primarily as a matter between colonized and colonizer. If the cold war influenced the literature of decolonization, I figured, it was primarily in ideological ways, with a smattering of writers lining up on one side or the other.

It took me a long time to make decent sense of the archival record I encountered. Ingrained habits of thought prevented me from understanding the data I found. I had to unlearn many of the assumptions I brought to the project. When I started working on cultural diplomacy initiatives, I was prepared to read every utterance through the lenses of conspiracy and cynicism. How did the United States and the Soviet Union coopt and defang and reroute the literature of decolonization, I wanted to know? How did the cold war's partisans recruit and corrupt intellectuals from the decolonizing world? The temptation to interpret the archival record from this perspective was even greater when I turned to the punitive measures state agencies visited upon writers. I anticipated writing a book detailing how large states first tried to bribe writers, resorting to coercion and intimidation when lavish conferences and generous book deals did not do the trick. There was, however, a problem. Neither the archives I consulted nor the literary texts themselves seemed to support such a reading. Far from controlling anticolonial writers, the cultural diplomacy programs I studied seemed to be waged from a position of relative weakness, not overwhelming strength. The more I looked, the more I encountered evidence that some of the same writers were happy to accept support from both US and Soviet diplomacy programs, which were in turn happy to pay court without making explicit demands or getting firm commitments from writers in the decolonizing world. Even more surprising was how ineffective censorship, intimidation, and surveillance proved, at least in terms of influencing the political content of literature from the global south. Rather than drawing ideological fences around literary enclaves, punitive state measures strengthened the narrative that intellectuals belonged to a nonaligned creative guild that trespassed national borders and narrow ideological affiliations. The tendency of nation-states to seize on the abuses of rival states—the United States was especially vulnerable on this score, as alliances with European imperialist nations, homegrown racial discrimination, and support for many ruthless dictators were noted by nonaligned figures—allowed dissident writers to mobilize cold war rivalries in their defense. This did not level the playing field in their disputes with the political police, but it allowed persecuted writers to find allies and audiences empathetic to their situation.

This process of discovery has led me to challenge some of the main assumptions in postcolonial and global literary studies. For instance, there is a long-standing belief that the United States, after World War II, gradually consolidated its status of an imperial power by taking over western European interests in Africa, Asia, and the Caribbean. Edward W. Said, the foremost scholar of postcolonial studies, pushed the consensus view that the United States inherited the mantle of British imperialism.[1] This may be true in terms of geopolitical history, broadly speaking, but does not explain the cultural and literary history of the twentieth century very well. Neither the United States nor the Soviet Union was able to dominate cultural production in the decolonizing world in the fashion of the departing European powers, which exported their languages, religions, books, and educational systems to their areas of influence, especially in settler colonies. Although cultural diplomacy programs brought outside interests into colonial areas, these outside interests were not in a position to dictate terms. More often than not, the opportunistic global south writers who became known overseas worked equally well with US and Soviet diplomacy networks. Cultural imperialism is not quite the right concept to explain the complexity of this situation.

Likewise, the dark side of state involvement in the arts—censorship, surveillance, and other punitive measures—did not allow large states and their proxies in the decolonizing world to assume full control of anticolonial literary forces. Very often, the effort to control writers backfired, creating new partnerships out of old rivalries. Studying attempts to intimidate writers in the decolonizing world allows us to complicate our narratives about intellectual life during this period. The United States and the Soviet Union, each of which made significant efforts to manage intellectual production within their own territories, exported their ideas about containing political dissent to the decolonizing world. In Africa and Asia, anti-Communist states were especially zealous in their attempts to limit intellectual autonomy. The difference in intellectual freedoms between so-called First, Second, and Third Worlds was much narrower than most studies of the century would have us believe. The FBI's harassment of Black writers and the anti-Communism of many regimes in the decolonizing world make it difficult to conclude that US defenses of intellectual freedom during the cold war were much more than disingenuous exercises in point scoring. The effects of this include the creation of global professional comradery among writers who worked in this period. The threat of censorship, deportation, and imprisonment meant that writers of nearly all political persuasions and national origins began to see themselves as part of an international system.

State intimidation channeled Thomas Mann, Susan Sontag, Arthur Koestler, Doris Lessing, Harold Pinter, Irina Ratushinskaya, Salman Rushdie, and Wole Soyinka into the same professional networks. Just as cultural diplomacy programs had a way of breaching ideological differences between writers, so too did the work of censors and the political police.

It took me a long time to accept that some of the key debates in postcolonial studies—especially those about autonomy and utilitarianism, and likewise those about indigeneity and hybridity—were formed in the crucible of the aesthetic cold war. I was long accustomed to seeing how modernist approaches to literature had informed anticolonial writing in metropolitan languages, but I had not given enough thought to how socialist aesthetic theory might have been perceived by writers in the decolonizing world. A few, isolated figures had declared their admiration for socialist realism and translated it across ideological borders, but I had never been convinced that this quirk of the Soviet apparatus had more than a limited influence on global letters of the twentieth century. What I did not appreciate is how much socialist aesthetic theory's approach to languages and literatures would be appealing to anticolonial writers who wanted to take stock of indigenous cultural resources. It gave writers suspicious of cosmopolitanism and hybridity a common language, a distinct and compelling answer to the problems of securing cultural autonomy.

Finally, this book proposes a different model for writing a global history of literature in the twentieth century. Putting the cold war and decolonization into the same frame permits us to see that cultural diplomacy programs and the political police had an equally sizable impact on the reorganization of global literary production during the twentieth century. The "world republic of letters" cannot be mapped by reference to a cultural "Greenwich meridian," a literary capital based in western Europe or North America, as Pascale Casanova would have it. Cairo, Hong Kong, Ibadan, Kampala, and Tashkent were as important as London, New York, or Paris when it comes to appreciating how writers and readers from decolonizing areas became integrated into world-literary space. Nor do Franco Moretti's graphs, maps, and trees furnish enough data about political conditions and cultural institutions to explain how and why literary practices move.[2] The aesthetic cold war, I have argued in this book, represents a distinct phase of global literary history. To understand it, we must acknowledge that geopolitical power affects literary exchange without then concluding that geopolitical power translates neatly into forms of cultural influence. In fact, archival and textual evidence suggests that the relationship between geopolitical power and literary practices is highly variable. Different chapters of this story will require different archives, different models of cultural exchange, and different accounts of the relationship between politics, aesthetics, and intellectual history. When I started my research for this project, I did not anticipate how the history of ideas and international politics would move in such different directions despite their symbiotic relationship during this period, when writers were courted and monitored by large states. It stands in marked contrast to our own moment, when most large states have lost interest in books and ideas.

NOTES

Chapter 1

1. Chinua Achebe, *Morning Yet on Creation Day* (Garden City, NY: Anchor, 1975), 29. Emphasis original, here and in all quoted material, unless otherwise noted. Additional references parenthetical. C. L. Innes puts lecture date at 1972. *Chinua Achebe* (Cambridge: Cambridge UP, 1990), 63.

2. Contemporaneous reports on and responses to the Bandung Conference include A. Appadorai, "The Bandung Conference," *India Quarterly: A Journal of International Affairs* 11.3 (1955): 207–35; Chong-ik Yi, "The Bandung Conference, April 18–24, 1955 and the United States Reaction," MA Thesis, University of Wisconsin-Madison (1957); Iqbal Hasan Burney, "Newspaper Coverage of the Bandung Conference," MA Thesis, Stanford University (1956); Richard Wright, *The Color Curtain: A Report on the Bandung Conference*, foreword Gunnar Myrdal (Cleveland: World Publishing, 1956). More recent attempts to think about the historical significance of the Bandung Conference include See Seng Tan and Amitav Acharya, eds., *Bandung Revisited: The Legacy of the 1955 Asian-African Conference for International Order* (Singapore: National U of Singapore P, 2008); Brian Russell Roberts and Keith Foulcher, eds., *Indonesian Notebook: A Sourcebook on Richard Wright and the Bandung Conference* (Durham: Duke UP, 2016); Luis Eslava, Michael Fakhri, and Vasuki Nesiah, eds., *Bandung, Global History, and International Law: Critical Pasts and Pending Futures* (Cambridge: Cambridge UP, 2017); Christopher J. Lee, ed., *Making a World after Empire: The Bandung Moment and its Political Afterlives* (Athens: Ohio UP, 2010); and David Scott, *Omens of Adversity: Tragedy, Time, Memory, Justice* (Durham: Duke UP, 2014).

3. "Final Communiqué of the Afro-Asian Conference of Bandung (24 April 1955)," in *Asia-Africa Speak from Bandung*, ed. Indonesian Ministry of Foreign Affairs (Djakarta: 1955), 161–69. https://www.cvce.eu/en/obj/final_communique_of_the_asian_african_conference_of _bandung_24_april_1955-en-676237bd-72f7-471f-949a-88b6ae513585.html.

4. George Padmore, *Pan-Africanism or Communism*, foreword Richard Wright, intro. Azinna Nwafor (1956; Garden City: Doubleday, 1971), xv.

5. Frantz Fanon, *The Wretched of the Earth*, trans. Richard Philcox, foreword Homi K. Bhabha, preface Jean-Paul Sartre (New York: Grove, 2004), 55. Additional references parenthetical.

6. Hannah Arendt, *The Origins of Totalitarianism*, "Preface to Part Two" (Orlando: Harvest, 1968), xix.

7. Odd Arne Westad is the preeminent historian of the relationship between the cold war and decolonization. See *The Global Cold War: Third World Interventions and the Making of Our*

Times, 2nd ed. (Cambridge: Cambridge UP, 2007) as well as *The Cold War: A World History* (New York: Basic Books, 2017).

8. Monica Popescu, *At Penpoint: African Literatures, Postcolonial Studies, and the Cold War* (Durham: Duke UP, 2020), 36.

9. There are many accounts of cold war cultural diplomacy. Some of the best of considerations of US activities include Penny M. Von Eschen, *Satchmo Blows Up the World: Jazz Ambassadors Play the Cold War* (Cambridge: Harvard UP, 2004); Greg Barnhisel, *Cold War Modernists: Art, Literature, and American Cultural Diplomacy* (New York: Columbia UP, 2015); Harris Feinsod, *Poetry of the Americas: From Good Neighbors to Countercultures* (Oxford: Oxford UP, 2017); Danielle Fosler-Lussier, *Music in America's Cold War Diplomacy* (Berkeley: U of California P, 2015); Serge Guilbaut, *How New York Stole the Idea of Modern Art: Abstract Expressionism, Freedom, and the Cold War*, trans. Arthur Goldhammer (Chicago: U of Chicago P, 1983); Catherine Gunther Kodat, *Don't Act, Just Dance: The Metapolitics of Cold War Culture* (New Brunswick: Rutgers UP, 2015).

10. See William J. Maxwell, *F.B. Eyes: How J. Edgar Hoover's Ghostreaders Framed African American Literature* (Princeton: Princeton UP, 2015); James Smith, *British Writers and MI5 Surveillance, 1930–1960* (Cambridge: Cambridge UP, 2013); Mary Helen Washington, *The Other Blacklist: The African American Literary and Cultural Left of the 1950s* (New York: Columbia UP, 2014); Simone Browne, *Dark Matters: On the Surveillance of Blackness* (Durham: Duke UP, 2015); and Claire A. Culleton and Karen Leick, eds., *Modernism on File: Writers, Artists, and the FBI, 1920–1950* (New York: Palgrave Macmillan, 2008). Additional references parenthetical.

11. Sarah Brouillette, "US-Soviet Antagonism and the 'Indirect Propaganda' of Book Schemes in India in the 1950s," *University of Toronto Quarterly* 84.4 (2015): 170–88.

12. See especially Pierre Bourdieu, *The Field of Cultural Production: Essays on Art and Literature*, ed. and intro. Randal Johnson (New York: Columbia UP, 1993) and *The Rules of Art: Genesis and Structure of the Literary Field*, trans. Susan Emanuel (Stanford: Stanford UP, 1996). Some of Bourdieu's most insightful readers, who have influenced my own thinking, include John Guillory, *Cultural Capital: The Problem of Literary Canon Formation* (Chicago: U of Chicago P, 1993); Pascale Casanova, *The World Republic of Letters*, trans. Malcolm DeBevoise (Cambridge: Harvard UP, 2004); James F. English, *The Economy of Prestige: Prizes, Awards, and the Circulation of Cultural Value* (Cambridge: Harvard UP, 2005); Mark McGurl, *The Program Era: Postwar Fiction and the Rise of Creative Writing* (Cambridge: Harvard UP, 2009); Sarah Brouillette, *UNESCO and the Fate of the Literary* (Stanford: Stanford UP, 2019). Additional references parenthetical.

Chapter 2

1. Aamir R. Mufti, *Forget English! Orientalisms and World Literatures* (Cambridge: Harvard UP, 2016) argues that indigeneity (or cultural authenticity) should not be regarded as the aesthetic antagonist of colonialism. European Orientalists, who were actively involved in imagining the modern idea of world literature, helped produce a discourse of cultural authenticity as part of the colonial enterprise, not as a form of resistance to it. Siraj Ahmed, *Archaeology of Babel: The Colonial Foundation of Humanities* (Stanford: Stanford UP, 2018) agrees broadly with this premise, but goes further in claiming that philology itself is a tool of colonial rule, and we would

do well to imagine what kinds of discursive knowledge we can generate without philological tools. By contrast, Peter D. McDonald, *Artefacts of Writing: Ideas of the State and Communities of Letters from Matthew Arnold to Xu Bing* (Oxford: Oxford UP, 2017), suggests that global literature is in many ways resistant to the machinations of states, creating readerly and writerly communities that cannot be contained by the apparatus of state rule.

2. Fredric Jameson, *Marxism and Form: Twentieth-Century Dialectical Theories of Literature* (Princeton: Princeton UP, 1971), ix.

3. Kay Boyle, Whit Burnett, Hart Crane, Caresse Crosby, Harry Crosby, Martha Foley, Stuart Gilbert, A. L. Gillespie, Leigh Hoffman, Eugene Jolas, Elliot Paul, Douglas Rigby, Theo Rutra, Robert Sage, Harold J. Salemson, and Laurence Vail. "Manifesto: The Revolution of the Word," in *Transition Workshop*, ed. Eugene Jolas (1929; New York: Vanguard, 1949), 173–74.

4. Marjorie Perloff's account still dominates the field. She suggests that if we pay too much attention to the supposed ideological messages of manifesto-art, we will miss the underlying formal similarities embedded in different instances of the genre. *The Futurist Moment: Avant-Garde, Avant Guerre, and the Language of Rupture*, 2nd ed. (Chicago: U of Chicago P, 2003). See also Janet Lyon, *Manifestoes: Provocations of the Modern* (Ithaca: Cornell UP, 1999), Martin Puchner, *Poetry of the Revolution: Marx, Manifestos, and the Avant-Gardes* (Princeton: Princeton UP, 2006), and Laura Winkiel, *Modernism, Race, and Manifestos* (Cambridge: Cambridge UP, 2008).

5. See also my previous book, *Commonwealth of Letters: British Literary Culture and the Emergence of Postcolonial Aesthetics* (Oxford: Oxford UP, 2013), which invokes the concept to explain how midcentury literary institutions facilitated collaboration between white metropolitan writers and their counterparts from the sub-Saharan Africa and Caribbean especially.

6. On the question of vernacular speech and global literature, see also Jahan Ramazani, *The Hybrid Muse: Postcolonial Poetry in English* (Chicago: U of Chicago P, 2001) and *A Transnational Poetics* (Chicago: U of Chicago P, 2009) and Matthew Hart, *Nations of Nothing but Poetry: Modernism, Transnationalism, and Synthetic Vernacular Writing* (Oxford: Oxford UP, 2010).

7. Andrei Zhdanov, Maxim Gorky, Nikolai Bukharin, Karl Radek, and Alexei Stetsky, *Problems of Soviet Literature: Reports and Speeches at the First Soviet Writers' Congress*, ed. H. G. Scott (New York: International Publishers, n.d.), 40. Additional references parenthetical. See also Régine Robin, *Socialist Realism: An Impossible Aesthetic*, trans. Catherine Porter, foreword Léon Robel (Stanford: Stanford UP, 1992), 31–36.

8. Franco Moretti, *Modern Epic: The World System from Goethe to García Márquez* (London: Verso, 1996) offers the most engaging account of epic as an important genre for the emergence of a world literary system. See also C. D. Blanton, *Epic Negation: The Dialectical Poetics of Late Modernism* (Oxford: Oxford UP, 2015). Influential treatments of epic include Erich Auerbach, *Mimesis: The Representation of Reality in Western Thought*, trans. Willard R. Trask, intro. Edward W. Said (Princeton: Princeton UP, 2003); Georg Lukács, *The Theory of the Novel: A Historico-Philosophical Essay on the Forms of Great Epic Literature*, trans. Anna Bostock (Cambridge: MIT Press, 1971); and M. M. Bakhtin, *The Dialogic Imagination: Four Essays*, ed. Michael Holquist, trans. Caryl Emerson and Michael Holquist (Austin: U of Texas P, 1981). Tragedy, as a modern genre, has witnessed a resurgence of interest as well. See Helene P. Foley and Jean E. Howard, coordinators, "Special Topic: Tragedy," *PMLA* 129.4 (2014): 617–741; Miriam Leonard, *Tragic Modernities* (Cambridge: Harvard UP, 2015); David Scott, *Conscripts of Modernity: The*

Tragedy of Colonial Enlightenment (Durham: Duke UP, 2004). Paul K. Saint-Amour also makes an insightful distinction between epic and the encyclopedia as modern genres in *Tense Future: Modernism, Total War, Encyclopedic Form* (Oxford: Oxford UP, 2015). Additional references parenthetical.

9. Steven S. Lee, "Modernist Indigeneity and World Revolution," conference presentation, MLA 2020, Seattle.

10. Joseph Stalin, *Marxism and the National and Colonial Question*, ed. A. Fineberg (New York: International Publishers, n.d.). See also Greg Castillo, "Peoples at an Exhibition: Soviet Architecture and the National Question," in *Socialist Realism without Shores*, eds. Thomas Lahusen and Evgeny Dobrenko (Durham: Duke UP, 1997), 91–119.

11. The contrasting perspectives of M. M. Bakhtin and Antonio Gramsci provide an interesting sidebar to this discussion. In "Epic and the Novel," Bakhtin celebrates the novel's radical form, which he attributes to the genre's polyglossia. In his notes on linguistics, by contrast, Gramsci argues that democracy will be extended in Italy when working-class people have better command of the hegemonic language, leaving regional dialects behind. Gramsci, *Selections from Cultural Writings*, eds. David Forgacs and Geoffrey Nowell-Smith, trans. William Boelhower (Cambridge: Harvard UP, 1985).

12. For a succinct overview of the Surrealist split, especially how it impacted francophone colonial intellectuals, see Carrie Noland, "Red Front / Black Front: Aimé Césaire and the Affaire Aragon," in *Voices of Negritude in Modernist Print: Aesthetic Subjectivity, Diaspora, and the Lyric Regime* (New York: Columbia UP, 2015), 176–203.

13. Aragon, W. H. Auden, José Bergamín, Jean Richard Bloch, Nancy Cunard, Brian Howard, Heinrich Mann, Ivor Montagu, Pablo Neruda, Ramón Sender, Stephen Spender, and Tristan Tzara, "Authors Take Sides on the Spanish War" (London: *Left Review*, 1937), n.p.

14. Oswald de Andrade, "Cannibalist Manifesto" [*Manifesto Antropófago*], trans. Leslie Bary, *Latin American Literary Review* 19.38 (1991): 39. Additional references parenthetical.

15. See Luís Madureira, *Cannibal Modernities: Postcoloniality and the Avant-Garde in Caribbean and Brazilian Literature* (Charlottesville: U of Virginia P, 2005); Valérie Loichot, *The Tropics Bite Back: Culinary Coups in Caribbean Literature* (Minneapolis: U of Minnesota P, 2013); and Njeri Githire, *Cannibal Writes: Eating Others in Caribbean and Indian Ocean Women's Writing* (Urbana: U of Illinois P, 2014) for three of the more recent studies of Andrade and Latin American literature's use of his concepts. Githire considers how Suzanne Césaire, Maryse Condé, Edwidge Danticat, and other anticolonial women writers have reworked the idea of cultural cannibalism first theorized by Andrade.

16. There is no certainty about when Césaire joined the Communist Party. The year 1942 comes from A. James Arnold, *Modernism and Negritude: The Poetry and Poetics of Aimé Césaire* (Cambridge: Harvard UP, 1981), 69. For Césaire's complicated and ever-evolving relationship to communism, see Césaire, *Solar Throat Slashed: The Unexpurgated 1948 Edition*, trans. and ed. A. James Arnold and Clayton Eshleman (Middletown: Wesleyan UP, 2011); Noland, *Voices of Negritude in Modernist Print*; Gary Wilder, *Freedom Time: Negritude, Decolonization, and the Future of the World* (Durham: Duke UP, 2015); Christopher L Miller, "The (Revised) Birth of Negritude: Communist Revolution and 'the Immanent Negro' in 1935," *PMLA* 125.3 (2010): 743–49; Raisa Rexer, "Black and White and Re(a)d All Over: *L'Étudiant noir*, Communism, and the Birth of Négritude," *Research in African Literatures* 44.4 (2013): 1–14; and Christian Filostrat,

Negritude Agonistes, Assimilation against Nationalism in the French-speaking Caribbean and Guyane (Cherry Hill, NJ: Africana Homestead Legacy Publishers, 2008), which reprints Césaire's first known use of negritude in "Conscience racial and révolution sociale." Arnold and his collaborator, Clayton Eshleman, have energetically pursued the argument that Césaire's poetry of the 1930s and '40s is "often violent, but not revolutionary in any political sense" (*Solar Throat Slashed* xviii), while Miller, Noland, and Rexer are more inclined to regard his early poetry as part of a close dialogue with communism. For more general treatments of negritude, especially on role of women in the movement, see T. Denean Sharpley-Whiting, *Negritude Women* (Minneapolis: U of Minnesota P, 2002) and Lori Cole, "*Légitime Défense*: From Communism and Surrealism to Caribbean Self-Definition," *Journal of Surrealism and the Americas* 4.1 (2010): 15–30.

17. Translation is from Rexer 8.

18. Translation is from Rexer 10.

19. For a detailed comparison of the Hindustani and English versions of the manifesto—which have significant differences—see Carlo Coppola, "The All-India Progressive Writers' Association: The European Phase," in *Marxist Influences and South Asian Literature*, vol. 1, ed. Carlo Coppola (East Lansing: Asian Studies Center Michigan State U, 1974): 1–34. I use the contested term Hindustani to describe the language because this is the term used by the participants themselves. For a set of discussions about the relationship between Hindustani, Hindi, and Urdu, see Sheldon Pollock, ed., *Literary Cultures in History: Reconstructions from South Asia* (Berkeley: U of California P, 2003), especially the final section, "The Twinned Histories of Urdu and Hindi."

20. Rakhshanda Jalil, *Liking Progress, Loving Change: A Literary History of the Progressive Writers' Movement in Urdu* (New Delhi: Oxford UP, 2014), 219. To my knowledge, Jalil is the first scholar to make extensive use of the intelligence files I quote, and for this I owe her a significant debt.

21. Sajjad Zaheer, "Reminiscences," in *Marxist Cultural Movement in India, Chronicles and Documents (1936–1947)*, vol. 1, ed. Sudhi Pradhan (Calcutta: Pradhan, 1979): 25–37 and *The Light: A History of the Movement for Progressive Literature in the Indo-Pakistan Subcontinent; a Translation of "Roshnai"*, trans. Amina Azfar, intro. Ahmad Ali Khan (Oxford: Oxford UP, 2006). See also Mulk Raj Anand's account of the founding of the group and the drafting of the manifesto in "Some Reminiscences of Sajjad Zaheer," *Lotus* 26 (October–December 1975): 44–51.

22. *Left Review* was part of the British wing of the International Union of Revolutionary Writers, a group with which the PWA was also affiliated. For connections between Anand, Fox, and Soviet-led cultural agencies, see Katerina Clark, "Indian Leftist Writers of the 1930s Maneuver among India, London, and Moscow: The Case of Mulk Raj Anand and His Patron Ralph Fox," *Kritika: Explorations in Russian and Eurasian History* 18.1 (2017): 63–87. For a fuller overview of *Left Review* and other radical little magazines of the period, see Peter Marks, "Art and Politics in the 1930s: *The European Quarterly* (1934–5), *Left Review* (1934–8), and *Poetry and the People* (1938–40)" in *The Oxford Critical and Cultural History of Modernist Magazines*, vol. 1, Britain and Ireland 1880–1955, eds. Peter Brooker and Andrew Thacker (Oxford: Oxford UP, 2009), 623–46 and Christopher Hilliard, "Producers by Hand and by Brain: Working-Class Writers and Left-Wing Publishers in 1930s Britain," *Journal of Modern History* 78.1 (2006): 37–64.

23. Lu Xun, "Silent China," in *Silent China: Selected Writings of Lu Xun*, ed. and trans. Gladys Yang (Oxford: Oxford UP, 1973), 165. Lu Xun, in turn, built upon his predecessors in the May

Fourth Movement, such as Hu Shi, who was arguing for a vernacular Chinese literature from the 1910s. See Chow Tse-tsung, *The May 4th Movement: Intellectual Revolution in Modern China* (Cambridge: Harvard UP, 1960).

24. Mulk Raj Anand, K. S. Bhat, J. C. Ghose, S. Sinha, M. D. Taseer, and S. S. Zaheer, "Manifesto of the Indian Progressive Writers' Association, London" *Left Review* 2.5 (1936): n.p. Additional references parenthetical. See also Jalil 219; Coppola; and Hafeez Malik, "The Marxist Literary Movement in India and Pakistan," *Journal of Asian Studies* 26.4 (1967): 649–64.

25. Zaheer, *The Light* 127.

26. As Zaheer says in "Reminiscences": "The most important thing that we learnt in Europe was that a progressive writers' movement could bear fruits only when it is propagated in various languages and when the writers of India realise the necessity of this movement and put in practice its aims and objects" (31).

27. Extract from Weekly Report of the Director, Intelligence Bureau, Home Department, Government of India, dated New Delhi, Thursday, 30 January 1936, No. 4. IOR/L/PJ/12/430.

28. Extract from Weekly Report of the Director, Intelligence Bureau, Home Department, Government of India, Dated New Delhi, Thursday, 16 April 1936, No. 15. IOR/L/PJ/12/499. The question of whether or not the PWA operated as a front for the Communist Party is a longstanding debate in Indian and Pakistani letters. For a quick overview, see Priyamvada Gopal, *Literary Radicalism in India: Gender, Nation and the Transition to Independence* (Abingdon: Routledge, 2005), 13–19 and Clark, "Indian Leftist Writers."

29. Letter from Home Department, Government of India to R. T. Peel, Secretary of P.&J. Department, India Office London 8 June 1936; Letter from Indian Progressive Writers' Association to [recipient unknown], 8 June 1936. IOR/L/PJ/12/499. For a fuller account of the development of the political police and the context of colonialism and anticolonialism, see James Hevia, *The Imperial Security State: British Colonial Knowledge and Empire-Building in Asia* (Cambridge: Cambridge UP, 2012) and Daniel Brückenhaus, *Policing Transnational Protest: Liberal Imperialism and the Surveillance of Anticolonialists in Europe, 1905–1945* (Oxford: Oxford UP, 2017).

30. The first document in the Progressive Writers' Association file among the India Office Records includes extracts from the manifesto. Extract from Weekly Report of the Director, Intelligence Bureau, Home Department, Government of India, dated New Delhi, Thursday, 2nd January 1936, No 1. IOR L/PJ/12/499.

31. Ruvani Ranasinha, *South Asian Writers in Twentieth-Century Britain: Culture in Translation* (Oxford: Oxford UP, 2007): 18.

32. George Orwell, "You and the Atom Bomb," in *George Orwell: Essays*, ed. and intro. John Carey, (New York: Knopf, 2002), 903–7.

33. *Mao Zedong's "Talks at the Yan'an Conference on Literature and Art": A Translation of the 1943 Text with Commentary*, trans. Bonnie S. McDougall (Ann Arbor: Center for Chinese Studies, U of Michigan, 1980), 88, n. 22. See also Lu Xun's short talk from 1927, "Silent China," in which he calls for traditional Chinese script to be abolished: "All we want is this: instead of overtaxing our brains to learn the speech of men long since dead, we should speak that of living men. Instead of treating language as a curio, we should write in the easily understood vernacular." *Silent China: Selected Writings of Lu Xun*, ed. and trans. Gladys Yang (Oxford: Oxford UP, 1973), 165. See also Auritro Majumder, *Insurgent Imaginations: World Literature and the Periphery* (Cambridge: Cambridge UP, 2021).

34. After the civil war, China translated large quantities of socialist realist fiction from the Soviet Union, but this lasted about a decade. See Y. P. Zhang, "The Emergence of the Global South Novel: *Red Sorghum, Présence Africaine*, and the Third Novelists' International," *Novel: A Forum on Fiction* 52.3 (2019): 347–68.

35. Alioune Diop, "Niam n'goura or *Présence Africaine*'s RAISON D'ÊTRE," trans. Richard Wright and Thomas Diop, *Présence Africaine* 1 (1947): 185. Additional references parenthetical.

36. Frank A. Collymore, "Note Book," *Bim* 4.15 (1951): 149.

37. Frank A. Collymore, "Notes for a Glossary of Words and Phrases of Barbadian Dialect," Parts 1–4, 5.17 (1952): 56–72, 5.18 (1953): 139–52, 5.19 (1953): 213–26, 5.20 (1954): 307–21.

38. Frank A. Collymore, "Editors' Blarney," *Bim* 2.6 [1945?]: 1.

39. Quoted in Peter Benson, *"Black Orpheus," "Transition," and Modern Cultural Awakening in Africa* (Berkeley: U of California P, 1986), 24. Additional references parenthetical.

40. Doris Lessing, "The Small Personal Voice," in *Declaration*, ed. Tom Maschler (New York: EP Dutton, 1958), 193. Additional references parenthetical.

41. See also Ezekiel [Es'kia] Mphahlele's "Writers and Commitment," *Black Orpheus* 2.3 (1969): 34–39, which suggests that poetry, rather than the novel form, allows committed African writers to communicate most directly with their audiences. Mphahlele's approach leans heavily on Trotsky's *Literature and Revolution*.

42. Aimé Césaire, "Letter to Maurie Thorez," trans. Chike Jeffers, *Social Text* 103.28.2 (2010): 145–52.

43. James Baldwin, "Letter from Paris: Princes and Powers," *Encounter* 8 (1957): 52.

44. W.E.B. Du Bois, "To the Congres des ecrivains et artistes noir," in "Messages," *Présence Africaine*, Congres issue 8/10 (1956): 383.

45. Juliana Spahr, *Du Bois's Telegram: Literary Resistance and State Containment* (Cambridge: Harvard UP, 2018), 4. Additional references parenthetical.

46. Foreword, *Présence Africaine* 1/2 (1955): 9. Additional references parenthetical.

47. C. D. Narasimhaiah, "A.C.L.A.L.S. Conference on Commonwealth Literature: Kingston, Jamaica, 3–9 January 1971," *Journal of Commonwealth Literature* 6.2 (1971): 121.

48. "Statement of Position to the Commonwealth Literature & Language Conference— Mona, January, 1971," *Journal of Black Poetry* 1.17 (1973): 29. Additional references parenthetical.

49. Ngũgĩ wa Thiong'o, *Decolonising the Mind: The Politics of Language in African Literature* (London: James Currey, 1986), 1.

50. Ngũgĩ wa Thiong'o, *Homecoming: Essays on African and Caribbean Literature, Culture and Politics* (London: Heinemann, 1972), 146.

51. Chinweizu, Onwuchekwa Jemie, and Ihechukwu Madubuike, "Towards the Decoloniza-tion of African Literature," *Transition* 48 (1975): 37. In a curious convergence, they, like Achebe, question the obscurantism of the early Okigbo but applaud the late Okigbo as an authentic and representative of West African oral traditions.

52. Wole Soyinka, "Neo-Tarzanism: The Poetics of Psuedo-Tradition," *Transition* 48 (1975): 44.

53. Robert Darnton, *Censors at Work: How States Shaped Literature* (New York: Norton), 234.

54. Evgeny Dobrenko, *The Making of the State Writer: Social and Aesthetic Origins of Soviet Literary Culture*, trans. Jesse M. Savage (Stanford: Stanford UP, 2001), xv. Additional references parenthetical. See also Robin, *Socialist Realism*.

55. Jean Bernabé, Patrick Chamoiseau, and Raphaël Confiant, *Éloge de la Créolité/In Praise of Creoleness*, trans. M. B. Taleb-Khyar (Baltimore: Gallimard and Johns Hopkins UP, 1990), 115. Additional references parenthetical.

56. Homi K. Bhabha and Paul Gilroy, perhaps the two most influential scholars of colonial and postcolonial literature of the 1990s, both espouse anti-nationalist, anti-essentialist positions. See Bhabha, *The Location of Culture* (London: Routledge, 1994) and Gilroy, *The Black Atlantic: Modernity and Double Consciousness* (Cambridge: Harvard UP, 1993).

Chapter 3

1. Ngũgĩ, *Decolonising the Mind* 5.

2. Makerere conference scripts. Discussants included Nkosi, Barry Reckord, Langston Hughes, Bernard Fonlon, and Christopher Okigbo (series I box 9 folder 3, TC papers).

3. "Transition Conference Questionnaire," *Transition* 5 (July–August 1962): 11–12.

4. Obiajunwa Wali, "The Dead End of African Literature?," *Transition* 10 (September 1963): 13–14. Additional references parenthetical.

5. See also McDonald, *Artefacts of Writing*, and Tobias Warner's thorough treatment of the language question in francophone African literature, *The Tongue-Tied Imagination: Decolonizing Literary Modernity in Senegal* (New York: Fordham UP, 2019).

6. The Congress for Cultural Freedom, "Manifesto," unanimously adopted in Berlin on 30 June 1950.

7. In western Europe, the Dreyfus affair set the pattern of the complicated relationship between autonomy, politics, and the practice of intellectuals. Pierre Bourdieu's reading of Émile Zola's contribution to the debate provides an informative overview of how intellectuals justified their public support of Dreyfus. In *The Rules of Art*, Bourdieu suggests that Zola attempted to preserve his status as a disinterested intellectual by intervening "*in the name of autonomy*," or as an objective intellectual who was defending universal values of truth against narrow political interests (129). To put this another way, Zola attempted to finesse his entry into the sordid field of politics by claiming he was motivated solely by nonpolitical criteria, that his attachment to objective standards of truth and fairness trumped any other concern. As we shall see, many African intellectuals of the 1960s generation embedded their political writings in the discourse of autonomy and intellectual detachment. See also Nicholas Brown, *Autonomy: The Social Ontology of Art under Capitalism* (Durham: Duke UP, 2019); Lisa Siraganian, *Modernism's Other Work: The Art Object's Political Life* (Oxford: Oxford UP, 2012); and Asha Rogers, *State Sponsored Literature: Britain and Cultural Diversity after 1945* (Oxford: Oxford UP, 2020).

8. Okigbo is quoted as saying, "the whole idea of a negro arts festival based on colour is quite absurd." Donatus Ibe Nwoga, ed., *Critical Perspectives on Christopher Okigbo* (Washington, DC: Three Continents, 1984), 33.

9. See Feinsod, *Poetry of the Americas;* Robyn Creswell, *City of Beginnings: Poetic Modernism in Beirut* (Princeton: Princeton UP, 2019); Giles Scott-Smith and Charlotte A. Lerg, eds., *Campaigning Culture and the Global Cold War: The Journals of the Congress for Cultural Freedom,* (London: Palgrave, 2017); Elizabeth M. Holt, "Al-Ṭayyib Ṣāliḥ's *Season of Migration to the North,* the CIA, and the Cultural Cold War after Bandung," *Research in African Literatures* 50.3 (2019): 70–90; and Patrick Iber, *Neither Peace nor Freedom: The Cultural Cold War in Latin America*

(Cambridge: Harvard UP, 2015). *Neither Peace nor Freedom* contrasts the work of the CCF in Latin America with that of the Soviet-sponsored World Peace Council and the Cuban *Casa de las Américas*.

10. As far back as May 1966, the editors of *Encounter* felt the need to deny rumors of CIA infiltration in a letter to the *New York Times*. Stephen Spender, Melvin J. Lasky, and Irving Kristol, "Freedom of *Encounter* Magazine," Letter to the Editor, *New York Times*, 10 May 1966. Less than a year later, the editors of *Ramparts* published "3 Tales of the CIA," *Ramparts* (April 1967): 15–28. This article revealed CIA funding of labor unions in the United States, and the story widened from there as the *New York Times* featured the program on the front page and in the letters to the editor, also reporting Spender's departure. Jerry M. Flint, "Ex-Official of C.I.A. Lists Big Grants to Labor Aides: Reuther Concedes Union Took $50,000 from Agency," *New York Times*, 8 May 1967; Sylvan Fox, "Stephen Spender Quits *Encounter*," *New York Times*, 8 May 1967; Max Frankel, "Ex-Official of C.I.A. Lists Big Grants to Labor Aides: Tells of Secret Subsidies to A.F.L.-C.I.O. to Fight Red Union Abroad," *New York Times*, 8 May 1967. Thomas Braden, a former CIA operative who had been associated with the CCF program (and later television co-host of CNN's *Crossfire*), made further public revelations with "I'm Glad the CIA is 'Immoral,'" *Saturday Evening Post* (20 May 1967): 10–14.

11. Neogy and Mphahlele, for example, were resolved that Neogy approached the CCF for funding (not the other way around), so it would have been impossible for his magazine to have started life as a CIA propaganda machine. In *"Black Orpheus," "Transition," and Modern Cultural Awakening in Africa*, Benson reiterates this claim, and the archival evidence I examined corroborates this (160–76). In a letter from CCF officer John Hunt to Neogy, during early negotiations related to *Transition* joining the network, Hunt said that the only requirements for accepting a grant would be to agree to cross-promotion of *Black Orpheus* and *Encounter*—and to keep the standards of the magazine high (12 September 1962; series 2 box 304 folder 4, CCF papers). At *Black Orpheus*, as I discuss later in this chapter, the nonpolitical character of the publication was perfect for the CCF agenda.

12. *Black Orpheus* and *Transition* were started without any funds from the CCF or the Farfield Foundation, the dummy nonprofit through which the CIA channeled funds to cultural organizations. From my archival research, corroborated by what Peter Benson reports, CCF funding for *Black Orpheus* began in 1961 with a grant of £2000, continuing at approximately this level for several years. See Beier to Josselson, 13 December 1960 (series 2 box 66 folder 3, CCF papers) and Hunt to Beier, 28 July 1961 (series 2 box 66 folder 4, CCF papers). Funding for *Transition* was more substantial, starting at about £2000 in 1962 and rising to about £4000 in 1964. See Hunt to Neogy, 3 December 1962 (series 2 box 304 folder 4, CCF papers); Farrand to Hunt, 13 October 1964; Farrand to Neogy, 24 March 1964 (both series 2 box 304 folder 5, CCF papers).

13. The Transcription Centre received a large annual grant compared to *Black Orpheus* and *Transition*—about £9000 in 1963. The higher costs of maintaining premises in London and purchasing recording equipment no doubt contributed to this. I was not able to ascertain an estimate of the cost for the Makerere conference, but the archives make it clear that the CCF underwrote the expenses. See Hunt to Duerden, 17 December 1962 (series 2 box 126 folder 3, CCF papers); Duerden to Hunt, 5 March 1963 (series 2 box 126 folder 5, CCF papers).

14. "Rajat Neogy on the CIA," interview with Tony Hall, *Transition* 32 (August–September 1967): 46.

15. Quoted in Benson 24.

16. Peter Coleman, *The Liberal Conspiracy: The Congress for Cultural Freedom and the Struggle for the Mind of Postwar Europe* (New York: Free Press, 1989); Frances Stonor Saunders, *The Cultural Cold War: The CIA and the World of Arts and Letters* (New York: The New Press, 1999); Giles Scott-Smith, *The Politics of Apolitical Culture: The Congress for Cultural Freedom, the CIA and Post-War American Hegemony* (London: Routledge, 2002); and Hugh Wilford, *The Mighty Wurlitzer: How the CIA Played America* (Cambridge: Harvard UP, 2008).

17. David Caute, *The Dancer Defects: The Struggle for Cultural Supremacy during the Cold War* (Oxford: Oxford UP, 2003); Katerina Clark, *Moscow: The Fourth Rome: Stalinism, Cosmopolitanism, and the Evolution of Soviet Culture, 1931–1941* (Cambridge: Harvard UP, 2011).

18. Kate A. Baldwin, *Beyond the Color Line and the Iron Curtain: Reading Encounters between Black and Red, 1922–1963* (Durham: Duke UP, 2002); Barbara Foley, *Spectres of 1919: Class and Nation in the Making of The New Negro* (Urbana: U of Illinois P 2003); William J. Maxwell, *New Negro, Old Left: African-American Writing and Communism Between the Wars* (New York: Columbia U P, 1999). For a more general account of visitors to the Soviet Union, see Michael David-Fox, *Showcasing the Great Experiment: Cultural Diplomacy and Western Visitors to Soviet Russia, 1921–1941* (Oxford: Oxford UP, 2012).

19. It is important to note that the State Department hit on the idea of jazz ambassadors in an effort to confront the so-called Achilles heel of foreign relations, namely racial discrimination in the United States. In the decolonizing regions of the world, the Soviets were continually pointing out US hypocrisy, citing poor treatment of African Americans and claiming the Communist movement was free of racial discrimination. As Penny Von Eschen points out, jazz ambassadors did not always toe the US foreign policy line, and often spoke their minds while on tour.

20. Irving Kristol and Stephen Spender, "After the Apocalypse: Editorial," *Encounter* 1 (1953): 1.

21. For a detailed examination of *Encounter*'s positioning as a curator of interwar modernism, see Greg Barnhisel, "*Encounter* Magazine and the Twilight of Modernism." *ELH* 81.1 (2014): 381–416.

22. Untitled chapter in *The God That Failed*, ed. Richard H. Crossman, foreword David C. Engerman (New York: Columbia UP, 2001), 272.

23. David Leeming, *Stephen Spender: A Life in Modernism* (New York: Henry Holt, 1999), 190.

24. Stephen Spender, *The Creative Element: A Study of Vision, Despair and Orthodoxy among some Modern Writers* (London: Hamish Hamilton, 1953), 14. Additional references parenthetical.

25. Memo, from British Committee for Cultural Freedom, undated, unsigned, probably early 1953 (series 2 box 129 folder 6, CCF papers).

26. Spender to Josselson, 22 October 1953 (series 2 box 129 folder 7, CCF papers); see also Spender to Josselson, 18 October 1953; Kristol to Josselson, 15 and 16 September [1953]; Josselson to Kristol, and Spender 1 February 1954; Kristol to Josselson, 25 February 1954; Josselson to Kristol, 25 February 1954; Kristol to Josselson, 1 March [1954]; Josselson to Kristol, 6 March 1954; Kristol to Josselson, 17 and 24 March [1954] (all series 2 box 129 folder 8, CCF papers); and many more in the files.

27. Josselson to Spender, 25 August 1959; 11 January 1960 (series 2 box 297 folder 4, CCF papers).

28. Josselson to Spender, 26 February 1960 (series 2 box 297 folder 4, CCF papers).

29. Spender to Josselson, 10 March [1960?] (series 2 box 297 folder, 4 CCF papers).

30. Josselson to Spender, 23 March 1960 (series 2 box 297 folder 4, CCF papers).

31. Thomas Borstelmann, *Apartheid's Reluctant Uncle: The United States and Southern Africa in the Early Cold War* (Oxford: Oxford UP, 1993).

32. Ezekiel Mphahlele, ed., *Conference of African Writers of English Expression, 11–17 June 1962*, Conference Proceedings (Kampala: Congress for Cultural Freedom, 1962).

33. Saunders Redding, "Trends in American Negro Writing," in Mphahlele, ed., *Conference of African Writers*, 5.

34. Arthur Drayton, "Socio-Historical Compulsion in the West Indian Novel," in Mphahlele, ed., *Conference of African Writers*, 8.

35. Gerald Moore, "Towards Realism in French African Writing," in Mphahlele, ed., *Conference of African Writers*, 3.

36. Ulli Beier, "Contemporary African Poetry in English," in Mphahlele, ed., *Conference of African Writers*, 6.

37. Lewis Nkosi, Press Report, Manchester *Guardian*, 8 August 1962, in Mphahlele, ed., *Conference of African Writers*.

38. Christopher Okigbo, *Labyrinths, with Path of Thunder* (New York and Ibadan: Africana Publishing and Mbari, 1971), 23.

39. See also Nathan Suhr-Sytsma, *Poetry, Print, and the Making of Postcolonial Literature* (Cambridge: Cambridge UP, 2017).

40. Duerden to Hunt, 19 September 1962 (series III box 21 folder 6, TC papers).

41. Patrick Jubb to S. E. Watrous, 22 June 1961 (series III box 23 folder 1, TC papers).

42. Quoted in Gerald Moore, "The Transcription Centre in the Sixties: Navigating in Narrow Seas," *Research in African Literatures* 33.3 (2002): 169. Additional references parenthetical.

43. Moore, "The Transcription Centre in the Sixties."

44. Hunt to Duerden, 25 September 1962 (series III box 21 folder 6, TC papers).

45. Hunt to Duerden, 26 June 1962 (series III box 21 folder 6, TC papers).

46. Duerden to Thompson, 7 July 1965 (series III box 23 folder 4, TC papers).

47. Dennis Duerden and Cosmo Pieterse, ed., *African Writers Talking* (New York: Africana Publishing, 1972).

48. Duerden to Bieber, 6 August 1964 (series III box 21 folder 3, TC papers).

49. Wole Soyinka, "From Africa to the 'Global Black,'" interview by Tommy Shelby, *Transition* 106 (2011): A-36.

50. Ulli Beier and Janheinz Jahn, "Editorial," *Black Orpheus* 1 (1957): 4. Additional references parenthetical.

51. Contract between Longman and Mbari, June 1963; see also letter John Hunt to Begum Hendrickse, 5 June 1963 (both series 2 box 235 folder 13, CCF papers).

52. Rajat Neogy, "7 T ONE = 7 E TON," *Transition* 1 (1961): 10.

53. Robie Macauley, "Little Magazines," *Transition* 9 (1963): 25.

54. Andrew N. Rubin, *Archives of Authority: Empire, Culture, and the Cold War* (Princeton: Princeton UP, 2012), 60; Spahr, *Du Bois's Telegram* 105. See also Bhakti Shringarpure, *Cold War*

Assemblages: Decolonization to Digital (New York: Routledge, 2019) and Caroline Davis, *African Literature and the CIA: Networks of Authorship and Publishing* (Cambridge: Cambridge UP, 2020). Rubin, Spahr, Shringarpure, and Davis all contend that the CIA selected a few African writers to promote—which is true—but also that the process of selection had clear political motives and effects—a conclusion with scant supporting evidence. Did Achebe or Sembène serve as apologists for US interests when they attended CCF events and then as apologists for Soviet interests when they accepted the Lotus Prize? In *Trumpism in Academe: The Example of Caroline Davis and Spahring Partners* (Ibadan: Bookcraft, 2021), Soyinka argues that these scholarly accounts show high levels of disrespect for the creativity and agency of African writers of his generation. Additional references parenthetical.

55. Eric Bulson, *little magazine, world form* (New York: Columbia UP, 2017).

56. Bessie Head, Letter to the Editor, *Transition* 17 (1964): 6.

57. Letter to *Présence Africaine*, 20 March 1964 (series 2 box 304 folder 5, CCF papers).

58. Letter to *Présence Africaine*, 20 March 1964 (series 2 box 304 folder 5, CCF papers). See Monica Popescu, *At Penpoint*, for an instructive comparison between the CCF African network and *Présence Africaine* (56–58).

59. Biodun Jeyifo, *Wole Soyinka: Politics, Poetics and Postcolonialism* (Cambridge: Cambridge UP University Press, 2004) 42–43.

60. Wole Soyinka, "The Writer in an African State," *Transition* 31 (1967): 11.

61. Beier to Josselson, 18 August 1960 (series 2 box 66 folder 3, CCF papers).

62. Ezekiel Mphahlele, *Down Second Avenue* (London: Fabers, 1959), 1. Additional references parenthetical.

63. Ezekiel Mphahlele, *Voices in the Whirlwind and Other Essays* (New York: Hill and Wang, 1972), 158.

64. Simon Gikandi, "Modernism in the World," *Modernism/modernity* 13.3 (2006): 420.

65. Michaela Bronstein, "Ngũgĩ's Use of Conrad: A Case for Literary Transhistory," *MLQ* 75.3 (2014): 411–37.

Chapter 4

1. Sometimes called the Afro-Asian Writers' Union or Movement. The *Présence Africaine* group and the Tricontinental are the only potential rivals to this claim of significance.

2. The first six issues of the magazine are called *Afro-Asian Writings*, this main title being repurposed as a subtitle when the journal was renamed *Lotus* with issue 7 [sometimes labelled volume 2, issue 1] (January 1971). From 1971, the editorial board tightened the erratic publishing schedule, bringing out the magazine on a quarterly basis.

3. Plans to publish the magazine in a fourth language, Russian, are in AAWA literature, but I have not uncovered any extant issues in languages other than Arabic, English, and French. See Alex La Guma, "Report of the General Secretary to the Seventh General (25th Anniversary) Conference Tashkent Uzbekistan September-October 1983," *Lotus* 56 (1985): 191.

4. On the CCF background of *Season of Migration to the North*, see Elizabeth M. Holt, "Al-Ṭayyib Ṣāliḥ's *Season of Migration to the North*." In "A New Collection of Arab Literature," a book review of *Selected Works of Middle-East Writers* (in Russian; Moscow: Progress Publishers, 1978), Abou Bakr Youssef discusses the inclusion of Salih's novel as part of an Afro-Asian book series in Russian. *Lotus* 38/39 (October 1978–March 1979): 126–8.

5. The first issue of *Afro-Asian Writings* (March 1968) names the Congress for Cultural Freedom as a neocolonialist front funded by US intelligence services (142), while the second issue labels the CCF-sponsored little magazine *Hiwar* (Lebanon) a cover for "Western intelligence services" (189). See also Siddheswar Sen, "Writers' Freedom and Commitment," *Lotus* 20 (April–June 1974) 34–38.

6. "Editor's Note," *Lotus* 9 (July 1971): 6–7. Even in 1977, El-Sebai was still complaining that a commercial distributor had not been found for the English and French versions. "Editor's Note," *Lotus* 31 (January–March 1977): 4–5.

7. See Sophia Azeb, "Crossing the Saharan Boundary: *Lotus* and the Legibility of Africanness," *Research in African Literatures* 50.3 (2019): 91–115, and Hala Halim, "Translating Solidarity: An Interview with Nehad Salem," *Critical Times* 3.1 (2020): 131–47.

8. Nikolai Tikhonov, "Editorial: The Great Brotherhood of Literatures Born of the October Revolution," *Lotus* 34 (October–December 1977): 11. Additional references parenthetical.

9. Vijay Prashad, *The Darker Nations: A People's History of the Third World* (New York: New Press, 2007), 12. See also Anne Garland Mahler, *From the Tricontinental to the Global South: Race, Radicalism, and Transnational Solidarity* (Durham: Duke UP, 2018), which traces nonaligned radicalism through the Tricontinental movement, which overlapped with the AAWA project in a few key areas.

10. The status of Asian nations within and bordering the Soviet Union is an interesting question, not fully pursued in this chapter, which focuses instead on the anglophone writers who participated in the AAWA network. Nergis Ertürk describes the Russian and Turkish revolutions, ideologically different but historically and geographically proximate, "entangled revolutions." "Nâzım Hikmet and the Prose of Communism," *boundary 2* 47.2 (2020): 153. Gül Bilge Han also considers Hikmet's participation in AAPSO and AAWA in "Nazım Hikmet's Afro-Asian Solidarities," *Safundi* 19.3 (2018): 284–305. Leah Feldman, *On the Threshold of Eurasia: Revolutionary Poetics in the Caucasus* (Ithaca: Cornell UP, 2018), documents the complex aesthetic interplay between Russian and Asian poetry within the Soviet Union. Likewise, the cluster of documents gathered in a 2014 issue of *Modernism/modernity*, led by Harsha Ram's "Introducing Georgian Modernism," give a sense of how modernist aesthetics and revolutionary politics combined in the early twentieth century. *Modernism/modernity* 21.1 (2014) 283–359.

11. Wai Chee Dimock, *Through Other Continents: American Literature across Deep Time* (Princeton: Princeton UP, 2006), 4; Nicolai Volland, *Socialist Cosmopolitanism: The Chinese Literary Universe, 1945–1965* (New York: Columbia UP, 2017), 52.

12. My account of *Lotus* and the uneven temporalities of decolonization is influenced by many recent efforts to stretch linear accounts of literary and intellectual history. See Leah Feldman, "Global Souths: Toward a Materialist Poetics of Alignment," *boundary 2* 47.2 (2020): 199–225; Adom Getachew, *Worldmaking after Empire: The Rise and Fall of Self-Determination* (Princeton: Princeton UP, 2019); Achille Mbembe, *On the Postcolony* (Berkeley: U of California P, 2001); David Scott, *Conscripts of Modernity* and *Omens of Adversity*; Pheng Cheah, *What is a World? On Postcolonial Literature as World Literature* (Durham: Duke UP, 2016); Yogita Goyal, *Romance, Diaspora, and Black Atlantic Literature* (Cambridge: Cambridge UP, 2010); Greg Forter, *Critique and Utopia in Historical Postcolonial Fiction: Atlantic and other Worlds* (Oxford: Oxford UP, 2019); as well as Mufti, *Forget English!*; Dimock, *Through Other Continents*; Saint-Amour, *Tense Future*; and Wilder, *Freedom Time*. Additional references parenthetical.

13. J. M. Coetzee, "Man's Fate in the Novels of Alex La Guma," in *Doubling the Point: Essays and Interviews*, ed. David Attwell (Cambridge: Harvard UP, 1992), 344. Additional references parenthetical.

14. See Graham Huggan, *The Postcolonial Exotic: Marketing the Margins* (London: Routledge, 2001); Gail Low, *Publishing the Postcolonial: Anglophone West African and Caribbean Writing in the UK, 1948–1968* (Abingdon: Routledge, 2011); Caroline Davis, "The Politics of Postcolonial Publishing: Oxford University Press's Three Crowns Series 1962–1976" *Book History 8* (2005): 227–44; J. Dillon Brown, *Migrant Modernism: Postwar London and the West Indian Novel* (Charlottesville: U of Virginia P, 2013); and Kalliney, *Commonwealth of Letters*.

15. Franco Moretti, "Conjectures on World Literature," *New Left Review* 1 (2000): 54–69, and "More Conjectures," *New Left Review* 20 (2003): 73–81. Additional references parenthetical.

16. Fredric Jameson, *A Singular Modernity: Essay on the Ontology of the Present* (London: Verso, 2002); Warwick Research Collective, *Combined and Uneven Development: Towards a New Theory of World Literature* (Liverpool: Liverpool UP, 2015). Additional references parenthetical.

17. Clark, *Moscow: The Fourth Rome*; Popescu, *At Penpoint*; Rossen Djagalov, *From Internationalism to Postcolonialism: Literature and Cinema between the Second and the Third Worlds* (Montreal & Kingston: McGill-Queen's UP, 2020); Steven S. Lee, *The Ethnic Avant-Garde: Minority Cultures and World Revolution* (New York: Columbia UP, 2015).

18. When I say that the Soviet Union was publishing roughly the same number of books as the United States, United Kingdom, France, and West Germany combined in 1961, I refer to the number of books originally published in that year, either in first or new editions. This does not refer to the number of books printed—new titles as opposed to print runs is the distinguishing factor. I follow UNESCO conventions here. It is worth noting that the United States dramatically increased its share of global book production in the 1960s, accounting for just over four percent of world book publishing in 1960, rising to about 12.5 percent in 1969. By the late 1970s, when the United States stopped reporting data to UNESCO, the Unites States and USSR were publishing about the same number of books per year, although the Soviet Union continued to publish far more literary books on average throughout this period (thirty to forty percent more annual releases). The print runs (as opposed to titles published) I refer to in the next paragraph come from a book series announcement in *Lotus*. *UNESCO Statistical Yearbook 1963, 1970, 1976, 1981* (Paris: UNESCO, 1964–1981). Pages consulted 1963: 344–99; 1976: 795–916; 1981: vol. 8, 23–149. See also Gretchen Whitney, "International Book Production Statistics," in *International Book Publishing: An Encyclopedia*, ed. Philip G. Altbach and Edith S. Hoshino (New York: Garland, 1995), 163–85.

19. Susanna Witt, "Between the Lines: Totalitarianism and Translation in the USSR," in Brian James Baer, ed., *Contexts, Subtexts, and Pretexts: Literary Translation in Eastern Europe and Russia* (Amsterdam/Philadelphia: John Benjamins, 2011), 150.

20. Victor Ramzes, "African Literature in Russia," *Transition* 25 (1966): 40–42. Ramzes reports an active translation scene since the Tashkent conference, with millions of volumes of books being published every year. According to the notes on contributors, Ramzes is Russian and works for the "Afro-Asian Department of the Foreign Commission of the USSR Union of Writers." *Transition* 25 (1966): 2.

21. "A Book on Kalidasa Opens a New Series," *Lotus* 34 (October–December 1977): 176.

22. Blanche La Guma, Preface to *A Soviet Journey*, by Alex La Guma, ed. Christopher J. Lee, foreword Ngũgĩ wa Thiong'o, (Lanham: Lexington Books, 2017), xiii. In his introduction, Lee quotes Blanche, who called her husband a "rouble millionaire" (29). See also Ngugi's foreword, which attests to the prominence of La Guma and the importance of Victor Ramzes. Fellow Lotus Prize winner, Sonomyn Udval, also reports that La Guma's work circulated widely in her native Mongolia. Sonomyn Udval, "Review of the New Mongolian Literature," *Lotus* 24/25 (April–September 1975): 146–49.

23. *And a Threefold Cord* (1964) was first published by Seven Seas, the East German publisher. The English- and French-language editions of *Lotus*, likewise, were printed in East Germany for most of the magazine's run. As B. Venkat Mani discusses in *Recoding World Literature: Libraries, Print Culture, and Germany's Pact with Books* (New York: Fordham UP, 2017), the East German book market was open to a wider range of writers than its West German counterpart. The La Guma papers contain contracts and copyright agreements on editions of several books for Eastern European markets, ranging from five thousand copies of *In the Fog of Seasons' End* in Slovenian; twenty-five thousand copies of the same novel in Hungarian; fifty thousand copies in Russian of *Time of the Butcherbird*; and a whopping seventy-five thousand copies of *A Soviet Journey*, in English, with Russian publisher Progress. See MCH 118 box 7 folder 4, multiple items.

24. Audre Lorde, "Notes from a Trip to Russia," in *Sister Outsider: Essays and Speeches*, foreword Cheryl Clarke (Berkeley: Crossing Press, 2007), 13–35. Additional references parenthetical.

25. Lydia H. Liu, "After Tashkent: The Geopolitics of Translation in the Global South," https://www.ici-berlin.org/events/lydia-h-liu/, accessed 8 June 2020.

26. Anatoly Sofronov, "Editor's Note," *Lotus* 34 (October–December 1977): 4; Tikhonov, "The Great Brotherhood" 5.

27. Alex La Guma, "What I Learned from Maxim Gorky" *Lotus* 34 (October–December 1977): 164–68.

28. "Special Section on: Lotus Award Winners for the Year 1975: Chinua Achebe, Faiz Ahmed Faiz, Kim Chi Ha, M. Mahdi El Gawahri," *Lotus* 30 (October–December 1976): 121.

29. C. J. George, *Mulk Raj Anand, His Art and Concerns: A Study of His Non-Autobiographical Novels* (New Delhi: Atlantic, 1994) 12–13. Anand names Zaheer as a fellow organizer in "Some Reminiscences of Sajjad Zaheer" (51).

30. M. V. Desai, "The Asian Writers' Conference December 1956—New Delhi," *Books Abroad* 31.3 (Summer 1957): 243–45. Mulk Raj Anand confirms this account in "Some Reminiscences of Sajjad Zaheer" (51). See also "Asian Writers' Conference," *Indian Daily Mail* 13 December 1956 (section 2—n.p.).

31. Quotations from Mulk Raj Anand, K. S. Bhat, J. C. Ghose, S. Sinha, M. D. Taseer, and S. S. Zaheer, "Manifesto of the Indian Progressive Writers' Association, London," *Left Review* 2.5 (1936): n.p.

32. Youssef El-Sebai, "The Role of AFRO-ASIAN Literature and the National Liberation Movements," *Lotus* 1 (March 1968): 11.

33. See also Warner, *Tongue-Tied Imagination*.

34. On the importance of the Non-Aligned Movement, see El-Sebai, "Editorial: Inspiration from the Colombo Meetings of the Non-Alignment Movement," *Lotus* 31 (January–March 1977): 6–7. On the significance of Afro-Asian Peoples' Solidarity Organization, see El-Sebai, "Twenty Years of Struggle for the Afro-Asian Peoples' Solidarity," *Lotus* 35 (January–March 1978): 114–23.

On the significance of Bandung, see El-Sebai, "Bandung . . . and the Afro-Asian Solidarity," *Lotus* 26 (October–December 1975): 20–23. The report of the UNESCO meeting is reproduced in *Lotus* as "Influence of Colonialism on the Artist, his Milieu, and his Public in Developing Countries," *Lotus* 18 (October 1973): 10–20.

35. Of the issues of *Lotus* I have read and the archival documents I have examined, the most comprehensive narrative history of the Afro-Asian movement written by a participant is Valentin Kotkin, *Path of Struggle and Victories: 25th Anniversary of the Afro-Asian Writers' Movement* (Moscow: Novosti Press Agency Publishing House, 1983). Held in La Guma papers, MCH 118 box 14 folder 4. See also "In Tashkent Young Writers from Africa and Asia Met," *Lotus* 32–33 (1977): 119–126; Hala Halim, "*Lotus*, the Afro-Asian Nexus, and Global South Comparatism," *Comparative Studies of South Asia, Africa and the Middle East* 32.3 (2012): 563–83; and Rossen Djagalov, "The Afro-Asian Association and Soviet Engagement with Africa," *Black Perspectives* 2 November 2017, https://www.aaihs.org/the-afro-asian-writers-association-and-soviet-engagement-with-africa/, accessed 19 December 2019. Djagalov also provides highlights of the Russian-language materials held at RGALI in *From Internationalism to Postcolonialism* 65–110.

36. Langston Hughes, *A Negro Looks at Soviet Central Asia*, (Moscow: Co-Operative Publishing Society of Foreign Workers in the USSR, 1934); *I Wonder as I Wander: An Autobiographical Journey*, intro. Arnold Rampersad (1956; New York: Farrar Straus, Giroux, 1984). See also David Chioni Moore, "Local Color, Global 'Color': Langston Hughes, the Black Atlantic, and Soviet Central Asia, 1932," *Research in African Literatures* 27.4 (1996): 49–70 and Baldwin, *Beyond the Color Line and the Iron Curtain*.

37. Confusingly, when the Chinese delegation led a breakaway group to form the Afro-Asian Writers' Bureau, the Soviet-backed group, which sponsored *Lotus*, became known as the Permanent Bureau of the Afro-Asian Writers' Association. On the Sino-Soviet split and its effect on Afro-Asian literature, see Pieter Vanhove, "'A World to Win:' China, the Afro-Asian Writers' Bureau, and the Reinvention of World Literature," *Critical Asian Studies* 51.2 (2019): 144–65; Duncan M. Yoon, "'Our Forces Have Redoubled': World Literature, Postcolonialism, and the Afro-Asian Writers' Bureau," *Cambridge Journal of Postcolonial Literary Inquiry* 2.2 (2015): 233–52; and Kotkin, *Path of Struggle*. Lydia H. Liu, "The Eventfulness of Translation: Temporality, Difference, and Competing Universals," *translation: a transdisciplinary journal* 4 (2014): 148–70, considers the impact of the AAWA on Chinese literature before the split.

38. Ratne Deshapriya Senanayake, ed., *Afro-Asian Poems: Anthology*, vol. 1, part 1 (Colombo: Afro-Asian Writers' Bureau, 1963), vii.

39. Youssef El-Sebai, "Editor's Note," *Lotus* 20 (April–June 1974): 6–7.

40. Youssef El-Sebai, "Report of the Secretary General [at Alma-Ata Afro-Asian conference 1973]," *Lotus* 20 (April–June 1974): 166–67.

41. Alex La Guma, "Report of the Secretary General to the Seventh General (25th Anniversary) Conference, Tashkent, Uzbekistan, September–October 1983," *Lotus* 56 (1985): 192.

42. Minutes from *Lotus* magazine working-group meeting, Moscow, 18 January 1985 (MCH 118 box 7 folder 3, La Guma papers).

43. Probably Ronnie Kasrils, who wrote poetry under the pen name A.N.C. Kumalo, although possibly Dumasani Kumalo (*Drum* journalist and anti-apartheid activist who lived in the United States during his exile).

44. Alex La Guma, "South African Writing under Apartheid," *Lotus* 23 (January–March 1975): 20. See also Nesrine Chahine, "Peter Abrahams and the Bandung Era: Afro-Asian Routes of Connection," *Critical Arts* 34.3 (2020): 30–40; Matthew Eatough, "The Critic as Modernist: Es'kia Mphahlele's Cold War Literary Criticism," *Research in African Literatures* 50.3 (2019): 136–56; Christopher J. Lee's introduction to La Guma's nonfiction writing from exile, "Distant Writing: African Literature and Its Cold War Itineraries," in Alex La Guma, *Culture and Liberation: Exile Writings, 1966–1985*, ed. and intro. Christopher J. Lee, foreword Albie Sachs, afterword Bill Nasson (London: Seagull, 2021), 15–51.

45. Dennis Brutus, "A Wrong Headed Bunch," *Lotus* 12 (April 1972): 158. Special section on South Africa runs 141–78.

46. This example provides both corollary and counterpoint to Jed Esty's account of decolonization and the *bildungsroman* in *Unseasonable Youth: Modernism, Colonialism, and the Fiction of Development* (Oxford: Oxford UP, 2012). Esty suggests, convincingly, that the narrative of the *bildungsroman* tends to stall as it grapples with the logic of development in colonial situations. If long-format fiction tends to present colonial situations as frozen in time, without a viable future, the poetry and short fiction of *Lotus* tends to represent the present as saturated by both past and future.

47. Joe Cleary writes that postcolonial studies has consistently favored the global south's experimental-modernist writers over those who inclined toward realism, leading him to conclude that this has produced a "detrimental effect" on postcolonial studies. "Realism after Modernism and the Literary World-System," *Modern Language Quarterly* 73.3 (2012): 265. See also Michael Denning, *Culture in the Age of Three Worlds* (London: Verso, 2004), 51–72.

48. Andrew van der Vlies provides an excellent account of La Guma's publication history. *South African Textual Cultures: White, Black, Read All Over* (Manchester: Manchester UP, 2007).

49. Alex La Guma, "The Exile," *Lotus* (1972): 68.

50. Mahmood Mamdani, *Citizen and Subject: Contemporary Africa and the Legacy of Late Colonialism*, 2nd ed. (Princeton: Princeton UP, 2018).

51. Hannah Arendt, *Between Past and Future: Eight Exercises in Political Thought*, 2nd ed. (New York: Viking, 1968), 13.

52. For example, Mbulelo Mzamane, a South African fiction writer of the next generation, says that *Time of the Butcherbird* "lacks authenticity and penetration of his earlier work in its evocation of the social milieu in which he characters move, a shortcoming which a number of his African readers close to the source will immediately recognize." This judgment approaches critical consensus of La Guma's later work. Mbulelo Vizikhungo Mzamane, "Sharpeville and Its Aftermath: The Novels of Richard Rive, Peter Abrahams, Alex La Guma, and Lauretta Ngcobo," *ARIEL* 16.2 (1985): 40.

53. Letter from Ezekiel Mphahlele to La Guma, 28 May 1962, written on CCF letterhead, congratulating La Guma on publication and stating that it will be "among the texts we shall examine at Makerere" (MCH 118 box 2 folder 7, La Guma papers).

54. Clipping (MCH 118 box 2 folder 7, La Guma papers). Review published 6 March 1962.

55. Alex La Guma, *A Walk in the Night and Other Stories* (Evanston: Northwestern UP, 1967), n.p.

56. Anthony Reed, *Freedom Time: The Poetics and Politics of Black Experimental Writing* (Baltimore: Johns Hopkins UP, 2014), 9.

57. Grant Farred, *Midfielder's Moment: Coloured Literature and Culture in Contemporary South Africa* (Boulder, CO: Westview, 2000), 36–37. See also Rita Barnard, *Apartheid and Beyond: South African Writers and the Politics of Place* (Oxford: Oxford UP, 2007), especially "Beyond the Tyranny of Place" and "The Location of Postapartheid Culture," 119–74.

58. Alex La Guma, *The Stone Country* (London: Heinemann, 1967), 7.

59. Christopher J. Lee, "The Workshop of Confinement: Political Quarantine and the Spatial Imagination in the Early Fiction of Alex La Guma," *Modern Fiction Studies* 67.2 (2021): 272–91.

60. Alex La Guma, *Time of the Butcherbird* (Oxford: Heinemann, 1979), 1.

61. In noting this, I am partly in alignment with Monica Popescu's reading of La Guma in *South African Literature beyond the Cold War* (New York: Palgrave Macmillan, 2010). Popescu reads La Guma's fiction as indebted to socialist realism, which has the tendency to be teleological and yet to derail "the seamless linear experience of time," with lots of speed-ups and fast-forwards (44). She reads *A Soviet Journey*, by contrast, as full of ghosts and revenants. I see many of the same time-bending tendencies in La Guma's texts, although I attribute this less to an engagement with socialist realism and more as a function of La Guma's exile and the cold war networks he traversed.

62. Abdul JanMohamed's influential account of La Guma's fiction is contradictory on the matter of temporality and the fullness (or poverty) of La Guma's fictional imagination. On one hand, JanMohamed writes that La Guma's South Africa is stark and abject, as in the passage quoted in the main text (257). On the other hand, in his reading of *In the Fog of Seasons' End*, he says that La Guma "mythologizes the African past for present consumption and then sacrifices the present for a future freedom. The presentation of these tensions and contradictions through swift juxtapositions and flashbacks is perfectly consonant with the discontinuous experience of the characters," a gloss that resonates with my own sense of the amplitude, rather than the thinness, of the *Lotus* aesthetic (262). *Manichean Aesthetics: The Politics of Literature in Colonial Africa* (Amherst: U of Massachusetts P, 1983). Kathleen Balutansky, likewise, shies away from labelling La Guma's fiction as straightforward socialist realism, but she does insist that his writing uses "dialectical movement" in order to "transcend the destructive and alienating effects of Apartheid" through his revolutionary aesthetics. *The Novels of Alex La Guma: The Representation of Political Conflict* (Boulder, CO: Three Continents Press, 1990), 106, 127. See also Cecil A. Abrahams, *Alex La Guma* (Boston: Twayne, 1985).

63. Roger Field, *Alex La Guma: A Literary and Political Biography* (Woodbridge: James Currey, 2010), 141; and Popescu, *South African Literature beyond the Cold War*, 25–53.

Chapter 5

1. Richard Jean So, *Transpacific Community: America, China, and the Rise and Fall of a Cultural Network* (New York: Columbia UP, 2016). By contrast, Nan Z. Da, *Intransitive Encounter: Sino-U.S. Literatures and the Limits of Exchange* (New York: Columbia UP, 2018), describes "a catalog of self-erasing Sino-U.S. literary interactions in the long nineteenth century," locating patterns of cultural exchange that were at once common and so inconsequential they "might as well not have happened" (2).

2. Christina Klein, *Cold War Orientalism: Asia in the Middlebrow Imagination, 1945–1961* (Berkeley: U of California P, 2003). See also Nicole Huang, *Women, War, Domesticity: Shanghai*

Literature and Popular Culture of the 1940s (Leiden: Brill, 2005), who regards Chang as an assertive symbol of women's literary culture in adverse wartime conditions. Conversely, in *The East Is Black: Cold War China in the Black Radical Imagination* (Durham: Duke UP, 2015), Robeson Taj Frazier documents relations between the Chinese Communist Party and the revolutionary segments of African diaspora, a competing network of China–US exchange in which Chang's writings did not circulate.

3. Eileen Chang, *Written on Water*, ed. Andrew F. Jones and Nicole Huang, trans. Jones (New York: Columbia UP, 2005), 156. Additional references parenthetical.

4. Eileen Chang, *Love in a Fallen City*, trans. Chang and Karen S. Kingsbury (New York: New York Review of Books, 2007), 1. The preface to and several of the stories from *Romances* are presented in the English collection, *Love in a Fallen City*. Additional references parenthetical.

5. Lu Xun was and remains a national literary giant, known for his portrayals of common people and his development of vernacular literature (*baihua wenxue*), as opposed to the highly stylized and refined literary language (*wenyan*) of the centuries-old Chinese canon. See Xiaojue Wang, *Modernity with a Cold War Face: Reimagining the Nation in Chinese Literature across the 1949 Divide* (Cambridge: Harvard U Asia Center, 2013), 23–53, for a helpful overview of the main debates in Chinese literature from 1911–49. For an overview of the League of Left-Wing Writers in English, see Wang-chi Wong, *Politics and Literature in Shanghai: The Chinese League of Left-Wing Writers, 1930–1936* (Manchester: Manchester UP, 1991). A widely cited passage from his oeuvre reveals that Lu Xun abandoned his medical studies after seeing a photograph of a Chinese man being executed for espionage by Japanese forces while a group of passive Chinese watch the spectacle apathetically. There and then he decided to serve his country as a writer by jolting it from its long stupor, turning a moment of shame and indignation into "an allegorical scene in which China's fate is illuminated," as David Der-wei Wang remarks in *The Monster That Is History: History, Violence, and Fictional Writing in Twentieth-Century China* (Berkeley: U of California P, 2004), 20. Lu Xun supported the national cause much like the James Joyce of *Dubliners*, that is by showing the Chinese to themselves in all their complacencies, disfigurements, and hypocrisies. In C. T. Hsia's estimation, Lu Xun at his best "is content to probe the disease without prescribing a cure: he has too high a respect for the art of fiction to present other than the unadorned truth" (*History of Modern Chinese Fiction*, 2nd ed. [New Haven: Yale UP, 1971], 46). Against this reading of Lu Xun as relatively detached, see Kang Liu, *Aesthetics and Marxism: Chinese Aesthetic Marxists and their Western Contemporaries* (Durham: Duke UP, 2000). Additional references parenthetical.

6. Although many of the first generation of Asian American intellectuals regard Buck as an Orientalist writer, trafficking in demeaning stereotypes, recent scholarly treatments of her show a more complicated figure who consciously resisted exotic caricatures. The novel presents bits of Chinese culture as fundamentally different than corresponding features in North American or western European cultures, but beyond these inessential curiosities exists a more fundamental common humanity. Quoting a passage from the novel, in which the poor, hardworking protagonist, Wang Lung, gives his wife some money to buy clothes for his child, will help me illustrate the point:

> Wang Lung sat smoking, thinking of the silver as it had lain upon the table. It had come out of the earth, this silver, out of his earth that he ploughed and turned and spent himself upon. He took his life from this earth; drop by drop by his sweat he wrung food from

270 NOTES TO CHAPTER 5

it and from the food, silver. Each time before this that he had taken the silver out to give to anyone, it had been like taking a piece of his life and giving it to someone carelessly. But now for the first time such giving was not pain. He saw, not the silver in the alien hand of a merchant in the town; he saw the silver transmuted into something worth even more than itself—clothes upon the body of his son.

In this scene, the narrator lays bare the protagonist's thoughts, which are utterly comprehensible. Long accustomed to poverty, he hates giving away money to others, but for the first time, when his hard-won earnings go to clothe and feed his family, he does not begrudge exchanging his money for useful things. Wang Lung acts and reasons in ways that are utterly familiar. The narrator patiently walks the reader through this process of thought. This transparency is reinforced by Buck's simplistic, no-frills prose: nothing is so strange or unusual that it calls for ornate syntax or farfetched metaphors. Everything is available for inspection, including what the main characters think and feel. Beneath the Chinese customs lies a common humanity that translates easily across cultural and linguistic barriers. Pearl S. Buck, *The Good Earth* (New York: Grosset & Dunlap, 1931), 38–39. See also Colleen Lye, *America's Asia: Racial Form and American Literature, 1893–1945* (Princeton: Princeton UP, 2005), 204–9. *The Good Earth*'s eminently readable main character provides a kind of foil for Eric Hayot's "hypothetical mandarin," a trope in the Euro-American imagination in which foreign, inscrutable, and non-Western cultural practices are gathered under the rubric of Chinese difference. Eric Hayot, *The Hypothetical Mandarin: Sympathy, Modernity, and Chinese Pain* (Oxford: Oxford UP, 2009).

7. In his controversial essay, "Third-World Literature in the Era of Multinational Capitalism," Fredric Jameson uses Lu Xun's "Diary of a Madman" as his principal example of a national allegory in Third-World writing. *Social Text* 15 (1986): 65–88. The essay prompted any number of rejoinders, the best of which is Aijaz Ahmad, "Jameson's Rhetoric of Otherness and the 'National Allegory,'" *Social Text* 17 (1987): 3–25. In *The Monster that is History*, David Der-wei Wang also reads Lu Xun's "Diary of a Madman" as national allegory. Shu-mei Shih and Leo Ou-fan Lee offer more complicated perspectives by noting that interwar Shanghai's literary culture afforded Chang unique opportunities to observe the nationalist movement firsthand while remaining in close contact with international circuits of literary production. Leo Ou-fan Lee, *Shanghai Modern: The Flowering of a New Urban Culture in China, 1930–1945* (Cambridge: Harvard UP, 1999); Shu-mei Shih, *The Lure of the Modern: Writing Modernism in Semi-Colonial China, 1917–1937* (Berkeley: U of California P, 2001).

8. Letter, Chang to Hsia, "Zhang Ailing gei wo de xinjian," (Eileen Chang's letters to me), *Unitas* 13.11 (September 1997), 70–71. Quoted in and translated by Xiaojue Wang 293.

9. Rey Chow, *Primitive Passions: Visuality, Sexuality, Ethnography, and Contemporary Chinese Cinema* (New York: Columbia UP, 1995), 112.

10. See also L. Maria Bo, who argues that Chang's technique of equivocal contrast provides a key for understanding her translation of Ernest Hemingway's *The Old Man and the Sea* into Chinese. "Freedom Over Seas: Eileen Chang, Ernest Hemingway, and the Translation of Truth in the Cold War," *Comparative Literature* 71.3 (2019): 252–71.

11. The most widely known of these is Frank Kermode, *The Sense of an Ending: Studies in the Theory of Fiction: with a new epilogue* (Oxford: Oxford UP, 2000). Others include Paul K. Saint-Amour, *Tense Future*; Steven Belletto, *No Accident, Comrade: Chance and Design in Cold War American Narratives* (Oxford: Oxford UP, 2012); Sarah Cole, *At the Violet Hour: Modernism and*

Violence in England and Ireland (Oxford: Oxford UP, 2012); Patrick Deer, *Culture in Camouflage: War, Empire, and Modern British Literature* (Oxford: Oxford UP, 2009); Marian Eide, *Terrible Beauty: The Violent Aesthetic and Twentieth-Century Literature* (Charlottesville: U of Virginia P, 2019); Daniel Grasuam, *On Endings: American Postmodern Fiction and the Cold War* (Charlottesville: U of Virginia P, 2011); Pearl James, *The New Death: American Modernism and World War I* (Charlottesville: U of Virginia P, 2013); Marina MacKay, *Modernism and World War II* (Cambridge: Cambridge UP, 2007); Alan Nadel, *Containment Culture: American Narratives, Postmodernism, and the Atomic Age* (Durham: Duke UP, 1995); Adam Piette, *The Literary Cold War: 1945 to Vietnam* (Edinburgh: Edinburgh UP, 2009); Vincent Sherry, *The Great War and the Language of Modernism* (Oxford: Oxford UP, 2003).

12. Shuang Shen, in *Cosmopolitan Publics: Anglophone Print Culture in Semi-Colonial Shanghai* (New Brunswick: Rutgers UP, 2009), 135–44, discusses the magazine's pro-Axis slant, although Chang herself did not publish anything that extolled the regimes of Nazi Germany or imperial Japan, to my knowledge. See also Huang, *Women, War, Domesticity*, for an account of Shanghai literary culture during wartime.

13. In his introduction to *The Rice-Sprout Song*, David Der-wei Wang describes these two texts as pro-Communist. Eileen Chang, *The Rice-Sprout Song*, foreword David Der-wei Wang (Berkeley: U of California P, 1998), xiv. Xiaojue Wang describes Chang's attendance at the Shanghai Writers' and Artists' conference (260). In the introduction to *Eileen Chang: Romancing Languages, Cultures and Genres*, Kam Louie also reports that Chang attended this conference (Hong Kong: Hong Kong UP, 2012), 9.

14. Eileen Chang, *Naked Earth*, intro. Perry Link (New York: New York Review of Books, 2015), xi. Additional references parenthetical.

15. For an account of the State Department's earliest efforts in cultural diplomacy, see Frank A. Ninkovich, *The Diplomacy of Ideas: U.S. Foreign Policy and Cultural Relations, 1938–1950* (Cambridge: Cambridge UP, 1981).

16. Mary L. Dudziak, *Cold War Civil Rights: Race and the Image of American Democracy*, 2nd ed. (Princeton: Princeton UP, 2011).

17. Nicholas J. Cull, *The Cold War and the United States Information Agency: American Propaganda and Public Diplomacy, 1945–1989* (Cambridge: Cambridge UP, 2008). As Cull documents, USIA was established as a separate entity in 1953, although the State Department continued to be actively involved in USIA programs. In Hong Kong, as in most other situations, USIA staff submitted their plans to the US Ambassador for final approval (for instance, see 8th Review of [USIA Hong Kong] Operations, 1 January—30 June 1957, RG 306 P131 box 99, NARA II). Jason C. Parker, *Hearts, Minds, Voices: US Cold War Public Diplomacy and the Formation of the Third World* (Oxford: Oxford UP, 2016), argues that the focus of US public diplomacy gradually shifted from Europe to the global south. For an overview of the USIA's documentary film program, see Tony Shaw, *Hollywood's Cold War* (Edinburgh: Edinburgh UP, 2007), 167–98.

18. Cull reports that the formation of USIA was a direct response to estimates that the Soviets were devoting vast resources to their book scheme, which was leaving US cultural diplomacy far behind (52).

19. For an overview of how the State Department and USIA made use of modernist literature, see Greg Barnhisel, *Cold War Modernists*. Eric Bennett, *Workshops of Empire: Stenger, Engle, and American Creative Writing during the Cold War* (Iowa City: U of Iowa P, 2015)

considers how the State Department and the CIA drafted creative writing programs into the cold war. Trysh Travis, "Middlebrow Print Culture in the Cold War: Books USA, 1967," (*PMLA* 128.2 [2013]: 468–73) provides a short overview of some of the public-private book schemes of the cold war.

20. Ellen D. Wu, "'America's Chinese': Anti-Communism, Citizenship, and Cultural Diplomacy during the Cold War," *Pacific Historical Review* 77.3 (2008): 391–422.

21. Josephine Nock-Hee Park, *Cold War Friendships: Korea, Vietnam, and Asian American Literature* (Oxford: Oxford UP, 2016), 11.

22. Richard M. McCarthy, interviewed by Jack O'Brien, Association for Diplomatic Studies and Training, Foreign Affairs Oral History Project, 28 December 1988. https://www.adst.org /OH%20TOCs/McCarthy,%20Richard%20M.toc.pdf?_ga=2.148614775.1564764507 .1565889797-212518284.1565889797.

23. Mei-Hsiang Wang, "Eileen Chang—The Unknown Story: *The Rice-Sprout Song* and the *Naked Earth* under the USIS Book Translation Program," *EurAmerica* 45.1 (2015): 73–137. The full story of USIA support for the novel is not known to my satisfaction. On one hand, there are suggestions that someone at USIA, probably McCarthy, supplied the outline of the plot for *Naked Earth* (see also Xiaojue Wang 267). On the other hand, if USIA had commissioned the novel and found it satisfactory—Chang remained a favorite of McCarthy's—it is likely that USIA would have made better arrangements for the publication and distribution of the book. As Barnhisel documents, USIA book production schemes were robust in the mid-1950s, and as a known author Chang could expect preferential treatment. A tantalizing letter by McCarthy reports that Scribner's wanted to see chapters of Chang's work in progress, probably *Naked Earth*, before making a final decision on whether to publish *The Rice-Sprout Song* (letter McCarthy to Franklin Steiner, 19 May 1954, RG 84 entry 2689 box 1 NARA II). Unfortunately, long-term closures of the NARA II facility due to the ongoing public health crisis severely limited my access to these materials.

24. The manuscript of Chang's short story "The Spyring," which is not dated, suggests that she sent the story to McCarthy. Chang also wrote scripts and provided translations for Voice of America, which also employed McCarthy at different points in his career. Finally, letters from Chang to C. T. Hsia in the 1960s report that McCarthy was trying to help Chang place *Book of Change* with a US publisher. http://www.zonaeuropa.com/culture/c20100824_1.htm.

25. In his introduction to *The Rouge of the North*, David Der-wei Wang says that Chang wrote scripts for Voice of America (ix). It also seems likely that Chang adapted *One Day in the Life of Ivan Denisovich* for Voice of America, although I have not been able to confirm this in the archives.

26. Memo, 13 January 1954, USIS [USIA] Hong Kong to USIA Washington, "IPS: *World Today* No. 44, dated January 1, 1954," included with copy of *World Today* 1. Additional references parenthetical. Internal memos and reports argue that *World Today* was successful precisely because the sponsorship of the United States government was open: "One of the principal reasons why our Chinese-language magazine *World Today* is so popular, we believe, is that it is attributed; many readers buy it primarily because they do regard it as an official spokesman for the United States." Semi-annual Report, USIS Hong Kong to USIA Washington, 14 March 1955, RG 84 entry 2689 Box 4, NARA II.

27. Memo from United States Embassy, Taipei, to United States Embassy, Hong Kong 25 March 1953, NARA II RG84 Entry 2689 Box 3.

NOTES TO CHAPTER 5   273

28. Eric Bennett, *Workshops of Empire* 103–16. See also Richard Jean So, "The Invention of the Global MFA: Taiwanese Writers at Iowa, 1964–1980," *American Literary History* 29.3 (2017): 499–520.

29. Letter Chang to Hsia, 31 December 1965. http://digitallibrary.usc.edu/cdm/compound object/collection/p15799coll92/id/175/rec/4.

30. Paul Nadal, "Cold War Remittance Economy: US Creative Writing and the Importation of New Criticism into the Philippines," *American Quarterly* 73.3 (2021): 557–95; Kalyan Nadiminti, "The Global Program Era: Contemporary International Fiction in the American Creative Economy," *NOVEL: A Forum on Fiction* 51.3 (2018): 375–98.

31. Richard Jean So, "Literary Information Warfare: Eileen Chang, the US State Department, and Cold War Media Aesthetics," *American Literature* 85.4 (2013): 719–44; David Der-wei Wang, Introduction to *The Rice-Sprout Song*; and Nicole Huang, "Worlding Eileen Chang (Zhang Ailing): Narratives of Frontiers and Crossings," in *Wiley Blackwell Companion to World Literature*, ed. Ken Seigneurie (https://doi.org/10.1002/9781118635193.ctwl0232) all say that Chang composed the novel in English and then translated it into Chinese. L. Maria Bo (252, note 2) and Hsia (389), on the other hand, say the novel was written in Chinese and translated into English. There are similar discrepancies in the secondary literature on *Naked Earth*.

32. Eileen Chang, *The Rice-Sprout Song* (New York: Charles Scriber's Sons, 1955), v-vi.

33. *The Rice-Sprout Song* (New York: Scribner's, 1955), v.

34. Further, as Bo points out, the conclusion of *The Rice-Sprout Song* differs in the Chinese and English versions (268–69). In the English version, we learn of Moon Scent's charred body being discovered in the aftermath of the granary fire. The Chinese version, however, leaves her ultimate fate a mystery.

35. Eileen Chang, "The Original Typewritten Manuscript of 'The Spyring,'" ESWN Culture Blog, accessed 25 June 2019, http://www.zonaeuropa.com/culture/c20081005_1.htm. The website informs readers that this version of the story was first published in the Hong Kong periodical *Muse* in April 2008. *Lust, Caution*, trans., foreword Julia Lovell, afterword Ang Lee (New York: Anchor, 2007).

36. See also Haiyan Lee, "Enemy under My Skin: Eileen Chang's 'Lust, Caution' and the Politics of Transcendence," *PMLA* 125.3 (2010): 640–56. Lee says that Chang began writing the story in Hong Kong in the early 1950s. She also reads the story as a protest against the instrumental use of women's bodies for the nationalist cause.

37. Tina Chen, *Double Agency: Acts of Impersonation in Asian American Literature and Culture* (Stanford: Stanford UP, 2005), xvii.

38. Letter Chang to C. T. Hsia, 16 October 1964. http://digitallibrary.usc.edu/cdm/compoundobject/collection/p15799coll92/id/250/rec/3.

39. The debates about translation and global literature are too involved to recapitulate in this space. To get a sense of the discussion, see Rebecca L. Walkowitz, *Born Translated: The Contemporary Novel in an Age of World Literature* (New York: Columbia UP, 2015); David Damrosch, *What Is World Literature?* (Princeton: Princeton UP, 2003); Emily Apter, *Against World Literature: On the Politics of Untranslatability* (London: Verso, 2013); Christopher GoGwilt, *The Passage of Literature: Genealogies of Modernism in Conrad, Rhys, and Pramoedya* (Oxford: Oxford UP, 2011); Gayle Rogers, *Incomparable Empires: Modernism and the Translation of Spanish American Literature* (New York: Columbia UP, 2016); Jahan Ramazani, *Poetry in a Global Age* (Chicago: U of Chicago P, 2020); and Haun Saussy, *Translation as Citation: Zhuangzi Inside Out*

(Oxford: Oxford UP, 2017). Saussy's thinking about loan words, calques, and macaronic texts is especially relevant to Chang's bilingualism: her English texts often import words, phrases, and metaphors directly from the Chinese.

40. Eileen Chang, "Chinese Translation: A Vehicle of Cultural Influence," ed. and intro. Christopher Lee, *PMLA* 130.2 (2015): 497. In addition to translating anglophone writers into Chinese, Chang translated some anticommunist novels, such as Chen Chi-ying's *Fool in the Reeds* (Hong Kong: Rainbow Press, 1959), into English.

41. Eileen Chang, *Half a Lifelong Romance*, intro. and trans. Karen S. Kingsbury (New York: Anchor, 2014), vii, x. David Der-wei Wang, in his foreword to *The Rouge of the North*, says that Chang was "forced" to insert "pro-communist messages" into her work from the early 1950s. Eileen Chang, *The Rouge of the North*, foreword David Der-wei Wang (Berkeley: U of California P, 1967, 1995), note 3, xxix.

Chapter 6

1. Doris Lessing, *Going Home* (1957; St Albans: Granada, 1968), 62. Additional references parenthetical.

2. Doris Lessing files, KV2/4054, /4055, /4056, /4057, and /4058, National Archives, United Kingdom.

3. 11 September 1952 (KV2/4054).

4. 29 July 1952 (KV2/4054).

5. 18 July 1955 (KV2/4055).

6. Report from Security Liaison Officer Central Africa to MI5 Head Office, 16 May 1956 (KV2/4056).

7. Letter from MI5 Director General to Commissioner of Police, Zanzibar, 29 Nov 1962 (KV2/4058).

8. Letter from Security Liaison Officer East Africa to MI5 Head Office and Security Liaison Officer Central Africa, 22 May 1956 (KV2/4056).

9. Unsigned note, 16 May 1956, on dossier's "Minute Sheet," or summary of contents (KV2/4056).

10. Cristina Vatulescu, *Police Aesthetics: Literature, Film, and the Secret Police in Soviet Times* (Stanford: Stanford UP, 2010).

11. Special Branch are the undercover political police, while CID work in plainclothes but remain part of the regular police force. Letter from B. M. de Quehen, Director F.I.S.B. to Prime Minister's Private Secretary, 30 April 1956 (KV2/4056).

12. The security files on Hogarth also make this apparent. Reports on Hogarth's doings are very meager in comparison with Lessing's file (KV2/4063).

13. Doris Lessing, *Walking in the Shade: Volume Two of My Autobiography, 1949–1962* (New York: HarperCollins, 1997), 206. See also her satirical story, "Spies I Have Known," in *Spies I Have Known and Other Stories* (Glasgow: Collins Educational, 1995), 171–93. Additional references parenthetical.

14. Doris Lessing, *The Golden Notebook* (1962; New York: Harper Perennial, 1990), xi. Additional references parenthetical.

15. Report from Central African Security Liaison to MI5 Head Office, 16 July 1956 (KV2/4056).

16. Lessing to Leonard Smith, 17 April 1948, Lessing papers (Sussex).

17. For instance, in the second book of *Children of Violence, A Proper Marriage* (1954), Martha Quest is thrilled when she attends her first left club meeting and discovers a space of racial equality, an entirely novel experience for her. By the end of the novel, however, she and her small band of White communists are struggling with the problem of cross-racial cooperation in the movement. It is much the same in *A Ripple from the Storm* (1955) and *Landlocked* (1965), with the added complication that the White progressive activists bicker and form splinter groups. The *Children of Violence* series: *Martha Quest* (1952; New York: HarperPerennial, 1964); *A Proper Marriage* (1954; New York: HarperPerennial, 1964); *A Ripple from the Storm* (1958; New York: HarperPerennial, 1966); *Landlocked* (1965; New York: HarperPerennial, 1966); *The Four-Gated City* (New York: Bantam, 1969). See also Lessing's account of this period in *Under My Skin: Volume One of My Autobiography, to 1949* (New York: HarperCollins, 1994), 258–92. Additional references parenthetical.

18. See also Lessing, *Walking in the Shade* 202–5.

19. Lessing to Leonard Smith, 5 June 1945, Lessing papers (Sussex).

20. Lessing to Leonard Smith, 7 October 1947, Lessing papers (Sussex).

21. Lessing to John Whitehorn, 25 March 1948, Lessing papers (UEA).

22. See Lessing's correspondence with members of the Soviet Union of Writers at RGALI, Russian State Archive of Literature and the Arts, f. 631, inv. 126 doc. 706.

23. Lessing to E. P. Thompson, 21 February 1957, Lessing papers (UEA). Also reproduced in *Walking in the Shade* 213–16.

24. Matthew Taunton, "Communism by the Letter: Doris Lessing and the Politics of Writing," *ELH* 88.1 (2021): 252.

25. In Lessing's file, for instance, there are transcripts of tapped phone calls about entirely unrelated matters. Lessing's file would receive a copy if she was mentioned by either of the speakers. The same is true of intercepted letters in which Lessing is mentioned.

26. Peter J. Kalliney, *Cities of Affluence and Anger: A Literary Geography of Modern Englishness* (Charlottesville: U of Virginia P, 2007).

27. Tommy makes occasional appearances in the notebooks, but the accounts in the notebooks contradict those in *Free Women*: the notebooks give different information about his age and activities. These differences are not, I think, crucial to the reading I offer here.

28. See also Sophia Barnes, "Readers of Fiction and Readers in Fiction: Readership and *The Golden Notebook*," in *Doris Lessing and the Forming of History*, eds. Kevin Brazil, David Sergeant, and Tom Sperlinger (Edinburgh: Edinburgh UP, 2016), 71–83.

29. Ato Quayson, *Aesthetic Nervousness: Disability and the Crisis of Representation* (New York: Columbia UP, 2007).

30. Tobin Siebers, *Disability Aesthetics* (Ann Arbor: U of Michigan P, 2010), 2–3.

31. Michael Trask, *Ideal Minds: Raising Consciousness in the Antisocial Seventies* (Ithaca: Cornell UP, 2020), 169.

32. Jeanne-Marie Jackson, *The African Novel of Ideas: Philosophy and Individualism in the Age of Global Writing* (Princeton: Princeton UP, 2021), 3.

33. See also Benjamin Kohlmann, "Toward a History and Theory of the Socialist Bildungsroman," *Novel: A Forum on Fiction* 48.2 (2015): 167–89, and Joseph R. Slaughter, *Human Rights, Inc.: The World Novel, Narrative Form, and International Law* (New York: Fordham UP, 2007).

34. David T. Mitchell and Sharon L. Snyder, *Narrative Prosthesis: Disability and the Dependencies of Discourse* (Ann Arbor: U of Michigan P, 2000), 164.

35. Doris Lessing, *Shikasta: Re: Colonised Planet 5* (New York: Vintage, 1979). In her preface, Lessing says clearly that novelists are increasingly experimenting by "'plug[ing] in' to an over-mind, or Ur-mind, or unconscious," and that science fiction offers some of the most exciting possibilities for understanding this development of consciousness (ix). Lynda Coldridge of *The Four-Gated City* even makes a few cameo appearances in *Shikasta*, where she is treated as something of a visionary whose mind was open to communications with alien species.

Chapter 7

1. Audre Lorde, *Zami: A New Spelling of My Name* (Freedom: Crossing Press, 1982), 159. Additional references parenthetical.

2. 9 September 1954, Audre Lorde FBI file.

3. 17 June 1957, Audre Lorde FBI file.

4. Audre Lorde, "Grenada Revisited," in *Sister Outsider* 177.

5. Mary Helen Washington, *The Other Blacklist*; Carole Boyce Davies, *Left of Karl Marx: The Political Life of Black Communist Claudia Jones* (Durham: Duke UP, 2007). Additional references parenthetical.

6. See James Baldwin, "Princes and Powers," which originally appeared in the CCF's flagship journal, *Encounter*. See also Hazel Rowley, *Richard Wright: The Life and Times* (New York: Henry Holt, 2001), 452–80.

7. C.L.R. James, *Mariners, Renegades and Castaways: The Story of Herman Melville and the World We Live in*, ed. and intro. Donald E. Pease (Hanover: UP of New England, 1953, 1978, 2001), 126. Additional references parenthetical.

8. Claudia Jones, "An End to the Neglect of the Problems of the Negro Woman!" (New York: National Women's Commission, CPUSA, 1949), 4. Additional references parenthetical.

9. 2 February 1942, Volume 1 Claudia Jones FBI file.

10. Davies speculates that she may have taken the alias Jones as part of her Party initiation (209).

11. 24 September 1946 and 16 June 1947, Volume 1 Claudia Jones FBI file.

12. [17?] May 1947, Volume 1 Claudia Jones FBI file.

13. See also Davies, *Left of Karl Marx* 196; Ellen Schrecker and Phillip Deery, *The Age of Mc-Carthyism: A Brief History with Documents*, 3rd ed. (Boston: Bedford-St Martin's, 2017), 42.

14. Although the files say she was arrested for the first time in 1948, by INS, the first "prosecutive summary" visible in her dossier is in fragments, coming later.

15. In a humorous scene in her prison memoirs, Elizabeth Gurley Flynn recalls a conversation with a potential legal representative who asks about the evidence against her and the other accused: "When we replied, 'Books,' he asked incredulously, 'Would I have to read books?' One of our amused committee said: 'Oh, yes, several hundred on politics, economics, world history, etc.' He replied scornfully: 'No, thanks. I don't like books. I like to fish.'" *The Alderson Story: My Life as a Political Prisoner* (New York: International Publishers, 1963), 14. At the trial, an FBI agent was responsible for carrying in and out a cartload of books "by Marx, Engels, Lenin, Stalin, and a few American writers," from which long and unintelligible passages were

recited, out of context, boring the jurors and spectators to the extent that the "newspapers lost interest" (22).

16. [Mid-1951?], Volumes 3–4 Claudia Jones FBI file.

17. 23 November 1951, Volume 5 Claudia Jones FBI file.

18. 7 February 1952, Volume 6 Claudia Jones FBI file. It does not appear that either of the prosecutors followed the full recommendations of the special agents. Although the librarians remain in the prosecutive summaries, a summary of the trial does not list the Librarian of Congress as a witness, and it does not appear that anyone from the New York Public Library testified, either. The prosecutors did, however, introduce a number of articles written by and about the defendants, some of them borrowed from the FBI's own holdings (23 March 1953 and 8 April 1953, Volume 7 Claudia Jones FBI file).

19. Flynn's memoir, *The Alderson Story*, details the warm friendship between the two women.

20. 3 November 1955, Volume 8 Claudia Jones FBI file.

21. If MI5 opened a file on Jones, which is extremely likely, it has not been made available to researchers. Unlike the United States, where many FBI files are available with Freedom of Information Act requests, MI5 files are released at the discretion of Her Majesty's Government. While C.L.R. James's and Doris Lessing's MI5 files have been released to the National Archives as a matter of public interest, Jones's file, if it exists, remains officially under wraps.

22. Davies, *Left of Karl Marx* 169–70, and Marika Sherwood (with Donald Hines, Colin Prescod, and the 1996 Claudia Jones Symposium), *Claudia Jones: A Life in Exile* (London: Lawrence and Wishart, 1999), 62–89.

23. 25th Congress papers, "Sunday Morning No 14, Claudia Jones" (CP/CENT/CONG/10/08 2–4, National Museum of Labour History).

24. Letter to Ben Davis, 15–16 May 1957 (Ben Davis papers, Schomburg Center). Quoted by Sherwood et al. (76).

25. Donald Hinds reports that Jones formulated the idea after hearing a comment at a community meeting. "The *West Indian Gazette*: Claudia Jones and the Black Press in Britain," *Race and Class* 50.1 (2008): 92.

26. Sherwood et al. 41–42. See also correspondence in Jones papers at Schomburg Library, which contain references to sporadic gifts from friends and comrades from the United States.

27. Quoted in Davies, *Left of Karl Marx* 69.

28. For an informative summary of the paper's coverage of the anticolonial struggle, see Bill Schwarz, "'Claudia Jones and the *West Indian Gazette*': Reflections on the Emergence of Postcolonial Britain," *Twentieth Century British History* 14.3 (2003): 264–85. Additional references parenthetical.

29. Whereas I read Jones's support for the West Indian Federation as a form of solidarity with national liberation projects, Joseph Keith reads Federation as a loose, transnational assemblage, inherently distinct from nationalist aspirations. His interpretation hinges on a delicate reading of James's *Mariners, Renegades, and Castaways*, and although I think he overemphasizes the anti-nationalist component of James's project, he provides a compelling reading. *Unbecoming Americans: Writing Race and Nation from the Shadows of Citizenship, 1945–1960* (New Brunswick: Rutgers UP, 2013), 131–62.

30. Carole Boyce Davies, ed. *Claudia Jones: Beyond Containment* (Banbury: Ayebia Clarke, 2011), 166.

31. Brent Hayes Edwards, *The Practice of Diaspora: Literature, Translation, and the Rise of Black Internationalism* (Cambridge: Harvard UP, 2003), 243.

32. Michelle Ann Stephens, *Black Empire: The Masculine Global Imaginary of Caribbean Intellectuals in the United States, 1914–1962* (Durham: Duke UP, 2005), 6.

33. See James's biographers Paul Buhle, *C.L.R. James: The Artist as Revolutionary* (London: Verso, 1988); Farrukh Dhondy, *C.L.R. James: A Life* (New York: Pantheon, 2001); and Kent Worcester, *C.L.R. James: A Political Biography* (Albany: SUNY Press, 1996). Robert A. Hill describes James of this period as operating almost exclusively within the confines of the small Marxist organization, a political institution systematically understudied. "In England 1932–1938," in Paul Buhle, ed., *C.L.R. James: His Life and Work* (London: Allison and Busby, 1986), 61–80.

34. FBI director J. Edgar Hoover encouraged INS to round up radical aliens for deportation; it would appear that James was caught in this dragnet. See letter from US Attorney General to Director of FBI, [29?] October 1947 (box 24 folder 37, James papers).

35. Box 24 folder 34, James papers.

36. Appendix A to Appellant's Brief in James v. Shaughnessy Civil Case No 76–205, US Court of Appeals Second Circuit (box 24 folder 32, James papers). He feared deportation more than prison, or so he says in a letter to Constance Webb on the day war was declared in Europe: "I don't mind going to prison here or in England. But my nightmare is that I will be deported to the W. Indies and be out of everything." James to Webb, 1 September 1939 (box 1 folder 1, James letters).

37. Donald E. Pease provides an overview of the contradictions of James's prosecution in his introduction to *Mariners, Renegades and Castaways* and also in "Doing Justice to C.L.R. James's *Mariners, Renegades and Castaways*," *boundary 2* 27.2 (2000): 1–19. See also the papers related to James's defense in his papers, box 24 folder 32, in which his attorneys argue that James did not, in fact, belong to the Communist Party, and so could not be acting as its agent.

38. 22 July 1947 (box 24 folder 34, James papers).

39. 18 October 1949 (box 24 folder 34, James papers).

40. Appendix C to Appellant's Brief James v. Shaughnessy, Civil Case number 76–205 (box 24 folder 32, James papers).

41. Appendix C to Appellant's Brief James v. Shaughnessy, Civil Case number 76–205 (box 24 folder 32, James papers).

42. Memo from SAC [special agent in charge] Newark NJ to Director FBI, 16 October 1953 (box 24 folder 36, James papers).

43. 23 February 1939, KV2–1824. KV2–1824 and–1825. James's MI5 files contain several exchanges between the US Foreign Service's London Attaché and MI5. London also sent that information to Jamaica, Trinidad, Barbados, and British Guiana. The FBI dossier has similar materials, including correspondence dated 17 November 1961 and 25 January 1963 (box 24 folder 37, James papers).

44. 9 July 1958 (box 24 folder 34, James papers).

45. 18 October 1949 (box 24 folder 34, James papers).

46. Box 24 folders 35–37 especially, James papers.

47. FBI summary of James's activities sent to MI5, 11 May 1953 (KV2–1825).

48. C.L.R. James, *The Black Jacobins: Toussaint L'Ouverture and the San Domingo Revolution*, 2nd ed. revised (New York: Vintage, 1963), 85–86; C.L.R. James, *A History of Negro Revolt* (New York: Haskell House, 1938, 1969), 8–9. See also Priyamvada Gopal, *Insurgent Empire: Anticolonial*

Resistance and British Dissent (London: Verso, 2019), which offers a revisionist account of how anticolonial resistance altered the political and intellectual history of metropolitan Britain.

49. See Buhle 110–11; Dhondy 110–14; Worcester 110–15; and Timothy Brennan, *At Home in the World: Cosmopolitanism Now* (Cambridge: Harvard UP, 1997), 224.

50. See also Raphael Dalleo, *American Imperialism's Undead: The Occupation of Haiti and the Rise of Caribbean Anticolonialism* (Charlottesville: U of Virginia P, 2016) and Laurent Dubois, *Avengers of the New World: The Story of the Haitian Revolution* (Cambridge: Harvard UP, 2004). On the genre of tragedy in postcolonial contexts, also see Ato Quayson, *Tragedy and Postcolonial Literature* (Cambridge: Cambridge UP, 2021).

51. Georg Lukács, *The Theory of the Novel: A Historico-Philosophical Essay on the Forms of Great Epic Literature*, trans. Anna Bostock (Cambridge: MIT Press, 1971), 17. Important studies of modern epic include Moretti, *Modern Epic*; C. D. Blanton, *Epic Negation: The Dialectical Poetics of Late Modernism* (Oxford: Oxford UP, 2015); and Mark Steven, *Red Modernism: American Poetry and the Spirit of Communism* (Baltimore: Johns Hopkins UP, 2017). Additional references parenthetical.

52. See also Jed Esty, "Global Lukács," *Novel: A Forum on Fiction* 42.3 (2009): 366–72.

53. Incidentally, James here anticipates the arguments of Amitav Ghosh, who in *The Great Derangement: Climate Change and the Unthinkable*, notes that people in the global south are the first to experience the direct effects of rising seawaters and other environmental catastrophes (Chicago: U of Chicago P, 2016).

54. Georg Lukács, *The Historical Novel*, trans. Hannah and Stanley Mitchell, intro. Fredric Jameson (Lincoln: U of Nebraska P, 1983), 36–37.

Chapter 8

1. Pramoedya Ananta Toer, *The Mute's Soliloquy: A Memoir*, trans. Willem Samuels (New York: Penguin, 1999), 35.

2. For a succinct overview of the role of testimonial writing in midcentury human rights campaigns, see Mark Philip Bradley, *The World Reimagined: Americans and Human Rights in the Twentieth Century* (Cambridge: Cambridge UP, 2016).

3. Mark Greif, *The Age of the Crisis of Man: Thought and Fiction in America, 1933–1973* (Princeton: Princeton UP, 2015). See also Leela Gandhi, "Postcolonial Theory and the Crisis of European Man," *Postcolonial Studies* 10.1 (2007): 93–110.

4. Barbara Harlow, "From the Women's Prison: Third World Narratives of Prison," *Feminist Studies* 12.3 (1986): 506.

5. Barbara Harlow, *Resistance Literature* (New York: Methuen, 1987), 124.

6. See also Oliver Lovesey, "Chained Letters: African Prison Diaries and 'National Allegory,'" *Research in African Literatures* 26.4 (1995): 31–45; Daniel Roux, "Writing the Prison," in *Cambridge History of South African Literature*, ed. David Attwell and Derek Attridge (Cambridge: Cambridge UP, 2012), 545–63; Paul Gready, *Writing as Resistance: Life Stories of Imprisonment, Exile, and Homecoming from Apartheid South Africa* (Lanham: Lexington Books, 2003); Rachel Knighton, *Writing the Prison in African Literature* (Oxford: Peter Lang, 2019); Geula Elimelekh, *Arabic Prison Literature: Resistance, Torture, Alienation, and Freedom* (Wiesbaden: Harrassowitz Verlag, 2014).

7. Jack Mapanje, ed., *Gathering Seaweed: African Prison Writing* (Harlow: Heinemann, 2002), xvii.

8. Ngũgĩ wa Thiong'o, *Detained: A Writer's Prison Diary* (Oxford: Heinemann, 1981), xi. Additional references parenthetical.

9. The name of PEN, which is now called PEN International, has changed through the years, so for convenience I refer to it as PEN throughout this chapter.

10. For accounts of the role of international human rights in African decolonization, see Getachew, *Worldmaking after Empire,* and Bonny Ibhawoh, *Imperialism and Human Rights: Colonial Discourses of Rights and Liberties in African History* (Albany: SUNY Press, 2007).

11. The historical debates about the relationship between the human rights and anticolonial movements are extremely lively. For instance, in *The Last Utopia: Human Rights in History* (Cambridge: Harvard UP, 2010), Samuel Moyn includes a chapter called "Why Anticolonialism Wasn't a Human Rights Movement." Critics of Moyn's position here include Joseph R. Slaughter, "Hijacking Human Rights: Neoliberalism, the New Historiography, and the End of the Third World" (*Human Rights Quarterly* 40.4 [2018]: 735–75) and Antony Anghie, "Whose Utopia? Human Rights, Development, and the Third World" (*Qui Parle* 22.1 [2013]: 63–80). Both Slaughter and Anghie suggest that Moyn's argument depends far too much on a metropolitan perspective, and the strongest criticisms, including Slaughter's, suggest that human rights abet neoliberal capitalism and the hollowing out of the Bandung project. Moyn himself responds to some of these criticisms in *Not Enough: Human Rights in an Unequal World* (Cambridge: Harvard UP, 2018). Getachew takes something of a compromise position, demonstrating how European states used the notion of human rights to limit or encumber sovereignty in the decolonizing parts of the world. The chapter is informed by these debates throughout, and I return to them explicitly in my concluding thoughts. See also Eleni Coundouriotis, *Narrating Human Rights in Africa* (Abingdon: Routledge, 2021); Slaughter, *Human Rights, Inc.*; Elizabeth Anker, *Fictions of Dignity: Embodying Human Rights in World Literature* (Ithaca: Cornell UP, 2012); and Lyndsey Stonebridge, *Placeless People: Writing, Rights, and Refugees* (Oxford: Oxford UP, 2018). Additional references parenthetical.

12. https://pen-international.org/who-we-are/history. Accessed 6 April 2020.

13. Galsworthy outlined the principles in the charter at the 1926 PEN Congress and ratified in 1948. https://pen-international.org/who-we-are/the-pen-charter. Accessed 6 April 2020.

14. See Rachel Potter, "Modernist Rights: International PEN 1921–1936," *Critical Quarterly* 55.2 (2013): 66–80 and "International PEN: Writers, Free Expression, Organisations," in *A History of 1930s British Literature*, ed. Benjamin Kohlmann and Matthew Taunton (Cambridge: Cambridge UP, 2019), 120–33.

15. The Executive Committee wrote to Franco in 1937, reporting in its minutes that although they had not received a reply, Koestler appeared to be alive and as well as anyone might be in a Spanish jail. There is also discussion about whether advocacy of Koestler violated the nonpolitical spirit of the organization as envisioned by founder and first president Galsworthy, HRC box 235 folder 4 English PEN EC Minutes Volume 1, 1931–37: 104–5. See also Koestler's letter of thanks to PEN, *PEN News* 90 (July 1937): 5. References to *PEN News* and PEN Executive Committee minutes are available for inspection at the Harry Ransom Center's online archive, HRC PN 121 P22, https://hrc.contentdm.oclc.org/digital/collection/p15878coll97/search.

16. Koestler was elected as a PEN member in July 1943, HRC box 235 folder 6, Executive Committee Minutes Volume 2, 1937–43: 116. A list of Koestler's PEN wartime activities include: "Literature and the World after the War," *PEN News* 119 (August 1941); "The PEN of the Future Conference and Writers in Freedom Symposium," *PEN News* 125 (October 1942); "Why has the Intelligentsia Fallen into Disrepute," *PEN News* 134 (May 1944); a conference celebrating the anniversary of publication of John Milton's "Areopagitica," *PEN News* 135 (August 1944).

17. "Presentation to Herman Ould," *PEN News* 143 (April 1946): 7.

18. "Fund for Intellectual Freedom," *PEN News* 181 (November 1952): 19–20. PEN members debated whether or not to take over administration of this fund, wondering if it would compromise the political neutrality of the organization, but ultimately accepted the responsibility.

19. "P.E.N. Fund for Exiled Writers," *PEN News* 195 (November 1957): 15 and "P.E.N. Fund for Exiled Writers," *PEN News* 196 (Spring 1958): 51.

20. H. G. Wells was invited to the 1934 Soviet Writers Congress but could not attend due to scheduling conflicts. Wells hoped to establish a Soviet PEN, but only on principle of free association for all writers of any political persuasion. *PEN News* 66 (October 1934): 5. For reports on negotiations to bring PEN to the Soviet Union, see *PEN News* 132 (December 1943): 9, and minutes of Annual General Meeting, 1964, HRC box 225, folder 3: 9.

21. PEN established centers in Hungary, Bulgaria, and Czechoslovakia before the war. They were dormant for a long time, through 1952. PEN kept these open, despite political changes, as part of an open-door policy toward the Warsaw Pact nations. *PEN News* 193 (October 1956): 48.

22. Lessing, *Walking in the Shade*, 64–68.

23. "Annual Report of the General Secretary, 1960–61," *PEN News* 201 (Autumn 1962): 51. See also Peter Finn and Petra Couvée, *The Zhivago Affair: The Kremlin, the CIA, and the Battle over a Forbidden Book* (New York: Pantheon, 2014), 51–53.

24. Melvin J. Lasky, "*Der Monat*, memorandum to Mr. Herman Ould, International Secretary, and to the National Secretaries of the P.E.N. Chapters," *PEN News* 157 (October 1948): 8.

25. "Secretary's Annual Report," *PEN News* 198 (Winter 1958–59): 20. Koestler's attacks on the Soviets are alluded to in the appendices to the executive committee minutes, note 27.

26. Saunders depicts PEN as resolutely anti-Communist, suggesting that the CCF was brought in to help them be more tolerant of different viewpoints and to stimulate East-West dialogue. My interpretation of the evidence revises this account, suggesting instead that PEN had a long history of trying to generate dialogue; the CCF pushed them to stiffen their anti-Communist position (*Cultural Cold War*, 363–67).

27. Alexei Surkov, "Literary Reactionaries are Stirring up Troubled Waters," originally published in *Isvestia*, 4 January 1964, reproduced in Appendices to English PEN Executive Committee Meeting Minutes—19 March 1964, in PEN Executive Committee Minutes 1963–65, Volume 10: 1. Additional references parenthetical.

28. David Carver, "Letter to the Editor," *Isvestia* (no evidence of publication), 14 February 1964, reproduced in Appendices to English PEN Executive Committee Meeting Minutes—19 March 1964: 6.

29. Saunders, *Cultural Cold War* 362.

30. South Africa so often provides exceptions. See Peter D. McDonald's critical appraisal of PEN South Africa in *The Literature Police*. He describes the White-dominated PEN as

"complicit" in apartheid in general and as active participants in the regime's censorship apparatus. *The Literature Police* 171.

31. Koestler's prison memoir, by contrast, is far less influential than *Darkness at Noon*, perhaps because his nonfictional account is boring in comparison. This is partly a question of narrative flair: the memoir is in essence a diary, chronological in presentation and drily factual in its representation of life as a political prisoner. *Dialogue with Death: The Journal of a Prisoner of the Fascists in the Spanish Civil War*, trans. Trevor and Phyllis Blewitt, intro. Louis Menand (Chicago: U of Chicago P, 1966).

32. Arthur Koestler, *Darkness at Noon*, trans. Daphne Hardy (1941; New York: Scribner, 1968), 112, 247. Additional references parenthetical.

33. Saunders, *The Cultural Cold War* 366.

34. Bruce King to Melvin Lasky, 20 October 1965 (series II box 18 folder 1, TC papers).

35. Letter and attachment from Soyinka to Duerden, 26 October [1965] (series II box 18 folder 1, TC papers).

36. Duerden to Schwarz, 8 November 1965 (series II box 18 folder 1, TC papers).

37. Soyinka to Aminu Abdulahi, 17 August 1967 (series II box 18 folder 1, TC papers).

38. Peter Elstob to PEN Writers in Prison Committee, 10 November 1967 (series II box 18 folder 1, TC papers). Dennis Duerden must have been carbon copied on the letter for it to be deposited in the Transcription Centre papers.

39. Peter Elstob to PEN Writers in Prison Committee, 10 November 1967 (series II box 18 folder 1, TC papers). See also Duerden to Ivan Katz (of CCF), 9 November 1965 (series II box 18 folder 1, TC papers), which includes further information about the letter campaign.

40. Series II box 18 folder 1, TC papers.

41. Wole Soyinka, *The Man Died* (New York: Farrar, Straus and Giroux, 1972), Appendix A, 290. Additional references parenthetical.

42. Jack Mapanje, *And Crocodiles Are Hungry at Night* (Banbury: Ayebia Clarke, 2011), 24, 363. Additional references parenthetical.

43. Soyinka's reflexive attitude about race as a binding agent is summed up in a letter to Duerden. Duerden proposed to do a production of several of Soyinka's plays with an international, all-Black cast. Soyinka replied, "A company like this, unified only by pigmentation is immediately hollow at the core." Soyinka to Duerden, 20 January 1964 (series II box 18 folder 1, TC papers).

44. Simon Gikandi, *Ngugi wa Thiong'o* (Cambridge: Cambridge UP, 2000), 200.

45. In *Writers in Politics: A Re-engagement with Issues of Literature and Society*, Ngũgĩ cites Kariuki's prison memoir as the foundational text of Kenyan literature (Oxford, Nairobi, and Portsmouth: James Currey, East African Educational Publishers, and Heinemann, 1981, 1997), 110–11. See also Josiah Mwangi Kariuki, *'Mau Mau' Detainee: The Account by a Kenya African of His Experiences in Detention Camps, 1953–1960*, foreword by Margery Perham (London: Oxford UP, 1963).

46. Nawal El Saadawi, *Memoirs from the Women's Prison*, trans. Marilyn Booth (Berkeley: U of California P, 1983, 1986), 129. Additional references parenthetical.

47. See also Magalí Armillas-Tiseyra, *The Dictator Novel: Writers and Politics in the Global South* (Evanston: Northwestern UP, 2019). Armillas-Tiseyra reads the dictator novel across Latin American and African contexts, recognizing that this subgenre offers a space for reflecting

on politics and national culture in the post-colony, beyond providing mere reportage on the excesses of actual dictators.

48. "Letters of Thomas Mann," *Encounter* 19.6 (December 1962): 3–15.

49. Jini Kim Watson, *Cold War Reckonings: Authoritarianism and the Genres of Decolonization* (New York: Fordham UP, 2021), 57–58.

50. Crystal Parikh, *Writing Human Rights: The Political Imaginaries of Writers of Color* (Minneapolis: U of Minnesota P, 2017), 3.

Conclusion

1. See Edward W. Said, *Orientalism* (New York: Vintage, 1994), 1–6 and 284–328, and also the introduction to *Culture and Imperialism* (New York: Vintage, 1993).

2. Franco Moretti, *Graphs, Maps, Trees: Abstract Models for Literary History* (London: Verso, 2005).

BIBLIOGRAPHY

Archival Materials

Citations of archival materials appear in endnotes.

Communist Party of Great Britain records. People's History Museum (National Museum of Labour History archive). Cited as CPGB records in notes.

Foreign Affairs Oral History Collection, Association for Diplomatic Studies and Training, Arlington, VA, www.adst.org.

Intelligence Bureau (India—colonial) records. IOR/L/PJ/12, India Office Records and Private Papers, British Library. Cited as IOR in notes.

International Association for Cultural Freedom (Congress for Cultural Freedom) papers. The Hanna Holborn Gray Special Collections Research Center, University of Chicago. Cited as CCF papers in the notes.

C.L.R. James papers. MS#1529, Rare Book and Manuscript Library, Columbia University Libraries. Includes FBI files on James and Forest-Johnson Tendency of which James was a leading member. Cited as James papers in the notes.

C.L.R. James letters. Sc MG 132, Schomburg Center for Research in Black Culture, Manuscripts, Archives and Rare Books Division, New York Public Library. Cited as James letters in the notes.

Claudia Jones Memorial Collection. Sc MG 692, Schomburg Center for Research in Black Culture, Manuscripts, Archives and Rare Books Division, New York Public Library. Cited as Jones collection in the notes.

Alex La Guma Collection. MCH 118 Mayibuye Center Archives, University of the Western Cape. Cited as La Guma papers in the notes.

Doris Lessing correspondence with Soviet Union of Writers. f 631, inv 126 doc 706, The Russian State Archive of Literature and Arts. Cited as Lessing letters (RGALI) in the notes.

Doris Lessing archive (University of East Anglia). British Archive for Contemporary Writing, University of East Anglia. Cited as Lessing papers (UEA) in the notes.

Doris Lessing papers (Sussex). SxMs62, The Keep, University of Sussex Library. Cited as Lessing papers (Sussex) in the notes.

National Archives and Records Administration II, College Park, Maryland. Cited as NARA II archives in the notes.

PEN archives. Manuscript Collection MS-03133, Harry Ransom Center, The University of Texas at Austin. Cited as PEN archives in the notes.

Transcription Centre papers. Harry Ransom Center, The University of Texas at Austin. Cited TC papers in the notes.

United Kingdom. Security Service (Military Intelligence Section 5). Paul Hogarth file. KV 2/4059, /4060, /4061, /4062, /4063, /4064. National Archives. Assorted documents dated 1939–1964. Internal case file PF 290880.

United Kingdom. Security Service (Military Intelligence Section 5). C.L.R. James file. Assorted documents dated 1932–54. KV2/1824, /1825. National Archives. Internal case file PF 44572.

United Kingdom. Security Service (Military Intelligence Section 5). Doris Lessing file. Assorted documents dated 1943–1962. KV2/4054, /4055, /4056, /4057, /4058. National Archives. Internal case file PF 97471.

United States. Federal Bureau of Investigation. Audre Lorde file obtained under provisions of Freedom of Information Act. Assorted documents dated 1954–1972. Internal case file number NY 100–122142.

United States. Federal Bureau of Investigation. Claudia Jones file obtained under provisions of Freedom of Information Act. Assorted documents dated 1942–1965. Internal case file number 100–72390 and NY 100–18676.

Zhang Ailing (Eileen Chang) papers. Collection 3032, East Asian Library, Special Collections, USC Libraries, University of Southern California. Available online: http://digitallibrary.usc.edu/cdm/landingpage/collection/p15799coll92, USC Digital Library. Cited as Chang papers in the notes.

Works Cited

"3 Tales of the CIA." *Ramparts*, April 1967: 15–28.

Abrahams, Cecil A. *Alex La Guma*. Boston: Twayne, 1985.

Achebe, Chinua. *Morning Yet on Creation Day*. Garden City, NY: Anchor, 1975.

Adéèkó, Adélékè. *Proverbs, Textuality, and Nativism in African Literature*. Gainesville: UP of Florida, 1998.

Ahmad, Aijaz. "Jameson's Rhetoric of Otherness and the 'National Allegory.'" *Social Text* 17 (1987): 3–25.

Ahmed, Siraj. *Archaeology of Babel: The Colonial Foundation of Humanities*. Stanford: Stanford UP, 2018.

Anand, Mulk Raj. "Some Reminiscences of Sajjad Zaheer." *Lotus* 26 (October–December 1975): 44–51.

———. *Untouchable*. New York: Penguin, 1935.

Anand, Mulk Raj, K. S. Bhat, J. C. Ghose, S. Sinha, M. D. Taseer, and S. S. Zaheer. "Manifesto of the Indian Progressive Writers' Association, London." *Left Review* 2.5 (1936): n.p.

Anderson, Benedict. *Imagined Communities: Reflections on the Origin and Spread of Nationalism*. New edition. London: Verso, 2006.

Andrade, Oswald de. "Cannibalist Manifesto" [*Manifesto Antropófago*]. Translated by Leslie Bary. *Latin American Literary Review* 19.38 (1991): 38–47.

Anghie, Antony. "Whose Utopia? Human Rights, Development, and the Third World." *Qui Parle* 22.1 (2013): 63–80.

Anker, Elizabeth. *Fictions of Dignity: Embodying Human Rights in World Literature*. Ithaca: Cornell UP, 2012.

Appadorai, A. "The Bandung Conference." *India Quarterly: A Journal of International Affairs* 11.3 (1955): 207–35.

Appiah, Kwame Anthony. *In My Father's House: Africa in the Philosophy of Culture*. Oxford: Oxford UP, 1992.

Apter, Emily. *Against World Literature: On the Politics of Untranslatability*. London: Verso, 2013.

Aragon, W. H. Auden, José Bergamïn, Jean Richard Bloch, Nancy Cunard, Brian Howard, Heinrich Mann, Ivor Montagu, Pablo Neruda, Ramón Sender, Stephen Spender, and Tristan Tzara. "Authors Take Sides on the Spanish War." London: *Left Review*, 1937.

Arendt, Hannah. *Between Past and Future: Eight Exercises in Political Thought*. 2nd ed. New York: Viking, 1968.

———. *The Origins of Totalitarianism*. Orlando: Harvest, 1968.

Armillas-Tiseyra, Magalí. *The Dictator Novel: Writers and Politics in the Global South*. Evanston: Northwestern UP, 2019.

Arnold, A. James. *Modernism and Negritude: The Poetry and Poetics of Aimé Césaire*. Cambridge: Harvard UP, 1981.

"Asian Writers' Conference." *Indian Daily Mail*, 13 December 1956, n.p.

Auerbach, Erich. *Mimesis: The Representation of Reality in Western Thought*. 1953. Translated by Willard R. Trask. Introduction by Edward W. Said. Princeton: Princeton UP, 2003.

Azeb, Sophia. "Crossing the Saharan Boundary: *Lotus* and the Legibility of Africanness." *Research in African Literatures* 50.3 (2019): 91–115.

Bakhtin, M. M. *The Dialogic Imagination: Four Essays*. Edited by Michael Holquist. Translated by Caryl Emerson and Michael Holquist. Austin: U of Texas P, 1981.

Baldwin, James. "Letter from Paris: Princes and Powers." *Encounter* 8.1 (1957): 52–60.

Baldwin, Kate A. *Beyond the Color Line and the Iron Curtain: Reading Encounters between Black and Red, 1922–1963*. Durham: Duke UP, 2002.

Balutansky, Kathleen. *The Novels of Alex La Guma: The Representation of Political Conflict*. Boulder, CO: Three Continents Press, 1990.

Barnard, Rita. *Apartheid and Beyond: South African Writers and the Politics of Place*. Oxford: Oxford UP, 2007.

Barnes, Sophia. "Readers of Fiction and Readers in Fiction: Readership and *The Golden Notebook*." In *Doris Lessing and the Forming of History*. Edited by Kevin Brazil, David Sergeant, and Tom Sperlinger, 71–83. Edinburgh: Edinburgh UP, 2016.

Barnhisel, Greg. *Cold War Modernists: Art, Literature, and American Cultural Diplomacy*. New York: Columbia UP, 2015.

———. "Encounter Magazine and the Twilight of Modernism." *ELH* 81.1 (2014): 381–416.

Beier, Ulli and Janheinz Jahn. "Editorial." *Black Orpheus* 1 (1957): 4.

Belletto, Steven. *No Accident, Comrade: Chance and Design in Cold War American Narratives*. Oxford: Oxford UP, 2012.

Bennett, Eric. *Workshops of Empire: Stenger, Engle, and American Creative Writing during the Cold War*. Iowa City: U of Iowa P, 2015.

Benson, Peter. *"Black Orpheus," "Transition," and Modern Cultural Awakening in Africa.* Berkeley: U of California P, 1986.

Berlin, Isaiah. *Four Essays on Liberty.* Oxford: Oxford UP, 1969.

Bernabé, Jean, Patrick Chamoiseau, and Raphaël Confiant. *Éloge de la Créolité/In Praise of Creoleness.* Translated by M. B. Taleb-Khyar. Baltimore: Gallimard and Johns Hopkins UP, 1990.

Bhabha, Homi K. *The Location of Culture.* London: Routledge, 1994.

Blanton, C. D. *Epic Negation: The Dialectical Poetics of Late Modernism.* Oxford: Oxford UP, 2015.

Bo, L. Maria. "Freedom Over Seas: Eileen Chang, Ernest Hemingway, and the Translation of Truth in the Cold War." *Comparative Literature* 71.3 (2019): 252–71.

"A Book on Kalidasa Opens a New Series." *Lotus* 34 (October–December 1977): 176.

Borstelmann, Thomas. *Apartheid's Reluctant Uncle: The United States and Southern Africa in the Early Cold War.* Oxford: Oxford UP, 1993.

Bourdieu, Pierre. *The Field of Cultural Production: Essays on Art and Literature.* Edited and introduced by Randal Johnson. New York: Columbia UP, 1993.

———. *The Rules of Art: Genesis and Structure of the Literary Field.* Translated by Susan Emanuel. Stanford: Stanford University Press, 1996.

Boyle, Kay, Whit Burnett, Hart Crane, Caresse Crosby, Harry Crosby, Martha Foley, Stuart Gilbert, A. L. Gillespie, Leigh Hoffman, Eugene Jolas, Elliot Paul, Douglas Rigby, Theo Rutra, Robert Sage, Harold J. Salemson, and Laurence Vail. "Manifesto: The Revolution of the Word." 1929. In *Transition Workshop*, edited by Eugene Jolas, 173–74. New York: Vanguard, 1949.

Braden, Thomas W. "I'm Glad the CIA is 'Immoral.'" *Saturday Evening Post*, 20 May 1967: 10–14.

Bradley, Mark Philip. *The World Reimagined: Americans and Human Rights in the Twentieth Century.* Cambridge: Cambridge UP, 2016.

Brathwaite, Kamau. *The Arrivants: A New World Trilogy.* Oxford: Oxford UP, 1973.

Brennan, Timothy. *At Home in the World: Cosmopolitanism Now.* Cambridge: Harvard UP, 1997.

Breton, André and Diego Rivera. "Manifesto for an Independent Revolutionary Art." 1938. https://www.marxists.org/subject/art/lit_crit/works/rivera/manifesto.htm

Bronstein, Michaela. "Ngũgĩ's Use of Conrad: A Case for Literary Transhistory." *MLQ* 75.3 (2014): 411–437.

Brouillette, Sarah. *UNESCO and the Fate of the Literary.* Stanford: Stanford UP, 2019.

———. "US-Soviet Antagonism and the 'Indirect Propaganda' of Book Schemes in India in the 1950s." *University of Toronto Quarterly* 84.4 (2015): 170–88.

Brown, J. Dillon. *Migrant Modernism: Postwar London and the West Indian Novel.* Charlottesville: U of Virginia P, 2013.

Brown, Nicholas. *Autonomy: The Social Ontology of Art under Capitalism.* Durham: Duke UP, 2019.

Browne, Simone. *Dark Matters: On the Surveillance of Blackness.* Durham: Duke UP, 2015.

Brückenhaus, Daniel. *Policing Transnational Protest: Liberal Imperialism and the Surveillance of Anticolonialists in Europe, 1905–1945.* Oxford: Oxford UP, 2017.

Brutus, Dennis. "A Wrong Headed Bunch." *Lotus* 12 (April 1972): 158.

Buck, Pearl S. *The Good Earth.* New York: Grosset & Dunlap, 1931.

Buhle, Paul. *C.L.R. James: The Artist as Revolutionary.* London: Verso, 1988.

Bulson, Eric. *little magazine, world form.* New York: Columbia UP, 2017.

Burney, Iqbal Hasan. "Newspaper Coverage of the Bandung Conference." MA Thesis, Stanford University, 1956.

Carlston, Erin G. *Double Agents: Espionage, Literature, and Liminal Citizens*. New York: Columbia UP, 2013.

Casanova, Pascale. *The World Republic of Letters*. Translated by Malcolm DeBevoise. Cambridge: Harvard UP, 2004.

Castillo, Greg. "Peoples at an Exhibition: Soviet Architecture and the National Question." *Socialist Realism without Shores*. Edited by Thomas Lahusen and Evgeny Dobrenko, 91–119. Durham: Duke UP, 1997.

Caute, David. *The Dancer Defects: The Struggle for Cultural Supremacy during the Cold War*. Oxford: Oxford UP, 2003.

Césaire, Aimé. "Letter to Maurie Thorez." Translated by Chike Jeffers. *Social Text* 103.28.2 (2010): 145–52.

———. *Solar Throat Slashed: The Unexpurgated 1948 Edition*. Translated and edited by A. James Arnold and Clayton Eshleman. Middletown: Wesleyan UP, 2011.

Chahine, Nesrine. "Peter Abrahams and the Bandung Era: Afro-Asian Routes of Connection." *Critical Arts* 34.3 (2020): 30–40.

Chang, Eileen. "Chinese Translation: A Vehicle of Cultural Influence." Edited and introduced by Christopher Lee, *PMLA* 130.2 (2015): 488–498.

———. *Half a Lifelong Romance*. Introduced and translated by Karen S. Kingsbury. New York: Anchor, 2014.

———. *Love in a Fallen City*. Translated by Chang and Karen S. Kingsbury. New York: New York Review of Books, 2007.

———. *Lust, Caution*. Translated and foreword by Julia Lovell, afterword by Ang Lee. New York: Anchor, 2007.

———. *Naked Earth*. Introduced by Perry Link. New York: New York Review of Books, 2015.

———. *The Rice-Sprout Song* [first English edition]. New York: Charles Scribner's Sons, 1955.

———. *The Rice-Sprout Song*. 1955. Foreword by David Der-wei Wang. Berkeley: U of California P, 1998.

———. *The Rouge of the North*. 1967. Foreword by David Der-wei Wang. Berkeley: U of California P, 1998.

———. "The Original Typewritten Manuscript of 'The Spyring.'" ESWN Culture Blog, http://www.zonaeuropa.com/culture/c20081005_1.htm. Accessed 25 June 2019.

———. *Written on Water*. Edited by Andrew F. Jones and Nicole Huang. Translated by Jones. New York: Columbia UP, 2005.

Cheah, Pheng. *What is a World? On Postcolonial Literature as World Literature*. Durham: Duke UP, 2016.

Chen, Chi-ying. *Fool in the Reeds*. Translated by Eileen Chang. Hong Kong: Rainbow Press, 1959.

Chen, Tina. *Double Agency: Acts of Impersonation in Asian American Literature and Culture*. Stanford: Stanford UP, 2005.

Chinweizu, Onwuchekwa Jemie, and Ihechukwu Madubuike, "Towards the Decolonization of African Literature." *Transition* 48 (1975): 29–37 + 54 + 56–57.

Chow, Rey. *Primitive Passions: Visuality, Sexuality, Ethnography, and Contemporary Chinese Cinema*. New York: Columbia UP, 1995.

Chow, Tse-tsung. *The May 4th Movement: Intellectual Revolution in Modern China*. Cambridge: Harvard UP, 1960.

Clark, Katerina. *Moscow: The Fourth Rome: Stalinism, Cosmopolitanism, and the Evolution of Soviet Culture, 1931–1941*. Cambridge: Harvard UP, 2011.

———. "Indian Leftist Writers of the 1930s Maneuver among India, London, and Moscow: The Case of Mulk Raj Anand and His Patron Ralph Fox." *Kritika: Explorations in Russian and Eurasian History* 18.1 (2017): 63–87.

Cleary, Joe. "Realism after Modernism and the Literary World-System." *Modern Language Quarterly* 73.3 (2012): 255–68.

Coetzee, J. M. *Doubling the Point: Essays and Interviews*. Edited by David Attwell. Cambridge: Harvard UP, 1992.

Cole, Lori. "*Légitime Défense*: From Communism and Surrealism to Caribbean Self-Definition." *Journal of Surrealism and the Americas* 4.1 (2010): 15–30.

Cole, Sarah. *At the Violet Hour: Modernism and Violence in England and Ireland*. Oxford: Oxford UP, 2012.

Coleman, Peter. *The Liberal Conspiracy: The Congress for Cultural Freedom and the Struggle for the Mind of Postwar Europe*. New York: Free Press, 1989.

Collymore, Frank A. "Note Book," *Bim* 4.15 (1951): 149.

———. "Notes for a Glossary of Words and Phrases of Barbadian Dialect," Parts 1–4, 5.17 (1952): 56–72, 5.18 (1953): 139–52, 5.19 (1953): 213–26, 5.20 (1954): 307–21.

———. "Editors' Blarney," *Bim* 2.6 (1945?): 1.

Communist Party of France. *Pourquoi Je suis communiste* [*Why I am a Communist*]. Paris: Éditions du Parti Communiste Français, [1947].

The Congress for Cultural Freedom. "Manifesto." Berlin, 30 June 1950.

Coppola, Carlo. "The All-India Progressive Writers' Association: The European Phase." In *Marxist Influences and South Asian Literature*, vol. 1. Edited by Carlo Coppola, 1–34. East Lansing: Asian Studies Center Michigan State U, 1974.

Coundouriotis, Eleni. *Narrating Human Rights in Africa*. Abingdon: Routledge, 2021.

Creswell, Robyn. *City of Beginnings: Poetic Modernism in Beirut*. Princeton: Princeton UP, 2019.

Crossman, Richard H., ed. *The God That Failed*. 1949. Foreword by David C. Engerman. New York: Columbia UP, 2001.

Cull, Nicholas J. *The Cold War and the United States Information Agency: American Propaganda and Public Diplomacy, 1945–1989*. Cambridge: Cambridge UP, 2008.

Culleton, Claire A., and Karen Leick, eds. *Modernism on File: Writers, Artists, and the FBI, 1920–1950*. New York: Palgrave Macmillan, 2008.

Da, Nan Z. *Intransitive Encounter: Sino-U.S. Literatures and the Limits of Exchange*. New York: Columbia UP, 2018.

Dalleo, Raphael. *American Imperialism's Undead: The Occupation of Haiti and the Rise of Caribbean Anticolonialism*. Charlottesville: U of Virginia P, 2016.

Damrosch, David. *What Is World Literature?* Princeton: Princeton UP, 2003.

Darnton, Robert. *Censors at Work: How States Shaped Literature*. New York: Norton, 2014.

David-Fox, Michael. *Showcasing the Great Experiment: Cultural Diplomacy and Western Visitors to Soviet Russia, 1921–1941*. Oxford: Oxford UP, 2012.

Davies, Carole Boyce, ed. *Claudia Jones: Beyond Containment*. Afterword by Alrick X. Cambridge. Banbury: Ayebia Clarke, 2011.

———. *Left of Karl Marx: The Political Life of Black Communist Claudia Jones*. Durham: Duke UP, 2007.

Davis, Caroline. *African Literature and the CIA: Networks of Authorship and Publishing*. Cambridge: Cambridge UP, 2020.

———. "The Politics of Postcolonial Publishing: Oxford University Press's Three Crowns Series 1962–1976." *Book History* 8 (2005): 227–44.

Day-Lewis, Cecil. "Revolutionaries and Poetry." *Left Review* 1.10 (1935): 397–402.

Deer, Patrick. *Culture in Camouflage: War, Empire, and Modern British Literature*. Oxford: Oxford UP, 2009.

Denning, Michael. *Culture in the Age of Three Worlds*. London: Verso, 2004.

Desai, M. V. "The Asian Writers' Conference December 1956—New Delhi." *Books Abroad* 31.3 (Summer 1957): 243–45.

Dhondy, Farrukh. *C.L.R. James: A Life*. New York: Pantheon, 2001.

Dimock, Wai Chee. *Through Other Continents: American Literature across Deep Time*. Princeton: Princeton UP, 2006.

Ding Ling. *The Sun Shines over the Sanggan River*. Translated by Yang Xianyi and Gladys Yang. Beijing: Foreign Languages Press, 1984.

Diop, Alioune. "Niam n'goura or *Présence Africaine*'s RAISON D'ÊTRE." Translated by Richard Wright and Thomas Diop, *Présence Africaine* 1 (1947): 185–192.

Djagalov, Rossen. "The Afro-Asian Association and Soviet Engagement with Africa." *Black Perspectives* (November 2017). https://www.aaihs.org/the-afro-asian-writers-association-and-soviet-engagement-with-africa/. Accessed 19 December 2019.

———. *From Internationalism to Postcolonialism: Literature and Cinema between the Second and the Third Worlds*. Montreal & Kingston: McGill-Queen's UP, 2020.

Dobrenko, Evgeny. *The Making of the State Writer: Social and Aesthetic Origins of Soviet Literary Culture*. Translated by Jesse M. Savage. Stanford: Stanford UP, 2001.

Du Bois, W.E.B. "To the Congres des ecrivains et artistes noir." In "Messages." *Présence Africaine*, Congres issue 8/10 (1956): 379–401.

Dubois, Laurent. *Avengers of the New World: The Story of the Haitian Revolution*. Cambridge: Harvard UP, 2004.

Dudziak, Mary L. *Cold War Civil Rights: Race and the Image of American Democracy*. 2nd ed. Princeton: Princeton UP, 2011.

Duerden, Dennis and Cosmo Pieterse, eds. *African Writers Talking*. New York: Africana Publishing, 1972.

Eatough, Matthew. "The Critic as Modernist: Es'kia Mphahlele's Cold War Literary Criticism." *Research in African Literatures* 50.3 (2019): 136–56.

Edwards, Brent Hayes. *The Practice of Diaspora: Literature, Translation, and the Rise of Black Internationalism*. Cambridge: Harvard UP, 2003.

Eide, Marian. *Terrible Beauty: The Violent Aesthetic and Twentieth-Century Literature*. Charlottesville: U of Virginia P, 2019.

El Saadawi, Nawal. *Memoirs from the Women's Prison*. Translated by Marilyn Booth. Berkeley: U of California P, 1986.

El-Sebai, Youssef. "Bandung . . . and the Afro-Asian Solidarity." *Lotus* 26 (October–December 1975): 20–23.

———. "Editorial: Inspiration from the Colombo Meetings of the Non-Alignment Movement." *Lotus* 31 (January–March 1977): 6–7.

———. "Editor's Note." *Lotus* 9 (July 1971): 6–7.

———. "Editor's Note." *Lotus* 20 (April–June 1974): 6–7.

———. "Editor's Note." *Lotus* 31 (January–March 1977): 4–5.

———. "Report of the Secretary General [at Alma-Ata Afro-Asian conference 1973]." *Lotus* 20 (April–June 1974): 153–73.

———. "The Role of AFRO-ASIAN Literature and the National Liberation Movements." *Lotus* 1 (March 1968): 5–12.

———. "Twenty Years of Struggle for the Afro-Asian Peoples' Solidarity." *Lotus* 35 (January–March 1978): 114–23.

Elimelekh, Geula. *Arabic Prison Literature: Resistance, Torture, Alienation, and Freedom.* Wiesbaden: Harrassowitz Verlag, 2014.

English, James F. *The Economy of Prestige: Prizes, Awards, and the Circulation of Cultural Value.* Cambridge: Harvard UP, 2005.

Ertürk, Nergis. "Nâzım Hikmet and the Prose of Communism," *boundary 2* 47.2 (2020): 153–180.

Eslava, Luis, Michael Fakhri, and Vasuki Nesiah, eds. *Bandung, Global History, and International Law: Critical Pasts and Pending Futures.* Cambridge: Cambridge UP, 2017.

Esty, Jed. "Global Lukács." *Novel: A Forum on Fiction* 42.3 (2009): 366–72.

———. *Unseasonable Youth: Modernism, Colonialism, and the Fiction of Development.* Oxford: Oxford UP, 2012.

Fanon, Frantz. *The Wretched of the Earth.* Translated by Richard Philcox, foreword by Homi K. Bhabha, preface by Jean-Paul Sartre. New York: Grove Press, 2004.

Farred, Grant. *Midfielder's Moment: Coloured Literature and Culture in Contemporary South Africa.* Boulder: Westview, 2000.

Feinsod, Harris. *Poetry of the Americas: From Good Neighbors to Countercultures.* Oxford: Oxford UP, 2017.

Feldman, Leah. "Global Souths: Toward a Materialist Poetics of Alignment." *boundary 2* 47.2 (2020): 199–225.

———. *On the Threshold of Eurasia: Revolutionary Poetics in the Caucasus.* Ithaca: Cornell UP, 2018.

Field, Roger. *Alex La Guma: A Literary and Political Biography.* Woodbridge: James Currey, 2010.

Filostrat, Christian. *Negritude Agonistes, Assimilation against Nationalism in the French-Speaking Caribbean and Guyane.* Cherry Hill, NJ: Africana Homestead Legacy Publishers, 2008.

Finn, Peter and Petra Couvée. *The Zhivago Affair: The Kremlin, the CIA, and the Battle over a Forbidden Book.* New York: Pantheon, 2014.

First, Ruth. *117 Days: An Account of Confinement and Interrogation under the South African 90-Day Detention Law.* Introduction by Angela Y. Davis. New York: Penguin, 1965.

Flint, Jerry M. "Ex-Official of C.I.A. Lists Big Grants to Labor Aides: Reuther Concedes Union Took $50,000 from Agency." *New York Times,* 8 May 1967.

Flynn, Elizabeth Gurley. *The Alderson Story: My Life as a Political Prisoner.* New York: International Publishers, 1963.

Foley, Barbara. *Spectres of 1919: Class and Nation in the Making of The New Negro*. Urbana: University of Illinois Press, 2003.

Foley, Helene P. and Jean E Howard, coordinators. "Special Topic: Tragedy." *PMLA* 129.4 (2014): 617–741.

Forter, Greg. *Critique and Utopia in Historical Postcolonial Fiction: Atlantic and other Worlds*. Oxford: Oxford UP, 2019.

Fosler-Lussier, Danielle. *Music in America's Cold War Diplomacy*. Berkeley: U of California P, 2015.

Fox, Ralph. *The Novel and the People*. 1937. New York: International Publishers, 1945.

Fox, Sylvan. "Stephen Spender Quits Encounter." *New York Times*, 8 May 1967.

Frankel, Max. "Ex-Official of C.I.A. Lists Big Grants to Labor Aides: Tells of Secret Subsidies to A.F.L.-C.I.O. to Fight Red Union Abroad." *New York Times*, 8 May 1967.

Frazier, Robeson Taj. *The East Is Black: Cold War China in the Black Radical Imagination*. Durham: Duke UP, 2015.

Gandhi, Leela. "Postcolonial Theory and the Crisis of European Man." *Postcolonial Studies* 10.1 (2007): 93–110.

George, C. J. *Mulk Raj Anand, His Art and Concerns: A Study of His Non-Autobiographical Novels*. New Delhi: Atlantic, 1994.

Getachew, Adom. *Worldmaking after Empire: The Rise and Fall of Self-Determination*. Princeton: Princeton UP, 2019.

Ghosh, Amitav. *The Great Derangement: Climate Change and the Unthinkable*. Chicago: U of Chicago P, 2016.

Gikandi, Simon. "Modernism in the World." *Modernism/modernity* 13.3 (2006): 419–24.

———. *Ngũgĩ wa Thiong'o*. Cambridge: Cambridge UP, 2000.

Gilroy, Paul. *The Black Atlantic: Modernity and Double-Consciousness*. Cambridge: Harvard UP, 1993.

Ginzburg, Eugenia Semyonovna. *Journey into the Whirlwind*. Translated by Paul Stevenson and Max Hayward. San Diego: Harcourt, 1967.

Githire, Njeri. *Cannibal Writes: Eating Others in Caribbean and Indian Ocean Women's Writing*. Urbana: U of Illinois P, 2014.

Goble, Mark. *Beautiful Circuits: Modernism and the Mediated Life*. New York: Columbia UP, 2010.

GoGwilt, Christopher. *The Passage of Literature: Genealogies of Modernism in Conrad, Rhys, and Pramoedya*. Oxford: Oxford UP, 2011.

Goldstone, Andrew. *Fictions of Autonomy: Modernism from Wilde to de Man*. Oxford: Oxford UP, 2013.

Gopal, Priyamvada. *Insurgent Empire: Anticolonial Resistance and British Dissent*. London: Verso, 2019.

———. *Literary Radicalism in India: Gender, Nation and the Transition to Independence*. Abingdon: Routledge, 2005.

Goyal, Yogita. *Romance, Diaspora, and Black Atlantic Literature*. Cambridge: Cambridge UP, 2010.

Gramsci, Antonio. *Selections from Cultural Writings*. Edited by David Forgacs and Geoffrey Nowell-Smith, translated by William Boelhower. Cambridge: Harvard UP, 1985.

Grasuam, Daniel. *On Endings: American Postmodern Fiction and the Cold War*. Charlottesville: U of Virginia P, 2011.

Gready, Paul. *Writing as Resistance: Life Stories of Imprisonment, Exile, and Homecoming from Apartheid South Africa*. Lanham, MD: Lexington Books, 2003.

Greif, Mark. *The Age of the Crisis of Man: Thought and Fiction in America, 1933–1973*. Princeton: Princeton UP, 2015.

Guha, Ranajit. *Elementary Aspects of Peasant Insurgency in Colonial India*. Foreword by James Scott. Durham: Duke UP, 1999.

Guilbaut, Serge. *How New York Stole the Idea of Modern Art: Abstract Expressionism, Freedom, and the Cold War*. Translated by Arthur Goldhammer. Chicago: U of Chicago P, 1983.

Guillory, John. *Cultural Capital: The Problem of Literary Canon Formation*. Chicago: U of Chicago P, 1993.

Halim, Hala. "*Lotus*, the Afro-Asian Nexus, and Global South Comparatism." *Comparative Studies of South Asia, Africa and the Middle East* 32.3 (2012): 563–83.

———. "Translating Solidarity: An Interview with Nehad Salem." *Critical Times* 3.1 (2020): 131–47.

Han, Gül Bilge. "Nazım Hikmet's Afro-Asian Solidarities." *Safundi* 19.3 (2018): 284–305.

Harlow. Barbara. *Barred: Women, Writing, and Political Detention*. Hanover: Wesleyan UP and UP of New England, 1992.

———. "From the Women's Prison: Third World Narratives of Prison." *Feminist Studies* 12.3 (1986): 501–24.

———. *Resistance Literature*. New York: Methuen, 1987.

Hart, Matthew. *Nations of Nothing but Poetry: Modernism, Transnationalism, and Synthetic Vernacular Writing*. Oxford: Oxford UP, 2010.

Hayot, Eric. *The Hypothetical Mandarin: Sympathy, Modernity, and Chinese Pain*. Oxford: Oxford UP, 2009.

Head, Bessie. Letter to the Editor. *Transition* 17 (1964): 6.

Hepburn, Allan. *Intrigue: Espionage and Culture*. New Haven: Yale UP, 2005.

Hevia, James. *The Imperial Security State: British Colonial Knowledge and Empire-Building in Asia*. Cambridge: Cambridge UP, 2012.

Hill, Robert A. "In England 1932–1938." In *C.L.R. James: His Life and Work*, edited by Paul Buhle, 61–80. London: Allison and Busby, 1986.

Hilliard, Christopher. "Producers by Hand and by Brain: Working-Class Writers and Left-Wing Publishers in 1930s Britain." *Journal of Modern History* 78.1 (2006): 37–64.

Hinds, Donald. "The *West Indian Gazette*: Claudia Jones and the Black Press in Britain." *Race and Class* 50.1 (2008): 88–97.

Hobsbawm, Eric and Terence Ranger, eds. *The Invention of Tradition*. Cambridge: Cambridge UP, 1983.

Hofstadter, Richard. "The Paranoid Style in American Politics." *Harper's Magazine*, November 1964. https://harpers.org/archive/1964/11/the-paranoid-style-in-american-politics/

Holt, Elizabeth M. "Al-Ṭayyib Ṣāliḥ's Season of Migration to the North, the CIA, and the Cultural Cold War after Bandung." *Research in African Literatures* 50.3 (2019): 70–90.

Hsia, C.T. *A History of Modern Chinese Fiction*. 2nd ed. New Haven: Yale UP, 1971.

Huang, Nicole. *Women, War, Domesticity: Shanghai Literature and Popular Culture of the 1940s.* Leiden: Brill, 2005.

———. "Worlding Eileen Chang (Zhang Ailing): Narratives of Frontiers and Crossings." *Wiley Blackwell Companion to World Literature,* edited by Ken Seigneurie. https://doi.org/10.1002/9781118635193.ctwl0232

Huggan, Graham. *The Postcolonial Exotic: Marketing the Margins.* London: Routledge, 2001.

Hughes, Langston. *I Wonder as I Wander: An Autobiographical Journey.* Introduction by Arnold Rampersad. New York: Farrar, Straus, and Giroux, 1984.

———. *A Negro Looks at Soviet Central Asia.* Moscow: Co-Operative Publishing Society of Foreign Workers in the USSR, 1934.

Iber, Patrick. *Neither Peace nor Freedom: The Cultural Cold War in Latin America.* Cambridge: Harvard UP, 2015.

Ibhawoh, Bonny. *Imperialism and Human Rights: Colonial Discourses of Rights and Liberties in African History.* Albany: SUNY Press, 2007.

"In Tashkent Young Writers from Africa and Asia Met." *Lotus* 32–33 (1977): 119–26.

Indonesian Ministry of Foreign Affairs, ed. "Final Communiqué of the Afro-Asian Conference of Bandung (24 April 1955)," in *Asia-Africa Speak from Bandung.* Djakarta: Indonesian Foreign Affairs, 1955. 161–69. https://www.cvce.eu/en/obj/final_communique_of_the_asian_african_conference_of_bandung_24_april_1955-en-676237bd-72f7-471f-949a-88b6ae513585.html

Innes, C. L. *Chinua Achebe.* Cambridge: Cambridge UP, 1990.

Institute of Pacific Relations. *Selected Documents of the Bandung Conference: Texts of Selected Speeches and Final Communique of the Asian-African Conference, Bandung, Indonesia April 18–24, 1955.* New York: Institute of Pacific Relations, 1955.

Irele, F. Abiola. *The African Imagination: Literature in Africa and the Black Diaspora.* Oxford: Oxford UP, 2001.

Isherwood, Christopher. *The Berlin Stories: "The Last of Mr. Norris" and "Goodbye to Berlin".* New York: New Directions, 1954.

Jackson, Jeanne-Marie. *The African Novel of Ideas: Philosophy and Individualism in the Age of Global Writing.* Princeton: Princeton UP, 2021.

Jalil, Rakhshanda. *Liking Progress, Loving Change: A Literary History of the Progressive Writers' Movement in Urdu.* New Delhi: Oxford UP, 2014.

James, C.L.R. *Beyond a Boundary.* 1963. Introduction by Robert Lipsyte. Durham: Duke UP, 1993.

———. *The Black Jacobins: Toussaint L'Ouverture and the San Domingo Revolution.* 2nd ed. revised. New York: Vintage, 1963.

———. *A History of Negro Revolt.* New York: Haskell House, 1938.

———. *The Life of Captain Cipriani: An Account of British Government in the West Indies, with the pamphlet The Case for West-Indian Self Government.* 1932 and 1933. Introduction by Bridget Brereton. Durham: Duke UP, 2014.

———. *Mariners, Renegades and Castaways: The Story of Herman Melville and the World We Live in.* 1953. Edited and introduced by Donald E. Pease. Hanover: UP of New England, 2001.

———. *World Revolution, 1917–1936: The Rise and Fall of the Communist International.* 1937. Edited and introduced by Christian Høgsbjerg. Durham: Duke UP, 2017.

James, Pearl. *The New Death: American Modernism and World War I*. Charlottesville: U of Virginia P, 2013.

Jameson, Fredric. *Marxism and Form: Twentieth-Century Dialectical Theories of Literature*. Princeton: Princeton UP, 1971.

———. *A Singular Modernity: Essay on the Ontology of the Present*. London: Verso, 2002.

———. "Third-World Literature in the Era of Multinational Capitalism." *Social Text* 15 (1986): 65–88.

JanMohamed, Abdul. *Manichean Aesthetics: The Politics of Literature in Colonial Africa*. Amherst: U of Massachusetts P, 1983.

Jeyifo, Biodun. *Wole Soyinka: Politics, Poetics and Postcolonialism*. Cambridge: Cambridge UP, 2004.

Jones, Claudia. "An End to the Neglect of the Problems of the Negro Woman!" New York: National Women's Commission, CPUSA, 1949.

———. "West Indies Federation." *West Indian Gazette* (March 1958): 2.

Joyce, James. *Dubliners*. New York: Penguin, 1967.

———. *A Portrait of the Artist as a Young Man*. 1916. Edited and introduced by Seamus Deane. New York: Penguin, 1992.

———. *Ulysses: The Corrected Text*. 1922. Edited by Hans Walter Gabler with Wolfhard Steppe and Claus Melchoir. New York: Vintage, 1986.

Kalliney, Peter J. *Cities of Affluence and Anger: A Literary Geography of Modern Englishness*. Charlottesville: U of Virginia P, 2007.

———. *Commonwealth of Letters: British Literary Culture and the Emergence of Postcolonial Aesthetics*. Oxford: Oxford UP, 2013.

Kariuki, Josiah Mwangi. *'Mau Mau' Detainee: The Account by a Kenya African of His Experiences in Detention Camps, 1953–1960*. Foreword by Margery Perham. London: Oxford UP, 1963.

Keith, Joseph. *Unbecoming Americans: Writing Race and Nation from the Shadows of Citizenship, 1945–1960*. New Brunswick: Rutgers UP, 2013.

Kermode, Frank. *The Sense of an Ending: Studies in the Theory of Fiction: with a new epilogue*. Oxford: Oxford UP, 2000.

Khlebnikov, Velimir. "An Indo-Russian Union." 1918. In *Collected Works of Velimir Khlebnokov*, vol. 1: Letters and Theoretical Writings. Translated by Paul Schmidt, edited by Charlotte Douglas, 341–42. Cambridge: Harvard UP, 1987.

Klein, Christina. *Cold War Orientalism: Asia in the Middlebrow Imagination, 1945–1961*. Berkeley: U of California P, 2003.

Knighton, Rachel. *Writing the Prison in African Literature*. Oxford: Peter Lang, 2019.

Kodat, Catherine Gunther. *Don't Act, Just Dance: The Metapolitics of Cold War Culture*. New Brunswick: Rutgers UP, 2015.

Koestler, Arthur. *Darkness at Noon*. 1941. Translated by Daphne Hardy. New York: Scribner, 1968.

———. *Dialogue with Death: The Journal of a Prisoner of the Fascists in the Spanish Civil War*. 1946. Translated by Trevor and Phyllis Blewitt. Introduction by Louis Menand. Chicago: U of Chicago P, 1966.

Kohlmann, Benjamin. "Toward a History and Theory of the Socialist Bildungsroman." *Novel: A Forum on Fiction* 48.2 (2015): 167–89.

Kotkin, Valentin. *Path of Struggle and Victories: 25th Anniversary of the Afro-Asian Writers' Movement*. Moscow: Novosti Press Agency Publishing House, 1983.

Kristol, Irving and Stephen Spender. "After the Apocalypse: Editorial." *Encounter* 1 (1953): 1.

La Guma, Alex. *Culture and Liberation: Exile Writings, 1966–1985*. Edited and introduced by Christopher J. Lee, foreword by Albie Sachs, afterword by Bill Nasson. London: Seagull, 2021.

———. "The Exile." *Lotus* (1972): 68–74.

———. *In the Fog of Seasons' End*. Oxford: Heinemann Educational, 1972.

———. "Report of the General Secretary to the Seventh General (25th Anniversary) Conference Tashkent Uzbekistan September–October 1983." *Lotus* 56 (1985): 181–92.

———. "South African Writing under Apartheid." *Lotus* 23 (January–March 1975): 11–21.

———. *A Soviet Journey*. Edited and introduced by Christopher J. Lee, foreword by Ngũgĩ wa Thiong'o, preface by Blanche La Guma. Lanham, MD: Lexington Books, 2017.

———. *The Stone Country*. London: Heinemann, 1967.

———. *Time of the Butcherbird*. Oxford: Heinemann, 1979.

———. *A Walk in the Night and Other Stories*. Evanston: Northwestern UP, 1967.

———. "What I Learned from Maxim Gorky." *Lotus* 34 (October–December 1977): 164–68.

Lahusen, Thomas and Evgeny Dobrenko, eds. *Socialist Realism without Shores*. Durham: Duke UP, 1997.

Lee, Christopher J., ed. *Making a World after Empire: The Bandung Moment and its Political Afterlives*. Athens: Ohio UP, 2010.

———. "The Workshop of Confinement: Political Quarantine and the Spatial Imagination in the Early Fiction of Alex La Guma," *Modern Fiction Studies* 67.2 (2021): 272–91.

Lee, Haiyan. "Enemy under My Skin: Eileen Chang's 'Lust, Caution' and the Politics of Transcendence." *PMLA* 125.3 (2010): 640–56.

Lee, Leo Ou-fan. *Shanghai Modern: The Flowering of a New Urban Culture in China, 1930–1945*. Cambridge: Harvard UP, 1999.

Lee, Steven S. *The Ethnic Avant-Garde: Minority Cultures and World Revolution*. New York: Columbia UP, 2015.

———. "Modernist Indigeneity and World Revolution." Conference presentation, MLA 2020, Seattle.

Leeming, David. *Stephen Spender: A Life in Modernism*. New York: Henry Holt, 1999.

Leonard, Miriam. *Tragic Modernities*. Cambridge: Harvard UP, 2015.

Lessing, Doris. *The Four-Gated City*. New York: Bantam, 1969.

———. *Going Home*. 1957. St Albans: Granada, 1968.

———. *The Golden Notebook*. New York: HarperPerennial, 2008. First published by Simon and Schuster, 1962.

———. *The Grass Is Singing*. New York: HarperPerennial, 1950.

———. *Landlocked*. 1965. New York: HarperPerennial, 1966.

———. *Martha Quest*. 1952. New York: HarperPerennial, 1964.

———. *A Proper Marriage*. 1954. New York: HarperPerennial, 1964.

———. *A Ripple from the Storm*. 1958. New York: HarperPerennial, 1966.

———. *Shikasta: Re: Colonised Planet 5*. New York: Vintage, 1979.

———. "The Small Personal Voice." *Declaration*. Edited by Tom Maschler, 186–201. New York: E. P. Dutton, 1958.

Doris Lessing. "Spies I Have Known." In *Spies I Have Known and Other Stories*, 171–93. Glasgow: Collins Educational, 1995.

———. *Under My Skin: Volume One of My Autobiography, to 1949*. New York: HarperCollins, 1994.

———. *Walking in the Shade: Volume Two of My Autobiography, 1949–1962*. New York: Harper-Collins, 1997.

Levi, Primo. *If this Is a Man*. Translated by Stuart Wolf. In *The Complete Works of Primo Levi*, vol. 1, 1–205. Edited by Ann Goldstein. Introduction by Toni Morrison. 3 vols. New York: Liveright, 2015.

Liu, Kang. *Aesthetics and Marxism: Chinese Aesthetic Marxists and their Western Contemporaries*. Durham: Duke UP, 2000.

Liu, Lydia H. "After Tashkent: The Geopolitics of Translation in the Global South." https://www.ici-berlin.org/events/lydia-h-liu/. Accessed 8 June 2020.

———. "The Eventfulness of Translation: Temporality, Difference, and Competing Universals." *translation: a transdisciplinary journal* 4 (2014): 148–70.

Loichot, Valérie. *The Tropics Bite Back: Culinary Coups in Caribbean Literature*. Minneapolis: U of Minnesota P, 2013.

Lorde, Audre. *Sister Outsider: Essays and Speeches*. Foreword by Cheryl Clarke. Berkeley: Crossing Press, 2007.

———. *Zami: A New Spelling of My Name*. Freedom: Crossing Press, 1982.

Louie, Kam, ed. *Eileen Chang: Romancing Languages, Cultures and Genres*. Hong Kong: Hong Kong UP, 2012.

Lovesey, Oliver. "Chained Letters: African Prison Diaries and 'National Allegory.'" *Research in African Literatures* 26.4 (1995): 31–45.

Low, Gail. *Publishing the Postcolonial: Anglophone West African and Caribbean Writing in the UK, 1948–1968*. Abingdon: Routledge, 2011.

Lu Xun. *Silent China: Selected Writings of Lu Xun*. Edited and translated by Gladys Yang. Oxford: Oxford UP, 1973.

Lukács, Georg. *The Historical Novel*. Translated by Hannah and Stanley Mitchell. Introduction by Fredric Jameson. Lincoln: U of Nebraska P, 1983.

———. *The Theory of the Novel: A Historico-Philosophical Essay on the Forms of Great Epic Literature*. Translated by Anna Bostock. Cambridge: MIT Press, 1971.

Lye, Colleen. *America's Asia: Racial Form and American Literature, 1893–1945*. Princeton: Princeton UP, 2005.

Lyon, Janet. *Manifestoes: Provocations of the Modern*. Ithaca: Cornell UP, 1999.

Macauley, Robie. "The 'Little Magazines.'" *Transition* 9 (1963): 24–25.

MacKay, Marina. *Modernism and World War II*. Cambridge: Cambridge UP, 2007.

Madureira, Luís. *Cannibal Modernities: Postcoloniality and the Avant-Garde in Caribbean and Brazilian Literature*. Charlottesville: U of Virginia P, 2005.

Mahler, Anne Garland. *From the Tricontinental to the Global South: Race, Radicalism, and Transnational Solidarity*. Durham: Duke UP, 2018.

Majumder, Auritro. *Insurgent Imaginations: World Literature and the Periphery*. Cambridge: Cambridge UP, 2021.

Malik, Hafeez. "The Marxist Literary Movement in India and Pakistan." *Journal of Asian Studies* 26.4 (1967): 649–64.

Mamdani, Mahmood. *Citizen and Subject: Contemporary Africa and the Legacy of Late Colonialism.* 2nd ed. Princeton: Princeton UP, 2018.

Man with a Movie Camera. Directed by Dziga Vertov. 1929.

Mani, B. Venkat. *Recoding World Literature: Libraries, Print Culture, and Germany's Pact with Books.* New York: Fordham UP, 2017.

Mann, Thomas. "Letters of Thomas Mann," *Encounter* 19.6 (December 1962): 3–15.

Mao Zedong's "Talks at the Yan'an Conference on Literature and Art": A Translation of the 1943 Text with Commentary. Translated by Bonnie S. McDougall. Ann Arbor: Center for Chinese Studies, U of Michigan, 1980.

Mapanje, Jack. *And Crocodiles Are Hungry at Night.* Banbury: Ayebia Clarke, 2011.

———, ed. *Gathering Seaweed: African Prison Writing.* Harlow: Heinemann, 2002.

Marks, Peter. "Art and Politics in the 1930s: *The European Quarterly* (1934–5), *Left Review* (1934–8), and *Poetry and the People* (1938–40)." In *The Oxford Critical and Cultural History of Modernist Magazines,* vol. 1, Britain and Ireland 1880–1955. Edited by Peter Brooker and Andrew Thacker, 623–46. Oxford: Oxford UP, 2009.

Marx, Karl. *The Eighteenth Brumaire of Louis Bonaparte.* New York: International Publishers, 1963.

Maxwell William J. *F.B. Eyes: How J. Edgar Hoover's Ghostreaders Framed African American Literature.* Princeton: Princeton UP, 2015.

———. *New Negro, Old Left: African-American Writing and Communism Between the Wars.* New York: Columbia University Press, 1999.

Mbembe, Achille. *On the Postcolony.* Berkeley: U of California P, 2001.

McCarthy, Richard M. Interviewed by Jack O'Brien, Association for Diplomatic Studies and Training, Foreign Affairs Oral History Project, 28 December 1988. https://www.adst.org/OH%20TOCs/McCarthy,%20Richard%20M.toc.pdf

McDonald, Peter D. *Artefacts of Writing: Ideas of the State and Communities of Letters from Matthew Arnold to Xu Bing.* Oxford: Oxford UP, 2017.

———. *The Literature Police: Apartheid Censorship and its Cultural Consequences.* Oxford: Oxford UP, 2009.

McGurl, Mark. *The Program Era: Postwar Fiction and the Rise of Creative Writing.* Cambridge: Harvard UP, 2009.

McLuhan, Marshall. *Understanding Media: The Extensions of Man.* Edited by W. Terrence Gordon. Corte Madera, CA: Gingko Press, 1994.

Merrill, James. *The Changing Light at Sandover: Including the Whole of the Book of Ephraim, Mirabell's Books of Number, Scripts for the Pageant, and a New Coda, The Higher Keys.* New York: Knopf, 2001.

Miller, Christopher L. "The (Revised) Birth of Negritude: Communist Revolution and 'the Immanent Negro' in 1935." *PMLA* 125.3 (2010): 743–49.

Mitchell, David T. and Sharon L. Snyder. *Narrative Prosthesis: Disability and the Dependencies of Discourse.* Ann Arbor: U of Michigan P, 2000.

Moore, David Chioni. "Local Color, Global 'Color': Langston Hughes, the Black Atlantic, and Soviet Central Asia, 1932." *Research in African Literatures* 27.4 (1996): 49–70.

Moore, Gerald. "The Transcription Centre in the Sixties: Navigating in Narrow Seas." *Research in African Literatures* 33.3 (2002): 167–81.

Moretti, Franco. "Conjectures on World Literature." *New Left Review* 1 (2000): 54–69.

———. *Graphs, Maps, Trees: Abstract Models for Literary History.* London: Verso, 2005.

———. *Modern Epic: The World System from Goethe to García Márquez.* London: Verso, 1996.

———. "More Conjectures." *New Left Review* 20 (2003): 73–81.

Moyn, Samuel. *The Last Utopia: Human Rights in History.* Cambridge: Harvard UP, 2010.

———. *Not Enough: Human Rights in an Unequal World.* Cambridge: Harvard UP, 2018.

Mphahlele, Ezekiel [Es'kia], ed. *Conference of African Writers of English Expression, 11–17 June 1962,* Conference Proceedings. Kampala: Congress for Cultural Freedom, 1962.

———. *Down Second Avenue.* London: Fabers, 1959.

———. *Voices in the Whirlwind and Other Essays.* New York: Hill and Wang, 1972.

———. "Writers and Commitment." *Black Orpheus* 2.3 (1969): 34–39.

Mufti, Aamir R. *Forget English! Orientalisms and World Literatures.* Cambridge: Harvard UP, 2016.

Mzamane, Mbulelo Vizikhungo. "Sharpeville and its Aftermath: The Novels of Richard Rive, Peter Abrahams, Alex La Guma, and Lauretta Ngcobo." *ARIEL* 16.2 (1985): 31–44.

Nadal, Paul. "Cold War Remittance Economy: US Creative Writing and the Importation of New Criticism into the Philippines." *American Quarterly* 73.3 (2021): 557–95.

Nadel, Alan. *Containment Culture: American Narratives, Postmodernism, and the Atomic Age.* Durham: Duke UP, 1995.

Nadiminti, Kalyan. "The Global Program Era: Contemporary International Fiction in the American Creative Economy." *NOVEL: A Forum on Fiction* 51.3 (2018): 375–98.

Narasimhaiah, C. D. "A.C.L.A.L.S. Conference on Commonwealth Literature: Kingston, Jamaica, 3–9 January 1971." *Journal of Commonwealth Literature* 6.2 (1971): 120–26.

Neogy, Rajat. "7 T ONE = 7 E TON." *Transition* 1 (1961): 10.

———. "Rajat Neogy on the CIA." Interview with Tony Hall. *Transition* 32 (August–September 1967): 45–46.

Ngũgĩ wa Thiong'o. *Decolonising the Mind: The Politics of Language in African Literature.* London: James Currey, 1986.

———. *Detained: A Writer's Prison Diary.* Oxford: Heinemann, 1981.

———. *Homecoming: Essays on African and Caribbean Literature, Culture and Politics.* London: Heinemann, 1972.

———. *Weep Not, Child.* Oxford: Heinemann Educational Publishers, 1964.

———. *Writers in Politics: A Re-engagement with Issues of Literature and Society.* Revised edition. Oxford, Nairobi, and Portsmouth, NH: James Currey, East African Educational Publishers, and Heinemann, 1997.

Ninkovich, Frank A. *The Diplomacy of Ideas: U.S. Foreign Policy and Cultural Relations, 1938–1950.* Cambridge: Cambridge UP, 1981.

Noland, Carrie. *Voices of Negritude in Modernist Print: Aesthetic Subjectivity, Diaspora, and the Lyric Regime.* New York: Columbia UP, 2015.

"Notes on Contributors." *Transition* 25 (1966): 2.

Nwoga, Donatus Ibe, ed. *Critical Perspectives on Christopher Okigbo.* Washington, DC: Three Continents, 1984.

Okigbo, Christopher. *Labyrinths, with Path of Thunder.* New York and Ibadan: Africana Publishing and Mbari, 1971.

Orwell, George. *1984*. 1949. Afterword by Erich Fromm. New York: Harcourt Brace, 1977.

———. "You and the Atom Bomb." In *George Orwell: Essays*. Edited and introduced by John Carey, 903–7. New York: Knopf, 2002.

Padmore, George. *Pan-Africanism or Communism*. 1956. Foreword by Richard Wright, introduction by Azinna Nwafor. Garden City, NY: Doubleday, 1971.

Parikh, Crystal. *Writing Human Rights: The Political Imaginaries of Writers of Color*. Minneapolis: U of Minnesota P, 2017.

Park, Josephine Nock-Hee. *Cold War Friendships: Korea, Vietnam, and Asian American Literature*. Oxford: Oxford UP, 2016.

Parker, Jason C. *Hearts, Minds, Voices: US Cold War Public Diplomacy and the Formation of the Third World*. Oxford: Oxford UP, 2016.

Pease, Donald E. "Doing Justice to C.L.R. James's Mariners, Renegades and Castaways." *boundary 2* 27.2 (2000): 1–19.

PEN International. "PEN Charter." https://pen-international.org/who-we-are/the-pen-charter. Accessed on 6 April 2020.

———. "Our History." https://pen-international.org/who-we-are/history. Accessed on 6 April 2020.

Perloff, Marjorie. *The Futurist Moment: Avant-Garde, Avant Guerre, and the Language of Rupture*. 2nd ed. Chicago: U of Chicago P, 2003.

Piette, Adam. *The Literary Cold War: 1945 to Vietnam*. Edinburgh: Edinburgh UP, 2009.

Pollock, Sheldon, ed. *Literary Cultures in History: Reconstructions from South Asia*. Berkeley: U of California P, 2003.

Popescu, Monica. *At Penpoint: African Literatures, Postcolonial Studies, and the Cold War*. Durham: Duke UP, 2020.

———. *South African Literature beyond the Cold War*. New York: Palgrave Macmillan, 2010.

Potter, Rachel. "International PEN: Writers, Free Expression, Organisations." In *A History of 1930s British Literature*, edited by Benjamin Kohlmann and Matthew Taunton, 120–33. Cambridge: Cambridge UP, 2019.

———. "Modernist Rights: International PEN 1921–1936," *Critical Quarterly* 55.2 (2013): 66–80.

Pramoedya Ananta Toer. *The Mute's Soliloquy: A Memoir*. Translated by Willem Samuels. New York: Penguin, 1999.

Prashad, Vijay. *The Darker Nations: A People's History of the Third World*. New York: New Press, 2007.

Présence Africaine. Foreword. *Présence Africaine* 1/2 (1955): 8–10.

Puchner, Martin. *Poetry of the Revolution: Marx, Manifestos, and the Avant-Gardes*. Princeton: Princeton UP, 2006.

Quayson, Ato. *Aesthetic Nervousness: Disability and the Crisis of Representation*. New York: Columbia UP, 2007.

———. *Tragedy and Postcolonial Literature*. Cambridge: Cambridge UP, 2021.

Ram, Harsha. "Introducing Georgian Modernism." *Modernism/modernity* 21.1 (2014): 283–8.

Ramazani, Jahan. *The Hybrid Muse: Postcolonial Poetry in English*. Chicago: U of Chicago P, 2001.

———. *A Transnational Poetics*. Chicago: U of Chicago P, 2009.

———. *Poetry in a Global Age*. Chicago: U of Chicago P, 2020.

Ramzes, Victor. "African Literature in Russia." *Transition* 25 (1966): 40–42.

Ranasinha, Ruvani. *South Asian Writers in Twentieth-Century Britain: Culture in Translation.* Oxford: Oxford UP, 2007.

Reed, Anthony. *Freedom Time: The Poetics and Politics of Black Experimental Writing.* Baltimore: Johns Hopkins UP, 2014.

Rexer, Raisa. "Black and White and Re(a)d all over: *L'Étudiant noir*, Communism, and the Birth of Négritude." *Research in African Literatures* 44.4 (2013): 1–14.

Rive, Richard. *'Buckingham Palace', District Six*. Introduction by Robin Malan. Claremont, South Africa: David Philip, 1986.

Rizzuto, Nicole M. *Insurgent Testimonies: Witnessing Colonial Trauma in Modern and Anglophone Literature.* New York: Fordham UP, 2015.

Roberts, Brian Russell and Keith Foulcher, eds. *Indonesian Notebook: A Sourcebook on Richard Wright and the Bandung Conference.* Durham: Duke UP, 2016.

Robin, Régine. *Socialist Realism: An Impossible Aesthetic.* Translated by Catherine Porter, foreword by Léon Robel. Stanford: Stanford UP, 1992.

Rogers, Asha. *State Sponsored Literature: Britain and Cultural Diversity after 1945.* Oxford: Oxford UP, 2020.

Rogers, Gayle. *Incomparable Empires: Modernism and the Translation of Spanish American Literature.* New York: Columbia UP, 2016.

Roux, Daniel. "Writing the Prison." In *The Cambridge History of South African Literature.* Edited by David Attwell and Derek Attridge, 545–63. Cambridge: Cambridge UP, 2012.

Rowley, Hazel. *Richard Wright: The Life and Times.* New York: Henry Holt, 2001.

Rubin, Andrew N. *Archives of Authority: Empire, Culture, and the Cold War.* Princeton: Princeton UP, 2012.

Said, Edward W. *Culture and Imperialism.* New York: Vintage, 1993.

———. *Orientalism.* New York: Vintage, 1994.

Saint-Amour, Paul K. *Tense Future: Modernism, Total War, Encyclopedic Form.* Oxford: Oxford UP, 2015.

Saunders, Frances Stonor. *The Cultural Cold War: The CIA and the World of Arts and Letters.* New York: The New Press, 1999.

Saussy, Haun. *Translation as Citation: Zhuangzi Inside Out.* Oxford: Oxford UP, 2017.

Schrecker, Ellen and Phillip Deery. *The Age of McCarthyism: A Brief History with Documents.* 3rd ed. Boston: Bedford-St Martin's, 2017.

Schwarz, Bill. "'Claudia Jones and the *West Indian Gazette*': Reflections on the Emergence of Postcolonial Britain." *Twentieth Century British History* 14.3 (2003): 264–85.

Scott, David. *Conscripts of Modernity: The Tragedy of Colonial Enlightenment.* Durham: Duke UP, 2004.

———. *Omens of Adversity: Tragedy, Time, Memory Justice.* Durham: Duke UP, 2014.

Scott-Smith, Giles. *The Politics of Apolitical Culture: The Congress for Cultural Freedom, the CIA and Post-War American Hegemony.* London: Routledge, 2002.

Scott-Smith, Giles, and Charlotte A. Lerg, ed. *Campaigning Culture and the Global Cold War: The Journals of the Congress for Cultural Freedom.* London: Palgrave, 2017.

Sen, Siddheswar. "Writers' Freedom and Commitment." *Lotus* 20 (April–June 1974): 34–38.

Senanayake, Ratne Deshapriya, ed. *Afro-Asian Poems: Anthology*. Volume 1 Part 1. Colombo: Afro-Asian Writers' Bureau, 1963.

Sharpley-Whiting, T. Denean. *Negritude Women*. Minneapolis: U of Minnesota P, 2002.

Shaw, Tony. *Hollywood's Cold War*. Edinburgh: Edinburgh UP, 2007.

Shen, Shuang. *Cosmopolitan Publics: Anglophone Print Culture in Semi-Colonial Shanghai*. New Brunswick: Rutgers UP, 2009.

Sherry, Vincent. *The Great War and the Language of Modernism*. Oxford: Oxford UP, 2003.

Sherwood, Marika, with Donald Hines, Colin Prescod, and the 1996 Claudia Jones Symposium. *Claudia Jones: A Life in Exile*. London: Lawrence and Wishart, 1999.

Shih, Shu-mei. *The Lure of the Modern: Writing Modernism in Semi-Colonial China, 1917–1937*. Berkeley: U of California P, 2001.

Shringarpure, Bhakti. *Cold War Assemblages: Decolonization to Digital*. New York: Routledge, 2019.

Siebers, Tobin. *Disability Aesthetics*. Ann Arbor: U of Michigan P, 2010.

Siraganian, Lisa. *Modernism's Other Work: The Art Object's Political Life*. Oxford: Oxford UP, 2012.

Slaughter, Joseph R. "Hijacking Human Rights: Neoliberalism, the New Historiography, and the End of the Third World." *Human Rights Quarterly* 40.4 (2018): 735–75.

———. *Human Rights, Inc.: The World Novel, Narrative Form, and International Law*. New York: Fordham UP, 2007.

Smith, James. *British Writers and MI5 Surveillance, 1930–1960*. Cambridge: Cambridge UP, 2013.

So, Richard Jean. "The Invention of the Global MFA: Taiwanese Writers at Iowa, 1964–1980." *American Literary History* 29.3 (2017): 499–520.

———. "Literary Information Warfare: Eileen Chang, the US State Department, and Cold War Media Aesthetics." *American Literature* 85.4 (2013): 719–44.

———. *Transpacific Community: America, China, and the Rise and Fall of a Cultural Network*. New York: Columbia UP, 2016.

Sofronov, Anatoly. "Editor's Note," *Lotus* 34 (October–December 1977): 4.

Solzhenitsyn, Alexander. *One Day in the Life of Ivan Denisovich*. Translated by Ralph Parker, introduction by Yevgeny Yevtushenko, foreword by Alexander Tvardovsky, afterword by Eric Bogosian. New York: Penguin, 1991.

Soyinka, Wole. *Collected Plays 1*. Oxford: Oxford UP, 1973.

———. *Collected Plays 2*. Oxford: Oxford UP, 1974.

———. "From Africa to the 'Global Black.'" Interview by Tommy Shelby. *Transition* 106 (2011): A34-A44.

———. *The Man Died*. New York: Farrar, Straus and Giroux, 1972.

———. "Neo-Tarzanism: The Poetics of Pseudo-Tradition." *Transition* 48 (1975): 38–44.

———. *Trumpism in Academe: The Example of Caroline Davis and Spahring Partners*. Ibadan: Bookcraft, 2021.

———. "The Writer in an African State." *Transition* 31 (1967): 10–13.

Spahr, Juliana. *Du Bois's Telegram: Literary Resistance and State Containment*. Cambridge: Harvard UP, 2018.

"Special Section on: Lotus Award Winners for the Year 1975: Chinua Achebe, Faiz Ahmed Faiz, Kim Chi Ha, M. Mahdi El Gawahri." *Lotus* 30 (October–December 1976): 113–34.

Spender, Stephen. *The Creative Element: A Study of Vision, Despair and Orthodoxy among some Modern Writers*. London: Hamish Hamilton, 1953.

Spender, Stephen, Melvin J. Lasky, and Irving Kristol. "Freedom of Encounter Magazine." Letter to the Editor. *New York Times*, 10 May 1966.

Spivak, Gayatri Chakravorty. *A Critique of Postcolonial Reason: Toward a Vanishing History of the Present*. Cambridge: Harvard UP, 1999.

Stalin, Joseph. *Marxism and the National and Colonial Question*. Edited by A. Fineberg. New York: International Publishers, n.d.

"Statement of Position to the Commonwealth Literature & Language Conference—Mona, January, 1971." *Journal of Black Poetry* 1.17 (1973): 29–32.

Stephens, Michelle Ann. *Black Empire: The Masculine Global Imaginary of Caribbean Intellectuals in the United States, 1914–1962*. Durham: Duke UP, 2005.

Steven, Mark. *Red Modernism: American Poetry and the Spirit of Communism*. Baltimore: Johns Hopkins UP, 2017.

Stonebridge, Lyndsey. *Placeless People: Writings, Rights, and Refugees*. Oxford: Oxford UP, 2018.

Suhr-Sytsma, Nathan. *Poetry, Print, and the Making of Postcolonial Literature*. Cambridge: Cambridge UP, 2017.

Tan, See Seng and Amitav Acharya, eds. *Bandung Revisited: The Legacy of the 1955 Asian-African Conference for International Order*. Singapore: National U of Singapore P, 2008.

Taunton, Matthew. "Communism by the Letter: Doris Lessing and the Politics of Writing." *ELH* 88.1 (2021): 251–80.

Tikhonov, Nikolai. "Editorial: The Great Brotherhood of Literatures Born of the October Revolution." *Lotus* 34 (October–December 1977): 5–12.

"Transition Conference Questionnaire." *Transition* 5 (July–August 1962): 11–12.

Trask, Michael. *Ideal Minds: Raising Consciousness in the Antisocial Seventies*. Ithaca: Cornell UP, 2020.

Travis, Trysh. "Middlebrow Print Culture in the Cold War: Books USA, 1967." *PMLA* 128.2 (2013): 468–73.

Trotsky, Leon. *Literature and Revolution*. 1925. Edited by William Keach, translated by Rose Strunsky. Chicago: Haymarket, 2005.

Udval, Sonomyn. "Review of the New Mongolian Literature." *Lotus* 24/25 (April–September 1975): 146–49.

UNESCO. "Influence of Colonialism on the Artist, his Milieu, and his Public in Developing Countries." *Lotus* 18 (October 1973): 10–20.

———. *UNESCO Statistical Yearbook 1963, 1970, 1976, 1981*. Paris: UNESCO, 1964–1981.

van der Vlies, Andrew. *South African Textual Cultures: White, Black, Read All Over*. Manchester: Manchester UP, 2007.

Vanhove, Pieter. "'A World to Win:' China, the Afro-Asian Writers' Bureau, and the Reinvention of World Literature." *Critical Asian Studies* 51.2 (2019): 144–65.

Vatulescu, Cristina. *Police Aesthetics: Literature, Film, and the Secret Police in Soviet Times*. Stanford: Stanford UP, 2010.

Volland, Nicolai. *Socialist Cosmopolitanism: The Chinese Literary Universe, 1945–1965*. New York: Columbia UP, 2017.

Von Eschen, Penny M. *Race against Empire: Black Americans and Anticolonialism, 1937–1957*. Ithaca: Cornell UP, 1997.

———. *Satchmo Blows Up the World: Jazz Ambassadors Play the Cold War*. Cambridge: Harvard UP, 2004.

Wali, Obiajunwa. "The Dead End of African Literature?" *Transition* 10 (September 1963): 13–15.

Walkowitz, Rebecca L. *Born Translated: The Contemporary Novel in an Age of World Literature*. New York: Columbia UP, 2015.

Wang, David Der-wei. *The Monster That Is History: History, Violence, and Fictional Writing in Twentieth-Century China*. Berkeley: U of California P, 2004.

Wang, Mei-Hsiang. "Eileen Chang—The Unknown Story: *The Rice-Sprout Song* and the *Naked Earth* under the USIS Book Translation Program." *EurAmerica* 45.1 (2015): 73–137.

Wang, Xiaojue. *Modernity with a Cold War Face: Reimagining the Nation in Chinese Literature across the 1949 Divide*. Cambridge: Harvard U Asia Center, 2013.

Warner, Tobias. *The Tongue-Tied Imagination: Decolonizing Literary Modernity in Senegal*. New York: Fordham UP, 2019.

Warwick Research Collective. *Combined and Uneven Development: Towards a New Theory of World Literature*. Liverpool: Liverpool UP, 2015.

Washington, Mary Helen. *The Other Blacklist: The African American Literary and Cultural Left of the 1950s*. New York: Columbia UP, 2014.

Watson, Jini Kim. *Cold War Reckonings: Authoritarianism and the Genres of Decolonization*. New York: Fordham UP, 2021.

Westad, Odd Arne. *The Cold War: A World History*. New York: Basic Books, 2017.

———. *The Global Cold War: Third World Interventions and the Making of Our Times*. Cambridge: Cambridge UP, 2007.

Whitney, Gretchen. "International Book Production Statistics." In *International Book Publishing: An Encyclopedia*. Edited by Philip G. Altbach and Edith S. Hoshino, 163–85. New York: Garland, 1995.

Wilder, Gary. *Freedom Time: Negritude, Decolonization, and the Future of the World*. Durham: Duke UP, 2015.

Wilford, Hugh. *The Mighty Wurlitzer: How the CIA Played America*. Cambridge: Harvard UP, 2008.

Winkiel, Laura. *Modernism, Race, and Manifestos*. Cambridge: Cambridge UP, 2008.

Witt, Susanna. "Between the Lines: Totalitarianism and Translation in the USSR." In *Contexts, Subtexts, and Pretexts: Literary Translation in Eastern Europe and Russia*, edited by Brian James Baer, 149–70. Amsterdam/Philadelphia: John Benjamins, 2011.

Wollaeger, Mark. *Modernism, Media, and Propaganda: British Narrative from 1900 to 1945*. Princeton: Princeton UP, 2006.

Wong, Wang-chi. *Politics and Literature in Shanghai: The Chinese League of Left-Wing Writers, 1930–1936*. Manchester: Manchester UP, 1991.

Worcester, Kent. *C.L.R. James: A Political Biography*. Albany: SUNY Press, 1996.

Wright, Richard. *The Color Curtain: A Report on the Bandung Conference*. Foreword by Gunnar Myrdal. Cleveland: World Publishing, 1956.

Wu, Ellen D. "'America's Chinese': Anti-Communism, Citizenship, and Cultural Diplomacy during the Cold War." *Pacific Historical Review* 77.3 (2008): 391–422.

Yoon, Duncan M. "'Our Forces Have Redoubled:' World Literature, Postcolonialism, and the Afro-Asian Writers' Bureau." *Cambridge Journal of Postcolonial Literary Inquiry* 2.2 (2015): 233–52.

Youssef, Abou Bakr. "A New Collection of Arab Literature." Review of *Selected Works of Middle-East Writers*. *Lotus* 38/39 (October 1978–March 1979): 126–28.

Yi, Chong-ik. "The Bandung Conference, April 18–24, 1955 and the United States Reaction." MA Thesis, University of Wisconsin-Madison, 1957.

Zaheer, Sajjad. *The Light: A History of the Movement for Progressive Literature in the Indo-Pakistan Subcontinent; a Translation of "Roshnai"*. Translated by Amina Azfar. Introduction by Ahmad Ali Khan. Oxford: Oxford UP, 2006.

———. "Reminiscences." In *Marxist Cultural Movement in India, Chronicles and Documents (1936–1947)*, vol. 1, edited by Sudhi Pradhan, 25–37. Calcutta: Pradhan, 1979.

Zhang, Y. P. "The Emergence of the Global South Novel: *Red Sorghum*, *Présence Africaine*, and the Third Novelists' International." *Novel: A Forum on Fiction* 52.3 (2019): 347–68.

Zhdanov, Andrei, Maxim Gorky, Nikolai Bukharin, Karl Radek, and Alexei Stetsky. *Problems of Soviet Literature: Reports and Speeches at the First Soviet Writers' Congress*. Edited by H. G. Scott. New York: International Publishers, n.d.

INDEX

Abrahams, Peter, 101

Achebe, Chinua, 6, 8, 33, 40, 52, 77, 118;
"Africa and Her Writers," 3–5, 10, 17–18, 21,
29; at the Conference of African Writers
of English Expression, 1962, 51; debates
over language and, 45; on decolonization
and time, 108; defense of use of English,
46, 53; Ngũgĩ's criticism of, 41; work with
both CCF and AAWA, 84

Ademola, Frances, 52

aesthetic cold war, 5–7, 17–18; anticolonial
revolutionaries and, 24–31; cultural
decolonization and, 40–41; debate over
appropriate language for writing and
place of politics in literature during, 32;
interwar debates and, 18–24; language
and, 45–46

aesthetics: aesthetic autonomy, 4, 10–11, 18,
20, 23, 41, 45–47, 54–56, 61–63; aesthetic
utilitarianism, 10, 18, 46, 170, 205, 220,
224, 248; modernist aesthetics, 25, 58, 66,
77, 80–81; socialist aesthetics, 21–22, 24,
45, 84, 103–104, 164, 178, 248

Affaire Aragon, 19, 23

"Africa and Her Writers," 3–5, 10, 17–18,
21, 29

African literature, 3–5, 7, 17–18, 89;
censorship of, 43–44; indigeneity in,
77–82; little magazines and, 34–35,
51, 57–58, 73–74; poetry in, 42–43;
pseudo-traditionalism in, 43–44;
transition of English language in,
20–21

*African Novel of Ideas: Philosophy and
Individualism in the Age of Global Writing,
The*, 173

"African Writers and the English Language,"
20–21

African Writers of English Expression.
See Makerere conference

African Writers Talking, 69

Afro-Asian Peoples' Solidarity Organization
(AAPSO), 93, 96

Afro-Asian Poems: An Anthology, 97

Afro-Asian Poetry, 101

Afro-Asian Writer's Association (AAWA),
23, 37–38, 73; anticolonial writers working
with both CCF and, 84; charter of,
98–99; conference circuit and, 95–100;
cultural diplomacy through, 83–84,
92–95; global network of anticolonial
writers built by, 85. *See also Lotus*

Afro-Asian Writers' Bureau, 97

Aitmatov, Chinghiz, *104*

All-India Progressive Writers' Association
(PWA), 8, 24, 33; Communist Party and,
30; formation of, 28–29; intelligence
agencies investigations of, 29–31; *Lotus*
and, 92–95; manifesto of, 28–31, 94–95;
on utility of literature and indigenous
languages, 46

Alma-Ata conference, *98, 98–99, 99,
104*

"Aloeswood Incense: The First Brazier,"
123–124

American Civilization, 208

Amnesty International, 219

Anand, Mulk Raj, 24, 28, 31, 93, 96

And Crocodiles Are Hungry at Night, 220, 230–233, 238–239, 242

Anderson, Benedict, 88

Andrade, Oswald de, 24–26, 45

Anghie, Antony, 243–244

Angry Young Men, 35–36

anticolonialism, 4–5; AAWA network of writers in, 84–85; calls for abolishing study of English and, 41–42; consolidated, 1940–1956, 31–36; human rights and, 243–244; interwar era revolutionaries of, 24–31; modernity in, 208–215; novels of, 36; through prison writing, 218–219. *See also* colonialism

apartheid, 43, 63, 79, 88, 103, 105–111, 113, 116, 151, 229, 235–236. *See also* color bar; racism

archive, 11–13, 101, 245–249

Arendt, Hannah, 6, 107–108

Armstrong, Louis, 60

Arrivants, The, 102, 108

Asian literature, 88, 91–92, 103

Association for Commonwealth Literature and Language Studies (ACLALS), 37, 40

Auden, W. H., 23, 60

"Authors Take Sides on the Spanish War," 23

autochthony, 21

autonomy, aesthetic. *See* aesthetics

avant-garde, militant, 195

Baldwin, James, 37–38, 65, 182

Bandung conference, 5–6, 37, 88, 96, 244

Barnhisel, Greg, 129

Barred: Women, Writing, and Political Detention, 218

Barthes, Roland, 44

Beacon, The, 24

Beckett, Samuel, 23

Beier, Ulli, 35, 57, 59, 65, 70, 77

Bennett, Eric, 134

Bennett, Louise, 21

Benson, Peter, 57, 73, 75

Berlin, Isaiah, 224

Bernabé, Jean, 34, 44–45

Between Past and Future, 107–108

Beyond a Boundary, 194

Bieber, Marion, 223

Bim, 34–35

Birmingham Centre for Contemporary Cultural Studies, 32

Black Atlantic, 96, 203, 216; Caribbean national autonomy movement and, 193–195; language translation and, 29; literature of, 33; negritude movement and, 26–27; political police and, 184; *Présence Africaine* and, 31, 33–34, 182; *West Indian Gazette* and, 191

Black Atlantic, The, 194

Black Jacobins: Toussaint L'Ouverture and the San Domingo Revolution, The, 25, 182, 195, 202–205, 211–212; 1963 revisions to, 215–216

Black Orpheus, 34–35, 51, 53, 57, 59, 82, 85; aesthetic autonomy and, 104; Congress for Cultural Freedom and, 63–64, 70–76; La Guma in, 91; Okigbo and, 66

black radicalism, 194

Book of Change, The, 135, 144

Bourdieu, Pierre, 13

Braine, John, 164

Brathwaite, Kamau, 21, 35, 40, 102; on decolonization and time, 108

Breton, André, 19

Breytenbach, Breyten, 101

British Communist Party (CPGB), 151

British New Left, 35–36

British Writers and MI5 Surveillance, 1930–1960, 155

Brouillette, Sarah, 13

Brubeck, Dave, 60

Brutus, Dennis, 66, 84, 101–103, 217, 234–235

Buck, Pearl S., 118, 121–122

'Buckingham Palace', District Six, 110

Buhle, Paul, 196
Bukharin, Nikolai, 22–23, 92
Bull, Theodore, 52
Bulson, Eric, 74, 100
Buru Quartet, 217–218

Campaign for Nuclear Disarmament,
   164–166
Camus, Albert, 34
"Cannibalist Manifesto," 24–26
Canopus in Argos: Archives, 179
capitalism, 6, 40, 84; cultural cannibalism
   and, 26; world literature as symptom of
   global, 90
Carew, Jan, 184, 193
Caribbean Carnival celebration, London,
   193–194
Caribbean intellectuals: FBI surveillance of,
   183–184; on political autonomy, 193–194;
   significant 1950s, 183–185; *West Indian
   Gazette* and, 191–192
Caribbean Voices, 68–69
Carlston, Erin G., 143
Carver, David, 222–223
Casanova, Pascale, 13, 90, 117
*Case for West Indian Self Government,
   The*, 195
Castro, Fidel, 241–242; Toussaint and,
   215
*Censors at Work: How States Shaped
   Literature*, 43
censorship, 43–45, 159–160, 247–248
Central Intelligence Agency (CIA), 7,
   53–54, 60; Congress for Cultural
   Freedom and, 53, 57, 82; recruitment of
   Africans, 63–64
Césaire, Aimé, 26–27, 184, 216, 245; on
   decolonization and time, 108; resignation
   from the Communist Party, 37
Chamoiseau, Patrick, 34, 44–45
Chang, Eileen, 7, 227; autobiographical
   writing by, 120–121; Chinese diaspora
   and, 118, 120; cultural diplomacy and,
   139–140; desolation portrayed by,

125–127, 138; equivocal contrast used by,
   122–125, 139–143; lack of critical or
   commercial success in the United States,
   119; nonalignment of, 120, 122, 135;
   portrayals of life in China, 121–122;
   themes in writing by, 118–119; translations
   by, 118, 143–147; unpublished works of,
   135; working in two languages, 118,
   120–122; work with political interest
   groups, 127–135. *See also Naked Earth;
   Rice-Sprout Song, The*
Changing Light at Sandover, The, 173
Chemchemi, 53
Chen, Tina, 143
Children of Violence, 154, 163, 166, 173–175,
   179
Ch'indaba, 82
Chinese literature, 118–119, 121–122
Chinese May Fourth New Culture
   Movement, 24
Chinweizu, 42, 44, 46
Chow, Rey, 122
Christie, Agatha, 91
Clark, Katerina, 90
Clark-Bekederemo, John Pepper, 35,
   51, 66, 230
classical literary forms: epic, 22, 122,
   203–207; tragedy, 22, 122, 126, 203, 215
Cleary, Joe, 104
Coetzee, J. M., 89, 114
cold war: aesthetic, 5–7, 17–18, 32, 40–41, 45;
   anticolonialism consolidated during,
   1940–1956, 31–36; political, 5–7; postcolo-
   nial tradition, 1956–1990, 36–47
*Cold War Orientalism: Asia in the Middle-
   brow Imagination, 1945–1961*, 118–119
Coleman, Peter, 59
Collymore, Frank, 35
colonialism, 16, 38–39; censorship and, 44;
   cultural effects of, 96; La Guma on
   Soviet, 115; literary critics of, 35; racial
   hierarchies imposed by, 27. *See also*
   anticolonialism; decolonization;
   imperialism; neocolonialism

color bar, 151, 157, 161, 163. *See also* apartheid; racism

Commonwealth of Letters: British Literary Culture and the Emergence of Postcolonial Aesthetics, 62–63

Communism in Africa, 70

communist ideas, 24–26, 40; La Guma and, 88–89; late colonial and early postcolonial writers influenced by, 32

Communist Party, 24, 26, 96; British, 151, 184, 190; Césaire's resignation from, 37; Claudia Jones and, 185–187; Doris Lessing and, 156–158, 163–164; Indian, 30; Mary McCarthy and, 60; Rhodesian, 156–157, 162; USIA and US State Department efforts against, 129–130

comparatist nationalism, 86

Conference of African Writers of English Expression, 1962. *See* Makerere conference

conferences: literary, 19; political, 5–6

Confiant, Raphaël, 34, 44–45

Congress for Cultural Freedom, 7, 31, 37–38, 40; aesthetic autonomy and, 54–56, 61–62; anticolonial writers working with both AAWA and, 84; backing of *Black Orpheus* and *Transition* by, 63–64, 70–76; capitalism and, 85; CIA recruitment of Africans and, 63–64; drama competition sponsored by, 77; *Encounter* and, 53, 57–61; establishment and management of, 56–57; funding scandal of, 53–54, 56–57, 82; global network of, 59–63; International PEN and, 222–223, 227–228; little magazines and, 57–59; political affiliations of, 58, 60; prison writing and, 219; radio and, 58–59, 68–70

Connolly, Cyril, 23

Conrad, Joseph, 81

"Conscience Raciale et Révolution Sociale," 26–27

Conscripts of Modernity: The Tragedy of Colonial Enlightenment, 203, 215

conspiracy narrative, 166

Constantine, David, 242

cosmopolitanism, 17–18, 62, 81, 248

Creative Spirit, The, 62

creoleness, 44–46

Créolité, 34

Crossman, Richard, 60

cultural authenticity, 18, 21

cultural cannibalism, 26

cultural diplomacy, 7–8, 47, 248; Afro-Asian Writer's Association (AAWA), 83–84, 92–95; archives on, 11–13; CIA programs for, 60; Congress for Cultural Freedom, 7; Eileen Chang and, 139–140, 146–147; Langston Hughes and, 96–97; *Lotus* and, 83; modernist culture and, 61; USIA/US State Department, 7, 119–120, 127–134

cultural imperialism, 10, 27, 65, 247

cultural independence, 18, 40–41

cultural institutions: autonomous of colonialism, 57; patronage of, 53–54, 57

Cunard, Nancy, 23

Dada, 25

Daily Worker, 156, 180, 187–188

Damas, Léon Gontran, 26

Dance of the Forests, A, 77

Darkness at Noon, 169, 217–218, 220, 224–227, 230

Darnton, Robert, 43

Darwish, Mahmoud, 101

Davies, Carole Boyce, 181

Day-Lewis, Cecil, 19, 60, 164

Declaration, 35–36

Decolonising the Mind, 34, 41

decolonization, 3–5, 56, 245–246; African poetry and, 42–43; Bandung conference and, 5–6; CCF sponsorship of African magazines and, 74; Chinese literature and, 145; choosing between capitalism and socialism in, 6; class consciousness in, 27; cultural, 87–88; cultural autonomy achieved by, 40–41; cultural diplomacy and, 7–8; global south, 6, 134, 207, 244;

individual rights and collective responsibilities in, 218; interwar anticolonial revolutionaries and, 24–31; political, 101; self-determination and, 182, 214, 219, 244; socialist realism and, 103–104; support for writers of, 7–8
Delaney, Shelagh, 164
Denning, Michael, 104
Der Monat, 222
Detained, 234, 238–240
Deutsch, André, 51, 52
development, 15, 25, 28, 38, 77; underdevelopment, 12, 89
Dick, Philip K., 173
Dimock, Wai Chee, 88
Ding Ling, 121, 136
Diop, Alioune, 33–34, 37, 39
Djagalov, Rossen, 90
Dobrenko, Evgeny, 43
Doctor Zhivago, 222
Dos Passos, John, 221
dos Santos, Marcelino, 96, 101
double agency, 140–143
Dover, Cedric, 24
Down Second Avenue, 64, 78–81
Drayton, Arthur, 52, 65
Drum, 64
DuBois, W. E. B., 37, 96
Du Bois's Telegram: Literary Resistance and State Containment, 38
Dudziak, Mary L., 129
Duerden, Dennis, 52, 67–70, 69, 81, 227–229, 245

eclecticism, 81
economic imperialism, 6, 27, 62, 219
Edwards, Brent Hayes, 194
Eighteen Springs, 127, 145
Eighteenth Brumaire of Louis Bonaparte, The, 203
Eliot, T. S., 3
Éloge de la créolité, 44–45
El Saadawi, Nawal, 220, 229, 237–238, 244
El-Sebai, Youssef, 84, 95, 99

Elstob, Peter, 228–229
Encounter, 53, 57–61, 69, 71, 77, 119, 223, 241–242
"End to the Neglect of the Problems of the Negro Woman!, An," 185–186
Engels, Friedrich, 204
Engle, Paul, 134
English, James F., 13, 117
equivocal contrast, 122–125
Esty, Jed, 173
"Exile, The," 105–107
extroverted nationalism, 100

Fairfield Foundation, 53
Faiz, Faiz Ahmed, 8, 93, 96, 217
Fall of the Pagoda, The, 135, 144
Fanon, Frantz, 6, 32, 184–185, 193, 195, 242–243
Farred, Grant, 110
F.B. Eyes: How J. Edgar Hoover's Ghostreaders Framed African American Literature, 30
February, Basil, 102
Federal Bureau of Investigation (FBI), 8, 12, 180–184; Claudia Jones and, 183–184, 187–190; C. L. R. James and, 153, 155–156, 183–184, 196, 198
Feinberg, Barry, 102
Feldman, Leah, 88
Fiedler, Leslie, 60
Field, Roger, 114
First, Ruth, 8, 220, 229, 234–236
First International Congress of Black Writers and Artists, 37
First World Festival of Negro Arts, 1966, 37, 95
Fischer, Louis, 62
flashbacks, 233–236
Flynn, Elizabeth Gurley, 188
Fonlon, Bernard, 52
Ford Foundation, 82
formalism, 21–22
Forster, E. M., 31, 180
Four-Gated City, The, 154, 173–179

Fox, Ralph, 19, 28
Franco, Francisco, 221–222
Free Women, 160, 166–172
Frontiers of War, 161, 169
Fund for Exiled Writers, 221
Fund for Intellectual Freedom, 221

Galsworthy, John, 221
García Lorca, Federico, 221
Garvey, Amy Ashwood, 191
Garvey, Marcus, 216
Getachew, Adom, 88, 244
Ghosh, Jyotirmoy, 28
Gide, André, 34
Gikandi, Simon, 80, 234
Gillespie, Dizzie, 60
Gilroy, Paul, 184, 194
Ginzburg, Eugenia, 217
Glissant, Édouard, 44
global cold war, 5–7
Goble, Mark, 175
God That Failed, The, 31, 60, 62, 223
Going Home, 151–152
Golden Cangue, The, 143
Golden Notebook, The, 108, 154, 160–163, 166
Goldstone, Andrew, 73
Goodbye to Berlin, 175
Good Earth, The, 118, 121–122, 136
Gorky, Maxim, 21–23, 92–93
Grain of Wheat, A, 81
grammatical fictions, 236–244
Grass is Singing, The, 151, 156
Greif, Mark, 218
"Grenada Revisited: An Interim Report," 181
Guardian, 228
Guilbaut, Serge, 119
Guillory, John, 13

Half a Lifelong Romance, 145
Hall, Stuart, 32
Hans, 28
Harlow, Barbara, 218
Hawkes, Jacquetta, 164

Hemingway, Ernest, 118
Hepburn, Allan, 143
Hill, Robert A., 196
Historical Novel, The, 212–213
History of Negro Revolt, A, 196, 202, 205, 215–216
Hofstadter, Richard, 166
Hogarth, Paul, 151–153, 158–159
House Un-American Activities Committee, 58
Hsia, C. T., 121, 146
Hughes, Langston, 51–52, 69, 96, 115
Hu Lancheng, 127
humanism, 34, 218, 242–243
human rights, 6, 13; prison memoirs and, 15, 218–221, 229–232
Human Rights Watch, 219
Hunt, John, 68, 223
Hu Shi, 32
Hutchinson, Alfred, 102
Huxley, Aldous, 221
hybridity (cultural), 11, 18, 42, 170, 248

Ideal Minds: Raising Consciousness in the Antisocial Seventies, 172–173
If This Is a Man, 217–218
Imagined Communities, 88
imperialism, 4, 96, 156; cultural, 10, 27, 65, 247; economic, 6, 27, 62, 219; political, 70, 166, 181–182. *See also* colonialism; neocolonialism
indigeneity, 10–11, 18, 77–82
indigenous languages, 10, 14, 22, 41–42, 54, 115
"Indo-Russian Union, An," 24
Inostrannaya literatura, 91
Insurgent Testimonies: Witnessing Colonial Trauma in Modern and Anglophone Literature, 113
intelligence networks: Central Intelligence Agency (CIA), 7, 53–54, 57, 60, 63–64, 82; Federal Bureau of Investigations (FBI), 8, 12, 153, 155–156, 180–184, 196, 198–202; MI5 (Security Service), 8, 12, 153–155, 164–166,

196, 198–201; MI6 (Secret Intelligence
Service), 8, 157; PWA investigated by,
29–31. *See also* political police
International Association for Cultural
Freedom (IACF), 82
International Congress in Defense of
Culture, 19
internationalism, 194–195
internationalist nationalism, 86
International PEN, 219–220; Congress for
Cultural Freedom and, 222–223, 227–228;
core principles and activities of, 221–224;
Soyinka and, 227–229
intersectionality, 185–187
interwar era, the: anticolonial revolutionar-
ies of, 24–31; debates over aesthetic
autonomy during, 18–24
In the Fog of Seasons' End, 116
Isherwood, Christopher, 60, 175
Ivinskaya, Olga, 222
I Wonder as I Wander, 96

Jackson, Jeanne-Marie, 173
Jalil, Rakhshanda, 28
James, C. L. R., 8, 193, 217; anticolonial
modernity in writing by, 208–215; arrival
in the United States, 195–196; *Beyond a
Boundary,* 194; *The Black Jacobins:
Toussaint L'Ouverture and the San
Domingo Revolution,* 25, 182, 195, 202–205,
211–212, 215–216; on classical literary
forms, 126; Communist party and,
183–184; criticisms of metropolitan
modernism, 22, 24; deportation of,
183–184, 245; FBI surveillance of, 153,
155–156, 183–184, 196, 198–202; INS
records on, 196, 198; *Mariners, Renegades
and Castaways: The Story of Herman
Melville and the World We Live In,* 198,
205, 208–216; Marxist theory and, 195;
MI5 surveillance of, 196, 198–201;
proto-socialist revolutionaries as heroes
of, 202; revolutionary theory of, 202–207
James, Henry, 62, 118

Jameson, Fredric, 18, 90
JanMohamed, Abdul, 114
Jefferson, Thomas, 204
Jemie, Onwuchekwa, 42, 44, 46
Jim Crow system, 96, 129, 214
Johnson-Forest Tendency, 196
Jolas, Eugene, 74
Jones, Claudia, 8, 12, 153, 155–156, *192,* 217; in
Britain, 190–195; Caribbean Carnival
celebration, London, and, 193–194;
Communist Party USA and, 185–187;
criticisms of the Communist Party, 186;
deportation of, 183–184, 188–189, 192; on
exploitation of African American
women, 185–186; FBI surveillance of,
183–184, 187–190; intersectionality and,
185–187; on political autonomy in the
Caribbean, 193–194; *West Indian Gazette*
and, 191–192
Josselson, Michael, 63–64, 68, 223–224
Journey into the Whirlwind, 217
Joyce, James, 21–22, 62

Kafka, Franz, 62
Kanafani, Ghassan, 101
Kariuki, J. M., 234
Kazin, Alfred, 228
Kelman, James, 21
Kenyatta, Jomo, 191
Kenyon Review, The, 73
Kgositsile, Keorapetse, 102
Khlebnikov, Velimir, 24
Khrushchev, Nikita, 36–37, 91
King, Bruce, 228
King, Martin Luther, Jr., 191
Kingsbury, Karen S., 127
Klein, Christina, 118
Koestler, Arthur, 60, 217, 236, 248; *Darkness
at Noon,* 169, 217–218, 220, 224–227, 230;
work with International PEN, 220–224
Kongi's Harvest, 77
Kristol, Irving, 53, 63
Kumalo, A. N. C., 102
Kunene, Mazisi, 102

La Guma, Alex, 8, 51, 88–89, 92, 104, 217; critical reviews of, 113–114; *Lotus* and, 101–105; as realist fiction writer, 113–114; *A Soviet Journey*, 114–116; *The Stone Country*, 111; "The Exile," 105–107; *Time of the Butcherbird*, 111–114; *A Walk in the Night*, 51, 108–111, 114; work with both CCF and AAWA, 84, 117–118

La Guma, Blanche, 92

Lamming, George, 35, 193

language: aesthetic cold war and, 45–46; anglophone, 20–21, 41–42, 52–53, 65–66; debates, 32, 45, 51–53, 64–65; francophone, 26, 29; of humanism in prison writing, 218; indigenous, 10, 14, 22, 41–42, 54, 115; sinophone, 97, 118; transition of, 20–21; translation, 29, 85–86, 89–92, 143–147; vernacular, 14, 29, 121

Lao She, 118, 121, 129

La Revue du monde noire, 24, 33

Lasky, Melvin, 222–223, 228

Last Utopia, The, 243–244

League of Left-Wing Writers, 24, 28, 31, 121

Lee, Ang, 143

Lee, Christopher J., 88, 114

Lee, Steven S., 23, 90

Left Book Club, 19

Left Review, 19, 28, 31

Légitime Défense, 24

Lenin, Vladimir, 91

Leshoai, Bob, 52

Lessing, Doris, 8, 32, 35–36, 222, 245, 248; on aesthetic autonomy and linguistic centralization, 46; anti-communism of, 155–156; anti-racism of, 156–157; Campaign for Nuclear Disarmament and, 164–166; censorship and pressuring of, 159–160; *Children of Violence*, 154, 163, 166, 173–175, 179; Communist Party and, 156–158, 163–164; on decolonization and time, 108; followed by political police, 151–153, 158–159; *The Four-Gated City*, 154, 173–179; *Free Women*, 160, 166–172;

Frontiers of War, 161, 169; *Going Home*, 151–152; *The Golden Notebook*, 108, 154, 160–163, 166; letter of protest signed by, 229; MI5 and, 153–155; on political police, 155–166; private correspondence and fiction of, 161–162; on self-censorship, 44; space fiction and, 172–179

L'étudiant noir, 26

Levi, Primo, 217

Lewis, Wyndham, 60

Life of Captain Cipriani: An Account of the British Government in the West Indies, The, 195

Limits, 66

linguistic centralization, 46–47

linguistic plurality, 11

Link, Perry, 139

Lin Yutang, 118, 121

literature: African, 3–5, 7, 17–18, 20–21, 34–35, 42–43, 51, 54–58, 73–74, 77–82, 89; anticolonial, 36; archives on, 11–13; Asian, 88, 91–92, 103; autonomy and indigeneity in, 4, 10–11; Caribbean, 68–69, 183–194; censorship of, 43–45, 159–160, 247–248; Chinese, 118–119, 121–122; double agency in Asian American, 140–143; flashbacks in, 233–236; global, 89–92; grammatical fictions, 236–244; history of, 13–14; industrial translation of, 89–92; interwar, 18–24; metropolitan, 3–4, 164, 208, 232, 248; novels in, 36; paranoid style or conspiracy narrative in, 166; postcolonial tradition in, 1956–1990, 36–47; prison writing (*See* prison writing); protest writing, 65; relationship between decolonization and, 7–8, 245–246; space fiction, 172–179

Literature and Revolution, 19

Literature Police: Apartheid Censorship and its Cultural Consequences, The, 43

Little Ai, 127, 128

Little Reunions, 144

Littlewood, Joan, 193

Liu, Lydia H., 92

Lorde, Audre, 92, 180–183

Lotus, 7, 23, 73, 82, 99–100, 119, 245; aesthetic unity in, 87; Alex La Guma and, 88–89, 103–105, 107; archive, collection, or survey principle in, 101; celebration of October Revolution, 92; comparative nationalism and, 86; compared to *Transition,* 84–85; cultural decolonization and, 87–88; cultural inventories in, 101; design and layout of, 100; literary genres showcased by, 86–87; political decolonization and, 101; PWA and, 92–95; socialist realism in, 84–85, 103–105; South African activists and writers in, 101–103; Soviet book series in, 91–92; Soviet sponsorship of, 83, 100; trilingual scope of, 85–86. *See also* Afro-Asian Writer's Association (AAWA)

"Love in a Fallen City," 124–126, 138

Lowell, Robert, 228

Lukács, Georg, 205–207, 212–213, 215

"Lust, Caution," 141–143

Lu Xun, 28–29, 32, 121

Macauley, Robie, 73, 223

Madubuike, Ihechukwu, 42, 44, 46

magazines, little, 34–35, 51, 57–59, 66–67, 73–74

Maimane, J. Arthur, 102

Makerere conference, 37, 51–53; birth of postcolonial African literature in English and, 64–65; lack of political discussions at, 58–59; Okigbo and, 66–67

Manchanda, Abhimanyu, 193

Man Died, The, 220, 233–234, 240–243

"Manifesto for an Independent Revolutionary Art," 19

Manley, Norman, 191

Mann, Heinrich, 23

Mann, Thomas, 242, 248

Man with a Movie Camera, 175

Mao Dun, 96, 121

Mao Zedong, 28–29, 31–33

Mapanje, Jack, 218, 220, 229, 231, 236; *And Crocodiles Are Hungry at Night,* 220, 230–233, 238–239, 242

Mariners, Renegades and Castaways: The Story of Herman Melville and the World We Live In, 198, 205, 208–216

Marx, Karl, 203–204

Marxism and Form, 18

Marxist ideas, 18, 24–25; alienation, 26–27; C. L. R. James and, 195; negritude and, 34

Mau Mau Detainee, 234

Maxwell, William J., 8, 30, 181–182

May Fourth New Culture Movement, 28, 31, 121

Mbari clubs, 53, 59, 64–66, 70, 91

Mbembe, Achille, 116; on meaningful human expressions, 218

McCarran Internal Security Act of 1950, 196

McCarthy, Mary, 60

McCarthy, Richard M., 130, 134, 141, 144

McDonald, Peter D., 43

McGurl, Mark, 13, 134

McLuhan, Marshall, 175

Mehnert, Klaus, 127

Melville, Herman, 195, 208–215

Memoirs from the Women's Prison, 220, 236–237

Merrill, James, 173

metropolitan areas, 116; cultural values of, 44; global north, 34–36

metropolitan literature, 3–4, 164, 208, 232, 248

MI5 (Security Service), 8, 12, 153–155; Campaign for Nuclear Disarmament and, 164–166; C. L. R. James and, 196, 198–201

MI6 (Secret Intelligence Service), 8, 157

Minh, Ho Chi, 101

Mitchell, David T., 178

Moby-Dick, 195, 208–215

modernism, 3; aesthetic autonomy and, 54–56, 61–63; African varieties, 80–81; culture of artistic, 61; Euro-American varieties, 59, 208–209; metropolitan, 19–20, 23, 43, 182

Modernism, Media, and Propaganda: British Narrative from 1900–1945, 140
modernist aesthetics, 25, 58, 66, 77, 80–81
Modisane, Bloke, 51–52, 102; work with both CCF and AAWA, 84
Monroe Doctrine, 181
Moore, Gerald, 65–66, 68, 69
Moretti, Franco, 90
Moyn, Samuel, 243–244
Mphahlele, Es'kia, 8, 41, 51, 77, 82, 102; Congress for Cultural Freedom and, 53–54, 56, 64–65; *Down Second Avenue,* 64, 78–81; work with both CCF and AAWA, 84
Mufti, Aamir, 86
Murdoch, Iris, 164

Nabokov, Nicolas, 60
Nadal, Paul, 134
Nadiminti, Kalyan, 134
Naipaul, V. S., 40, 229
Naked Earth, 118, 127, 130, 135–136, 139; equivocal contrast in, 140–141
Nardal sisters, 24, 33
narrative prosthesis, 178
national culture, 194–195, 242
national governments: information collection by, 7–9, 12; propaganda by, 59–60
nationalism, 86–88; extroverted, 100; vernacular, 121
negritude movement, 26, 34, 65
Negro Looks at Soviet Central Asia, A, 96
neocolonialism, 4, 130, 244. *See also* colonialism; imperialism
Neogy, Rajat, 8, 51, 58, 66, 82, 84, 217; editorial evenhandedness of, 74–75; *Transition* magazine and, 57, 71–74
"Neo-Tarzanism: The Poetics of Pseudo-Tradition," 42
Neto, Agostinho, 92, 101
Neue Zürcher Zeitung, 242
New Indian Writing, 30
New Left Review, 32

New York Times, 53, 121
Ngaahika Ndeenda, 239–240
Ngũgĩ wa Thiong'o, 8, 34, 46, 51, 81, 92, 98, 217; call for decolonization, 41–42, 108; *Detained,* 234, 238–240; *A Grain of Wheat,* 81; prison writing by, 218–220, 227; publicity used by, 229; work with both CCF and AAWA, 84
1984, 141, 169, 217–218
Nkosi, Lewis, 51–52, 68, 102; work with both CCF and AAWA, 84
Nkrumah, Kwame, 74–75
Non-Aligned Movement, 96
nonalignment: aesthetic, 9, 13, 35–36, 40, 122–125, 135; humanism and ideological, 242–243; political, 5–6, 33–35, 38–40, 70, 120, 156
Notebook, 108
Novel and the People, The, 19
"Novelist as Teacher, The," 27
Nyerere, Julius, 74

Obote, Milton, 75
October Revolution, 92
Of Chameleons and Gods, 238–239
Okara, Gabriel, 41, 51
Okigbo, Christopher, 4, 6, 17–18, 33, 51, 82; Makerere conference and, 66–67; modernism of, 55
One Day in the Life of Ivan Denisovich, 217
117 Days, 220, 229, 234–236
"On National Culture," 185
"On the Abolition of the English Department," 41
On the Postcolony, 116
Orientalism, 91, 94–95
Origins of Totalitarianism, The, 6
Orwell, George, 31, 166, 217–218
Osborne, John, 193

Padmore, George, 6, 24, 184, 195, 216
Paine, Tom, 204
paranoid style, 166
Parikh, Crystal, 244

Park, Josephine Nock-Hee, 130
Pasternak, Boris, 222, 239
Path of Thunder, 17
p'Bitek, Okot, 21, 51
Pease, Donald E., 213
Pericles, 204
Pieterse, Cosmo, 84, 102
Pink Tears, 135, 143–144
Pinter, Harold, 229, 231, 248
Platen, August von, 240–242
poetry, African, 42–43
Police Aesthetics: Literature, Film, and the Secret Police in Soviet Times, 158
Political Affairs, 187
political imperialism, 70, 166, 181–182
political police, 12–13; Audre Lorde and, 180–182; Doris Lessing and, 152–166. *See also* intelligence networks
Popescu, Monica, 6–7, 90, 114
Popular Front, 18, 30
Portrait of the Artist as a Young Man, A, 102
postcolonial literary tradition, 36–47
Pramoedya Ananta Toer, 96, 217–218
Prashad, Vijay, 86
Présence Africaine: anticolonial movement and, 37–41, 70; Comité de Patronage, 38, 40; Frantz Fanon and, 185; on little magazines, 75; nonalignment of, 33–34, 95, 182; Richard Wright and, 31
Priestley, J. B., 164
prison writing: as anticolonial resistance, 218–219; *Darkness at Noon,* 169, 217–218, 220, 224–227; flashbacks used in, 233–236; grammatical fictions, 236–244; international campaigns in, 229–233; language of humanism in, 218; non-governmental organizations (NGOs) and, 219–220; by prominent activists, 217–218; by Soyinka, 220, 227–229; struggles of decolonizing peoples in, 219–220
Problems in Soviet Literature, 19
propaganda, 59–60, 139
protest writing, 65
pseudo-traditionalism, 43–44

PWA. *See* All-India Progressive Writers' Association (PWA)
Pynchon, Thomas, 166

racial reconciliation, 34
racism, 4, 26–27, 115; apartheid, 43, 63, 79, 88, 103, 105–111, 113, 116, 151, 229, 235–236; Claudia Jones on, 185–186; color bar, 151, 157, 161, 163; Doris Lessing on, 156–157
Radek, Karl, 21–22
radio, Congress for Cultural Freedom and, 58–59, 68–70
Ramzes, Victor, 91
Ranger, Terence, 44
Rao, Raja, 40
Ratushinskaya, Irina, 242, 248
Redding, Saunders, 65
Resistance Literature, 218
revolution: Alex La Guma and, 89, 111, 113; anticolonial revolutionaries and, 24–31; ballads of, 87; Claudia Jones and, 187, 191, 194–195; C. L. R. James and socialist, 183–184, 195–196, 198, 202–205, 208, 210, 213, 215–216; in Cuba, 185; cultural autonomy and, 88; cynicism about, 125; Doris Lessing and Central African, 152, 154, 162; Eileen Chang and, 125, 136, 140; George Lukács and, 205–207; in *The Golden Notebook,* 169; in Grenada, 181–182; interwar documents and gatherings, 19; language of, 19; *Lotus* and, 88–89, 96; Marxist tradition, 34, 92; in Russia, 92
"Revolutionaries and Poetry," 19
"Revolution of the Word," 19–23, 45, 71
Rhys, Jean, 108
Rice-Sprout Song, The, 118, 130, 131, 134–135; desolation mood in, 138; equivocal contrast in, 122–125, 139; inspired directly by propaganda stories, 139; plot of, 135–140
Rickshaw, 129
Rickshaw Boy, 121
Rilke, Rainer Maria, 62

Rimbaud, Arthur, 62
Rive, Richard, 84, 102, 110
Rivera, Diego, 19
Rizzuto, Nicole M., 113
Robeson, Paul, 191
Robinet, Françoise, 69
Romances, 121, 125
Rosenberg, Ethel, 60
Rosenberg, Julius, 60
Rouge of the North, The, 135, 144
Rubin, Andrew N., 73–74, 119
Rubin, Neville, 76
Rushdie, Salman, 21, 229, 248

Said, Edward W., 247
Saint-Armour, Paul K., 125
Salih, Tayeb, 84
Salkey, Andrew, 193
Saro-Wiwa, Ken, 229
Sartre, Jean-Paul, 32, 34
Saunders, Frances Stonor, 56, 59, 119
Schwarz, Walter, 228
science fiction, 114, 166; apocalyptic, 154;
    space fiction, 172–179
Scott, David, 88, 203, 211–212, 215
Scott-Smith, Giles, 59, 61
Season of Migration to the North, 84
self-censorship, 43–44
self-determination, 182, 214, 219, 244
Selvon, Sam, 193
Sembène Ousmane, 96, 97–99
Senanayake, Ratne Deshapriya, 98
Senghor, Léopold Sédar, 26, 41, 63
Shakespeare, William, 91
Shanghai Evening Post, 120–121
Shikasta: Re: Colonised Planet 5, 179
Sillitoe, Alan, 164
Silone, Ignazio, 222
Sitwell, Edith, 60
Slaughter, Joseph R., 244
Slow Lynching, A, 233–234
"Small Personal Voice, The," 35–36, 44
Smith, James, 8, 155
Smith, Leonard, 162

Smith Act, 1918, 188
Snow, C. P., 164
Snyder, Sharon L., 178
So, Richard Jean, 118, 134
socialism, 6, 19, 96; AAWA and, 85; C. L. R.
    James and, 195–196, 198; revolutionary,
    202
socialist aesthetics, 21–22, 24, 45, 84,
    103–104, 164, 178, 248
socialist realism, 11, 33, 43–44, 84, 103–104,
    209–210, 214
Socialist Workers Party, 196, 198–199
Solzhenitsyn, Alexander, 217
Sontag, Susan, 248
Soviet Journey, A, 114–116
Soviet Union, the: Bandung meeting and,
    6; CCF activities and, 60; cold war
    diplomacy of, 11; industrial translation in,
    90–92; International PEN and, 222–223;
    La Guma on, 114–116; *Lotus* sponsored
    by, 84–88; postcolonial literary tradition
    and, 36–37; presence in the global literary
    system, 12, 22–23; propaganda and,
    59–60, 68; PWA and, 28–29; responses to
    James Joyce's work, 21–22; Sino-Soviet
    split and, 97; sponsorship of Afro-Asian
    Writer's Association (AAWA), 83;
    writers of the decolonizing world
    supported by, 7–8
Soviet Writers Congress, 22, 28–29, 33
Soyinka, Wole, 8, 35, 46, 51, 76, 82, 92, 120,
    244, 248; on African pseudo-tradition,
    42–44; defense of using English
    language, 53; drama competition
    sponsored by CCF and, 77; *The Man
    Died*, 220, 233–234, 240–243; negritude
    movement and, 34; prison writing by,
    217, 220, 227–229, 236; "The Writer in an
    African State," 75–76; work with both
    CCF and AAWA, 84
space fiction, 172–179
Spahr, Juliana, 38, 74
Spark, Muriel, 166
Spender, Stephen, 23, 53, 61–64, 68, 77, 81, 155

Spio-Garbrah, Elizabeth, 76
"Spyring, The," 141–143
Stalin, Josef, 37, 61
Stead, Christina, 24
Stephens, Michelle Ann, 194
Stonebridge, Lyndsey, 227
Stone Country, The, 111
Suez Crisis, 36–37
Sun Shines over the Sanggan River, The, 135–136
Surkov, Alexei, 222–223
Surrealism, 19, 23, 25–26, 28
Sutherland, Efua, 84

Tagore, Rabindranath, 91
Taseer, M. D., 93
Taunton, Matthew, 164
Taylor, Bob, 245
temporality of thought, 107–108
Tense Future: Modernism, Total War, Enyclopedic Form, 125
Theory of the Novel, The, 205–207
Third Programme, 69
Thomas, Dylan, 60
Thompson, E. P., 164
Thu Bon, 98
Tikhonov, Nikolai, 92
Time of the Butcherbird, 111–114
Times, The, 229
Toller, Ernst, 221
Tolstoy, Leo, 91
"Towards the Decolonization of African Literature," 42
Transcription Centre, 68–70, 91, 227–228
Transition, 19, 23, 25, 42, 53, 57, 59, 61, 82, 228; aesthetic autonomy and, 104; compared to Lotus, 84–85; Congress for Cultural Freedom and, 70–76; editorial evenhandedness of, 74–75; Makerere conference and, 51–53, 64, 66–67; Neogy's writing in, 71–74; on the Soviet book market, 91
Transpacific Community: America, China, and the Rise and Fall of a Cultural Network, 118
Trask, Michael, 172–173

Trilling, Lionel, 228
Trotsky, Leon, 19
Tutuola, Amos, 21
Tynan, Kenneth, 229
Tzara, Tristan, 23

Ulysses, 21–22
Under Western Eyes, 81
UNESCO, 90, 95–96
Union of Soviet Writers, 28, 31
United Front, 30
United States, the: Bandung meeting and, 6; cold war diplomacy of, 11; House Un-American Activities Committee, 58; Immigration and Naturalization Service (INS), 184, 196, 198; imperialism of, 181–182; invasion of Grenada by, 181; Jim Crow system in, 96, 129, 214; presence in the global literary system, 12; propaganda and, 59–60; USIA/US State Department, 7, 119–120, 127–134; writers of the decolonizing world supported by, 7–8
Unseasonable Youth: Modernism, Colonialism, and the Fiction of Development, 173
Untouchable, 31
utilitarianism, aesthetic. See aesthetics

Vatulescu, Cristina, 158
vernacular language, 14, 29, 121
Vertov, Dziga, 175
Voice of America, 129–130
Volland, Nicolai, 88
Von Eschen, Penny, 60, 129

Wain, John, 164, 229
Walcott, Derek, 118
Wali, Obiajunwa, 52–54
Walk in the Night, A, 51, 108–111, 114
Walkowitz, Rebecca L., 86
Wang, David Der-wei, 127, 139
Wang, Mei-Hsiang, 130
Warsaw Pact, 8, 92
Washington, Mary Helen, 8, 181–182
Waste Land, The, 78

Watson, Jini Kim, 243

Webb, Constance, 195

Weep Not, Child, 37

Wells, H. G., 221

Wesker, Arnold, 164, 229

West Indian Gazette and Afro-Asian Caribbean News, 191–192

"What a Life! What a Girl's Life," 120–121

Whitehorn, John, 163

Whitman, Walt, 118

Why I am a Communist, 31–32

Wide Sargasso Sea, 108

Wilder, Gary, 88

Wilford, Hugh, 59, 119

Wilson, Angus, 229

Witt, Susanna, 91

Wollaeger, Mark, 140

Wong, Jade Snow, 130

World Republic of Letters, The, 90

World Revolution, 1917–1936: The Rise and Fall of the Communist International, 196, 198, 205

World Today, 130, 132, 132–133

Wretched of the Earth, The, 6, 242–243

Wright, Richard, 31–32, 38, 182

"Writer in an African State, The," 75–76

Writers and Scholars of the East, 91–92

Writers in Exile, 221

Writers in Prison, 227–228

Writers' Internationale, 92–95

"Writing of One's Own," 122, 126

Written on Water, 121

Wynter, Sylvia, 40, 184, 193

XXth Century, The, 127

Yan'an Forum on Literature and Art, 31, 33

Yeats, W. B., 60, 108

Yibao, 145

"You and the Atom Bomb," 31

Young Communist League, 187

Yuannu, 144

Zaheer, Sajjad, 8, 28–30, 93, 217

Zami: A New Spelling of My Name, 180

Zulfiya, 93